INVASION

**Recent Titles
in War, Technology, and History**

INVASION

The Conquest of Serbia, 1915

Richard L. DiNardo

War, Technology, and History

An Imprint of ABC-CLIO, LLC

Santa Barbara, California • Denver, Colorado

Library of Congress Cataloging-in-Publication Data

DiNardo, R. L.
    Invasion : the conquest of Serbia, 1915 / Richard L. DiNardo.
        pages cm. — (War, technology, and history)
    Includes bibliographical references and index.
    ISBN 978-1-4408-0092-4 (hard copy : acid-free paper) — ISBN 978-1-4408-0093-1 (ebook) 1. World War, 1914–1918—Campaigns—Serbia. 2. Serbia—Strategic aspects. 3. Serbia—History, Military—20th century. 4. Strategy—History—20th century. 5. Military weapons—Technological innovations—History—20th century. I. Title.
    D561.D485   2015
    940.4′24—dc23   2014049105

ISBN: 978-1-4408-0092-4
EISBN: 978-1-4408-0093-1

19 18 17 16 15   1 2 3 4 5

This book is also available on the World Wide Web as an eBook.
Visit www.abc-clio.com for details.

Praeger
An Imprint of ABC-CLIO, LLC

ABC-CLIO, LLC
130 Cremona Drive, P.O. Box 1911
Santa Barbara, California 93116-1911

This book is printed on acid-free paper ∞

Manufactured in the United States of America

For my wife Rita, the most patient
and loving person I know.

Contents

A photo essay follows page 120

Maps

Series Foreword

Military historians can be a contentious, feisty lot. There is little upon which they agree. The importance of attrition vs. maneuver, the relative qualities of "deep battle" and "Blitzkrieg," the command abilities of Patton and Montgomery: put two military historians in a room and you'll likely get three opinions on any of these questions. And yet, there is one thing that unites military historians across the spectrum. Virtually everyone within the field recognizes the crucial role that technology has played in the development of the military art. Indeed, this is almost axiomatic: the very first man who picked up a club against his neighbor was wielding "technology" of a sort. The outcome of wars has been profoundly affected by the technological context in which they were fought. From spoke-wheeled chariots to the M1A1 tank, from blades of Toledo steel to the AK-47, from primitive "bombards" to the MOAB ("mother of all bombs"), the problem of technology has stood at the forefront of military history.

Beyond that unifying proposition, however, problems can still arise in analyzing the precise role of technology. Consider for a moment the impact of the Industrial Revolution. Just as it transformed society, economy, and culture, it changed the appearance of war beyond all recognition. It was the age of the mass army, "railroads and rifles," and the telegraph. The growth of industry allowed military forces to grow to unheard-of size. In 1757, Frederick the Great triumphed over the French at Rossbach with an army that totaled 22,000 men; at Königgrätz in 1866, well over 400,000 men would be contesting the issue, and Austrian casualties alone, some 44,000 men, would be precisely twice as large as Frederick's victorious host at Rossbach. The railroad allowed these hordes to move, quite literally, 24 hours per day, and the problem of the slow-moving supply column that had bedeviled military operations from time out of mind seemed to have been solved. Moreover, the introduction of the telegraph meant that armies could be kept on a tight leash, even by commanders hundreds of miles away.

For each advantage of the new technology, however, there was a corresponding difficulty. It was soon clear that commanding and controlling the mass army was a huge, even insurmountable, problem. It is generally agreed that Napoleon I had serious problems in this area in 1812, and that he was at his best with armies that totaled 85,000 men or less. It was foolish to expect an army of several hundred thousand men to maneuver nimbly across the countryside, wheel like a company, and whack the opponent a surprise blow in the flank. In fact, getting them to maneuver at all was a stretch. The telegraph was a modern marvel, true, but the vision it offered of total control of far-flung operations turned out to be a mirage. Tied to a static system of poles and wires, it was far more useful to the defender than to the attacker, and it was nearly useless in any kind of mobile campaign. The mass army, then, was a huge body with a small brain, and had a very difficult time doing much more than marching straight ahead and crashing into whatever happened to be in front of it.

At that point, a mutual slaughter began. The other great technological advance of the era was introduction of new firearms—the rifled musket, or simply "rifle." It dramatically improved the range and firepower of infantry and the 1860s would see another breakthrough, the breech-loader, which greatly increased rate of fire. With long-range rifles now in the hands of the defenders, assault columns could theoretically be shot to pieces long before they struck home. In place of the old-style assault, there now arose the firefight, with extended skirmish lines on both sides replacing the formations of line and column. It was an "open order revolution," the logical culmination of tactical developments since the French Revolution. Open order tactics, however, rarely allowed enough concentration of fighting power for a successful assault. Both sides lined up and fired. There were casualties, enormous casualties, often for little gain. It was the great conundrum of the era. Clearly, technology was not so much a solution to a problem on the 19th century battlefield; it was more like the problem itself.

These are the issues that will form the heart of Praeger's new *War, Technology, and History* series. Books in the series will focus on the crucial relationship between warmaking and technological advance in the past 200 years. During that period, new machines like the rifle, the railroad, and the telegraph (in the nineteenth century) and the machine gun, the airplane, and the tank (in the twentieth) have transformed the face of war. In the young twenty-first century, the U.S. Army has been emphasizing the ways in which information technology can have an even more radical transformative impact. Historically, armies that have managed to integrate these new technologies have found corresponding success on the battlefield, and their victories have as often as not come at the expense of those who have failed to ground their warmaking doctrine squarely in the available technology. The question is, therefore, much wider than a simple list of technical "specs" for various weapons. Books in the series will link technology and doctrine—that is, the weapons and the manner in which they were employed on actual battlefields of the day. The series is intended for a wide readership, from buffs and wargamers to scholars and "operators"—military officers and policymakers.

It is hard to argue with the notion that technological change has held the key to understanding military history, and in our contemporary era of information management and smart weaponry, technology continues to change the face of battle. Questions remain, however. Is technology our master or our servant? Are there limits to its usefulness? Does it alter the nature of war, or is war based on timeless, unchanging principles? These are a few of the themes to be explored by the authors—recognized experts all—in this new series. It presents no party line or previously agreed-upon point of view. Nor does it offer any simple answers to any of these questions. Welcome to War, Technology, and History.

Acknowledgments

Writing a book is an activity that requires a considerable degree of solitude. In amassing the material that serves as the basis for the work, however, one benefits from the assistance of a great many people, and this book is no exception. My friends Rob Citino and Dennis Showalter, two of the best German military historians of their respective generations, have always been most supportive of the project. Bruce Gudmundsson was most generous in providing sources from his own enormous collection of material on the imperial German army. My old friend Jack Tunstall generously provided copies of documents from the Austrian military archives in Vienna. I would also like to acknowledge the valuable services of the staff at the Library of the Marine Corps at Quantico, Virginia. Rachel Kingcade and Cynthia Evans, in particular, were tireless in their pursuit of materials requested via interlibrary loan. Thanks are also due to the staff at the National Defense University Library, as well as the staff of the Army Heritage and Education Center at Carlisle, Pennsylvania.

Conducting archival research abroad is an activity that requires time and above all money. I am most grateful to the Marine Corps University and the Marine Corps University Foundation, both of which provided generous financial support for several trips to Germany. I would also like to give thanks to my friends and colleagues at the Marine Corps Command and Staff College, located at Marine Corps Base Quantico, Virginia, who were always supportive of the project. Most notable here are Colonel Mark J. Desens, USMC, and Colonel Steven Grass, USMC, both directors of the Command and Staff College, and the dean of academics at the college, Dr. Charles D. McKenna. These gentlemen gave me the flexibility needed to manage the time required to complete the manuscript, while still completing my required tasks that are a normal part of my duties.

I also thank a number of people across the Atlantic. The staff at the library of the Zentrum für Militärgeschichte und Sozialwissenschaften der Bundeswehr (ZMSB) (formerly the Militärgeschichtliches Forschungsamt) at Potsdam were most helpful in helping me with the innumerable regimental histories that are so critical to research on the imperial German army. Dr. Gerald Maier and the staff at the Landesarchiv for Baden-Württemberg were most helpful. Aided by a superb website and online finding aid, I was able to obtain documents from two collections of papers and for the Twenty-Sixth Infantry Division by mail, thus saving me much time and expense. Many thanks are also due to Dr. Lothar Saupe and his successor, Dr. Martina Haggenmüller, at the Bavarian Military Archive in Munich, for their help in locating records for the Bavarian units involved in the campaign. As always, the staff at the Bundesarchiv-Militärarchiv in Freiburg was most helpful. Special thanks are due to Colonel Gerhard P. Gross, of the ZMSB, who was kind enough to arrange for a work space for me in the ZMSB offices at Freiburg, while the reading room at the archive had very limited space due to renovations. Frau Cynthia Flohr provided an extraordinary degree of assistance. Research in Germany is always made more enjoyable by my friends in Freiburg. Jürgen Förster, Klaus Maier, Detlef and Johanna Vogel, Horst Boog, Norbert and Karin Wiggershaus, and Roland and Annie Foerster always made travel to Germany, a truly delightful experience. Sadly, Rolli was lost to us far too soon on March 11, 2014.

Friends have always been a source of support, and in this regard I would like to thank Al, Jay, Pat, Sheila, Scott, Mary, Martin, Karl, Karen, and Irving. Teachers have also played an important role in my life. Particularly important in this regard is Cynthia Whittaker, my old teacher and friend of over 40 years. Two other important influences were the late William O. Shanahan and my *Doktorvater*, the late David Syrett. Both men were exemplary teachers and mentors who influenced those of us who were privileged to study with them in so many ways.

I am fortunate in being able to count on the love and support of two families. My parents Louis and Ann DiNardo have always been supportive of my choice of career, although it may have given them some *angst* at times. Many thanks also to my brothers Robert and Jerry, and their respective wives JoAnn and Vinece. Thanks also go to my nephews Michael and Thomas and my niece Ann Marie and her husband, Brian Hardgrove, for their love and support. The Moxley family of Baltimore, Maryland, has also been a source of love and support. Of particular note here is the Farmer family, David

Farmer and Eileen Moxley Farmer, and their twin daughters Alison and Amanda, who are now at the start of their own respective treks through the pathways of academia. Of course the most important member of the Moxley family is my wife, Rita, a woman whose love and patience seem at times to be boundless. It is with love and gratitude that I dedicate this book to her.

While a sizeable number of people have been mentioned here, I alone wrote this book. I am therefore responsible for any errors and omissions in it.

Introduction

"The Balkans is not worth the bones of a single Pomeranian grenadier."

Otto von Bismarck[1]

"I have already informed Your Excellency that the German forces committed against Serbia are to be reinforced."

Erich von Falkenhayn, September 10, 1915[2]

Most human endeavors are attended with varying degrees of irony, but few activities are as loaded with incongruity as war and diplomacy. The French revolutionary government initiated war in 1792, for example, as a crusade against tyrannical European monarchies. By 1813 Russia, Prussia, Austria, and Britain were aligned against France under Napoleon, who by then had become the veritable symbol of despotism.[3] Adolf Hitler's willingness to act on his desire to eradicate the Soviet Union and the "Jewish Bolshevik" threat ultimately resulted in, to use Curzio Malaparte's phrase, "the Volga rising in Europe." Finally the course of Franco-Russian relations that eventually resulted in the Entente Cordiale in 1894 produced one of the most ironic scenes of diplomatic history. When he hosted a group of senior French naval officers at the Peterhof, Russian tsar Alexander III, the very epitome of reaction, stood bareheaded for the playing of the La Marseillaise, the great song of the most radical phase of the French Revolution.[4]

World War I itself had its share of ironies. The major powers envisioned a short war that turned out to be precisely the kind of bloody and prolonged conflict they sought to avoid. It came to be called "the war to end all wars," only to give rise to the conditions that resulted in an even bloodier conflict

20 years later. World War I has many other ironies, and among them is the invasion of Serbia in 1915, the subject of this book.

There are, to be sure, ironic aspects to the Serbian campaign of 1915. That the Germany military, at the behest of General der Infanterie Erich von Falkenhayn, the chief of the German General Staff, should undertake an invasion of the part of Europe that Otto von Bismarck had sought to avoid entanglement in says much about the evolution of both German diplomacy and wartime strategy.[5] These aspects, especially how this operation was related to the strategy of both the Central powers and the Triple Entente, will be discussed in chapter two. Another incongruity was the fact that after doing most of the heavy lifting in the campaign, Germany happily left the administration of the area to Austria–Hungary and Bulgaria.[6]

Perhaps the most ironic aspect of the Serbian campaign of 1915 was its aftermath. The offensive was the follow-on operation to the Gorlice–Tarnow campaign of May 1915, an offensive that resulted in the liberation of Austrian Galicia and the conquest of Russian Poland. These operations arguably constituted the high point of close cooperation between Germany and Austria–Hungary.[7]

Relations between Germany and Austria–Hungary looked much different by the end of 1915. Relations between Falkenhayn and his Austro-Hungarian counterpart, Generaloberst Franz Baron Conrad von Hötzendorf, always difficult even when times were good, deteriorated considerably in the aftermath of the Serbian campaign. There were deep disagreements over the course of action that should be pursued next. Instead of close discussion, by the end of the campaign each man was more secretive than ever in terms of revealing future plans to the other.[8] These issues were magnified when it came to the matter of war aims between the allies. Even within Germany, the completion of the Serbian campaign and its strategic consequences produced deep divisions between Falkenhayn and German chancellor Theobald von Bethmann-Hollweg. The critical issue here was how to make the best possible use of these gains.[9]

Irony aside, there are a number of other reasons that recommend one's attention to this campaign. First, the reasons for mounting the operation were central to Falkenhayn's conception of Germany's strategy at this point in the war.[10] Thus, a close look at the campaign provides a great opportunity to see how a particular operation fitted into Germany's overall strategy.

Operationally, the invasion of Serbia in 1915 was the final major operation planned and conducted by one of the more successful military marriages in German history, namely Generalfeldmarschall August von Mackensen and his chief of staff, Generalmajor Hans von Seeckt. This book will also seek to reevaluate the relationship between the two men. The campaign also involved the combined efforts of three of the Central powers: Germany; Austria–Hungary; and the newest member of the alliance, Bulgaria. How Mackensen and Seeckt rose to the complex challenges in the conduct of coalition warfare is always worthy of attention.[11]

In his classic work *Small Wars: Their Principles and Practice*, British Colonel (later Major General) Charles E. Callwell noted that campaigns in small wars, owing to the harsh environments, were conducted as much against nature as against hostile forces.[12] This applied to the Serbian campaign of 1915 as well. Mackensen's forces had to cross three wide and deep rivers, namely the Save, Danube, and Morava. Crossing the Danube was further complicated by the river's powerful current. Beyond the rivers was mountainous terrain, with movement through it enabled only by poor roads.[13] The geography, combined with stout Serbian resistance, had brought three Austro-Hungarian invasions to grief in 1914.

Conquering both the terrain and the Serbian enemy was made even more complicated by another element of Mother Nature, the weather. The operation was launched in the autumn, the time of year that was marked by the powerful storm known as the *Kossava*, which lashed the area with high winds and rain, often turning rivers into raging torrents. The prospect of poor fall weather and the onset of the harsh Balkan winter, plus the threat of Entente intervention, demanded that the campaign be conducted with as much speed as possible.[14]

For the Germans, Austro-Hungarians, and Bulgarians, success in this endeavor depended on transitory advantages conferred by three types of equipment. The first was aircraft, with its ability to secure air superiority, conduct reconnaissance, and attack various targets of tactical and operational importance. Although only a handful of aircraft and balloons were employed, they made a crucial difference, especially in the opening stages of the offensive.[15]

The second was artillery, especially heavy guns. These had proved crucial to the success of German and Austro-Hungarian operations conducted against the Russians in 1915. The advantage of heavy guns, however, was greatest during the opening phase of the offensive. The excellent Austro-Hungarian rail and road network allowed the Germans and Austro-Hungarians to assemble a large number of guns on their side of the respective rivers. Once across the Save and the Danube, however, displacing artillery forward was going to be a most difficult task.[16]

Finally, bridging technology was critical in getting forces across three major rivers and then enabling the continuation of operations once forces had secured their respective bridgeheads. While narrower water obstacles with slower currents presented no real problems, large rivers such as the Danube and Save presented some real technical challenges. Although the task of assembling material had been made easier by the advent of motor vehicles such as trucks and there had been some improvement in the bridging material, the process itself had not changed much in over a century.[17]

All these challenges made the Serbian campaign no mere matter of a hungry tiger devouring a sick fawn. Rather, the campaign was a challenging military operation that demanded the defeat of both enemy and terrain in as short a time as possible. Before proceeding to a brief examination of how the two sides arrived at this situation, a few words must be said about an issue common to most works written about this part of the world, which comes down to the matter of which name to use. The geographic area over which this campaign was fought has known numerous ruling authorities, many with rather dissimilar languages. Many number of places in this campaign have names in German, Magyar, Bulgarian, and Serbian. The simplest solution to this issue will be applied. The names that will be used are the names that were common in 1915.

Finally, for the sake of truth in advertising, it must be said that this book is first and foremost a work of military history. Although some attention will be devoted to the topic of diplomacy between various members of the Central powers, the focus of attention throughout will be on the preparation, execution, and aftermath of the campaign launched against Serbia in 1915. Although the story of relations between Germany and its allies in World War I is an interesting one, it must remain secondary to the primary subject at hand. Having set forth that caveat, we can now proceed to a short survey of Austria–Hungary's relations with Serbia, as well as the opening campaigns of the war.

Chapter 1

Scorpions in a Bottle: Austria–Hungary and Serbia, 1875–1914

> "an awakening of a lively consciousness of our national unity in the distant Serb lands which are subjected to foreign elements."
>
> Serbian Radical Party Program, 1881[1]

> "[A war with Serbia] either will leave only faint traces of the present Serbian state or will shake Austria–Hungary to its foundations."
>
> Leopold von Berchtold, November 1913[2]

Every age has its share of isms, broad ideologies that often serve as the catalysts for the defining events of an age, be they positive or negative. The period between the end of the Crimean War and the start of World War I veritably abounded in isms, including imperialism, Darwinism and—its ultimately terrifying offset—social Darwinism, socialism and its murderous offspring communism, the already deadly phenomenon of anarchism, and finally nationalism.

For the dual monarchy of Austria–Hungary, the rise of nationalism was easily the most potentially lethal. By the 1870s, Austria–Hungary had come to the end of a long period of development marked by a number of transitions centered on changes in the political structure of the area. In 1806 the efforts of Napoleon, crowned by his victory at Austerlitz on December 2, 1805, brought about the Treaty of Pressburg. The treaty officially brought to an end the oxymoronic polity centered in Vienna known as the Holy Roman Empire, thus making Francis I the last person to hold the title Holy Roman emperor.[3]

The newly refashioned Austrian Empire was able to recover from the disaster of 1805, sufficiently so that it challenged Napoleon, again without ultimate success, in 1809. In 1812 Napoleon, then related to the Habsburg family by marriage, coerced Austria into participating in the invasion of Russia.[4] The Austrian contingent, commanded by the cautious Prince Charles Schwarzenberg, was able to avoid major fighting in the campaign and withdraw successfully from southern Russia back to Austrian territory.

With Napoleon's forces in tatters after the disastrous 1812 campaign and retreat from Russia and Prussia then in revolt against Napoleon and allied with Russia, Austria was able to take a position of neutrality. When the initial phases of 1813 campaign in Germany failed to yield decisive results for either side, both sides agreed to temporary truce of nearly two months. The brilliant if cynical Prince Klemens Metternich was then the guiding hand of Austrian foreign policy, and he was able to maneuver Austria not only on to the side of the allies but also as the military leader of the coalition.

In August 1813 Austria once again took the field against Napoleon. The Austrian forces were once again commanded by Schwarzenberg, aided by his brilliant Chief of Staff Joseph Radetzky. Schwarzenberg also acted as the overall commander of the combined Austrian, Prussian, and Russian armies, but often plans could be arrived at only by consensus and often required the personal intervention of Russian Tsar Alexander I to get some positive results.[5] Nonetheless, the allied forces were able to defeat Napoleon at the titanic battle of Leipzig in October 1813, and Schwarzenberg successfully led the allied armies in the invasion of France the following year that resulted in Napoleon's first abdication.

With Napoleon safely confined to the island of Elba, the victorious allied powers met in Vienna. Metternich was able to obtain a political reorganization of Germany that suited Austria's interests. He also restored Austrian control over northern Italy, although popular local sentiment was dead set against this. To the east and southeast, the Habsburg family maintained its power over Hungary by virtue of fact that the emperor of Austria simultaneously held the position of king of Hungary, while Austria continued to hold gains in the Balkans that had been hard won over time from the Ottoman Turks. These circumstances remained undisturbed by Napoleon's escape from Elba, final defeat at Waterloo, and subsequent confinement on St. Helena.

The period of restoration that began with the end of the Napoleonic Wars was accompanied by a repressive system of royal absolutist governance that came to be symbolized by Metternich himself. Metternich attempted to keep the Austrian Empire in a relatively static position, even as Europe was seething with change. These sentiments manifested themselves in the revolutions of 1848 in much of western and central Europe. Metternich himself was driven from office, and Hungary, where revolutionary sentiment was most radical, came under unofficial but acknowledged leader of the Hungarian Diet, Lajos Kossuth, who eventually declared it an independent country. Equally troublesome was the meeting of the Pan-Slav Congress in Prague. Although the largest Slavic people in the empire, the Czechs, were not considering secession from the empire, they were seeking the same legal rights as those held by the Austrians.[6]

The Habsburg government, however, then under the tough-minded Prince Felix zu Schwarzenberg and the newly crowned young emperor Francis Joseph, was able to restore order over the period beginning in late 1848 and extending into 1849. While General Prince Alfred Windischgrätz proved an indifferent military commander, he was successful in reoccupying Prague, dispersing the Pan-Slav Congress and later retaking Vienna from the rebels. Hungary was invaded by Austrian forces led by the Croatian general Josef Jelačić and a Russian army dispatched by the gendarme of Europe himself, Tsar Nicholas I. Finally, the aged Radetzky, then a commander in his own right, decisively defeated an attempt by the Kingdom of Sardinia-Piedmont to wrest northern Italy from Austria's control.

From 1849 to 1867, Austria experienced decline in its international position and change internally. Schwarzenberg's sudden death in 1852 deprived Austria of its most able if erratic leader. The policy of armed neutrality adopted in response to the Crimean War earned Austria the enmity of not just Nicholas I but all of his successors. Count Carl Ferdinand Buol, who had succeeded Metternich as foreign minister, allowed Austria to be goaded by Sardinian prime minister Camillo Cavour into a war with France over northern Italy. The Austrian army was unprepared in terms of equipment, stuck with tactics that relied too heavily on the bayonet, and indifferently commanded; the Austrian troops fought bravely but were defeated in the bloody battles of Magenta and Solferino.[7] The ultimate result of the Franco-Austrian War of 1859 was Austria's loss of Lombardy. A newly created Italian state also hungered for Venetia.

Meanwhile Austria's position as the dominant power in Germany deteriorated and collapsed. Although Austria was able to fend off a challenge by Prussia for supremacy in Germany in 1850, its position eroded thereafter. In 1866 Austria accepted a challenge by both Prussia and Italy. Austria's loss of influence over the German states was confirmed by the defeat at Prussia's hands in 1866.

Domestically, Austria began the period after the suppression of the 1848 revolution with Schwarzenberg's "neoabsolutist" government. This government survived several years beyond Schwarzenberg's death and was replaced by a more liberal administration after 1860. The more liberal administration lasted until 1867. The defeat of Austria in 1866 gave Hungary a considerable degree of leverage against Vienna. The result was the compromise (*Ausgleich*) of January 1867, which established the dual monarchy of Austria–Hungary as the successor to the Austrian Empire. By the terms of the compromise, Austria and Hungary each maintained status as a sovereign country in its own right. Both governments had parallel organizations, including separate ministries for defense, foreign affairs, and so on, and each had a prime minister. The dual monarchy had two unifying elements. One was the General Staff, which controlled the development of war plans and the overall direction of military operations. The other was Francis Joseph, who, while already emperor of Austria, was then crowned in as king of Hungary on June 8, 1867. The emperor's position was bolstered by his wife, the lovely Empress Elisabeth, better known as Sissi, who was a very popular figure in both Austria and especially Hungary.[8]

The reorganization of the Austrian Empire into Austria–Hungary had major consequences for all the peoples who comprised the Austro-Hungarian people. That the Germans were the most powerful and privileged ethnic group in the dual monarchy was always a given. The *Ausgleich*, however, then elevated the Hungarians to such a status, and they were dead set on maintaining it vis-à-vis the other ethnic groups in the empire, especially the Slavic people who lived in its southernmost territories.[9]

The jealous guarding of rights and status by the Hungarians after 1867 served to undermine Austro-Hungarian foreign policy during the latter nineteenth century. Shut off from overseas colonial ventures by virtue of its geography and having lost the duel with Prussia for the dominant position in Germany, Austria–Hungary then oriented its foreign policy toward expansion into the Balkans. This put Austria–Hungary on a collision course with Russia, who also sought to expand into the area, as well as one of the rising new powers in the region, Serbia.[10]

The gradual ebbing of the Ottoman Turkish tide that had threatened Vienna in 1683 had two major results over the ensuing three centuries. The first was the expansion of Russian influence into the area over time, followed by Austria. The other major result was the creation of a series of countries in southeastern Europe who had been able to free themselves from Turkish rule. The first of these was Hungary, once Ottoman Turkey's most notable possession north of the Danube River.

During the nineteenth century, as the pace of Ottoman decline accelerated, new countries began to appear. Greece was the first to gain its independence, at least officially, in 1829, partly though Greek efforts and partly through Turkey's defeat at the hands of Russia in the 1828–1829 war. Later on Romania, Bulgaria, and Montenegro gained independence in 1878, while Albania became a sovereign nation in 1912.

Serbia's road from Turkish province to independent nation began in 1804, with a revolt directed against local authority, which was based on the Janissaries, who had become particularly oppressive. The revolt was led by a pig dealer named George Petrović Karageorge.[11] The Serb revolt, which had garnered little foreign support, collapsed in 1813. Almost immediately thereafter, however, the Serbian revolt reignited in 1815, led by Miloś Obrenović. The renewed Serb revolt enjoyed greater success and had two major results.

The first was that by 1817 Serbia, although still a province of the Ottoman Empire, had been able to gain autonomous status under Obrenović. The other major result was bad blood between the Obrenović and Karageorge families, touched off when some of Obrenović's supporters murdered Karageorge. The rivalry between the two families dominated Serbian politics over the ensuing eight decades.[12]

Although the Turkish flag continued to fly in Belgrade, during the years after 1817 the Serbs went about creating a distinctive national culture and identity. Much of this revolved around language and literature and was based on the efforts of Vuk Stefanović Karadžić. Serbian nationalists, like others in that day and age, emphasized an idealized distant historical past that looked back to the medieval Serbian Empire of Stefan Dušan that stretched from the Save to the Danube, and from the Adriatic Sea to the Aegean Sea. Youth in Serbia were inculcated with the notion of the heroic past. Serbian national pride was also enhanced by the fact that of all the Balkan peoples, the Serbs were the only ones who were able to achieve a de facto independence without the aid of one or more foreign powers.[13]

Serbia's initial attempt to cast off the facade of Turkish suzerainty occurred in 1875, as part of a combined revolt with Montenegro and Bulgaria against the Turks. The joint efforts of the three peoples, however, came a cropper against the Turks. The failure of the revolts, plus the rising tide of Pan-Slavic feeling in Russia, drove Tsar Alexander II to intervene against Turkey. The ensuing Russo-Turkish War, which began in 1877, ultimately revolved around the siege of Plevna. After a siege of almost two months, the Russian forces were able to capture Plevna and the Turkish forces defending the town. This, plus the subsequent Russian victory at Shipka Pass, put the Russian army almost at the gates of Constantinople.[14]

Faced with British intervention on the side of Turkey, the Russians sought to impose a treaty on Turkey as quickly as possible. The resulting Treaty of San Stefano gave Russia everything it desired in regard to the Balkans. The other major powers of Europe found this unacceptable. Otto von Bismarck, wearing the hats of both Germany's chancellor and foreign minister, organized a conference of the major European powers in Berlin that met from mid-June to mid-July 1879. The Congress of Berlin, with Bismarck as the most prominent participant, modified the Treaty of San Stefano. Russia's territorial gain was limited to Bessarabia. An independent Bulgaria was created, and Serbia and Montenegro were also enlarged. Austria–Hungary was compensated by being given de facto control of Bosnia–Herzegovina, with its large Serbian population, although the area remained in name a part of Ottoman Turkey.[15]

Feelings in Russia ran high against the other European powers in general and against Bismarck in particular. The Russo-Turkish War and its aftermath resulted in the collapse of the League of the Three Emperors, although it was based more on the personal relationships of Alexander II, Germany's Wilhelm I, and Francis Joseph than formal obligations implied by the title.[16] Given the implosion of the multilateral arrangement, Bismarck thought the time was right to sign a 20-year secret alliance with Austria–Hungary. Bismarck's purposes in securing the alliance were twofold. First, from the standpoint of language and culture, Austria–Hungary was Germany's closest natural ally in Europe. Second, Bismarck saw the terms of the alliance, which called for each ally to come to the other's aid *if attacked* by Russia, and staying neutral in a war against any other power, as the best way to check Austro-Hungarian expansionist intentions in the Balkans. Thus the alliance served to prevent a conflict with Russia, while keeping France in a state of diplomatic isolation. From the Austro-Hungarian standpoint, having Germany as a potential ally in a conflict with Russia was comforting, even if Austria–Hungary would have to play the role of second fiddle.[17]

The alliance was a tough sell in both Berlin and Vienna. Wilhelm I, mortified at the prospect of an alliance directed against Russia, was so inclined against the treaty that Bismarck could only get his way by threatening to resign.[18] Austro-Hungarian foreign minister Julius Andrássy had already incurred the wrath of German and Hungarian nationalists and liberals over the occupation of Bosnia. Aged and ill, Andrássy resigned the day after the treaty was signed. Although Francis Joseph approved the agreement, he was unhappy at the humiliating prospect of coordinating Austro-Hungarian foreign policy with that of Germany.[19]

With Austria–Hungary locked up diplomatically, Bismarck then sought to repair relations with Russia. He was able to negotiate a new League of the Three Emperors with the Russian and Austro-Hungarian foreign ministers. Alexander II and Francis Joseph both approved, and the agreement was quickly signed by new tsar Alexander III, despite his reservations, after Alexander II was assassinated in St. Petersburg on March 1, 1881.[20]

Bismarck's second attempt to bring Germany, Austria–Hungary, and Russia together in a multilateral arrangement proved no more successful than his first. Russian and Austro-Hungarian interests clashed again over the Balkans. Austria–Hungary's concern about Russia's desire to both enlarge Bulgaria and turn it into a client state drove the dual monarchy to give limited support to Serbia, then under the control of King Milan Obrenović. Serbian opposition to the incorporation of eastern Rumelia into Bulgaria resulted in a Serbian invasion of Bulgaria on November 14, 1885.[21]

Contrary to Serbian expectations of an easy victory, the Bulgarian army, led by Bulgaria's new sovereign, Prince Alexander of Battenberg, quickly turned the tables on the Serbians. Within a week, Alexander inflicted a major defeat on the Serbians at Slivnica. The Bulgarians sought to follow this up by crossing the Serbian frontier and advancing on Niš. There was considerable concern on the part of both the Serbian and Austro-Hungarian governments that if Niš fell, the Bulgarian advance would continue toward Belgrade. The Bulgarian advance, however, was halted by an ultimatum from Vienna, threatening intervention on Serbia's behalf.[22]

The outcome of the brief war between Serbia and Bulgaria and its aftermath had far-reaching consequences. The most immediate was the collapse of the League of the Three Emperors. Conflicting interests over the Balkans made it impossible for Russia and Austria–Hungary to remain in any kind of formal diplomatic arrangement. Although the Russians were able to foment a coup against Alexander of Battenberg and topple him from the throne, it turned out to be a Pyrrhic victory.[23] The new Bulgarian monarch, Ferdinand of Saxe-Coburg-Gotha, supported by Austria–Hungary and Germany, was officially elected by the Bulgarian National Assembly. He proved even less acceptable to the Russians, but they ultimately had to live with him.

With the League of the Three Emperors then a shambles, Bismarck decided to go to the next best alternative. While maintaining the alliance with Austria–Hungary, Bismarck negotiated a bilateral agreement with his Russian counterpart Nicholas K. Giers, the Reinsurance Treaty. Each party promised to take a neutral stance if the other became involved in a war with a third party. The only two exceptions to this treaty were a Russian attack on Austria–Hungary and a German attack on France.[24] Because one of the two exceptions involved a Russian attack on Austria–Hungary, Bismarck thought it compatible with the original intent of the alliance with Austria–Hungary, which was to check Austro-Hungarian expansionist policy in the Balkans. It was in this context that Bismarck famously commented in a speech to the Reichstag about the Balkans not being worth a Pomeranian grenadier's bones.[25]

The Reinsurance Treaty proved to be Bismarck's last major act of foreign policy. William I died on March 9, 1888. His successor, Crown Prince Friedrich Wilhelm, ascended to the throne as Friedrich III. Already stricken with throat cancer, he died on June 15, 1888. The third German emperor to take the throne in that eventful year was Friedrich III's 29-year-old son, Wilhelm II. The new emperor, young and headstrong, immediately clashed with Bismarck. The aged chancellor, then in his 75th year, regarded the new sovereign as impulsive, indiscreet, and callow. For his part, Wilhelm, egged on by Bismarck's enemies at court and in the government, thought the old chancellor as haughty and arrogant.[26] Arguably Wilhelm and Bismarck were both right. Ultimately, however, only one could hold the center stage, and it was the kaiser. Over a dispute concerning domestic policy, Wilhelm demanded and received Bismarck's resignation on March 16, 1890. German foreign policy then took a different course.

The first major foreign policy issue for the new government, headed by Leo von Caprivi with Friedrich von Holstein as foreign minister, was the renewal of the Reinsurance Treaty. Although the Russians expressed some interest in renewing the agreement, Wilhelm and Holstein, eager to break with any number of Bismarck's notions in foreign policy, let the treaty lapse. Now a diplomatic free agent and unhindered by any prior agreements, Alexander III's Russia gravitated toward an alliance with France, a prospect that became a fact in 1894.[27]

The kaiser followed this alliance with a series of missteps that culminated in his decision to build a navy, urged on by Alfred von Tirpitz, that would be "second to none." The ensuing naval race with Britain and its outcome is too well known to bear repeating here.[28] The end result of the series of errors committed by the kaiser and the series of German governments between 1890 and 1905, culminating in the first Moroccan Crisis, was that Germany was then the isolated power in Europe. Thus it was all the more imperative for Germany to adhere to the alliance with Austria–Hungary. The dual monarchy increasingly found itself drawn into conflict with Serbia.

Although Austria–Hungary had supported Serbia in a limited fashion, after the conclusion of Bulgarian crisis, relations between Austria–Hungary and Serbia eroded badly. Serbia came to look at Bosnia–Herzegovina as unredeemed Serbia. This sentiment was magnified by the role that Bosnia–Herzegovina had played in the development of Serbian language and culture. Matters were not helped by Austro-Hungarian policy in the two provinces. During the late nineteenth century, Austro-Hungarian policy was to play the Serbs and Croats off against each other.[29]

By the early twentieth century, however, the Croats and Serbs had drawn closer to each other. In addition, on June 11, 1903, King Alexander I of Serbia and his wife were assassinated. The assassins were part of a conspiracy hatched by a cabal of army officers. The murders effectively removed the house of Obrenović from power. Alexander's successor was King Peter I, of the Karageorge family. The policy of the Serbian government then took a decidedly pro-Russian and anti-Austro-Hungarian cast.[30]

Anti-Austrian feeling in Serbia was heightened by the policies of the dual monarchy. Serbians who lived in the southern reaches of Hungary were impacted by the policy of "Magyarization" promulgated by the government of Kálmán Tisza, in which the learning of Hungarian was made compulsory for all children, regardless of nationality. Both Hungarian public opinion and government officials strongly opposed any attempt to give Serbians living in the dual monarchy rights and political power equal to those enjoyed by the Hungarians. Thus especially after 1908, when Bosnia–Herzegovina was officially annexed to Austria–Hungary, Serbs who lived within Austria–Hungary looked increasingly to Serbia to deliver them from an oppressive and tyrannical government that aimed to eradicate their culture.[31]

Austria–Hungary regarded Serbia as a mortal threat. Serbia was considered an expansionist power, backed by Russia, seeking territorial gain at the expense of either Austria–Hungary or Ottoman Turkey. As early as 1909 the chief of the General Staff of the Austro-Hungarian army, Feldzeugmeister Franz Baron Conrad von Hötzendorf, was arguing for a preemptive war against Serbia.[32]

The image of Serbia as an aggressive and expansionist power threatening the Austro-Hungarian Empire was confirmed by the Balkan Wars. Serbia, in combination with Montenegro, Bulgaria, and Greece, abetted by Russia, attacked and defeated Ottoman Turkey. With the Turkish presence virtually eliminated from Europe, the victors fell to squabbling over the spoils and a second Balkan War broke out, this time with Serbia, Montenegro, Greece, and Romania ranged against Bulgaria.[33] Serbia ended up gaining about half of Macedonia. The Serbian desire to gain access to the Aegean Sea was frustrated by an Austro-Hungarian ultimatum in October 1913, supported by Germany. Austro-Hungarian foreign minister Leopold von Berchtold succeeded in creating the small and barely viable kingdom of Albania to thwart Serbia's desire for a presence on the Aegean. The outcome of the Balkan Wars left Serbia furious with what was regarded as high-handed behavior by Austria–Hungary, but also with a strengthened sense that Serbia was then the leader of the South Slavs.[34]

Conrad, for whom Serbia was then an obsession, had hoped that Serbia would reject the October 1913 ultimatum, allowing Austria–Hungary to crush Serbia under what Conrad considered favorable circumstances. He even called for war at a Common Ministerial Council meeting held while Serbian prime minister Nikola Pašić was in Vienna on a diplomatic visit. The ministers, both Austrian and Hungarian, did not respond enthusiastically to Conrad's bellicosity. Nonetheless, it was clear that the situation had reached an impasse. Austria–Hungary could not simply let Bosnia and Herzegovina go, as that would begin the unraveling of the empire. Serbia was regarded as a mortal threat, and some major political and military figures, most notably Conrad, believed that the only way to deal with the threat was to invade Serbia and incorporate it into the empire. For its part, the Serbian government, headed by the pro-Russian combination of King Peter with Pašić as his prime minister, regarded Austria–Hungary as a declining power, the new "sick man of Europe."[35]

The story of the assassination of Archduke Franz Ferdinand and his wife Sophie in Sarajevo on June 28, 1914, is too well known to bear repeating here. It is simply sufficient to say that the war party saw the assassination as a chance to resolve the Serbian problem in a definitive fashion. The opposition of the Hungarian prime minister, István Tisza, was overcome by Berchtold's promise that no Serbian territory would be annexed, thus preserving the privileged status held by the Hungarians.[36] The threat of Russian intervention on Serbia's behalf was mitigated by the promise of full German support. The state of Germany's position in Europe virtually demanded that Austria–Hungary be supported, even if the consequences meant a widening of the war, although such an eventuality was certainly desired by some in Berlin.[37] Clearly the nature of the alliance between Germany and Austria–Hungary had departed from Bismarck's original vision.

As the desires of the war party at the Ballplatz became reality and dual monarchy moved toward war with Serbia and probably Russia, diplomacy faded to the background, replaced by the execution of mobilization and war plans. For Austria–Hungary, this had been a particularly tricky issue. Individual plans had to be devised for possible wars against Italy, Russia, and Serbia, or against any combination of these powers. Planning had to be done in some degree of consultation with Germany, especially in regard to Russia.

The story of cooperation (or lack thereof) between the respective general staffs of both Austria–Hungary and Germany and the relationships between the various chiefs of the general staffs between 1879 and 1914 is beyond the scope of this study.[38] It is sufficient to say that neither ally was entirely honest with the other. Although contact between the elder Moltke and his Austro-Hungarian counterpart Feldmarschall Friedrich Baron von Beck-Rzikowsky was regular and detailed, that type of relationship did not last long after Moltke's retirement in 1888. When the secretive Generalfeldmarschall Alfred von Schlieffen became chief of the General Staff in 1891, he recast the direction of German war planning. German war planning, especially after 1896, took on a focus oriented toward France. At the same time, Schlieffen's relationship with Beck took on a character that could be described as nugatory, with contacts reduced to only the most perfunctory sort.[39]

An improvement in matters was expected with the near simultaneous appointments of Conrad as chief of the Austro-Hungarian General Staff and Colonel General Helmuth von Moltke, the nephew of the victor of 1866 and 1870 (known as "Moltke the Younger"), as chief of the German General Staff in 1906.[40] The two men met much more often than their predecessors, but the relationship was far from trusting. Moltke gave Conrad a broad outline of the Schlieffen Plan but never provided details. Moltke simply assured Conrad in February 10, 1913, letter that the fate of Austria–Hungary would be determined by events on the Seine River as opposed to the Bug. Conrad, however, continued to believe that the Germans would make a major effort in the east.[41]

Moltke's unwillingness to divulge details certainly seemed wise when a highly placed staff officer, Colonel Alfred Redl, was arrested on May 24, 1913. Redl, a homosexual blackmailed into espionage by the Russians, had divulged a great deal of information about Austro-Hungarian war plans to both the Russians and the Serbians.[42] Conrad interrogated Redl, facilitated his suicide, and then tried to cover up the matter. Although the Germans were informed of Redl's arrest, details regarding his activities were withheld and Conrad did little more than give Moltke vague assurances trying to minimize the damage.[43] The result of all the reciprocal mistrust and deceit was that when the war began, neither army was quite sure what exactly the other would do. One thing was certain, however. If Austria–Hungary and Germany were involved in a war against France, Russia, and Serbia, the Serbian front would be handled exclusively by Austria–Hungary.

The Austro-Hungarian effort against Serbia was complicated by Conrad's own misjudgments concerning mobilization. Although it was clear that the Austro-Hungarians had decided on war against Serbia in early July, it was also clear two weeks later, before mobilization was declared, that war with Russia also loomed as a distinct possibility.[44] Thus the question revolved around two related issues, namely how large a force should be sent against the Russians and Serbians and what posture the forces should adopt once they deployed on their respective fronts.

Austria–Hungary declared war against Serbia on July 28, 1914. The next day Conrad issued the order for mobilization, which was followed by the partial Russian mobilization the same day. Conrad decided on the mobilization schedule that would send the Austro-Hungarian Second Army to the Serbian front. With a full Russian mobilization looming and Moltke urging him to undertake a larger concentration against the Russians, Conrad changed his mind two days later. He decided to send the Second Army to the Galician frontier, only to be told by the railway section of the General Staff that such a request was impossible, because mobilization was already under way.[45] Thus the Second Army would have to go down to the Serbian border, off load from their trains, and then reboard trains to go to the Galician border. Even though the Austro-Hungarians would have to proceed against Serbia with a smaller force, Conrad still assured Francis Joseph that a decisive victory over Serbia could be secured quickly.[46]

The prospect of a quick victory lay generally in the hands of the Austro-Hungarian Sixth Army in general and in particular in the hands of its commander, Feldzeugmeister Oskar Potiorek. Born on November 20, 1853, Potiorek had enjoyed a very successful career in the army, mostly in staff positions. His assignments included serving as deputy to Beck during his tenure as chief of the General Staff. This may have worked against him when Archduke Franz Ferdinand had to choose between Potiorek and Conrad as Beck's successor. Potiorek was embittered by Conrad's selection and was effectively bought off with the command on the Serbian border. It was this position that gave Potiorek the responsibility for Franz Ferdinand's security arrangements for the Archduke's visit to Sarajevo, not exactly a glittering success.[47]

Although he had very limited command experience, Potiorek was then entrusted with the overall command of the Austro-Hungarian Fifth and Sixth armies. Both armies were small, each with two corps attached. Potiorek had a total of about 10 infantry divisions, backed up by a number of reserve brigades, all together about 140,000 men, supported by 258 guns. A large number of formations had sizeable percentages of soldiers of southern

Slavic ethnicity, a factor that called their willingness to fight against Serbia into question.[48]

Opposing the Austro-Hungarian forces was the Serbian army. The Serbians fielded 11 infantry divisions, 6 first line and 6 second line. Fifteen third-line regiments were also available. The Serbians also had a first-line cavalry division on hand. These units gave the Serbian army a total strength of over 400,000 officers and men, many of whom had combat experience. These forces were supported by a reasonable amount of field artillery, plus fifty-two 120-mm guns and howitzers mainly of French manufacture, along with a battery of six 150-mm howitzers.[49]

The soul of the Serbian defense effort, however, was its commander. Voivode (Marshal) Radomir Putnik. Born in 1847 in the Serbian arsenal town of Kragujevać, Putnik began his career in the Serbian army as an artillery officer. His distinguished service against the Turks marked him for high rank. Putnik's association with the Radical Party, however, made him run afoul of the Obrenović dynasty. The return of the Karageorge family to power in 1903 brought Putnik back to prominence. When the first Balkan War began in 1912, Putnik led the Serbian army in the field and defeated the Turkish army at Kumanovo. He also produced a victory over Bulgaria in the Second Balkan War in 1913. Worn out from his exertions and in poor health, Putnik was taking the waters at Bad Gleichenberg in Austria when war broke out between Serbia and Austria–Hungary. Putnik was allowed to cross the border after the personal intervention of Francis Joseph with Austro-Hungarian border officials.[50]

Potiorek had very little if any margin for error. He sought to improve this by holding on to as much of the Second Army as possible, before the rest of it reboarded trains to head off to Galicia. Ultimately Potiorek used his considerable influence at court to keep four divisions, much to Conrad's dismay. The additional divisions raised Potiorek's manpower to 400,000, although this included a number of reserve and garrison units of dubious quality. The added units also brought Potiorek over 200 more guns. More important, Potiorek also used his clout to make his command effectively independent of Conrad Austro-Hungarian supreme headquarters, Armee Oberkommando or AOK.[51]

The Austro-Hungarian declaration of war against Serbia found Potiorek's units generally unprepared for immediate offensive action. To administer some instant punishment to the Serbians, Portiorek decided to use his available artillery, plus Austro-Hungarian navy monitors in the Save and Danube Rivers. Shells began hitting Belgrade on July 28 and continued with varying degrees of intensity over the next 36 days. By October 1914, 640 private houses and 60 government buildings had been hit. One structure that was damaged was the Austro-Hungarian consulate, which was hit by two shells. The buildings that housed the Russian and English legations were also damaged.[52]

This punitive if indiscriminate action was followed by the first Austro-Hungarian invasion. Although Potiorek had increased his forces, Montenegro's support of Serbia meant that Potiorek then had to defend a 400-mile border: Montenegro, Serbia, and Bosnia–Herzegovina. Nonetheless, Potiorek pressed ahead, sending the Austro-Hungarian Fifth Army under General der Infanterie Liborius *Ritter* von Frank across the upper Drina and Save Rivers on August 12, a crossing that was not completed until August 15. The Fifth Army was followed later by Potioek's own Sixth Army across the lower Drina, on the Fifth Army's right. Elements of the Second Army crossed the Danube near Belgrade. Conrad had allowed Potioriek the use of parts of the Second Army until August 18, when it had to be transferred to Galicia. Although Potiorek's original concept was to draw Serbian forces to the Fifth Army and the strike the Serbian left flank with the Sixth Army, events forced Potiorek into precisely the opposite course.[53]

Putnik had the luxury of time, intelligence, and topography. He was aware from a combination of local intelligence and information that had been supplied by Redl that the Austro-Hungarian Second Army was due to head off to Galicia in a very short time. In addition, the fact that Bulgaria had declared neutrality alleviated the need to employ large forces along the lengthy border between Serbia and Bulgaria. Thus Putnik had little to worry about over his right flank, allowing him to mass his forces against Potiorek's center, taking advantage of the gap between Frank's Fifth and Potiorek's Sixth armies.[54]

On August 16, 1914, the Serbian Second and Third armies attacked the Austro-Hungarian Fifth Army at Jadar on the Cer plateau. The attack caught Frank's forces in a somewhat scattered condition. In addition, the Austro-Hungarian troops were ill-equipped for mountain warfare. The Austro-Hungarian forces, having outrun their supplies and harassed by Serbian civilians fighting as guerrillas, fell apart quickly. The Austrian Twenty-First Infantry Division in particular suffered heavy casualties.

Putnik then turned his attention to the Austro-Hungarian Sixth Army. Although the Sixth Army was able to win some local actions, the result was yet another Austro-Hungarian retreat. By the end of August, all of Potiorek's forces were back across the rivers. Putnik, pressed by Russian calls for help, sent forces across the Drina into Bosnia. The Serbian invasion failed to arouse the Bosnian population against the Austro-Hungarians, and Potiorek was able to mount a defense, forcing the Serbs back across the river. Potiorek's first invasion had failed, losing some 600 officers and 22,000 men in about two weeks.[55]

Undeterred, Potiorek convinced AOK to allow him another crack at invading Serbia. This time the Potiorek's forces attempted a night crossing of the Drina and then crossed the Save. Launched on September 8, this attempt had even less success than Potiorek's first try. Shallow bridgeheads were created and promptly became magnets for Serbian counterattacks.

Rainfall turned the ground into a bog, restricting mobility for both sides. For four days the Austro-Hungarian Sixth Army and the Serbian First Army slugged it out for possession of Jagodnja Mountain, with heavy losses on both sides before the Austro-Hungarians gained control.[56]

Once again Putnik tried to counter Potiorek's invasion with an offensive of his own into Bosnia and even Hungary. On September 23, units from Serbian army group Užice, supported by Montenegrin troops, were able to get back into southeastern Bosnia.[57] Potiorek, using a combination of field formations and troops drawn from various fortresses, was able to drive the Serbians and Montenegrins back across the Drina during the first half of October.

Unwilling to accept the stalemate and perhaps realizing that his chance to supplant Conrad at AOK was slipping away, Potiorek launched yet another offensive against Serbia. Starting on November 6, the Fifth and Sixth armies were able to make slow but painful progress. Belgrade fell to Potiorek on December 2, and he announced its capture with great fanfare to Francis Joseph. Vienna responded with major celebrations, including a torchlight parade. Potiorek received all manner of honors, and Francis Joseph, apparently without even a hint of irony, named a street for Potiorek in Sarajevo.[58]

Celebrations of Austro-Hungarian success, however, were short-lived. The Austro-Hungarians were at the end of their logistical tether. Many soldiers were still wearing summer uniforms, suffering in the cold and often snowy weather. Aided by a timely French delivery of artillery ammunition, Putnik, showing an excellent sense of timing, unleashed four armies with 200,000 men a week after the occupation of Belgrade. On December 15, Belgrade came back into Serbian hands. The Austro-Hungarians found themselves right back where they had started from in August.[59]

Potiorek's campaigns against Serbia proved to be as costly as they were reckless. His armies reached a maximum strength of around 450,000 men during the summer of 1914. By the end of December Austro-Hungarian losses reached almost 274,000. These included almost 30,000 killed, over 122,000 wounded, and almost 75,000 missing, the vast majority of whom were captured. Also troubling was the fact that almost 47,000 were sick. Losses were so heavy that the Sixth Army was dissolved, and its remnants were subsumed into the Fifth Army. Conrad admitted in private to Lieutenant Colonel Karl von Kageneck, the German military attaché to Vienna that the dual monarchy had paid a high for acting on the desire to "slap Serbia."[60]

The final casualty was Potiorek himself. He had been able to make himself independent, or at least autonomous, from AOK. That position allowed Potiorek to ignore Conrad's order in October to adopt a defensive posture. If Potiorek was going to topple Conrad from his place at AOK, he had to produce results; the three invasions of Serbia brought about precisely the opposite of results desired. Because Potiorek had made himself independent of AOK, he then had to bear the responsibility for the disasters in Serbia, although that did not stop Potiorek from cashiering Frank in an attempt to shift blame. On December 17 Potiorek was relieved of command. He was succeeded by General der Kavallerie Archduke Eugen, who assumed command of a battered Fifth Army.[61]

Although Serbia had won a major victory, success too came at a considerable cost. The 1914 campaigns had cost Putnik over 163,000 casualties, including 69,000 fatalities from combat and sickness. The Austro-Hungarians also took some 19,000 prisoners. The Serbian army had also lost 60 guns. Although some material came in from Britain and Russia, losses had to be replaced by pressing captured Austro-Hungarian pieces into service, a measure that is always a second best course of action. Nonetheless, by the end of 1914 it was clear that Serbia had won a major victory and the prestige of Austro-Hungarian arms, not high to begin with, had suffered accordingly.[62]

Although the defeats suffered by Potiorek's forces were bad enough, far worse were the disasters inflicted by the Russians against Conrad's armies in Galicia. A confused mobilization made worse by Conrad's whipsawing of the Second Army between Serbia and Galicia and pointless cavalry raid left Conrad's armies, both outnumbered, virtually blind. Although outnumbered, Conrad, ever the believer that the best defense is a good offense, took the aggressive. Although General der Kavallerie Viktor Dankl's Austro-Hungarian First Army won an early success against the Russians at Kraśnik, the tide of war turned against Conrad. A series of at times confused actions were fought along the border east of the San River. The campaign culminated with the battle of Rava-Ruska on September 8, which was won decisively by the Russians. The defeat was made all the more personal for Conrad when his son Herbert was killed in the action.[63]

Conrad pulled his battered armies back across the San, abandoning Lemberg, the capital of Galicia. He also moved AOK from Przemysl to Teschen, while also leaving a large garrison in the fortress to hold it against the Russians. Buoyed by German victories to the north, Conrad reorganized and reinforced his armies. After consultation with his German allies, Conrad launched an offensive on September 30, 1914, as the German commander in the east, Generalfeldmarschall Paul von Hindenburg, undertook an offensive against Warsaw. The combined offensive made good initial progress; Conrad's armies relieved Przemysl on October 9. After that, however, the offensive foundered. Austro-Hungarian efforts to cross the San at other points failed, and Hindenburg's offensive into Russian Poland encountered increasingly stout opposition.[64]

The Russian commander-in-chief, Grand Duke Nicholas, had completed a complicated reorganization and repositioning of his armies. In mid-October the Russians went over to the offensive all along the front. As the Germans were driven away from Poland, the Austro-Hungarians were forced back from the San. Przemysl, with its garrison of over 120,000 men, was once again laid siege to by the Russians. By the time Conrad was able to check the Russian offensive at Limanowa-Lapanow in December, the Austro-Hungarian armies had been forced back into the Carpathian passes.[65] There the campaign ended.

While the Serbian campaigns were costly, the battles in Galicia were beyond disastrous. Austro-Hungarian losses in Galicia in 1914 were over 2,500,000, including well over 500,000 prisoners. Another 120,000 men were besieged in Przemysl. Huge amounts of material had been lost. By the end of 1914 the total strength of the Austro-Hungarian forces in the Carpathians was less than 300,000 men.[66] Even worse, the Russian Southwest Front was poised for a potential offensive from the Carpathian passes into the Hungarian plain.

The 1914 campaigns marked the culmination of the struggle between Austria–Hungary and Serbia that began essentially in 1879, with the dual monarchy's acquisition of Bosnia–Herzegovina. Despite Bismarck's diplomatic efforts, the coming clash could not be avoided. Ultimately the Austria–Hungary had no better alternative than to invade Serbia in an attempt to crush it. There was discussion in the Ballplatz about annexing Serbia to Austria–Hungary, although it is difficult to see how the dual monarchy could have profited from incorporating millions of restive Serbs into it, especially given Hungarian opposition to such a course of action. Even Conrad, the most ardent advocate of war against Serbia, later conceded that the long-term existence of the dual monarchy was essentially hopeless.[67]

Regardless of the prospects for the dual monarchy's survival, the execution of the Austro-Hungarian war plan and the subsequent campaigns in Galicia and Serbia left much to be desired. Austria–Hungary's army was capable of a major effort on only one front. That front should have been Galicia, especially after the specter of Russian involvement became apparent. Conrad's first error was to send the Second Army to Serbia and then send it back to Galicia. The court and Conrad compounded this error by letting Potiorek retain first all of the Second Army and later parts of it. Conrad's subsequent errors and misjudgments regarding the campaign in Galicia lie beyond the scope of this study.

Potiorek's mistakes were even less understandable than Conrad's. Even though he was going to be able to retain part of the Second Army, Potiorek's margin for error against the Serbian army was still slim. In addition his troops were ill-equipped for mountain warfare. Once the first invasion failed, Potiorek would have been wiser to adopt a defensive posture, as Conrad eventually suggested. In addition, Potiorek's securing a position autonomous from if not independent of AOK made him fully responsible for results. Ultimately Potiorek's dismissal was well deserved. From Conrad's perspective Potiorek's fall cemented his position as the de facto head of AOK, while Conrad was also able to dissociate himself from the defeats on the Serbian front.[68]

From the Serbian perspective the 1914 campaigns had an optimal outcome but still provided cause for concern. Bulgarian neutrality allowed Putnik to concentrate his forces against Potiorek. The voivode showed an excellent sense of timing in ordering counterattacks, particularly in December. The continuation of the attempted invasion of Bosnia was probably unwise, especially once the population showed an attitude of indifference. Also, although the 1914 campaigns were successful, victory still had its price and losses, in both men and material, were not easily replaced.

Both Germany and Austria–Hungary had entered the war with relatively clear strategic priorities. By the beginning of 1915 those priorities had shifted, and the position of Serbia among those priorities had also shifted. The reshuffling of priorities and how Serbia fit into the issue must now be addressed.

Chapter 2

Setting the Target: Strategic Priorities and Decisions, March–September 1915

> "Strategy is a system of expedients. It is . . . the continued development of the original leading thought in accordance with the constantly changing circumstances. It is the art of acting under the pressure of the most difficult conditions."
>
> Helmuth von Moltke the Elder, 1871[1]

By the end of 1914 if one thing had become absolutely clear to all of the major powers involved in World War I, it was that all of their war plans had miscarried to one degree or another. In this regard the power that was the worst off was Austria–Hungary. While any attempts by Serbia to make inroads into Bosnia and Herzegovina had been thwarted, all three Austro-Hungarian invasions of Serbia had ended in punishing defeats. Even worse, the disasters suffered in Galicia left the Russians in the Carpathian passes, threatening to erupt on to the Hungarian plain. At the same time, the fortress of Przemysl, with its large garrison and immense amounts of equipment, was besieged by the Russian Eleventh Army.

Germany was in a situation that was as difficult as it was complex. Although Germany had occupied almost all of Belgium and an important part of northeastern France, victory in the west was a long way off. Although the German forces in the east under Hindenburg and his chief of staff Erich Ludendorff had enjoyed success at Tannenberg, the attempt to take Warsaw had miscarried and Russian forces were still on Prussian soil. Turkey had joined the Central powers in October 1914 but was in an isolated situation, as there was no secure land route of communication between Germany and

Turkey. Between the two allies were two countries, hostile Serbia and neutral Bulgaria.

The two men most responsible for finding a way out of this situation to victory were General der Infanterie Erich von Falkenhayn and his Austro-Hungarian counterpart, Conrad von Hötzendorf. Erich von Falkenhayn was born on November 11, 1861, to a large (he had six siblings) and old aristocratic West Prussian family whose history was marked by a record of distinguished military service. General officers in the family included Falkenhayn's grandfather and several of his brothers.[2]

As befitting the scion of a military family, Falkenhayn attended the most important of the cadet schools in Germany, the one in Lichterfelde, near Berlin. After gaining his commission in the infantry as a lieutenant on April 17, 1880, Falkenhayn enjoyed a most successful career in the German army, including a considerable amount of time overseas. After his graduation in 1890 from the Kriegsakademie, Falkenhayn spent time in Chile as an instructor and in China, including a tour as a staff officer with the international force created to crush the Boxer Rebellion in China. After returning from Asia Falkenhayn was promoted to colonel in 1908 and given command of the Fourth Guards Regiment. A successful command stint resulted in Falkenhayn's promotion to Generalmajor in 1912.[3]

Falkenhayn's service in the Far East brought him to the attention of the Hohenzollern court. Both Wilhelm II and his brother Prince Heinrich thought Falkenhayn a most impressive individual and worthy of high position in the government. To the surprise of many, Wilhelm II appointed Falkenhayn Prussian minister of war on July 7, 1913, a position normally reserved for an officer with higher rank than a relatively junior Generalmajor. To preserve appearances, Wilhelm quickly promoted Falkenhayn to Generalleutnant.[4]

Although rather young for his position, Falkenhayn clearly reflected the innate conservatism that was a hallmark of imperial Germany. He sought to minimize the influence that the Reichstag might exercise over military policy and maintain the kaiser's privileges in that area as well. His approval of the army's heavy-handed crackdown on protesters in Alsace in the Zabern affair also illustrated his conservatism, which also earned him the enmity of the Social Democrats in the Reichstag. Militarily, the only major initiative undertaken by Falkenhayn as war minister was to increase the number of artillery shells per gun, although that step had not been completed when war broke out in 1914.[5]

During the first campaign in the west, Falkenhayn traveled with the Oberste Heeresleitung (OHL), the German supreme headquarters. By the middle of September it was clear that the stresses of the campaign had broken Moltke's health both physically and psychologically. Wilhelm II had been satisfied by Falkenhayn's tenure as Prussian war minister and was impressed by his energy. Perhaps sensing that the position of chief of the General Staff required a younger, more vigorous man, Wilhelm II made his choice. After a rather awkward period in October where Falkenhayn exercised de facto power while Moltke was still at OHL headquarters, the kaiser passed over a number of more senior generals once again and made Falkenhayn the new head of OHL, effective November 1, 1914.[6] To appease the objections of a number of people, including Chancellor Theobald von Bethmann-Hollweg and Ludendorff, Falkenhayn relinquished the post of Prussian war minister. Adolf Wild von Hohenborn, a close associate of Falkenhayn, was appointed Prussian war minister in January 1915. The issue of rank was also solved in January 1915 by a quick promotion for Falkenhayn to General der Infanterie.[7]

Falkenhayn, a tall man with an impassive countenance, a steely gaze, and a crew cut, was someone who rarely evoked indifference among his fellow officers. He had a talent for making enemies that bordered on genius. To be sure, some of this was a matter of circumstance. Appointed head of OHL at the age of 53 and of relatively junior rank, it is fair to say that a good many people with greater seniority were rankled by the mere fact that Wilhelm II had violated a treasured principle of military etiquette, namely seniority, by advancing someone so young to such a high position.[8] At this point in the war, however, the kaiser still mattered, and his support sustained Falkenhayn against the intrigues of his critics.[9]

The principal base of opposition to Falkenhayn was the German headquarters in the east, Ober Ost. Headed by Paul von Hindenburg and his chief of staff Erich Ludendorff, Ober Ost was established, ironically enough, by Falkenhayn in the fall of 1914, as the growth of German forces on the eastern front demanded the creation of a formal headquarters to direct the operations of several German armies on the eastern front.[10] The climate of opinion at Ober Ost was that the war should be won in the east and that Russia could be knocked out of the war. Thus the preponderance of German forces should be placed in the hands of the Hindenburg and Ludendorff duumvirate. Both men still believed in the concept of a decisive battle of annihilation, so dear to Schlieffen's thinking, and that it could be achieved against Russia. Ludendorff was also a firm advocate of expansion eastward, given his own proclivities and ties to pan-German organizations.[11]

Falkenhayn saw the war very differently. After the attempt to fight one last decisive battle in the west in 1914 resulted in the costly failure at Ypres, Falkenhayn decided to reconsider Germany's strategy. Where Schlieffen had considered France, Germany's most implacable enemy, an opinion shared by Moltke, Falkenhayn saw Britain in that role. With a continuous front in the west now a reality, the possibility of achieving a decisive result in the west was highly unlikely in the present circumstances.[12]

Although Falkenhayn desired to come to grips with Britain, he realized that this was not possible in the immediate situation. The next steps undertaken by Germany strategically were determined by situations regarding Galicia,

Turkey, and Italy. Of these, Galicia was the most important. During the winter and early spring of 1915 Conrad launched a series of offensives against the Russian forces in the Carpathian passes in a desperate attempt to relieve Przemysl, then besieged by the Russian Eleventh Army. Conrad's three offensives, launched in late January and continuing to late March, resulted in the worst of all possible worlds; each successive attack failed, and Przemysl fell on March 23, 1915. Taken all together, between Conrad's Carpathian campaigns and the fall of Przemysl, the Austro-Hungarian army suffered almost a million casualties.[13]

Although a Russian attempt to advance from the Carpathian passes into the Hungarian plain failed narrowly, the situation Austria–Hungary faced was dire. During late March and early April, August von Cramon, the German liaison officer at Armee Oberkommando (AOK), sent reports to OHL that described the state of the Austro-Hungarian army in alarming terms. Conrad also now sought German assistance, as much as it pained him to do so. Help had to be sent quickly, lest a renewed Russian breakout from the Carpathians cause an Austro-Hungarian collapse.[14]

Another situation that commanded Falkenhayn's attention concerned that of Turkey. The Ottoman Empire, still smarting from its recent defeats, looked to Germany for help in modernizing and upgrading the Turkish army. The most apparent manifestation of this assistance was the German Military Mission headed by Otto Liman von Sanders, sent to Constantinople by the kaiser in late 1913. The German military presence aroused Russian suspicion.[15]

The entry of Turkey on the side of the Central powers was by no means a certainty when war broke out in July and early August, although the new war minister, Young Turk leader Enver Pasha, was anxious to bring Turkey in. Conrad also wanted Turkey to join the Central powers, but only in the context of a fanciful notion (as only Conrad could dream up) of using some 50,000 Turkish troops and some Ukrainians to raise a revolt among the Kuban Cossacks against the tsar. The Porte's hand, however, was forced by the German navy, with the arrival of the light cruisers *Goeben* and *Breslau* under Rear Admiral Wilhelm Souchon and the granting of entry into the straits by the Turkish government.[16] Turkey's entry was confirmed by the delivery of a large amount of gold from Germany to Turkey, and Enver's ordering Souchon into the Black Sea to attack Russian ships and ports. By November 2, 1914, Turkey was at war with Russia and the other entente powers.[17]

Turkey's entry provided both positives and negatives for Germany. With Turkey then on Germany's side, Germany had a means through which the British Empire could be challenged directly, as some German military thinkers had envisioned before the war. This certainly fit well with Falkenhayn's concept of strategy for the war.[18]

Any advantages that Turkey brought to the Central powers, however, were offset by some serious disadvantages. The most prominent of these was geography. With Bulgaria still neutral and Serbia unconquered, there was no direct line of communication by land between Berlin and Constantinople. Although the Anglo-French naval thrust up the Straits of the Dardanelles on March 18, 1915, came to naught against modern Turkish artillery and mines, Falkenhayn still had to be concerned about the ability of the Turks to fend off a determined thrust by the entente toward Constantinople in the future. British forces under Sir John Nixon seemed poised to press up from Basra to take Baghdad. Although the Turkish army had adequate stocks of ammunition in early 1915, Turkey's isolation could place it in a dangerous situation if those stocks were consumed in a couple of major campaigns. In addition, German intelligence was reporting that the Russians were assembling a large force in Odessa for a descent on the Turkish coast. Without additional aid from Germany, Turkey's prospects for remaining in the war for the long haul were dim indeed.[19]

Still another concern for Falkenhayn was the attitude of Italy. A signatory to the Triple Alliance in 1882 with Germany and Austria–Hungary, Italy had been steadily backing away from that arrangement, especially after 1908.[20] Although German war planning, especially under Moltke the Younger, had taken Italy's possible defection into account, the actual declaration of neutrality by the government of Antonio Salandra left a bitter taste. Moltke vented his rage against Italy especially after the 1914 campaign in the west had miscarried.[21]

By the spring of 1915, it was becoming increasingly clear that Italy was moving toward becoming an active member of the entente. Falkenhayn urged the Austro-Hungarians to try to buy off the Italians with territorial concessions in the Tirol. That suggestion brought the sarcastic rejoinder from Conrad that Germany should cede Alsace-Lorraine back to France.[22] Because a diplomatic solution between Austria–Hungary and Italy was not possible, some major military success by Germany and Austria–Hungary might dissuade Italy from taking the plunge into war.

Such a situation required close cooperation between Germany and Austria-Hungary. That would be a difficult proposition given the personality of Falkenhayn's Austro-Hungarian counterpart, the ever-controversial Franz Baron Conrad von Hötzendorf. Born on November 11, 1852, Conrad was the son of Franz Xaver Conrad von Hötzendorf, a Napoleonic War veteran and professional cavalry officer until injury caused his retirement in 1848.

Conrad's military service began at the Wiener Neustadt Military Academy in 1867, and he graduated in 1871. After his first posting as a lieutenant with the 11th Field Jäger Battalion, Conrad enjoyed a most successful career over the ensuing four decades. Posted as an instructor to the Austrian War College from 1888 to 1892, Conrad developed a reputation as one of the major thinkers in the Austro-Hungarian army. Later on, commanding at both the regimental and divisional level, Conrad was regarded as an innovative officer and an inspiring leader. He was also able to create a coterie of officers, many of whom were his former students, who were devoted to Conrad.[23]

Conrad was appointed chief of the General Staff in November 1906, mainly on the recommendation of Archduke Francis Ferdinand and some other members of the royal family. Conrad held the position, with the exception of one short break, almost continuously from the time of his appointment until his dismissal in early 1917. Perhaps the one trait that most distinguished Conrad during his tenure was the phenomenon of obsession. Conrad's first fixation was on Serbia. He had been an ardent proponent of war against Serbia since 1909.[24] In 1914 he finally had that desire satisfied. The object of Conrad's next obsessive urge was Gina von Reininghaus, the beautiful wife of Austria's biggest hotel magnate, Hans von Reininghaus. Conrad eventually satisfied that want, marrying his mistress later in 1915, after Gina's divorce was granted. Gina's appearance at AOK in early 1915 and the happy couple's setting up housekeeping at AOK in Teschen, a practice emulated by other senior officers at AOK, was regarded as scandalous by German liaison officers there.[25]

By early 1915 Conrad had moved on to two new obsessions. The first was the besieged fortress of Przemysl.[26] Conrad mounted several offensives to relieve Przemysl but succeeded only in bleeding his army white as the Russians eventually occupied the fortress on March 23, 1915. Conrad's other obsession, and a much more long-lasting one, concerned Italy. From the time of his tour as a brigade commander in Trieste 1899, especially after some civil disturbances there in 1902, Conrad nurtured a hatred of all things (with the exception of Gina) Italian.[27] Conrad's fixation with Italy only increased as Italy moved from a position of neutrality toward belligerence.

Falkenhayn and Conrad were not well suited to working together to meet the demands of coalition warfare. The two men were not exactly contemporaries, as Conrad was almost a decade older. More than that, Conrad was a man of the nineteenth century. He generally preferred personal meetings. Once a meeting was over, Conrad followed it up with a lengthy memorandum, often written in the kind of florid style more common to the nineteenth century. Because the Serbian campaigns in 1914 had been Potiorek's exclusive responsibility, Conrad spent most of his time at Teschen.[28]

Falkenhayn's situation was rather different. Although Hindenburg and Ludendorff ran operations on the eastern front at Ober Ost, Falkenhayn had to divide his time between OHL headquarters on the western front at Meziéres, Berlin, Allenstein (Ober Ost's headquarters), and OHL's eastern front headquarters at Pless, about one hour's drive away from Teschen. All this meant extensive travel by train and automobile.[29] Given these circumstances, Falkenhayn considered face-to-face meetings too wasteful of precious time. For him, if a personal conversation was required, that was something that could be handled by telephone, a device with which Conrad was never comfortable. When it came to written communications, Falkenhayn regularly redefined the meaning of the word *terse*.[30]

Given the differences in age, outlook, and style, it should have come as no surprise that the relationship between the two men was difficult. It got off to as poor a start as possible when Falkenhayn invited Conrad in late October 1914 to come to Berlin to discuss the situation on the eastern front. Instead of making the trip, Conrad sent his aide, Lieutenant Colonel Rudolf Kundmann, as his representative. Gerhard Tappen, Falkehayn's operations officer, noted Kundmann's attendance at the meeting but simply listed him as "Conrad's adjutant," not even mentioning Kundmann by name. Although the meeting was conducted in a manner that was civil enough, there was no doubt that OHL in general and Falkenhayn in particular were livid at what could rightly be considered a childish snub by Conrad. This could hardly be considered a positive omen for the development of a good working relationship.[31]

Over the first three months of 1915, as events in the Carpathians and the siege of Przemysl ran their respective courses, Falkenhayn set his strategic priorities. Three people figured prominently in these decisions. The first was Colonel (later Generalmajor) Ernst Wrisberg. Head of the army section in the war ministry, Wrisberg had come up with a plan for reorganizing the German army. Falkenhayn met Wrisberg on February 22, 1915, and Falkenhayn approved the plan, which also met with Wilhelm II's concurrence.[32]

Wrisberg's plan, which also applied to the military establishments of Bavaria, Saxony, and Württemberg, reorganized the German army's divisions. In 1914 the German army went to war with divisions that used a "square pattern" organization. Each infantry division consisted of two brigades, with each brigade containing two regiments, usually with three battalions each. Thus, the standard German infantry division based its combat power on 12 infantry battalions.

Under Wrisberg's plan, each division would give up a brigade headquarters plus one infantry regiment. The divisions losing units would be compensated by getting additional trained replacements as well as extra machine guns. The detached regiments would be used to create new divisions. It was hoped that the reorganization would produce as many as 24 new divisions, which would fill the role of Germany's strategic reserve.[33]

In actual execution, Wrisberg's plan took a bit more time to execute, as it had to be carried out gradually. In addition, there was difficulty in providing the equipment needed to fully outfit the newly created divisions. Some units, such as the Bavarian 11th Infantry Division, were not created until March 21, 1915. In the end, Wrisberg's plan yielded only 14 divisions.[34] Nonetheless, by the spring of 1915 Falkenhayn had a strategic reserve at his disposal.

While Germany's new strategic reserve was being formed, Falkenhayn turned to Colonel (later Generalmajor) August von Cramon. Born on April 7, 1861, Cramon was commissioned as a lieutenant on February 13, 1883.

Cramon spent his career as an up and coming officer in the cavalry, eventually reaching the rank of colonel on January 1, 1912, after doing a tour as commander of the Guards Cuirassier Regiment. When war broke out in 1914, Cramon was the chief of staff of the VII Corps. On October 21, 1914, Cramon was appointed commander of the Third Cavalry Brigade. After a short combat tour in France, on January 30, 1915, Cramon was appointed the OHL representative to AOK in Teschen.[35]

Cramon as OHL's representative at AOK proved to be a felicitous choice. As the German liaison officer at AOK, Cramon was able to gain the trust of both Falkenhayn and Conrad. In addition, Cramon was able to develop excellent relationships with members of the AOK staff. This enabled Cramon to provide Falkenhayn with timely, accurate, and detailed information.[36] During late March, Falkenhayn asked Cramon for a good deal of detailed information regarding the overall state of the Austro-Hungarian forces on the eastern front and the Russian forces opposing them. Cramon's responses apparently gave Falkenhayn precisely what he was looking for.[37]

With that information in hand, Falkenhayn next went to Colonel Wilhelm Groener, the chief of the railway section of the General Staff. Falkenhayn asked to examine Groener to look at three different courses of action in regard to moving forces to the east. The three alternatives were the Nieman River, a sector on both sides of the Pilica River, or against Serbia. At the end of March, Falkenhayn narrowed Groener's task to that of moving German forces into upper Silesia and Galicia.[38]

Once he had all of the facts at hand, Falkenhayn made his decision. He sounded out Cramon on April 4, 1915, on the idea that a German force of four corps, over half of Germany's strategic reserve, would be committed to an offensive in the sector between the towns of Gorlice and Tarnow. Cramon agreed with Falkenhayn's idea, noting that sufficient Austro-Hungarian forces were available to support it. Conrad was briefed on the plan, and he approved it at the meeting in Berlin on April 14, 1915.[39] This attack, supported by the Austro-Hungarian Fourth and Third Armies, if successful would drive the Russians back to the San, thus outflanking the forces in the Carpathians.

Although Falkenhayn had decided that action against the Russians in Galicia had to take the highest priority, Serbia was still very much uppermost in Falkenhayn's mind. The same day Falkenhayn was sounding out Cramon about the Gorlice attack, he met Conrad in Berlin. It is difficult to tell if Falkenhayn sent his April 4 message to Cramon before or after the meeting with Conrad. In any case, at the meeting Falkenhayn raised the possibility of an eventual attack on Serbia. Conrad responded that the Austro-Hungarian forces on the Serbian border were insufficient for conducting an offensive. Such an operation might be possible if done in cooperation with German and Bulgarian forces. A few days later Falkenhayn was informed by his intelligence officer, Colonel Richard Hentsch, that the water level of the river was so high that any kind of offensive action by either side was out of the question until mid-April at the earliest. Serbia was important but would have to wait.[40]

Falkenhayn's decision to commit reserves to the eastern front was opposed by many at OHL, including Tappen and Wild.[41] Nonetheless German Eleventh Army, commanded by Generaloberst August von Mackensen with Colonel Hans von Seeckt as his chief of staff, containing about 130,000 Germans and Austro-Hungarians, arrived in its assembly area in late April. Mackensen's trump card was his superiority in artillery, especially heavy calibers. With the support of the Austro-Hungarian Fourth and Third Armies, Mackensen had over 1,000 guns at his command.[42]

Using a carefully considered tactical plan, Mackensen's force attacked on May 2, 1915. After four days a hole of several miles had been torn in the Russian lines and large parts of the Russian Third Army had been severely mauled. Mackensen, partly on his own initiative and later at the direction of Falkenhayn and Conrad, pressed on to the San. In late May the Eleventh Army swung part of its forces to the southeast to approach Przemysl. In a short siege the German heavy artillery battered Przemysl's forts. The Russian defense collapsed under a German infantry assault, and, by June 3, 1915, Przemysl was once again in the hands of Austro-Hungarian authorities.

Mackensen and Seeckt argued that the Germans and Austro-Hungarians should press on to retake Lemberg, the capital of Austrian Galicia. Falkenhayn agreed after Tappen visited Eleventh Army headquarters in late May and heard the views of Mackensen and Seeckt. Thus, when Conrad wrote to suggest that a meeting be held to discuss further operations, Falkenhayn already had a proposal at hand.[43]

Presented with a fait accompli by Falkenhayn, Conrad had little choice but to agree. Mackensen, then entrusted with an army group consisting of the German Eleventh Army, the Austro-Hungarian Fourth Army and the Austro-Hungarian Second Army, drove forward on Lemberg.[44] Reinforced and with ammunition stocks rebuilt, Mackensen's offensive was launched on June 13, 1915. Once again the combination of thorough reconnaissance, careful employment of artillery, good tactics, and judicious operational pauses brought success. A mere eight days after the start of the offensive, the last Russian position west of Lemberg collapsed. The capital of Austrian Galicia was retaken by elements of the Austro-Hungarian Second Army on June 22, 1915, a major morale boost for Austria–Hungary.[45]

Even before Lemberg was taken, Seeckt was considering how to keep the momentum of the offensive going. He advocated redirecting Mackensen's forces to the north, into the southern flank of Russia's Polish salient. Seeckt gained Mackensen's support for the plan, and Falkenhayn as well as Conrad quickly responded favorably as well. Falkenhayn got the plan officially approved by the kaiser in a meeting on July 2, 1915, over the objections of Ober Ost.[46]

Launched on July 13, 1915, the offensive, which involved several of Ober Ost's armies as well as Mackensen's army group, made slow progress initially. Eventually, however, German superiority, especially in heavy artillery, again took its toll and the Russian defenses began to crumble. By the first week of August the Russians were in full retreat from Poland. Warsaw fell on August 5. Russian fortresses such as Novogeorgievsk were crushed by German and Austro-Hungarian heavy artillery. The last major fortress in Poland, Brest-Litovsk, fell to the Austro-Hungarian VI Corps on August 26.[47] That marked the effective end of the campaign.

The success of the campaigns in Galicia and Poland produced mixed results strategically and far-reaching consequences operationally. Mackensen's victories in May failed to deter Italy from entering the war. Italy declared war against Austria–Hungary only on May 23, 1915. Although it was well known that Italy was going to declare war, the Italian army and its chief, General Luigi Cadorna, required some time to mobilize forces and set them in motion. This fatal delay allowed Conrad to organize forces in the Carnic Alps. Eventually the Austro-Hungarian Fifth Army, ably commanded by the tough-minded Svetozar Boroević von Bojna, set its defensive lines up along the Isonzo River, where it brought Cadorna's offensive to a halt by early July 1915.[48]

Events in Galicia and Poland had more positive results in regard to Romania. A prolonged Russian presence in the Carpathians, or a penetration into Hungary, plus the example of Italy, might have persuaded Romania's pro-entente prime minister Ion Brătianu to enter the war. Mackensen's victories, however, plus Italy's failure to make any major headway, and the dispatching of some German divisions to southern Hungary persuaded Romania to maintain its policy of neutrality.[49]

The neutral country most powerfully impacted by Gorlice–Tarnow and its aftermath was Bulgaria. When Przemysl fell to the Russians on March 23, 1915, the government of Minister President Vasil Radoslavov initiated tentative negotiations to join the entente. Bulgaria changed course, however, over the spring and summer of 1915. Radoslavov had hedged his diplomatic bets anyway, also exploring what he could get from the Central powers. The size and scope of German victories over Russia certainly made a profound impression on Bulgaria, as King Ferdinand later told Mackensen. That impression was reinforced when it became clear that the British effort at Gallipoli had resulted in a stalemate that was as bloody as it was inconclusive. Finally, Bulgarian policy makers realized that with Serbia on the side of the entente, it would be difficult for Bulgaria to realize its foreign policy aims. Thus by the summer of 1915 the prospects of Bulgaria joining the Central powers had increased considerably.[50]

Operationally, the campaigns in the east produced critical results but with a potentially important negative trade-off. The elimination of the Russian-held salient in Poland shortened the line considerably. The straightening of the line gave Falkenhayn the ability to draw some forces and headquarters from the eastern front for the new effort against Serbia as well as strengthening the western front, as a new Anglo-French offensive was expected momentarily.[51]

The trade-off in regard to any offensive against Serbia concerned time. Continuing the campaign on the eastern front meant that operations would continue to almost the end of the summer. Thus any offensive against Serbia could not be undertaken until the autumn, a chancy proposition given the difficulty of the terrain and the vagaries of the weather at that time of the year.

Falkenhayn had made it clear to Conrad in April 1915 that Serbia was to be dealt with decisively once the impending offensive against the Russians against Gorlice–Tarnow had run its course. Conrad noted that any operation against Serbia would require Bulgarian participation.[52] As operations in Poland proceeded over the course of July and into August, Falkenhayn returned again to the subject of Serbia. Conrad, however, had returned to his obsession with Italy. Throughout May and June Conrad was calling for the buildup of a force of at least 20 divisions, including German units, for an offensive against Italy.[53]

Falkenhayn was able to scotch this notion of Conrad in two ways. First, Falkenhayn took advantage of the fact that while Italy had declared war against Austria–Hungary, no such declaration had been issued against Germany. Falkenhayn made sure that Germany did not declare war against Italy. German actions against Italy amounted solely to the severing of diplomatic and economic ties. In addition, although Falkenhayn was willing to provide some forces to aid Austria–Hungary's defense, the forces were minimal and were subject to severe restrictions on how they could be used. Thus Conrad was compelled to confine the Austro-Hungarian forces on the Italian front to a defensive posture.[54]

On June 13, 1915, Falkenhayn informed Conrad that Serbia would be the next target of the Central powers. Falkenhayn's desire for invading Serbia was motivated by continuing concern over the situation of Turkey. Such concern was heightened by the British landings in the Gallipoli Peninsula in mid-April. Although the dauntless defense mounted by the Turks under Mustafa Kemal brought the British operation to a standstill, Falkenhayn was still concerned. Operations at Gallipoli had consumed large amounts of ammunition, and fighting had resulted in heavy casualties. Liman, Kemal's principal German military advisor, sent Falkenhayn worried missives about the shortage of artillery ammunition.[55]

Conrad and Falkenhayn agreed that for an invasion of Serbia, the participation of Bulgaria was a critical prerequisite. As Mackensen's victories took shape over the late spring and early summer of 1915, the Bulgarians began to sound out the Germans and Austro-Hungarians about the prospects of Bulgaria entering the war. In late July Lieutenant Colonel Petur Ganchev was sent to Germany to begin talks. Ganchev was a judicious choice in this regard;

he had been an adjutant to King Ferdinand, and Ganchev had served as military attaché to Germany.[56]

For his part, Falkenhayn was ready to receive Ganchev with a proposal of his own. This included the stipulations that Bulgaria not only go to war with Serbia but also exert pressure on Romania to either join the Central powers or at the least permit the right of transit. Also within six weeks of signing a military convention, Germany and Austria–Hungary would each provide six divisions for the invasion of Serbia, while Bulgaria would provide five divisions. Overall command would be entrusted to Mackensen. Falkenhayn duly transmitted this proposal to AOK.[57]

The Austro-Hungarian reaction was not positive. For one thing Conrad was still preoccupied with Italy. Earlier in June Conrad had suggested to Arthur Baron von Bolfras, the head of Francis Joseph's military chancery, that some peaceful solution with Serbia be sought that would result in some sort of political union between Austria–Hungary and Serbia. This was a fanciful notion to say the least but indicative of how much Conrad's focus had shifted from Serbia to Italy. Conrad's position was also contrary to that of the Austro-Hungarian foreign ministry, which advocated a much harder line toward Serbia.[58]

Conrad also objected to the fact that a German commander would be in overall charge of the effort. The Austro-Hungarians regarded the Balkans as their area of influence and resented what was considered a German intrusion. Even more galling to Conrad was the command arrangement. Mackensen was subject to the orders of AOK and OHL, and any kind of directive from AOK required the approval of OHL. Although this kind of system had been used in Galicia and Poland with success, it was still extremely irksome to Conrad. Nonetheless, AOK had to go along with the proposal.[59]

Ganchev arrived at Pless on August 3, armed with Radoslavov's demands, which included an immediate loan of 200,000,000 francs, plus guarantees of German support for Bulgaria against any intervention by Greece and Romania and German military assistance for the defense of the Black Sea coast against the Russians.

When Ganchev returned to Sofia on August 10, the position of Radoslavov's government had moved decisively toward joining the Central powers. By that time, Warsaw had fallen and it was clear the Russians were being run completely out of Poland. In addition, Radoslavov realized that the only way Bulgaria could realize its foreign policy aims in regard to Serbia and Macedonia was by allying itself with Germany and Austria–Hungary. Finally, a British attempt to launch a coordinated attack with forces in Gallipoli with a new amphibious effort at Suvla Bay had failed. With the war going Germany's way in any case, taking the plunge into war did not seem to be that big a risk.[60]

Events moved swiftly thereafter, and much to Falkenhayn's satisfaction. Mistrustful of Austria–Hungary's motives and military competence, Ganchev declared decisively that Bulgaria would never agree to the invasion being led by an Austro-Hungarian commander. Thus Bulgaria agreed to the command arrangements suggested by Falkenhayn. At a personal level, Falkenhayn was indignant at Conrad's demand that an Austro-Hungarian general be entrusted command of the invasion, especially given the fact that Germany would be providing at least half of forces. Falkenhayn's desire to wrap up the negotiations had to be heightened over Turkey's situation. Although it was clear by the end of August 1915 that the Turkish defenses had indeed held, Turkey's isolation had to be overcome. Finally, there was some concern that the Allies might try to get aid directly to Serbia. Indeed, David Lloyd George had just proposed such a concept to the British War Council in early 1915. Joffre also wanted help sent to Serbia, although on a minimal scale.[61]

On September 6, 1915, the three powers signed the military convention at Pless. The three signatories were Falkenhayn, Conrad, and Ganchev. Germany and Austria–Hungary pledged to advance against Serbia within 30 days of the signing of the agreement, while Bulgaria would advance within 35 days. Germany and Austria–Hungary would each provide six divisions, while Bulgaria would contribute another four divisions. The goal was to provide a numerical superiority of two to one over the Serbs. As per Falkenhayn's initial proposal, Mackensen would be in overall command and armed with the authority to issue orders to Austro-Hungarian and Bulgarian units as well as German. In addition, once the route to Bulgaria was open, a German brigade would be sent to Varna and Burgas, and possibilities of introducing German U-boats into the Black Sea would be investigated. Finally, Bulgaria would get its requested 200,000,000 franc loan from Germany and Austria–Hungary.[62]

The convention and the manner by which it was negotiated and signed is worthy of several comments. The first is the total absence of civilian policy makers from the negotiations, even though it was Bethmann who had first proposed an attack on Serbia in November 1914. That the convention was negotiated by Falkenhayn indicated just how much the making of foreign policy and the making of military strategy were divorced from each other.[63] The issue of Serbia also revealed the complete disconnect between the military planners at AOK in Teschen and the foreign policy establishment at the Ballplatz in Vienna. Burian, for example, thought that the attack on and occupation of Serbia was a good idea; it should be done solely with Austro-Hungarian troops, a notion that Conrad scoffed at.[64]

The discussions between OHL and AOK revealed just how much of junior partner Austria–Hungary was becoming in the alliance. Conrad was well aware of this but frankly admitted that there was very little he could do in this regard. The Bulgarians also probably sensed this as well, as they were reasonably satisfied with the fact that Mackensen would be in overall command.[65]

Finally, the timing of the convention had the advantage of preempting the entente. To some degree this reflected poorly on French and British policy makers. The British military attaché to Bulgaria, Lieutenant Colonel H.D. Napier, noticed Ganchev boarding a train for Berlin in civilian clothes, something that Napier regarded as ominous.[66] During the late summer of 1915, French military and political leaders discussed the idea of sending an expedition to Serbia's aid. General Maurice Sarrail, recently relieved by Joffre as commander of the French Third Army, put forth a proposal that Joffre regarded as extravagant, but that found favor ultimately with French political leaders. Meanwhile Napier noted a significant increase in German diplomatic activity in Sofia during August 1915.[67]

The signing of the convention, however, forced the French to move their plans ahead at a faster pace. The first move, to make vague promises to Bulgaria after the convention had been signed, was a classic case of too little, too late. The British would also now be included in the military operation, although there was not much enthusiasm for the idea among some British military leaders.[68] Thus the convention initiated a race between the Central powers and the entente. Could the Germans, Austro-Hungarians, and Bulgarians assemble a force and undertake the invasion of Serbia faster than the French and British send a force to Serbia via Greece? Serbia's fate depended on this question.

Chapter 3

Forces, Plans, and Preparations: September 1915

"The Army was generously reinforced with heavy artillery and technical troops."

Max von Gallwitz[1]

"The mission of Generalfeldmarschall von Mackensen is: to defeat the Serbian Army wherever he finds it and to open and secure land communications between Hungary and Bulgaria as quickly as possible."

OHL Directive, September 15, 1915[2]

"This army is Serbia's last. There are no more men available to replace losses suffered in the next campaign."

OHL Intelligence Report, September 10, 1915[3]

Once a decision has been made, it must be carried out. In the case of the invasion of Serbia, the decision in question was made by the military convention agreed to by Germany, Austria–Hungary, and Bulgaria. Each of the Central powers committed themselves to provide a particular number of divisions to the operation; Germany and Austria–Hungary would provide six divisions each, while the Bulgarians would provide four.[4] Now the matter became finding those divisions.

Finding forces to execute the operation called for by the convention was not as simple a matter as one might think. As both Falkenhayn and Conrad had to worry about multiple fronts, the margins both men had to work with were

-

rather thin. In early September, for example, Falkenhayn and Conrad were dickering over the status of the Austro-Hungarian Second and Ninth Cavalry Divisions and the shifting of the two units from Brest-Litovsk to Kovel.[5] That the two chiefs of their respective general staffs would devote that kind of attention to a seemingly trivial matter is telling.

For Conrad, the latest consumer of resources was the Italian front. Although the Austro-Hungarian forces under the redoubtable Svetozar Boroević had held off the Italians in the second battle of the Isonzo, losses were heavy.[6] As a result, the Austro-Hungarian Fifty-Ninth and Sixty-First Infantry Divisions plus the Nineteenth Mountain Brigade were dispatched to the Italian front from the Serbian border. Given other commitments on the eastern front, Conrad had to ask for the Germans to send more forces to the Serbian theater than had already been agreed on. Falkenhayn assented to the request but also restated the importance of invading Serbia.[7]

Conrad complicated his own problems by acting in a typical way. Ever desirous of scoring a victory of his own, Conrad once again launched an offensive on the eastern front in the south, looking to advance all the way to Kiev. Beginning on August 26, the "Black-Yellow" offensive proved typical of so many of Conrad's ideas, a grandiose concept beyond the capability of his forces. The execution, as was so often the case for the Austro-Hungarian army, yielded results that were incommensurate with the casualties suffered to attain them. Some territorial gains were made, but at heavy cost. Someone in the manpower section at AOK admitted to Cramon that Conrad's Ukrainian adventure had cost the Austro-Hungarian army about 200,000 men. In point of fact losses were a bit larger than that, totaling about 230,000. More disturbing was the fact that almost half of the losses suffered were in the form of prisoners taken by the Russians. Falkenhayn noted that the collapse of the Austro-Hungarian Fourth Army was large enough that it demanded the shifting of German troops to shore up the Austro-Hungarian position.[8]

Aside from the limited if dearly bought gains outlined earlier, Conrad's offensive also had two other results. One was that renewed Austro-Hungarian failure served only to exacerbate the contempt of the Germans, ranging from Ludendorff to Falkenhayn. The other result was that since Austria–Hungary could not provide the troops called for by the convention, Falkenhayn would have to come up with the extra divisions needed to replace them.[9]

Rustling up the additional troops was not as easy a task for Falkenhayn as one might think. For one thing, as noted earlier, he was operating with very little in the way of strategic reserves. Many of the divisions created by the Wrisberg plan had been committed to the western front to cover the troops withdrawn to form the German Eleventh Army, while other divisions were sent directly to the eastern front. To cover the Serbian border sector previously held by Austro-Hungarian units sent to Italy, in late August 1915 Falkenhayn shifted the 103rd Infantry Division from the eastern front.[10] Although the French offensives in Champagne and Artois were thwarted, and the British attack at Loos was also defeated, German forces in the west were drawn into serious combat. Thus the western front would not have much to spare in the way of troops.[11]

The other source of divisions for the offensive against Serbia was the eastern front. Some could be shifted from Poland as the straightening front freed up both divisions and higher headquarters for use elsewhere. More problematic was the drawing of divisions from that part of the eastern front under the control of Ober Ost. As the offensive into Poland wound down, Hindenburg and Ludendorff undertook a further attack into Lithuania, a project near and dear to the heart of the latter. This attack, described by Seeckt in a letter to his wife as Ludendorff's private war and being of "little value," did bring further territorial gains but also required the commitment of additional divisions.[12]

Fortunately for Falkenhayn, the course of operations in Galicia and Poland over the spring and summer shortened the line sufficiently to free up troops for the Serbian operation. Falkenhayn was able to reunite the Forty-Third Reserve Division, which had been divided between the eastern and western fronts. The Bavarian 11th Infantry Division as well as the 44th Reserve and 25th, 101st, 105th, and 107th Infantry Divisions were earmarked to join the 103rd Infantry Division, which had already been dispatched to the Serbian border. To augment these forces Falkenhayn was able to move the Sixth Infantry Division from the western front, and he was even able to pry the Twenty-Sixth Infantry Division out of Ober Ost. Four corps headquarters, the III, IV, X, and XXII Reserve, were assigned to the operation, under the direction of the German Eleventh Army. The German Eleventh Army was reinforced later by the newly formed Alpine Corps, then operating in the Tirol.[13] The Austro-Hungarian contribution to the invasion was the Austro-Hungarian Third Army, the organization of which will be discussed in more detail later in this chapter.

The final part of the invasion force was the Bulgarian army. In 1915 the Bulgarian army could field 10 infantry divisions. Like the other armies that had fought in the Balkan Wars, the Bulgarian army had still not totally recovered from the strain imposed. Nonetheless, Conrad had thought that a renewed invasion of Serbia could not be undertaken without Bulgarian participation. Bulgaria's part of the invasion, as called for by the convention, would be the Bulgarian First Army, consisting of the First, Sixth, Eighth, and Ninth Infantry Divisions. The Bulgarian First Army could bring over 100,000 men to the fight, supported by over 200 light field guns of French and German manufacture, including material captured in the Balkan Wars. Commanding the Bulgarian First Army was Generalleutnant Kliment Bojadiev.[14]

The inclusion of the Bulgarians, plus the additional German divisions to cover Austro-Hungarian shortfalls, provided Falkenhayn with as many as

300,000 soldiers, a total he regarded as adequate to defeat a Serbian army with an estimated strength of 190,000 to 220,000 troops. The most important advantage lay in artillery. The German Eleventh and Austro-Hungarian Third Armies fielded about 1,200 guns, including some 36 batteries of heavy artillery, meaning pieces ranging in caliber from 150 mm up to 420 mm.[15] In addition to artillery, another advantage for the Central powers was air power. Although Bulgaria had no aircraft to speak of, the German Luftstreitkräfte assigned the First, Twenty-Eighth, Thirtieth, Fifty-Seventh, Sixty-Sixth, and Sixty-Ninth Aviation Detachments, administered by a headquarters and maintained by the Thirteenth Army Aircraft Park. The Austro-Hungarian Third Army was supported by the Third, Sixth, Ninth, and Fifteenth Aviation Companies. Thus Mackensen had at his disposal probably anywhere between 150 and 200 German and Austro-Hungarian aircraft. Finally, Mackensen also had available to him the Austro-Hungarian navy's Danube Flotilla, including its 10 monitors, a source of potentially powerful artillery support.[16]

This formidable array of military power was commanded by a group of officers whose abilities ranged from the brilliant to the workmanlike. The offensive would be in the hands of two officers who constituted one of Germany's most successful military marriages, namely Generalfeldmarschall August von Mackensen and his chief of staff, Generalmajor Hans von Seeckt.

Mackensen, born on December 6, 1849, hailed from a prosperous if nonnoble Saxon family. On October 6, 1869, just two months short of his 20th birthday, Mackensen joined the Prussian army as a one-year volunteer. Serving with the Second Life Hussars, Mackensen saw action in the Franco-Prussian War. After the war Mackensen enrolled as a student at the University of Halle. In 1873, however, Mackensen abandoned academia for the army, obtaining a regular commission as a lieutenant. Like most officers in the imperial German army, Mackensen did not attend the Kriegsakademie. Nonetheless, in 1880 he was assigned to the Great General Staff as captain. The section to which Mackensen was posted dealt with Russia, Austria–Hungary, and the Balkans. After his tour on the Great General Staff was over, Mackensen wrote analytical pieces on the Serbo-Bulgarian War for the German army's professional publication, *Militär Wochenblatt.*[17]

With his stint on the Great General Staff concluded, Mackensen then moved back to field duties with his beloved Second Life Hussars, eventually commanding the regiment and writing a history of it. Success with the Second Life Hussars brought Mackensen to the attention of the highest authorities in Germany, resulting in his serving as an adjutant, first to Schlieffen and later Wilhelm II. The latter posting, combined with a close association with the kaiser, helped him earn a patent of nobility on November 12, 1899. After stints in command at the brigade and division levels, Mackensen was appointed a General der Kavallerie and given command of the XVII Corps, a rather unusual assignment for a cavalry general.[18]

Before 1914 Mackensen's appointment might have been seen as a nice way to bring a fine military career to a close. The events of 1914, however, changed all that. After an initial setback at Gumbinnen, Mackensen led the XVII Corps with distinction, playing a critical role at Tannenberg. He then moved up to army command, leading the German Ninth Army, first in Hindenburg's unsuccessful attempt to take Warsaw, later in the Lodz campaign, capturing the city on December 6, 1914. Mackensen also commanded the Ninth Army in a limited attack in January 1915, marked by the first use of poison gas in warfare.[19]

Now a Generaloberst, Mackensen was slated to play a much more prominent role in 1915. Given command of the newly created German Eleventh Army, Mackensen was tasked with commanding the critical attack at Gorlice. Its success, outlined in the previous chapter, eased Austria–Hungary's situation as the Russians were driven from the Carpathians. After capturing Przemysl, Mackensen forces drove forward and took Lemberg, a victory that earned Mackensen a promotion to Generalfeldmarschall. He then led an army group into southern Poland, eventually capturing Brest-Litovsk. Mackensen was then tasked to command the invasion of Serbia and in fact was specifically named as the commander of the invasion force in the military convention.[20]

Mackensen had enjoyed a rather rapid rise in rank. In less than a year he had advanced in rank from a General der Kavallerie to a Generalfeldmarschall. The levels of command had also increased, from a corps of two divisions to an army group of three field armies. Mackensen had proven himself equal to the challenges each new level of command imposed. As a corps commander, he was the quintessential hard charger, often leading from the front.[21] His understanding of army level command was well illustrated in a letter written at the start of the Lodz campaign quoted at length:

> It seems quite strange to me, that I sit here at my desk and map table, while my troops fight between the Warthe and the Vistula. But such is the conduct of modern warfare. The distances of the march routes and the battlefield, the extent of the latter and the whole technical apparatus of the modern army brings it out so. Hohensalza is very good in this respect. It is valuable for the conducting of business when a headquarters remains in the same place for a longer time and becomes a traffic center. Units report by telephone and wireless radio and receive their orders by the same means. One is far from particular staffs and still speaks constantly with them and is constantly in contact with the battle front.
>
> The business area of my headquarters is here in a Gymnasium. All of my sections make demands on my time. I work in the room with the directors. It is regrettable that the days are so short that it limits tactical success and the day's accomplishments.[22]

Likewise the prospect of commanding a group of armies did not daunt the old hussar, and he was able to make that transition well, handling a group of four armies (two German and two Austro-Hungarian) into southern Poland, a situation marked by complexity and risk.[23] By the autumn of 1915 Mackensen had established himself as one of Germany's most capable field commanders.

Outside of sheer professional competence, Mackensen had several other qualities that recommended him for this particular assignment. As a general, Mackensen had very few idiosyncrasies, or "vanities," as Seeckt put it, to appease.[24] Undoubtedly the most notable quirk in which Mackensen indulged was his preference in uniforms. He preferred the uniform of the Second Life Hussars, marked by its headgear, the Death's Head fur busby. This, plus his size, deep-set eyes, and handlebar mustache, gave Mackensen a kind of "theatrical" appearance and evoked memories of the Napoleonic Wars and the Prussian hero of that age, Gebhard von Blücher, and accounted for Mackensen's popular nickname, the "new Marshal forwards."[25]

The two most notable qualities Mackensen possessed in abundance were character and tact. Many, but not all, of Mackensen's contemporaries regarded him as a brilliant soldier, an appellation applied even by some as parsimonious with compliments as Ludendorff.[26] There was unanimity, however, about Mackensen the person. Everyone admired the old hussar. Seeckt and the major German commanders who worked for him all thought highly of Mackensen's character. Even Wilhelm II's adjutant, the ancient Generaloberst Hans von Plessen (age 74), regarded Mackensen as a commander of average ability, but considered him "a splendid man."[27]

Mackensen also had an abundance of tact, a trait that was an absolute necessity in his position. His service at the Hohenzollern court served him well in understanding the importance of protocol and observing the diplomatic niceties, critical aspects in the conduct of coalition warfare. Mackensen had thus far been able to avoid becoming embroiled in the controversies between Conrad and Falkenhayn. While Mackensen had offended the Austrians with a somewhat tactless message to the Habsburg court and AOK announcing the fall of Przemysl, relations improved with the advance into Galicia in June.[28] He contrived to give the Austro-Hungarians the honor of recapturing Lemberg. This proved a major boost to Austro-Hungarian morale and made Mackensen a very popular figure in Vienna.

The popularity of Mackensen with Germany's ally was confirmed on his trip to Vienna, a journey made at the expressed wish of Francis Joseph, who wanted to convey his thanks to the man responsible for the liberation of Galicia. Arriving in Vienna aboard a special train on September 24, 1915, he was escorted to the Hofburg, where Francis Joseph greeted him most warmly. After awarding Mackensen the Grand Cross of the Order of Saint Stephan, a small dinner party (15 people total in attendance) was held. The old emperor then invited Mackensen back to his private quarters for a private audience, which lasted about 30 minutes. Mackensen's "elegant appearance and courtly charm" won him not only the affections of Francis Joseph but many of the emperor's military retinue as well.[29] Given his ability to work with the Austro-Hungarians and the reputation he enjoyed after the victories in Galicia, Mackensen was perhaps the only realistic choice to command the invasion.

Mackensen's alter ego in this venture was his chief of staff, Generalmajor Hans von Seeckt. Born on April 22, 1866, Seeckt was the latest addition to a family that was part of the Pomeranian nobility. The son of an army officer, Seeckt followed his father's vocation and joined the Kaiser Alexander Guards Regiment in 1885 as an officer cadet. First commissioned in 1887, Seeckt entered the Kriegsakademie in 1893 and graduated three years later. Seeckt rose through the army in a series of command and staff positions and by 1914, he was the chief of staff of the III Corps. Successful tactical actions at Vailly in October 1914 and Soissons in January 1915 confirmed Seeckt's reputation as a brilliant staff officer and planner. On March 9, 1915, Falkenhayn, also a close acquaintance of Seeckt, appointed him as chief of staff for the then-forming German Eleventh Army.[30] The victories in Galicia brought promotion to Seeckt as well, attaining Generalmajor the same day Mackensen was appointed Generalfeldmarschall. This led Seeckt to muse somewhat cynically to his wife that he and Macksensen were being set up by Falkenhayn as some sort of counterweight to Hindenburg and Ludendorff.[31]

The relationship between Mackensen and Seeckt, like that of other World War I German commanders and their chiefs of staff, has occasioned much comment. Older scholarship has often depicted commanders such as Mackensen, Crown Prince Rupprecht of Bavaria, and especially Hindenburg as mere medal-bedecked front men for their chiefs of staff, including officers such as the brilliant Seeckt, the sagacious Hermann von Kuhl, and especially the driven and ambitious Ludendorff. This image was exemplified in earlier works such as John Wheeler-Bennett's biography of Hindenburg. The only purpose Hindenburg served, it seemed, was to keep the high-strung Ludendorff on an even keel during times of crisis. In the case of Mackensen and Seeckt, B. H. Liddell Hart referred to Seeckt as "Mackensen's guiding brain."[32]

This image is as misleading as it is insulting. Men such as Hindenburg, Mackensen, and Rupprecht, were professional officers who had served many years and with distinction. Able officers with command experience are promoted to general officer rank because of their intelligence, not because of their lack of it. In Mackensen's case, his knowledge of the area and the Serbian and Bulgarian armies has already been mentioned. Seeckt noted that Mackensen's range of knowledge, both theoretical and practical, was "impressive."[33] Experience in the 1914 and 1915 campaigns had given both Mackensen and Seeckt a profound appreciation for the potential of relatively new technology, to include aircraft, heavy artillery, and telephone.

Temperamentally Mackensen and Seeckt were well suited to each other. They had known each other professionally since 1901. Under the strain of battle, Mackensen proved every bit as stoic as his sphinx-like chief of staff, although Seeckt did think that Mackensen was given at times to melancholy.[34] The team of Mackensen and Seeckt had shown itself as a most formidable combination during the offensives in Galicia and Poland. They would now apply their abilities and forces at their command against Serbia.

The principal German headquarters earmarked for the invasion of Serbia was that of the German Eleventh Army. Commanded by Mackensen for the campaigns in Galicia and Poland, for the Serbian operation it came under Generaloberst Max von Gallwitz. Like Mackensen, Max Gallwitz came from a nonnoble background. Gallwitz was born on May 2, 1852, in Breslau. His father was a noncommissioned officer (NCO) in the Tenth Landwehr Regiment, while Gallwitz's maternal grandfather was an NCO in the First Cuirassier Regiment.[35]

Pursuing a military career was a good way for a young man in the middle class to improve his social status. An aptitude for mathematics drew Gallwitz into the artillery. On August 13, 1870, Gallwitz reported for duty with the Replacement Battalion of the Ninth Schleswig-Holstein Field Artillery Regiment. Gallwitz quickly found himself being sent to the siege of Metz, but his introduction to combat did not occur until the end of October. In December 1870 Gallwitz fought in the battle of Orleans. By May 1871 he was an ensign commanding a gun crew. After the war Gallwitz pursued a career in the artillery, eventually becoming head of the artillery section in the war ministry, where he proved a staunch advocate of modernization of the artillery.[36]

After a stint as a division commander, Gallwitz was ennobled on June 16, 1913. At the outbreak of the war Gallwitz took command of the Guard Reserve Corps, leading it with distinction on both the western and eastern fronts. By 1915 he was commanding an army-size force designated Army Group Gallwitz, which was later renamed as the German Twelfth Army. Gallwitz led the Twelfth Army as it fought along the Narew River in the summer offensive in Russian Poland.[37]

Gallwitz was an officer who was certainly devoted to his branch, so much so that he named his first daughter Barbara, after the patron saint of the artillery. Nonetheless, Gallwitz was no parochial officer. He had a great many interests. His contemporaries universally held him in high regard. Ludendorff described Gallwitz as "the best commander in our army," a view Mackensen shared. On September 30, 1915, OHL assigned Gallwitz to the command of the Eleventh Army.[38]

Assisting Gallwitz was his chief of staff, Colonel Gottfried Marquard. Born on June 2, 1864, in Braunschweig, Marquard entered the army in 1883. In 1892 he was admitted to the Kriegsakademie as a student. After a company level assignment with the Fifty-Fourth Infantry Regiment, Marquard filled a steady string of staff assignments, including a stint on the Great General Staff and a tour as an instructor at the Kriegsakademie. On March 18, 1915, Marquard, by now a colonel, was assigned as Gallwitz's chief of staff.[39]

Marquard was the type of professional staff officer that the German army excelled in creating.

Gallwitz had at his command the III, IV, and X Reserve Corps. The III Corps was commanded by General der Infanterie Ewald von Lochow. Born on April 1, 1855, in Petkus, Brandenburg, Lochow obtained his first commission as a lieutenant in the Second Foot Guards on April 19, 1873. After attending the Kriegsakademie, Lochow filled a number of staff positions, including a tour on the Great General Staff. From there his career took more of a direction toward command, holding such positions at battalion and regimental level. Success in these endeavors led to Lochow's promotion to Generalmajor and appointment to command of Nineteenth Infantry Brigade on June 14, 1906. After a stint as commander of the Second Guard Division, Lochow was appointed commander of the III Corps on September 13, 1912, and promoted to General der Infanterie in June 1913. Lochow led the III Corps in 1914, with none other than Hans von Seeckt as his chief of staff. By 1915 Lochow had a well-earned reputation as an able combat commander.[40]

The III Corps' two divisions were the Sixth Infantry and Twenty-Fifth Reserve, commanded by Generalmajors Richard Herhudt von Rohden and Thaddäus von Jarotsky, respectively. Richard Herhudt von Rohden was the embodiment of the German infantryman, the *Landser*. Born on November 16, 1857, Herhudt entered the Corps of Cadets and obtained his commission as a second lieutenant on April 15, 1876, serving in the Sixty-Third Infantry Regiment. Herhudt then served his entire career in the infantry. He commanded at every level from company through regiment. Instead of doing a tour of staff duty, Herhudt served in faculty or command positions at schools, including the School of Marksmanship. His promotion to Generalmajor on October 1, 1912, coincided with his appointment as commandant of the Infantry School. At the onset of war, Herhudt was appointed to command of the Sixth Infantry Division. He was probably one of the most experienced of Gallwitz's division commanders.[41]

Jarotsky, born April 27, 1858, was an experienced officer who had commanded at every level. He had led Twenty-Fifth Reserve Division since November 25, 1914. The division had served in the Carpathians in early 1915 as part of the Beskiden Corps, backstopping the Austro-Hungarians.[42]

The second of Gallwitz's three corps was the IV Reserve Corps, commanded by Generalleutnant Arnold von Winckler. Born on February 17, 1856, Winckler obtained his first commission in 1874. A graduate of the Kriegsakademie, after pursuing a standard career path of command and administrative posts, Winckler was appointed commander of the Second Guard Division in 1912. He led the division through the opening campaigns in the west. In 1915 Winckler's division, part of the Guard Corps, played an important role in the Gorlice–Tarnow offensive, gaining a critical bridgehead over the San River. Winckler's performance earned him command of the

XXXXI Reserve Corps in July 1915. After the completion of the offensive into Poland, he took over the IV Reserve Corps. Winckler was the embodiment of the Prussian military tradition of a subordinate commander who acts aggressively on his own initiative while keeping within the overarching framework of a plan.[43]

Winckler's two divisions were the Bavarian 11th Infantry and the 105th Infantry Division. The Bavarians were commanded by Generalleutnant Paul Ritter von Kneussl. Born on June 27, 1862, Kneussl pursued a career in the Bavarian army, obtaining his first commission in 1884. On March 27, 1913, he was promoted to Generalmajor and named commander of the Bavarian Eighth Infantry Brigade. Success in brigade command led to Kneussl's appointment as commander of the newly forming Bavarian Eleventh Infantry Division on March 25, 1915. Commanding his division as well as an ad hoc corps, Kneussl was promoted to Generalleutnant on May 19, 1915. Kneussl's signal success in the Gorlice operation was the capture of Przemysl. He later led the division into Poland.[44]

The commander of the 105th Infantry Division was Generalmajor Adolf von der Esch. Like Mackensen and Gallwitz, Esch, born on March 4, 1861, hailed from a middle-class family in Stettin. Esch joined the army as a cadet in 1879 and enjoyed a successful career in the infantry. A Kriegsakademie graduate, Esch later returned to the school as its director, a position held by Carl von Clausewitz himself. Ennobled in 1892, Esch was eventually promoted to Generalmajor on March 22, 1913; he had commanded the Forty-First Infantry Brigade and later the Thirty-Eighth Infantry Division in combat. Esch took command of the newly formed 105th Infantry Division on June 1, 1915, and led it in its initial combat action in Galicia.[45]

The last of Gallwitz's three corps was the X Reserve Corps, commanded by Generalleutnant Robert Kosch. Born in Glatz on April 5, 1856, Kosch was a career infantryman. Like most officers, he did not attend the Kriegsakademie, but nonetheless enjoyed a steadily upward trajectory in his profession, both in rank and in position. Promoted to Generalleutnant on April 22, 1912, he later led Tenth Infantry Division. During the opening campaigns in the east Kosch commanded at the division level. Promoted to corps command, Kosch led the I Corps during the Second Masurian Lakes campaign with some distinction. Appointed to command of the X Reserve Corps on June 11, 1915, Kosch led the corps in the advance into Russian Poland in the summer of 1915, and the X Reserve Corps performed well enough to earn a fulsome congratulatory order from Mackensen.[46] While not brilliant, Kosch was the kind of steady, workmanlike general officer the German army also excelled at creating.

Kosch's two principal subordinates were Generalleutnant Richard von Kraewel, commanding the 101st Infantry Division and Generalmajor Ludwig von Estorff, commanding the 103rd Infantry Division. Kraewel, born August 17, 1861, entered the army as a cadet and obtained his first commission as a lieutenant on November 16, 1880. A Kriegsakademie graduate, Kraewel prospered in the infantry and was ultimately promoted to Generalmajor on April 22, 1912. A command tour of the Thirty-Fourth Infantry Brigade followed. After a short stint as commander of the Seventeenth Reserve Division, Kraewel was assigned as the chief of staff to the incoming military governor of Belgium, Generaloberst Moritz Freiherr von Bissing. His tenure as Bissing's chief of staff, however, was rather short, as Kraewel was appointed to the command of the 101st Infantry Division on September 17, 1915. Thus he had little time to prepare for his first major operation as a division commander.[47]

Ludwig von Estorff, born in 1859, had followed a very different career path. Unlike many of his contemporaries Estorff, although a Kriegsakademie graduate, had spent several years in the colonies, manly in both German East and Southwest Africa. During the Hottentot Rebellion and the Herrero War, Estorff proved to be a veritable magnet for bullets, being wounded three times. After his return to Germany, he was promoted to Generalmajor in 1912 and took command of a brigade. In the opening battles of 1914, Estorff was severely wounded. He returned to action, this time in command of the 103rd Infantry Division, leading it with success in Galicia.[48]

The German Eleventh Army had one unattached division, namely the 107th Infantry Division, commanded by Generalmajor Otto von Moser. Born on March 21, 1860, Moser obtained his first commission as a second lieutenant on October 7, 1878. He then filled a series of staff and command positions in infantry units. Although Moser did not attend the Kriegsakademie, after his promotion to lieutenant colonel in April 1906 he was posted there as an instructor. Promoted to Generalmajor on October 1, 1912, Moser took command of the Fifty-Third Infantry Brigade four months later. While leading the brigade in combat, Moser was severely wounded on September 2, 1914. His return from convalescence was capped by taking command of the newly forming 107th Infantry Division. The Serbian operation was Moser's first action on the battlefield since his wounding. Aside from the 107th Infantry Division, Gallwitz's army also had control of Group Fülöpp, a division-sized unit commanded by Feldmarschalleutnant Artur Fülöpp.[49]

The second major unit in Army Group Temesvár, as Mackensen's force was called, was the Austro-Hungarian Third Army.[50] In early 1915, the Austro-Hungarian Third Army was commanded by Generaloberst Karl Tersztyánsky von Nadas. Tersztyánsky had submitted a plan for a new invasion of Serbia in June 1915, but AOK showed little interest.[51] As the tempo of planning picked up over the late summer of 1915, Tersztyánsky was slated to command the Austro-Hungarian Third Army in the invasion. In September 1915, however, a conflict arose between Tersztyánsky and Tisza over the issue of using civilian workers for military purposes. To appease the powerful Tisza, Francis Joseph removed Tersztyánsky from his post. To fill the post of Third Army commander, on September 20, 1915, AOK selected General der Infanterie Hermann Baron Kövess von Kövessháza.[52]

The new commander of the Third Army hailed from one of Hungary's oldest families, one whose name went all the way back to the first siege of Vienna by the Turks in 1529. Herman Kövess was born on March 31, 1854. His father Albin was a career infantry officer who had served in the 1848, 1849, 1959, and 1866 campaigns, ultimately achieving general officer rank and ennoblement on November 25, 1873. Following his father's footsteps, Kövess entered the Hainburg Militär Kadetten Institut in 1865, moving from there to the Engineering and Artillery Academy in 1869.[53]

After obtaining his first commission, Kövess enjoyed a moderately successful career in the Austro-Hungarian army. As a junior officer, he was able to attend the Kriegsschule (the Austrian equivalent of the German Kriegsakademie). Prospects for long-term service on the General Staff, however, were marred by Kövess's failure in the examination for major on the General Staff. With that path for his career closed off, Kövess moved into the infantry. In the infantry Kövess enjoyed considerable success, holding a series of command positions from battalion up to corps level, attaining the rank of General der Infanterie on November 1, 1911. Although he enjoyed good connections with the Habsburg court and was regarded highly by Conrad, it seemed likely that Kövess's career was going to end at the rank of General der Infanterie.[54]

Like Mackensen, Kövess's career profited from the outbreak of war. He distinguished himself as commander of the XII Corps. Later the XII Corps was reinforced with a division and renamed Army Group Kövess. During the offensive into Poland in the summer of 1915, Kövess's force captured the fortress of Ivangorod, a success that earned Kövess a good deal of notoriety. Now the man of the moment in Vienna, Kövess was appointed to command the Third Army and sent to the Balkans. His chief of staff was Generalmajor Theodor Konopicky.[55]

Kövess and Mackensen were well acquainted with each other. When Mackensen commanded the German Ninth Army in Poland and launched his limited attack in late January 1915, Kövess, then exercising temporary command of the Austro-Hungarian Second Army, put in an attack in support of Mackensen's effort. Seeckt described Kövess as "very sympathetic."[56]

The Austro-Hungarian Third Army was something of a lash up. Its major Austro-Hungarian components were the Austro-Hungarian VIII and XIX Corps, commanded by Feldzeugmeister Viktor von Scheuchenstuel and Feldmarschalleutnant Ignaz Trollmann, respectively. Of these two, only the VIII Corps had the normal compliment of two infantry divisions. In addition, both the Fifty-Seventh Infantry Division, commanded by Feldmarschalleutnant Heinrich Goiginger, and Feldmarschalleutnant Lukas Snjarić's Fifty-Ninth

Infantry Division, were composed of alpine units. The Austro-Hungarian XIX Corps had only one division, Generalmajor Heinrich von Pongrácz's Fifty-Third Infantry, which also had alpine units. The rest of the XIX Corps consisted of several separate infantry brigades.

Aside from the VIII and XIX Corps, the other Austro-Hungarian components of Kövess's army consisted of the newly created Sixty-Second Infantry Division, commanded by Feldmarschalleutnant Franz von Kalser, and two division size equivalents, Groups Streith and Sorsich, commanded by Generalmajor Rudolf Streith and Feldmarschalleutnant Bela Sorsich von Severin, respectively.[57]

Because Conrad had already asked Falkenhayn for additional German divisions to supplement the invasion force, the Austro-Hungarian Third Army was given an oversized German component. The German XXII Reserve Corps was commanded by General der Kavallerie Eugen von Falkenhayn. The older brother of the chief of the General Staff, Eugen von Falkenhayn, was born on September 4, 1853. After obtaining his first commission in December 1870, Falkenhayn spent the next 10 years in the cavalry. After a short stint as commander of the Eleventh Infantry Division, on September 10, 1914, Falkenhayn took command of the XXII Reserve Corps and was promoted to General der Kavallerie two weeks later. Falkenhayn led the corps with some distinction in both Galicia and Poland.[58]

Unlike the average German corps, which usually possessed two divisions, Falkenhayn had three infantry divisions. The Forty-Third Reserve Infantry Division was commanded by Generalmajor Hermann von Runckel. Born on August 25, 1863, Runckel obtained his first commission as a lieutenant in 1882 and was admitted to the Kriegsakademie six years later. After a series of staff assignments, including a stint on the Great General Staff, Runckel moved into the command track, holding command positions successively at battalion, regiment, and brigade level. He took over the Forty-Third Reserve Division at the end of October 1914 and had led it since.[59]

The peculiarities of the imperial German military system were evident in the career of the commander of the Forty-Fourth Reserve Division, Generalleutnant Eugen von Dorrer. Born on November 18, 1857, Dorrer was an artilleryman. A native Württemberger, Dorrer had spent his career in Württemberg's army. He served as Württemberg's military representative on the Great General Staff, adjutant to Wilhelm II, king of Württemberg and later as Württemberg's military representative in Berlin. Already experienced as a division commander, Dorrer took command of the Forty-Fourth Reserve Division on September 1, 1914.[60]

Württemberg's army was also represented in the commander of Falkenhayn's third division, the Twenty-Sixth Infantry Division, commanded by Generalleutnant Wilhelm von Urach, duke of Württemberg, the nephew of king Wilhelm II of Württemberg. Urach was born on March 3, 1864, in

Monaco, as his mother was Princess Florestine of Monaco. Entering the army of Württemberg on October 1, 1883, Urach spent much of his early career in the cavalry, making the rank of captain (Rittmeister) on June 13, 1891. After serving at field grade ranks and commanding the Twenty-Sixth Cavalry Brigade, Urach was promoted to Generalmajor on March 22, 1910. Attaining the rank of Generalleutnant on September 13, 1912, Urach was appointed commander of the Twenty-Sixth Infantry Division. He led the division through the campaigns in the west in 1914 and Poland in 1915.[61]

Taken all together, the German commanders involved in the operation were generally a very experienced lot, although this marked Winckler's first major operation as a corps commander. The only possible drawback was that some of the division commanders were taking charge of their units only days before the start of the operation, not exactly the most propitious time for a change of commanders.

Shifting these forces was a massive undertaking. The key officer here was perhaps one of the most controversial figures of the war, Richard Hentsch. Born December 18, 1869, Hentsch was the son of a sergeant. Hentsch entered the Saxon army in 1888 and later attended the Kriegsakademie. After service on the staff of the XII Corps, in April 1914 Hentsch was assigned to the Great General Staff as the head of the intelligence section, with the rank of lieutenant colonel. Hentsch continued in that position after the outbreak of war, as the Great General Staff became OHL. In September 1914 Moltke sent Hentsch to visit the German First and Second Armies at the height of the crisis on the Marne. The outcome of Hentsch's tour was the decision, made by a combination of Hentsch and the commander of the German Second Army to retreat from the Marne, effectively ending Germany's chance for a decisive victory in 1914.[62] While the controversy associated with the decision ultimately led Hentsch to demand a court of inquiry to clear his name, Hentsch remained in his position.

Hentsch's first visit to the Serbian theater was in late 1914, when he and the chief of the Balkan section of AOK, Lieutenant Colonel Alfred Purtscher, visited Potiorek's headquarters. In the spring of 1915 Falkenhayn sent Hentsch down to the Serbian border once again. He reported to Falkenhayn that the state of the river precluded offensive action by either side, thus aiding Falkenhayn's decision to commit Mackensen's forces to action in Galicia.[63]

After making his report, Hentsch remained in the Serbian area of operations to plan the offensive with a small staff that was, officially at least, attached to Tersztyánsky's headquarters. One of Hentsch's staff officers was Major Scheunemann, who had been the chief engineer on Gallwitz's staff in Poland. Scheunemann's task was to locate suitable locations for crossing the Danube between Belgrade and the Iron Gates. Meanwhile Hentsch, described by Falkenhayn as a "farsighted officer," then oversaw the preparations for the Eleventh Army's arrival. Four railroad companies were sent to the Hungarian

Banat to make the local rail stations capable of receiving German troop trains of 50 cars each. German railroad authorities also worked with their Austro-Hungarian counterparts to resolve any issues involved in moving German troops into and through Austro-Hungarian territory.[64]

The invasion force was assembled with an interesting combination of haste and secrecy. On September 16, 1915, Mackensen, returning from a week's leave (his first break since the onset of war) in Germany, as well as Seeckt, reported to OHL headquarters on the eastern front in Allenstein, East Prussia. There the old hussar was given his mission regarding Serbia. The directive, published by OHL the day before, put Mackensen's mission very simply, "the mission of Generalfeldmarschall Mackensen is: to defeat the Serbian army wherever he finds it and to open and secure land communications between Hungary and Bulgaria as quickly as possible." The forces subordinate to Mackensen were precisely laid out along with his command authority regarding the Austro-Hungarian and Bulgarian forces under him. The details were hashed out by Seeckt and Tappen.[65]

With their mission now before them, Mackensen and Seeckt now set to work. Arriving in Temesvár on September 18, Mackensen's headquarters, located in a large "magnificent" building that once housed a bank, then incorporated Hentsch's small staff into its organization. Seeckt undertook several personal reconnaissance trips to crossing locations and oversaw the formulation of detailed plans, based on Hentsch's initial work. Meanwhile Mackensen saw to the more diplomatic aspects of his position, including his aforementioned trip to Vienna.[66]

Mackensen's staff was both large and unique, at least relative to that period of the war, in that it was a combined staff.[67] The staff was drawn from that of the army group that Mackensen had commanded in Poland. It was then supplemented by Hentsch's small staff, and by an Austro-Hungarian contingent of staff officers, headed by the Austro-Hungarian liaison officer, Colonel Julius Lustig-Prean von Preansfeld. Austro-Hungarian General Staff officers were assigned to various sections of the army group staff, such as Captain Alfred Jansa, who was posted to the operations section. The army group headquarters was also home to both Bulgarian and Turkish liaison officers, namely Lieutenant Colonel Tantisloff and Major Hüsni, respectively.[68]

Planning was a fairly constant activity. Jansa noted that often in the operations section breakfast was a working affair. One officer, Captain Dunst, spent much of the day on the telephone, checking in with subordinate headquarters and passing on short verbal orders issued by the head of the section, Major Fedor von Bock. On one occasion, when Jansa was celebrating his posting to the operations section with some champagne at breakfast for him and his colleagues, Mackensen walked in unannounced. Noticing the bottle, the old hussar asked in a somewhat surly voice what was the meaning of this. Jansa stepped forward and explained the nature of the occasion. Mackensen cautioned the captain "in a less surly manner" about "bringing temptation" into the austere Prussian atmosphere of the headquarters and then disappeared into Seeckt's office. Emerging two minutes later, Mackensen walked through the area, turned to Jansa, and nodded his welcome. Bock then took a glass and drank a toast to Jansa.[69]

The time the entire staff got together was for dinner. Jansa was struck at how large the staff was. Meals were often accompanied by music or sometimes singing. Mackensen usually presided at these affairs. In his absence Seeckt took on that duty. After dinner work resumed. Reports were collected and read, and the situation map was updated, with input from the head of the intelligence section, Major Frederici. Meanwhile, the army group's subordinate armies, corps, and divisions formulated their own plans that ultimately translated the concepts of Hentsch, Mackensen, and Seeckt into a campaign.[70]

As in any large combined staff, the atmosphere was not always harmonious. Seeckt and Lustig developed a mutual dislike, for reasons Jansa could not discern. Jansa often found himself having to defend the honor of the Austro-Hungarian army after its latest setback. According to Jansa, even Mackensen on occasion was given to "Prussian spitefulness." Although Seeckt never made disparaging remarks about the Austro-Hungarian army to Jansa and the army group war diarist, Captain Blankenhorn, exhibited Badenese tact, the young Austrian often got into arguments with Dunst, a loose-tongued Berliner. Bock supported Dunst initially but then sought to squelch these arguments by giving Dunst or Jansa jobs that kept them away from each other. An exasperated Seeckt finally told the operations section via Bock to stop the nonsense altogether.[71]

While plans were refined, the troops assembled. The first to arrive were the engineers. For German pioneers like Bavarian Joseph Huber, the withdrawal of his company from France raised the expectation among the men that they were headed to the eastern front. Much to the surprise of the Bavarians, their train headed toward Weisskirchen (Fehértemplom), the rail station that served as the most forward offloading stop for the Mackensen's German forces. Once there, the local Austro-Hungarian troops oriented them as to the terrain, and they set to work improving railroad stations, roads, and bridges.[72]

The infantry and artillery began assembling later in September. Some of these trips were not without incident. The Third Field Artillery Regiment, assigned to the Forty-Fourth Reserve Division, had its entraining in Cambrai interrupted by a French bombing raid, which caused no casualties. The 205th Reserve Infantry Regiment, also part of 44th Reserve Division coming from Poland, lost 3 men killed and 13 injured when the Machine Gun Company and the 2nd Battalion were involved in a railway accident near Nasielsk.[73]

Units coming from Poland also had to make one mandatory stop on their way out of the theater. All units on their way out the eastern front had to halt at a delousing station. The men were deloused, and the horses were "sanitized."

All clothing was cleaned in a steam chamber. This reflected both the cultural attitude of the Germans toward the east as a generally unclean and uncivilized place and the real concern of the German army over noncombat casualties in units already worn down by months of fighting. In the case of the Fifty-Second Reserve Infantry Regiment, the delousing experience at Czestochau was made more pleasant afterward by being served coffee and having the opportunity to mingle briefly with the pretty women in the village.[74]

For the troops entraining, whether in Poland or France, their ultimate destination was a mystery. Natural speculation was that troops being pulled out from the eastern front were heading to the west, while the reverse applied for troops coming from the west. The men of the 203rd Reserve Infantry Regiment, for example, were hoping for a quiet period of rest on the Dutch border after the rigors of active operations on the eastern front. Commanders were often equally in the dark. Robert Kosch, commander of the X Reserve Corps, wrote to his wife on September 3, 1915, that his corps was going to be withdrawn from Poland and sent to another front, but he did not know where. Only on September 12 was Kosch informed of his new assignment. Kosch's uncertainty was reflected in the orders issued to the corps. Security was further enhanced by the ordering of officers and men not to post any cards or letters or give any information about their destination.[75] The officers and men of the Twentieth Infantry Regiment, coming from the western front with the Sixth Infantry Division, did not realize they were being committed to Serbia until the fourth day of their rail journey, when they crossed the Hungarian border. Once the trains turned south, however, the troops were certain that they were headed for unfamiliar territory. The author of the 205th Reserve Infantry Regiment's history noted that as the regiment moved further into Hungary, the trains passed through small stations with names that were "unpronounceable."[76]

Mackensen's forces assembled in southern Hungary over the second and third weeks of September. The 105th Infantry Division, for example, arrived in Hungary in stages between September 18 and 23. On average, a German division required around 70 trains to move. To preserve secrecy, trains ran only in the daylight hours as far as Budapest. Rail movements near the Serbian border, offloading, and marches to bivouac areas were conducted at night. These treks often had to be made with the use of a compass, and German troops had to employ their nonverbal communication skills in trying to gain information from the local population, most of whom were utterly unfamiliar with German.[77]

Most of the German troops detrained and then bivouacked in areas away from the rivers that would have to be crossed. Several divisions detrained at Versecz, about 30 miles north of Weisskirchen.[78] Once the troops had reached their bivouac areas, they were prepared rather quickly for the new campaign. This began with the exchanging of equipment. Infantry regiments exchanged their Mauser rifles for a shorter carbine version of the weapon. Appropriate clothing was also issued. After months of combat on the eastern front, the new clothing was regarded as particularly welcome. The uniforms of the Twenty-Ninth Field Artillery, for example, were so worn out that they "barely covered the skin." Wagons were also exchanged for lighter local peasant carts, and mules were provided, to be handled by local Hungarians or Bosnian and Croatian Muslims. Many of these men showed up wearing uniforms that one regimental history described as "fantastic." Aside from their Hungarian, Bosnian, or Croation mule handlers, the Germans also employed prisoners of war. In the X Reserve Corps at least, each division was assigned some 200 Russian prisoners to be used as wagon drivers.[79]

In addition, divisions received replacements. The 122nd Fusiliers received a particularly large consignment of 67 officers and 1,600 men, allowing the regiment to build its combat strength back up to over 4,000. Replacements arrived throughout the period before the operation. The Fifty-Second Reserve Infantry Regiment, for example, received some 463 replacements the evening before the unit was slated to cross the Danube. Divisions also had independent units attached to them, especially alpine machine gun companies. Heavy batteries were also attached. Finally, for the crossing of the rivers, each division received 32 German pontoons, 41 Austro-Hungarian half pontoons, 20 to 30 local river craft known as *Zillen*, 240 rowers, and 100 Austro-Hungarian sailors.[80]

Once the new equipment and weapons had been issued, the troops began a period of intense training. Franz Giese, a veteran and historian of the 227th Reserve Infantry Regiment, provided a good description of a typical training day. The day began at 7:30 a.m. with an hour-long class on Serbian tactics and the attitude of the Serbian population, drawn from the Austro-Hungarian experience of 1914. The classes, conducted by Austro-Hungarian officers, stressed that the soldiers should expect all manner of bad or underhanded behavior by both Serbian soldiers and civilians.[81] Such practices included misuse of flags of truce or surrender, gruesome mistreatment of the wounded, and attacks by civilians, including women and even children. From 9:30 a.m. to noon soldiers engaged in one of three activities, namely physical training, rifle practice, or hikes with full field kit. After lunch, from 3:00 p.m. to 4:30 p.m. there were inspections by various high ranking officers and dignitaries. Giese then spent the late afternoon in an hour of pleasant conversation over a glass of wine with the landlord of the house where he was quartered. This was typical of other German infantry regiments as well.[82]

This period of training had lighter moments as well. During a hike through mountainous terrain, the men of the 146th Infantry Regiment, part of the 101st Infantry Division, encountered the occasional bear. Captain Behrends organized a hunting party to go after a large female bear spotted by a noncommissioned officer. Three shots from Behrends's newly issued carbine, however, missed at a range of 100 to 150 yards, and the captain was left surprised at how fast a bear could run.[83]

Kövess's Austro-Hungarian Third Army also assembled in southern Hungary. The concentration of Austro-Hungarian forces near Belgrade proceeded smoothly. The biggest concern was over the total amount of bridging material that had to be divided between the two armies. The German Eleventh Army was demanding more bridging assets for itself than were on hand for both armies.[84]

As in Galicia before the Gorlice–Tarnow offensive, the German army was deploying troops on the territory of an ally. Because the troops would be quartered in Hungarian villages, soldiers were given some detailed instructions on behavior and deportment. Kosch's X Reserve Corps, for example, ordered troops not to enter the private gardens and vineyards in their bivouac areas without the permission of the owner. This order was apparently not followed with precision, as there were a number of complaints from civilians in Weisskirchen and the surrounding area of German X Reserve Corps soldiers doing exactly what they had been told not to do. Corps headquarters urged units to investigate such incidents and punish offenders. Such niceties, however, disappeared when the units ultimately deployed for the start of the operation. A good firing position was a good firing position, even if it is in someone's vineyard.[85]

Being deployed to southern Hungary was also a new experience for the German soldiers both socially and culturally. The civilians in the area, be they Hungarian, Bosnian, or Croatian, were happy to see the German army appear in force. For the local inhabitants, a successful offensive against Serbia would move the war well away from them.[86] For their part, German troops regarded the local population with a combination of curiosity and contempt. Many noted the colorful attire worn by the inhabitants. Kosch, who was something of a shutterbug, used his camera to take a number of portrait photos of local civilians. A lack of facility with the German language led many of them to consider the local Hungarians rather primitive folk. The 227th Reserve Infantry Regiment, for example, was quartered in the village of Nagy-Szam, near the Serbian border. On October 3 a ball was held at the hotel for the officers of the regiment. Also in attendance were the leading men of the village ("fat bourgeois"), their wives, and their daughters. The regimental historian noted that the younger generation spoke German poorly and danced German dances equally badly.[87]

The British theorist of irregular warfare, C. E. Callwell, as noted previously, once stated that in "small wars" an army had to contend with both the enemy and nature.[88] Almost as if they had taken Callwell at his word, the Austro-Hungarians, Bulgarians and Germans in particular, were training and equipping to deal with the Serbian army and the environment. The Serbian army in 1915 could be considered formidable but fragile. By 1915 the Serbian army could field 11 infantry divisions, one cavalry division, and a number of smaller detachments. Although Serbia had mobilized just over 700,000 men by the spring of 1915, the Serbian army's strength was anywhere between 250,000 and 270,000. In addition there were an unknown number of irregular fighters, known as *Komitadjis*, feared and hated by the Austro-Hungarians.[89]

The Germans regarded the Serbian army as a tough opponent. The average soldier, usually of peasant background, was inured to hardship and infused with a fierce nationalist spirit. Well experienced and disciplined, the forte of the Serbian soldier was on the defense and in the counterattack. They were also regarded as masters of field fortification and skilled in the art of camouflage.[90]

The Serbian commanders, like their German, Austro-Hungarian, and Bulgarian opponents, were experienced and skilled in the ways of modern warfare. Prime among them was the commander of the Serbian army, Voivode Radomir Putnik. His victories over the Austro-Hungarians in 1914 elevated him to almost iconic status in Serbia. Nonetheless, his infirm health, exacerbated by an attack of influenza, precluded him from playing a major role in the campaign.[91]

Putnik's two major subordinate commanders were Voivode Živojin Mišić and Voivode Stepan Stepanović. Based on the reports of agent Albin Kutschbach, posted in Niš, plus an analysis of earlier operations, the intelligence section of OHL was able to provide lots of biographical details, plus careful judgments on the abilities of these men. Although Kutschbach regarded Mišić very highly, German intelligence was more circumspect. While noting his bravery, German intelligence believed him lacking the qualifications for high command.

Stepanović was much more highly regarded, considered by the Germans to be a "clever, energetic officer with a full understanding of high command." The Germans also had information on key high-level staff officers, such as Božidar Terzić.[92]

Although the Serbian army had proven itself a formidable force in 1914, there were also some very fragile aspects to it. This applied especially to the elements of artillery and support infrastructure. In 1914 the Serbian army fielded some 768 guns of calibers ranging from 75 mm to 150 mm, primarily of French and German manufacture. The artillery also included guns captured from the Turkish army during the Balkan Wars. The 1914 campaigns resulted in the capture of a number Austro-Hungarian guns, but the Serbians lost some 60 guns themselves. Thus by the summer of 1915, the Serbian army was supported by about 780 guns, of which 240 were heavy.[93]

The number of guns available to the Serbians was inadequate, especially when it had to be spread to guard against Austro-Hungarian, German, and Bulgarian threats. Prewar ammunition stocks had been depleted by the 1914 campaigns, and shortages had only been covered by the timely arrival of munitions from France. The only facility capable of producing artillery shells, the arsenal at Kragujevać, could not meet the ferocious demands of modern warfare in both artillery and small arms ammunition.[94] Serbia had no air force to speak of. A small detachment of some 30 French aircraft operated out of Serbia, staffed by about 60 officers and men. Although lightly damaged aircraft could be repaired, spare parts had to be imported.[95]

Aside from the French aviation detachment, foreign aid to Serbia was also present in the form of the Russian, French, and British naval missions. The Russian and French naval missions were comparatively small affairs, although the French mission was the most efficiently run organization of the three. In terms of equipment, the French and Russian missions brought with them heavy naval guns, which were deployed near Belgrade.[96]

The British Naval Mission was the most comprehensive in its approach. Commanded initially by Commander Hubert Cardale and later by Rear Admiral Ernest Troubridge, RN, the British naval mission employed a combination of mines, small river craft capable of firing torpedoes, fixed torpedo stations set up on the banks of the Save and Danube, plus several naval guns. Troubridge was a figure of some controversy. In command of the Mediterranean squadron at the outbreak of war, Troubridge failed to prevent the German light cruisers *Goeben* and *Breslau* from reaching Constantinople. A court of inquiry resulted in a court martial in early November 1914, which acquitted Troubridge of the charge of negligence but ended his career afloat. Command of the naval mission was regarded by the Admiralty as a rather minor position that had to be filled.[97]

The mission of the British, French, and Russian naval forces sent to Serbia was a simple one. It was to assist the Serbians in defending the line of the Save and Danube Rivers against a renewed crossing by the Central powers. The Allied naval missions were there also to hold the Austrian Danube Flotilla at bay.[98]

The Serbian army was also short of all kinds of other equipment. The medical services were in poor shape. The Serbians were fortunate that their allies provided generous support in this regard. The Russians sent two field hospitals and several mobile kitchens. The French sent some 100 doctors, including some of their top specialists. The biggest effort was made by the British Red Cross, which set up no less than 16 field hospitals. These were supplemented by philanthropic efforts financed by wealthy Britons. Neutral countries, most notably the United States, also pitched in. Altogether over 2,000 foreigners went to render medical aid to Serbia. Often Austro-Hungarian prisoners were used to help staff many of these facilities.[99]

Manpower was also a major concern. Victory in 1914 had come with a high price in blood, in the form of over 120,000 casualties. The mobilization of so many men by the spring of 1915 had brought all economic activity to a complete halt. Matters were made worse by multiple epidemics in the spring of 1915. Numbers of men were struck down, including medical personnel, by typhus, cholera, and dysentery. Finally, the Serbian army had been forced to draft men from territories taken in the Balkan Wars. These included large numbers of Macedonians and Bulgarians, who the Germans and Austro-Hungarians expected to be of dubious reliability. These were supplemented by various small detachments of foreign volunteers, including some 1,500 Americans. Given all these circumstances, both German and Austro-Hungarian intelligence recognized that given Serbia's manpower situation, this was the last force Serbia was able to field.[100]

The entry of Bulgaria into the war on the side of the Central powers forced the Serbians to spread their forces. By the late summer of 1915 the Serbian forces were deployed in a long line resembling an expanded version of an inverted and backward "J." The short end of the "J" was western Serbia, opposite Bosnia, where small forces were posted to contest a limited Austro-Hungarian via Višegrad. Opposing the Austro-Hungarian Third and German Eleventh Armies were the Serbian First and Third Armies, commanded by Mišić and Pavel Jurišić-Sturm, respectively. Between them the two armies, plus the garrison of Belgrade and a division assigned by Serbian General Headquarters as a reserve, fielded about 143 infantry battalions, of which over 100 were first line or second line, meaning the best-equipped and manned formations. Some 362 guns were deployed in support of about 150,000 men.[101]

The long side of the "J" was the line that faced the Bulgarian border. The principal Serbian formation here was Stepanović's Second Army, along with the Timok Group under General Ilija Gojković. The forces the Bulgarians faced consisted of just over 100 infantry battalions as well as the majority of the Serbian cavalry. Supporting this 100,000 men were 238 guns. Finally there was a small force in Macedonia, composed of 26 third-line battalions (staffed by older men) and a number of recruit battalions under General Damljan Popović.[102]

The Serbian army's well-documented defensive capabilities were made even more formidable by the forbidding terrain over which the campaign was fought. This began with the natural moat protecting northern Serbia, formed by the Save and Danube Rivers. The rivers, which joined just east of Belgrade, were both wide. The average width of the Save was 300 to 700 yards, whereas that of the Danube could be over a mile in places. Although both rivers had numerous islands that could provide some cover for the invading forces, strong currents made bridging them no sure thing. The average current was almost three miles per hour and over four miles per hour when the river was high. As one German engineer put it, the technical circumstances for crossing were "hardly favorable."[103]

South of the rivers, the Serbians enjoyed the advantage of mountains that afforded excellent positions for observation and fire. Once through the mountains, Serbia was cut by three rivers, the Nišava, Morava, and Ibar, that ran roughly parallel to each other in a north to south course. Further to the southeast, the Bulgarians would have to force the passes of the Rhodope Mountains and then advance over difficult terrain to the Nišava River and the Serbian capital of Niš. Serbia's railroad network was underdeveloped and designed for a country whose economy was based on agriculture. The roads were also very poor, often amounting to little more than rudimentary tracks.[104]

Both Germany and Austria–Hungary had been contemplating a renewed offensive against Serbia, and each power had developed a similar concept. Tersztyánsky and his staff had developed a conceptual plan that evidently presumed Bulgarian participation. Serbia would be dispatched by a concentric attack from both the north and east by a force of 390 battalions against an estimated force of 230 Serbian battalions.[105]

After their arrival, Hentsch and his small staff began more detailed planning, to include the reconnoitering of crossing sites. While Tersztyánsky believed that a force of some 19 divisions was needed to invade Serbia, Hentsch regarded a dozen German and Austro-Hungarian divisions as sufficient for the purpose. This force would be supplemented by a Bulgarian force attacking from the east and an Austro-Hungarian division attacking from Bosnia. The ultimate goal was to trap and destroy the Serbian forces in the Kragujevać—Ćuprija area, while the Bulgarian forces would seize Niš and move on the key Serbian arsenal at Kragujevać. A smaller Bulgarian force would hold the valley of the Vardar River, the sole approach route for any entente force coming up from Salonika. Most critical to the success of the plan was the restoration of the rail line from Niš to Sofia, thus opening communications to Bulgaria and Turkey, while severing rail communications between Niš and Salonika.[106]

By the last week of September Mackensen's forces were ready. The rapid assembly and reequipping of the German Eleventh Army and the XXII Reserve Corps showed the German army at its most agile in a strategic sense. The matter of Serbia then became something akin to a race, with the Central powers competing against the Serbian army, the possibility of nature intervening in the form of the *Kossava*, and the increasingly likely arrival of an Anglo-French relief force at Salonika.[107] That race was now about to begin.

Chapter 4
The Opening Moves: September 25–October 12, 1915

"The operations of the Army Group began on 6 October."

Hans von Seeckt[1]

"Early today I stood for the first time on Serbian soil."

Robert Kosch, October 10, 1915[2]

As the German troops began arriving over the course of September in their assembly areas, preparations concomitant with the impending river crossing were also put in hand. Troop movements within the assembly areas were conducted at night. The training described in the previous chapter was done in areas well away from the rivers. As German and Austro-Hungarian air power became more active, the French aircraft operating out of Požarevac (Passarowitz), which had been active in flying reconnaissance over the area north of the rivers, were effectively driven out. French air power, scarce as it was, was further diluted when Bulgaria joined the Central powers. A detachment of eight French aircraft had to be dispatched to the Bulgarian border to keep track of Bulgarian military activities.[3]

With German aerial dominance then assured, the work of extended reconnaissance could begin. German and Austro-Hungarian aircraft, operating from airfields north of the river, flew numerous reconnaissance sorties. Aviation detachments attached to individual corps were tasked with conducting reconnaissance of the corps' respective sector. Roads and Serbian positions were to be photographed. Pilots also worked closely with the staff officers of the heavy artillery batteries, to ensure that every heavy artillery round had some effect. More distant reconnaissance was left to the Thirtieth Aviation Detachment, operating out of Weisskirchen. The detachment's aircraft ranged as far afield as Kruševac, about 90 miles from Weisskirchen.

The goal of all this aerial activity was to search for and keep track of the movements of any Serbian reserves. All aerial reconnaissance reports were to be reproduced in 15 copies for subordinate units, with reports being delivered personally by aviation detachment staff officers. Later on, as the date for the start of the operation neared, tethered observation balloons were raised, the view from which also offered a good view of the Serbian defenses. Aside from examining Serbian positions and movements, aerial reconnaissance flights also looked for sites for future airfields on Serbian territory. The First Aviation Detachment decided that its next base would be Požarevac, while the Sixty-Sixth Aviation Detachment chose Gradiste for its future location.[4]

While German and Austro-Hungarian aircrew were examining Serbian defenses from a bird's eye view, the ground officers were also conducting a reconnaissance of the prospective crossing points. Aside from examining the river-crossing sites, officers were also trying to acquaint themselves with the roads in the area, especially when it turned out that the maps they had were inaccurate. As they had prior to the Gorlice–Tarnow offensive, German officers reconnoitering near the river took the precaution of wearing all or parts of Austro-Hungarian uniforms, especially its distinctive hat. In addition, reconnaissance trips were timed to coincide with the serving of food to Serbian troops.[5]

As the onset of the operation approached, more senior officers made personal reconnaissance trips. Kosch, for example, undertook a reconnaissance of the 107th Infantry Division's crossing points on September 30, 1915, accompanied by Moser, the division's commander. Later on Gallwitz, Seeckt, and Mackensen as well reconnoitered the crossing points. The occasional French aircraft trying to snoop around the German positions were driven off, either by German aircraft or by antiaircraft fire.[6]

While reconnaissance missions were being flown, German aircraft were also undertaking another mission, namely bombing. The most favored targets were Požarevac, the principal Serbian airfield near the river, and Kragujevać, with its arsenals and ammunition production facilities. German attacks were conducted by flights of three to six aircraft. Bomb loads were small. One of the standard German aircraft of the period, the Halberstadt biplane, had a very limited bomb load capacity. On September 30, 1915, for example, six German aircraft from the Thirtieth Aviation Detachment attacked Kragujevać. A total of 30 bombs were dropped, an average of five bombs per aircraft.[7]

The bombs dropped by the Germans were relatively primitive. During the first half of the war, the Germans used high explosive bombs that ranged in size from 4.5 kilograms (just over 9 pounds) to 50 kilograms (110 pounds). More common were the 10-kilogram (22 pounds) and 20-kilogram (44 pounds) bombs.

Fuses at that stage in the war were notoriously unreliable, and this impacted the effectiveness of the bombs. By the end of September 1915 the Germans had dropped 2,400 kilograms (5,291 pounds) on Serbian targets. According to the German official history, only about half of the bombs actually exploded. The bombs that did explode failed to do any major damage.[8]

Serbian efforts at aerial defense rested largely on the employment of Turkish antiaircraft guns captured in the Balkan Wars. During the September 30, 1915, raid against Kragujevać the Serbian air defenses scored their lone success, shooting down a German Albatross. Both German crewmen, Warrant Officer Otto Krisch and Captain Kurt von Scheffer (pilot and observer, respectively), were killed.[9]

During the first days of October the Germans intensified their bombing operations but still obtained meager results. Continued Serbian antiaircraft efforts likewise yielded no successes. While the desultory bombing campaign continued, aerial reconnaissance continued to track Serbian troop movements, and any information gained was passed on as far down as to individual divisions.[10]

Meanwhile, the Germans and Austro-Hungarians completed their preparations for the river crossing. The divisions slated to make the crossing began moving to their respective assault positions. Once there, the troops also amassed their river-crossing material. The Austro-Hungarian Danube Flotilla continued its work of clearing the river of mines and occasionally tangling with a river craft that was part of one of the Allied naval missions. In addition, the Danube Flotilla sent out wooden decoys in the hopes that by firing at them, Serbian artillery batteries would disclose their positions.[11]

The heavy artillery was rolled into firing positions, and ammunition stocks were built up. As in the Gorlice–Tarnow attack, the opening barrage was planned to be short but intense. By early October each division had several thousand rounds for each type of artillery employed in the coming offensive amassed, with up to about 1,000 rounds placed in a battery's firing position.[12]

The artillery was a critical component of the German plan. Jansa expressed his concern to Seeckt about the Austro-Hungarian VIII Corps having to cross Save River and assault Belgrade directly. Kövess himself wrote to a friend that his mission to "stir up the nest of hornets." Seeckt and the army group's artillery officer Richard von Berendt assured Jansa that there was a sufficient amount of heavy artillery available to eliminate any threat to the Austro-Hungarian effort.[13]

The artillery itself was given specific targets to strike, according to the type of piece used. The heavy guns, meaning anything larger than 120 mm, had the lowest number of shells available, were thus directed to fire slowly and deliberately against known Serbian trenches and defensive positions, such as the old Turkish castles like the Kalemegdan at Belgrade. Aircraft were specifically assigned to observe the fall of the shells and then communicate the results, so that proper adjustments could be made. Medium artillery, usually in the range of 100 mm to 105 mm, was tasked with counterbattery fire against any Serbian guns capable of reaching the heavy guns. The soldiers manning the observation posts for these batteries hoped for some Serbian reaction while it was still dark. Once the Serbian gun flashes were spotted, the distance to them could be calculated and fire could be directed against them. The light artillery, short-range mortars, and flat trajectory weapons would employ direct fire against Serbian defenses covering the riverbank. This included the monitors of the Danube Flotilla, whose shallow draught (just under four feet) allowed them to get close of the Serbian shore.[14]

On September 28, 1915, Mackensen set the date for the start of the operation as October 5 or 6. The assertion that the original date for the operation was October 10, but moved up because of entente forces landing at Salonika, is not supported by documentary evidence.[15] Both OHL and AOK were concerned about the possibility of Greece joining the entente and some kind of move to aid Serbia directly; thus keeping Turkey isolated was part of the calculations at OHL as well as in Temesvár. News of the landing at Salonika, as well as concerns about the weather, merely confirmed the wisdom of Mackensen and Seeckt setting the date for the operation as they did.[16]

The plan first envisaged by Tersztyánsky and later fleshed out by Hentsch called for a concentric attack by the Austro-Hungarian and German forces from the north, with a limited thrust from the west, while the Bulgarian forces would attack from the east. Mackensen's staff, under Seeckt's direction, then worked in some important details. The original idea, at least implicitly, suggested that the attacks by Germany, Austria–Hungary, and Bulgaria be simultaneous. Because the military convention called for Bulgaria to be ready for military action 35 days after signing it, while Germany and Austria–Hungary were to be ready by 30 days after signature, the timing of the operation was altered.[17]

Instead of simultaneous thrusts, Mackensen's army group would execute a series of attacks with carefully staggered timing. Kövess's Austro-Hungarian Third Army would begin its artillery bombardment on October 5 and cross to the Serbian side of the Save just west of Belgrade on the 7th. Gallwitz's German Eleventh Army's crossing would also be staggered, with the X Reserve Corps, after artillery preparation beginning on October 6, crossing the Danube River on October 7. The IV Reserve and III Corps would start their artillery preparation on the 7th and then cross the Danube on the 8th. The idea was to draw the bulk of the Serbian forces north to oppose the armies of Kövess and Gallwitz, who would fix the Serbian forces along the Save and Danube. This would facilitate the attack of Bojadjev's Bulgarian First Army, advancing directly west from the Bulgarian border against the Serbian capital of Niš, cutting the Serbian army's lines of communication to the south. From Mackensen's standpoint, the most favorable outcome would be a decisive action in the Morava valley, resulting in the destruction of the Serbian forces in the area between Kragujevać and Ćuprija.[18]

With more distant operational plans in hand Mackensen and Seeckt then set forth the plans for the immediate task at hand. The mission for both the Austro-Hungarian Third and German Eleventh Armies was, simply stated, to cross the river before it. Once across, each army was to secure the high ground beyond the Serbian shore. With the bridgeheads established, the pontoon bridges could be built without interruption.[19]

With the date for the crossings then set, the initial steps preceding the crossing to the south bank of the Save and Danube were undertaken. The preliminary measures centered on seizing the large islands in the rivers. For the Austro-Hungarian Third Army, the islands in question were Little Zigeuner (Gypsy) and Big Zigeuner, located in the German XXII Reserve Corps' sector, just west of Belgrade. The German Eleventh Army had to take Semendria Island in the III Corps sector. More important, Winckler's IV Reserve Corps had to seize Temesziget, a large island of just over 23 square miles sitting in the Danube about 10 miles from Požarevac. Kosch's X Reserve Corps had to take the island of Cibuklia.[20]

Taking the islands served two purposes. First, seizing the islands would provide cover for Mackensen's forces assembling on the north bank of the Save and Danube. The islands effectively divided each river into a shorter northern arm and a wider southern arm. Once the islands were in German or Austro-Hungarian hands, the northern arm could be bridged without Serbian interference. Assault troops could then assemble on the islands and prepare for the crossing of the wider southern arm to the Serbian shore. Second, once the islands had been secured, the larger ones could also serve as platforms for the lighter artillery pieces.

Of all the islands in question, the most important was Temesziget. Over 12 miles long and up to 3 miles across at its widest point, its capture was critical to the IV Reserve Corps' crossing operations. The island's importance could be gauged by the fact that Seeckt took time from his personal reconnaissance to brief the plan for the seizing of Temesziget to the Bavarian Eleventh Infantry Division. Also some concern was expressed over the fact that enemy aircraft had been reconnoitering over the island as well.[21]

On the night of September 24–25 the first crossings were made to Temesziget by elements of the Bavarian Eleventh Infantry Division. The Serbian outposts on the island were overwhelmed. By September 28 about half of the division had been moved to the island, including four batteries of artillery. For a combination of humanitarian reasons and security, Winckler ordered the civilian population of Temesziget to be evacuated.[22] The other islands could be taken closer to the start of the operation.

As the divisions slated to make the crossing continued their preparations, military commanders and diplomats also got ready for the operation. In another classic example of too little, too late, on October 3 the Russians sent Bulgaria an ultimatum, trying to dissuade Bulgaria from going to war.

Napier described the Bulgarian response to the Russian ultimatum as "impertinent."[23] The following day Mackensen and Seeckt met with Kövess and Konopicky at Temesvár to discuss the details of the Austro-Hungarian Third Army's crossing. Mackensen, Gallwitz, and their chiefs of staff also got out to meet with their key subordinate officers.[24]

Other issues that were decided between AOK and OHL were turned into policies that the troops would put into practice. Any prisoners captured in Serbia would be turned over to Austro-Hungarian authorities. Places where such turnovers would occur would be named later. In addition, any unit that captured equipment could make use of it as the unit saw fit. This had been something of a sticky problem during the campaigns in Galicia and Poland and had produced some awkward moments.[25]

There were also some last-minute tweaks to the plan. The most notable change was the reduction of the role of the Austro-Hungarian Sixty-Second Infantry Division. Originally it was slated to cross the Drina at Višegrad. Once it became clear that the unit lacked the combat power to make an opposed crossing, the division's attack was postponed by two days.[26]

During the first five days of October, preparations were completed. Guns were deployed, and ammunition stockpiled by the pieces. The craft needed to cross the river were collected near the crossing sites but were kept hidden as much as possible. Some regiments, like the German 227th Reserve Infantry, continued to receive replacements. Reconnaissance, both aerial and ground, was conducted of both the islands and the Serbian shore. Even the most minute of changes in enemy dispositions were noted. Assuming that heavy fighting would be required and that regular supply would not be available immediately, troops slated to make the crossing were issued additional ammunition, plus regular rations for two days and combat (referred to as "iron") rations for an additional four days. Finally, units made sure their numbers of telephone stations were established, to facilitate the transmission of orders and reports between higher and lower headquarters.[27]

During the night of October 5–6 the final reconnaissance trips were made. Some ventured by boat close to the Serbian shore to gauge the state of the defenses on the river and to see if any new mines had been laid. A patrol composed of volunteers from the Seventy-First Infantry Regiment led by Sergeant Mackenrodt returned from its trip to find Mackensen and Estorff there to receive their findings. Subordinate commanders such as Falkenhayn also moved their headquarters as close as possible to the north bank of both rivers. Efforts were also made to ensure that forward command posts and headquarters alike had telephone communications.[28]

The artillery spent October 5 firing registration fire. With the guns registered against designated targets, fire for effect began on the afternoon of October 6. Although the morning had been foggy, by the afternoon the weather had cleared enough for German and Austro-Hungarian spotter aircraft to get aloft. Troubridge noted that at Belgrade, the Austro-Hungarian and German heavy guns quickly got a fix on the Serbian antiaircraft guns and destroyed them.[29] With the only threat to them eliminated, the spotter aircraft could circle at leisure, observing the fall of each shot. Data could then be passed to the batteries either by landing near the position or dropping a note tied to a weighted object. Thus the heavy artillery could shoot slowly and deliberately. The Germans and Austro-Hungarians could then make every heavy artillery shell, a precious commodity outside the western front, count.[30]

The heavy artillery, because it had the longest range, concentrated on known Serbian gun positions and against identified defensive positions. At Ram and Semendria the heavy guns paid considerable attention to the Serbian positions at Gorica and Avala Mountains, respectively, as these overlooked the river. Belgrade was especially hard hit. General Mihailo Živković, commander of Belgrade's defenses, reported that some 15,000 shells hit the city. The naval guns sent as part of the Russian naval mission to Serbia were quickly destroyed. The same fate befell the French naval guns at Belgrade as well. Searchlights and torpedo and mining stations were also severely battered, presumably by the smaller caliber guns.[31]

As darkness fell on October 6 the artillery continued to fire against their targets on the Serbian shore; the infantry of Kövess's army swung into action. The infantry began to move first to the islands in the river and then to the Serbian shore. It was simultaneously aided and hindered by a strong storm that broke over the area that night. The Forty-Fourth Reserve Division was Falkenhayn's lead unit. At 3:30 a.m. on October 7, the 208th Reserve Infantry Regiment put 15 pontoons into the water, each carrying 10 men. Over the course of a long day, one battalion was able to secure the western part of cigar-shaped Big Zigeuner Island (over 2.5 miles long), while the First Battalion gained a foothold on the Serbian shore west of Belgrade. German artillery effectively protected the front of the German bridgehead, while the rest of the regiment moved to the Serbian side.[32]

Although the Germans had gained a foothold, the situation was still tenuous. The number of pontoons was limited, so German units had to be crossed in relays. Although the Serbian artillery response was weak, Serbians maintained a lively machine gun and rifle fire and used hand grenades liberally. A number of pontoons were damaged, and one hit a mine and sank. Falkenhayn had to ask Kövess for additional pontoons and bridging equipment.[33]

Tactically, the situation was still a problematic one for the German XXII Reserve Corps. The Serbians still held large parts of Big and Little Zigeuner Islands, and those two islands had to be cleared before the bridges spanning the river could be built. Runckel's Forty-Third Reserve Division was then committed to securing the islands. This required some difficult fighting. Several attempts were required just to land troops on Little Zigeuner Island

and some hard fighting to secure it. On Big Zigeuner Island a combination of German infantry and engineers drove the Serbians back from their positions. The Serbian survivors were ultimately able to retreat to the Serbian shore on a temporary bridge built before the German operation began. Success here was costly for the German engineers. Of the 80 committed to the fighting on Big Zigeuner Island, 56 were casualties. A number of German soldiers drowned as well.[34]

While Falkenhayn's XXII Reserve Corps was dealing with the Serbian forces on the islands and on the Serbian side of the river west of Belgrade, the Austro-Hungarian elements of Kövess's Austro-Hungarian Third Army made their attempts to cross the Save. The effort met with mixed success. Trollmann's Austro-Hungarian XIX Corps shifted its crossing site a bit to the east, from Kupinovo to Progar for Pongrácz's Fifty-Third Infantry Division and further east to Boljevci for the 205th Landsturm Brigade. Two other Landsturm brigades, the Twentieth and Twenty-First, were held in reserve. The shift to the east, which was approved by Kövess, provided the usual set of trade-offs that are a part of a river crossing. Although the new sites had better approach routes for Trollmann's troops and the river at Progar allowed monitors to work close to the Serbian bank, the swampy ground on the Serbian side limited routes away from the river. The result was that the XIX Corps crossed essentially unopposed but were stopped short of Obrenovac by the Serbian Drina Division II, part of Mišić's First Army.[35]

A far more dramatic scene was being played out at Belgrade. Kövess had entrusted the crossing of the Save River at Belgrade to the Austro-Hungarian VIII Corps, commanded by Feldzeugmeister Viktor *Graf* von Scheuchenstuel. Born in 1857, Scheuchenstuel had led divisions successfully in combat. His first mission as a corps commander was a daunting one.[36] Like Falkenhayn's XXII Reserve Corps, Scheuchenstuel's troops had to simultaneously take Great War Island at the confluence of the Save and Danube Rivers and gain a lodgment on the Serbian shore just below Belgrade itself.

Although elements of Snjarić's Fifty-Ninth Infantry Division were able to secure Great War Island, which provided a forward platform for light artillery, getting a lodgment on the Serbian side proved costly and difficult. A light rain served to ground spotter aircraft. Also Belgrade's defenses were stoutly manned and supported by artillery. Although a number of guns had been silenced, enough Serbian pieces remained in action and thus made life miserable for Snjarić's battalions that were crossing the river. By nightfall on October 8 the Fifty-Ninth Infantry Division was established on the Serbian shore at the foot of the hill looking up at the walls of the Kalemegdan fortress. Austro-Hungarian losses in both men and pontoons was considerable.[37]

The course of October 9 brought Kövess's army a hard-won success. Falkenhayn's German XXII Reserve Corps advanced to the east and south. Runckel's Forty-Third Reserve Division moved into the western part of

Belgrade, occupying the *Konak*, King Peter's official residence. The German flag was raised early on October 9. Runckel's troops, with the German Forty-Fourth Reserve Division covering their right flank, occupied the Banovo Mountain, overlooking the city from the southwest.[38]

The Austro-Hungarian Fifty-Ninth Infantry Division spent October 9 fighting its way into Belgrade and the Kalemegdan in bitter house-to-house combat. Snjarić's troops were also ably supported by two monitors from the Danube Flotilla. By the evening of October 9 the Austro-Hungarian flag flew over the rubble of the Kalemegdan. Živković pulled his troops out of Belgrade to the hills south and southeast of the city, where they joined the Timok II Division.[39]

Kövess's forces that were already across the river would continue attacking on October 10. The Austro-Hungarian XIX Corps would resume its attack. Kövess rejected a suggestion by Conrad that Trollmann's corps be removed and shifted to Belgrade. Falkenhayn's German XXII Reserve Corps would move south. The Austro-Hungarian VIII Corps, with only one division in Belgrade, would stay put. More disappointing was the fact that the Austro-Hungarian Sixty-Second Infantry Division would be unable to take any offensive action for at least a week. Meanwhile the units still on the north side of the Save would cross to the Serbian side.[40]

Even this limited action proved overly ambitious. Falkenhayn's corps made only a few local advances. The Twenty-Sixth Infantry Division was able to get across the river. Likewise the remaining infantry units of the Forty-Third and Forty-Fourth Reserve Divisions also entered the bridgehead. Scheuchenstuel was able to bring Goiginger's Fifty-Seventh Infantry Division across the river.[41]

Trying to bring material across the river was proving difficult. Although a pontoon bridge to Big Zigeuner Island had been completed and a Serbian bridge for foot traffic from Big Zigeuner to the Serbian side had been captured, this helped only a little. Bad weather was already setting in, and rising water was flooding parts of the islands in the river and washing out the roads. Getting heavy artillery across was especially problematic. Kövess decided to postpone the attack scheduled for October 11 to the next day.[42]

The attack on October 12 brought mixed success. The German XXII Reserve Corps, supported by a carefully planned and executed artillery preparation, drove the Serbians back a couple of miles to the south, securing the Petlovo Hills and the town of Zeleznik. The Austro-Hungarian VIII Corps, on Falkenhayn's left, made much slower progress. Part of the problem there was that the deteriorating conditions on the river made it difficult for the Austro-Hungarian monitors to support the ground troops effectively. The stormy weather also interfered with the clearing of mines.[43]

By the evening of October 12 Kövess could be reasonably satisfied with the progress of the Austro-Hungarian Third Army. Although the Scheuchenstuel's VIII Corps had taken more losses than anticipated, Belgrade and the area immediately south of the city were in the hands of the Central powers. Aside from the problems with the Sixty-Second Infantry Division, the only other sticking point for Kövess was the situation Trollmann's XIX Corps faced. Having made no progress on October 12, Kövess now returned to Conrad's earlier suggestion to reposition the corps. Mackensen and Seeckt agreed with the idea, with the proviso that sufficient force be left to hold the bridgehead already won. The main concern here was that complete abandonment of the river bank by Trollmann's troops would give the Serbians a propaganda victory.[44]

The seizure of Belgrade brought about a new set of issues for Mackensen. One problem for Mackensen concerned public relations. After the course of operations on October 9, Mackensen was able to report the fall of Belgrade to both OHL and AOK.[45] Both OHL and AOK, however, reported that only their troops took the city. Kövess likewise also put out a release crediting Snjarić's division with the capture. A visibly annoyed Mackensen trooped into the operations section of his headquarters demanding to know how this occurred. Jansa pointed out that while the German troops took the western part of the city, the Austro-Hungarians had successfully stormed the Kalemegdan. That mollified the old hussar for the moment.[46]

The fall of Belgrade also raised the issue of the treatment of the civilian population. Before the war Belgrade had a population of about 92,000. The chaos of the initial Austrian invasions and occupations, however, had reduced the city's population to a mere 10,000, some of whom had participated in Belgrade's defense.[47] Mackensen's headquarters issued a proclamation over his signature to the Serbian population. It noted occasions where civilians had engaged in combat with German and Austro-Hungarian troops. The document proclaimed that the invading forces only sought to fight the Serbian army. If Serbian civilians, however, were found to be engaging in resisting, they would be subject to the harshest measures, including hanging and shooting. The house of the offending civilian's family would also be destroyed.[48]

About 50 miles to the east, Gallwitz's German Eleventh Army was crossing the Danube on a wide front. The Eleventh Army's crossing operation was to be executed in a staggered fashion. Kosch's X Reserve Corps would cross at Ram, while Winckler's IV Reserve Corps would cross to the south bank of the Danube via the newly occupied Temesziget Island. Lochow's III Corps, on Gallwitz's right, originally scheduled to cross on October 7, would cross two days later at Semendria.[49]

The crossing of the X Reserve Corps was probably considered the most important of the Eleventh Army's crossings, given that both Mackensen and Gallwitz were in attendance with Kosch to observe the proceedings.[50] The initial plan called for the 103rd Infantry Division to seize Cibuklia Island, so that the crossing at Ram just to the east could proceed without any interference from Serbian troops there. Meanwhile the 101st Infantry Division would cross the Danube a few miles to the east at Bazias. Once on the south bank, the troops would secure the Gorica Hills, which loomed some 1,100 feet high and overlooking the river. East of the X Reserve Corps, Group Fülöpp would demonstrate to fix any Serbian troops in the area.[51]

Of all the Eleventh's Army's crossings, the X Reserve Corps crossing at Ram proved to be the easiest. Cibuklia was quickly secured by one company each from the Thirty-Second and Seventy-First Infantry Regiments. Some batteries from the 205th Field Artillery Regiment also moved to the island. As the German barrage reached its height, the Estorff's lead element, the Seventy-First Infantry Regiment, put its first echelon, the Fifth Company into the river at 6:45 a.m. A few minutes later the Thirty-Second Infantry Regiment put its lead pontoons in the water. As the engineers and sailors guided the infantry filled pontoons across the river, the soldiers occasionally had to duck down as some German shells fell short and landed in the water.[52]

The errant German shell notwithstanding, the 103rd Infantry Division's crossing at Ram was an unqualified success. Serbian resistance was negligible on the southern bank. The Second Battalion of the Seventy-First Infantry Regiment quickly drove away the few defenders present taking 10 prisoners and capturing two old French made guns after an engineer used a grenade to drive off or disable the crews. The rest of the regiment followed as quickly as number of available craft allowed. The Thirty-Second Infantry Regiment also continued sending troops across. With the two regiments on the southern bank of the Danube, they quickly moved against the Gorica Hills, securing them by 10 a.m. To reinforce the infantry, Austro-Hungarian mountain artillery now assembled on the northern bank.[53]

While Estorff's 103rd Infantry Division was enjoying success at Ram, Kraewel's 101st Infantry Division met equally light resistance in its crossing. The departure point for the division was the village of Bazias, where the width of the Danube was about 1,100 yards. Serbian resistance was so light, however, that by the afternoon of October 7 major elements of the 101st Division were across and had linked up with the 103rd Division.[54] Only at around dusk did the Serbians act, launching an attack of about regimental strength through a high cornfield to retake the Gorica Hills. Launched without artillery support, the Serbian effort proved something of a forlorn hope, especially since the German infantry battalions had been reinforced with the Seventy-First Regiment's machine gun company. The attack was beaten off with heavy losses to the Serbians.[55]

Having fended off the Serbian effort, regiments on Serbian soil sought to exploit the situation. The elements of the 101st Infantry Division that were across the river, the 45th, 59th, and one battalion of the 146th Regiments, expanded the division's bridgehead to the south. The 103rd Infantry Division attempted to move against the Anatema Hills, the next hill mass south of the Gorica Hills. The effort was stopped short of its objective, however, by a then-aroused

Serbian artillery and a new Serbian defensive position. A 10 p.m. counterattack, plus a worrisome gap opening between the Seventy-First and Thirty-Second Regiments, brought an end to a very busy day.[56]

By the end of October 7, Kosch and his commanders had every reason to be satisfied. Some 14 battalions were then across the river, and some Austro-Hungarian mountain artillery had been brought to the Serbian side as well. In addition, telephone lines were also extended to the south bank of the Danube. Although the number of prisoners taken (25 total) was disappointing, German losses were very light. The Thirty-Second Infantry Regiment, for example, lost only one officer, and four men were killed and six were wounded.[57]

With a firm presence on the Serbian side of the Danube then established, Kosch endeavored to expand his bridgehead. The goal of this expansion centered on taking the Anatema Hills. This would effectively put his crossing sites beyond the range of the Serbian heavy artillery, then still firing on them.[58] After spending October 8 building up his force, Kosch launched his attack the next day.

Over the course of October 9 and 10, the 103rd and 101st Infantry Divisions moved forward, contending with the hilly terrain and stout Serbian resistance. The two divisions were able to establish contact with each other, and they slowly drove the Serbian defenders out of their positions and the small villages that dotted the hills. As before, the German trump card was its heavy artillery. One regimental history noted that the topographical peak of the Anatema Hills was turned into a crater by a direct hit from a Krupp 420-mm howitzer, popularly known as a "Big Bertha."[59]

Heavy fighting continued on October 12, and only short gains were made by the X Reserve Corps. Nonetheless, with the Anatema Hills in his possession and pontoon bridges completed, Kosch could now order the heavy equipment, artillery and baggage for his corps across the river. A visit to the Serbian side on October 10 confirmed Kosch's impression that the X Reserve Corps had accomplished its first mission in the campaign.[60]

Originally, Winckler's IV Reserve Corps was not supposed to make its crossing on October 8. Kosch's success at Ram, however, led Winckler to move up his operation by 24 hours. This kind of aggressiveness had been a hallmark of Winckler during the offensive in Galicia, when he was commander of the Second Guard Division.[61]

Having occupied Temesziget Island, the IV Reserve Corps crossing now resolved itself into two crossings. While elements of the 105th Infantry Division moved on to Temesziget, the rest of Winckler's corps moved up to the north bank of the Danube. Having already crossed to Temesziget Island, two regiments of the Bavarian Eleventh Infantry Division and two from the 105th would cross from the south side of Temesziget Island to the south bank of the river. The 107th Infantry Division also moved up to the north bank of the Danube at Dunadombo, behind the 105th Infantry Division. Kneussl decided that Petka would be the immediate objective for his Bavarians, while Esch's 105th Infantry Division would make for the Leštar Hills, which overlooked the river. Another important target to take was the glass works at Kostolac, atop the hills. Reconnaissance missions conducted by 105th Infantry Division concluded that the Serbian forces covering the river in the IV Reserve Corps sector amounted to about four battalions, backed by two machine gun companies.[62]

Fire for effect began on the afternoon of October 7 and continued into the night. Meanwhile the infantry slated to cross from the south side of Temesziget Island gathered their pontoons, *Zillen* and other river craft. On the morning of October 8 the river was covered by low-hanging cloud and fog. Although this hindered the ability of spotter aircraft to work with their assigned heavy batteries, the cloud and fog also served to obscure the German crossing of the river.

The Serbian response to the German bombardment was negligible. As the German craft nosed into the Serbian bank, they could hear sporadic rifle and machine gun fire. Fanning out from their boats, the soldiers of the Bavarian Third and Twenty-Second Regiments quickly overran the Serbian positions closest to the river bank. Meanwhile the lead element of the 105th Infantry Division, the 129th Infantry Regiment, crossed the river in relays of one or two companies at a time. Like the Bavarians, the Prussians of the 129th Regiment quickly drove off the weak Serbian patrols and established a line.[63]

Once ashore, however, the course of events went somewhat differently for the two divisions. The 105th Infantry had a relatively smooth day. Once on Serbian soil in strength, the 129th Infantry Regiment moved into the Leštar Hills quickly. By noon Kostolac and its glass works were in the hands of the Third Battalion. The regiment was poised to move south the next day. Elements of the 122nd Fusilier Regiment also moved to the south bank. Meanwhile the Fifty-Second Infantry Regiment, having just assigned recently arrived replacements to the various companies, moved to its crossing point with its 50 pontoons. The regiment would cross to the Serbian side on October 9.[64]

The Serbians seemed to be much more cognizant of the Bavarian presence on the south side of the river. By mid-morning the Serbian defenses were becoming much more active. Although losses in men were light, a pontoon was damaged and a *Zillen* was destroyed. The Serbians attempted to attack into a gap between the Bavarian Third and Twenty-Second Infantry Regiments, requiring Kneussl to commit a battalion from the Bavarian Thirteenth Infantry Regiment. By nightfall on October 8, after some tough fighting, were in position to storm Petka the next day. Meanwhile, the 107th Infantry Division moved to its crossing point on the north bank of the river.[65]

Winckler's assault on October 9 was delayed in its start by heavy fog. The fog finally began lifting late in the morning, and the division commanders issued their orders accordingly. Kneussl, for example, issued his attack order at 10:30 a.m.. Artillery preparation began at noon, and the infantry attack began at 2:30 p.m.[66]

Matters did not get off to an auspicious start when German artillery, owing to poor observation, dropped some shells on the most forward company of the 2nd Battalion of the 122nd Fusiliers. Taking advantage of the confusion, the Serbians launched a large-scale attack along almost the whole of Winckler's front, aided by the high cornfields that masked their own positions. The Serbian infantry was finally driven off by the combination of German machine gun fire and artillery fire from both the north bank of the Danube and Temesziget.[67] Winckler's troops then went over to the attack, advancing through the cornfields the Serbians had used earlier.

Winckler's soldiers had to fight their way into the Serbian trenches dug into the cornfields, hidden by the high autumn corn. Ably supported by artillery, the Germans fought their way through the Serbian positions over the course of the late afternoon. Kneussl's Bavarians eventually levered the Serbians out of Petka, while Esch's 105th Infantry Division secured the Leštar Hills. The ferocity of the fighting was reflected in the casualties. The Bavarian Eleventh Infantry Division lost 750 men over the course of October 8 and 9. The Bavarians counted some 1,080 Serbian dead.[68]

Winckler's troops spent the next three days making short advances against light resistance. Occasionally the Serbians launched a counterattack, but these efforts were done with weak forces and easily beaten off. By the end of October 12, the 105th Infantry Division had moved south from the Leštar Hills, while Kneussl's Bavarians had reached the outskirts of Požarevac.

About 19 miles to the west, Lochow's III Corps made its crossing at Semendria. Lochow decided to wait until October 9 to make his crossing to the Serbian side. All of his heavy artillery firing positions were easily visible from the Serbian side. In addition, October 8 was consumed in having the Twenty-Fifth Reserve Division seize the western end of Semendria Island.[69]

Lochow's concerns proved to be justified. Although the German artillery was able to deploy without trouble, getting the infantry across proved to be problematic. Jarotzky's Twenty-Fifth Reserve Infantry Division in particular had a difficult time. The 168th Infantry Regiment (a Hessian outfit) was able to get a reinforced battalion on to Semendria Island, where the Germans encountered tough Serbian resistance. One company ended up on the south bank of the Danube but was able to hunker down for the night. Matters were made worse by the fact that several pontoons were destroyed by Serbian fire. A number of others were carried away in the strong current.[70]

Nonetheless, the III Corps was able to cross the river successfully on October 9. The Serbian artillery response was weak, so the powerful German guns had it all their own way. Known Serbian artillery positions were struck, and the old Turkish castle at Semendria, which overlooked the river, was pummeled by the German heavy guns. The Sixth Infantry Division was able to reach its departure point, Kevevára, and then cross the river without difficulty. While the 168th Infantry Regiment was able to get the rest of its men to the Serbian side of the river, Lochow decided to move the remaining units of the Twenty-Fifth Reserve Division to Kevevára and follow the Sixth Infantry Division's route across the river. The detachment on Semendria Island was also withdrawn back to the north bank.[71]

With the III Corps now across the river, Lochow moved on his first objective, Semendria itself. The 25th Reserve and 6th Infantry Divisions moved in from the east, while the 168th Infantry Regiment improved its precarious position on the south bank. The major obstacle to be overcome then was the Jezava River, a tributary of the Danube, 100 yards wide and swollen from rains. On October 11 the 168th Infantry Regiment attacked and occupied the old Turkish castle, while the rest of Jarotzky's infantry crossed the Jezava and fought their way into the town after an artillery bombardment. Herhudt's Sixth Infantry Division attacked the area southwest of Semendria, in particular the village of Lipe. By late afternoon the Twentieth and Twenty-Fourth Infantry Regiments had finally driven the Serbians from Lipe after some costly fighting. The Twentieth Infantry Regiment alone lost 12 killed and 68 wounded.[72]

With the Serbians then ejected from Belgrade and its environs and Gallwitz's Eleventh Army across the Danube, Mackensen's forces got on to other tasks. The railroad troops had to bring the railroad forward to the north bank of each river. Meanwhile, the corps commanders with bridgeheads to worry about sought to improve their respective logistical situations, building up their ammunition supplies. The goal was to get about four to five days' worth of ammunition to the south bank. Artillery ammunition, especially for the heavy caliber guns, was also cause for concern. Corps commanders ordered artillery units to report the status of their ammunition stocks by the end of the day. Getting ammunition across often involved using the hard-pressed pioneers to continue to ferry material to the south bank. Meanwhile, pontoon bridges were also built, mostly from the north bank of the Save and Danube to the large islands in the river, although two bridges had been built to the south bank at Belgrade.[73]

Commanders also now had to deal with the Serbian civilian population. Mackensen's proclamation, alluded to earlier, also applied to the smaller towns and villages as well as to large cities such as Belgrade. In general, however, Gallwitz's corps commanders were ordered to avoid contact with Serbian civilians. In addition, while corps commanders could order the evacuation of villages, they were prohibited from evacuating Serbian civilians to the north bank of the Danube. The only Serbians who would be sent to the prisoner collection point at Weisskirchen were captured soldiers or any male between ages 16 and 60 who were found to be armed.[74] The limiting of contact with civilians was for a practical reason. German intelligence was well aware that Serbia had suffered severely from epidemics in the winter and spring.

Limiting contact with civilians was seen as the best way to reduce the potential impact of disease on Mackensen's forces. More pleasantly, German soldiers found that incidents of Serbian civilians sniping at them to be relatively rare, contrary to expectations.[75]

At the higher levels of command, the river crossings were regarded with some satisfaction. The capture of Belgrade afforded the Wilhelm another opportunity to deplete OHL's stock of pink champagne. There was some concern at OHL, then located in Charleville, over what was perceived as the slow Austro-Hungarian advance and the fact that the Bulgarian army's offensive had still not begun. There was grim satisfaction in Teschen and Vienna that the Serbian "viper" was now going to be crushed, but unhappiness at the fact that the campaign was confirming Austria–Hungary's status as the junior partner in the alliance.[76]

Although matters had generally gone well in crossing the rivers, Mackensen also had some issues that were related to coalition warfare. The old hussar had gotten past his annoyance with Kövess over the latter's public announcement of the taking of Belgrade. Thus it was all smiles, at least publicly, when Mackensen and Seeckt went to Belgrade to congratulate Kövess on the city's capture on October 11.[77]

Privately, however, Kövess complained to Mackensen about the behavior of German troops, particularly those of Falkenhayn's XXII Reserve Corps. Kövess complained that German troops would often steal equipment and supplies from Austro-Hungarian soldiers. When Austro-Hungarian officers and NCOs tried to intervene and stop this, the German soldiers cursed at them and even threatened them with weapons.[78] Presumably Mackensen and Seeckt, both of whom were blessed with a degree of tact, spoke with Falkenhayn about the matter privately, as there is no mention of the embarrassing episode in the memoirs of either man.

Contretemps such as that between Kövess and Falkenhayn's soldiers notwithstanding, Mackensen and Seeckt had reason to be pleased. The crossings of the Save and Danube had gone about as well as they could have, with a few exceptions. Perhaps the most notable was the failure of Austro-Hungarian Sixty-Second Infantry Division to accomplish anything positive on the Drina, despite the prodding of the army group. It was simply not up to the task. Another problem was the losses suffered by Snjarić's Austro-Hungarian Fifty-Ninth Infantry Division at Belgrade. The German Twenty-Fifth Reserve Infantry Division's problems at Semendria ultimately proved to be a relatively minor annoyance.[79]

There were a number of reasons for German and Austro-Hungarian success. Operationally, the agreement between Falkenhayn and Conrad's that any renewed invasion of Serbia required Bulgarian participation paid considerable dividends. The mere presence of the Bulgarian "army in being" forced Putnik to have to devote a major part of his available troops and especially his heavy artillery to cover Serbia's eastern border. Likewise a considerable portion of the French aviation detachment also had to be dispatched to the Bulgarian border. Thus, when the Austro-Hungarian and German Eleventh Armies launched their respective river crossings, they were opposed by a total of only four Serbian divisions.[80]

Careful preparation by the Germans and Austro-Hungarians also paid off in the execution of the river crossings. German and Austro-Hungarians air superiority generally kept French reconnaissance aircraft from snooping around suspected assembly areas. Although the bombing campaign fizzled, aerial reconnaissance provided much needed information, especially as maps provided by the Austro-Hungarians often proved rather inaccurate. German reconnaissance efforts were aided by well-established practices, such as using all or part of Austro-Hungarian uniforms. The Serbians contributed to German reconnaissance efforts by falling into a rigid routine, especially when it came to feeding their own troops. Consequently, while the Serbians were well prepared at some places most notably Belgrade, they were caught completely off guard at Ram.[81]

In the conduct of the crossing, heavy artillery proved to be the trump card for Mackensen and Seeckt, as it had in Galicia and Poland. When it came to heavy guns, the Serbians simply had nothing that could compare to the resources available to the Central powers, especially in terms of numbers. The weather held long enough to allow German aircraft to spot for heavy batteries, a critical advantage. The lighter caliber guns, with a rapid rate of fire, played an important role in thwarting the counterattacks that the Serbians did mount.[82]

Finally, Mackensen and Seeckt received some sterling assistance from their Austro-Hungarian allies. Despite the failures of the Austro-Hungarian Sixty-Second Infantry Division and the difficulties of the XIX Corps and the VIII Corps in their respective crossings, Austro-Hungarian assistance was invaluable. The railroad authorities were able to enable the deployment of the Austro-Hungarian Third and German Eleventh Armies to their assembly areas in a smooth manner.[83]

The materials provided by the Austro-Hungarians for the river crossing, employed by German and Austro-Hungarian engineers, also proved to be excellent. Regimental histories noted that the pontoons provided by the Austro-Hungarians proved to be excellent, very stable in the water with little rocking, even when loaded with heavily equipped infantry. The small steamers also provided critical service in the powerful currents. Finally the monitors of the Austro-Hungarian Danube Flotilla provided excellent support in terms of naval gun fire and mine clearance.[84]

At the beginning of October 1915 two near simultaneous occurred, namely the Franco-British landing at Salonika and Army Group Mackensen's crossing of the Save and Danube Rivers. Mackensen and Seeckt calculated that perhaps as many as 150,000 French and British troops would be available for a thrust up the Vardar River Valley toward the Serbian border. In actual fact, the number of troops that did land was much smaller. For their part the Serbian

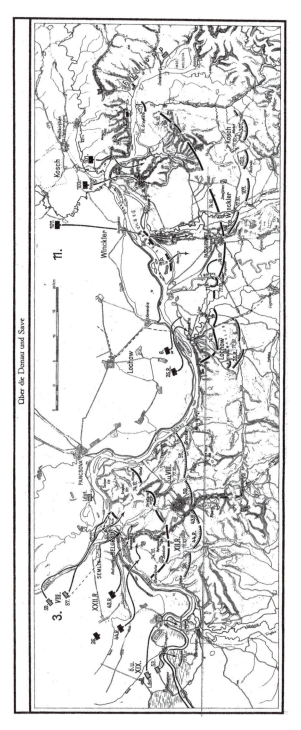

The Crossing of the Save and Danube, October 5–14, 1915. (Adapted from Foerster, Wolfgang, ed. *Mackensen: Briefe und Aufzeichnungen des Generalfeldmarschalls aus Krieg und Frieden*. Bonn: Wahlband der Buchgemeinde, 1938.)

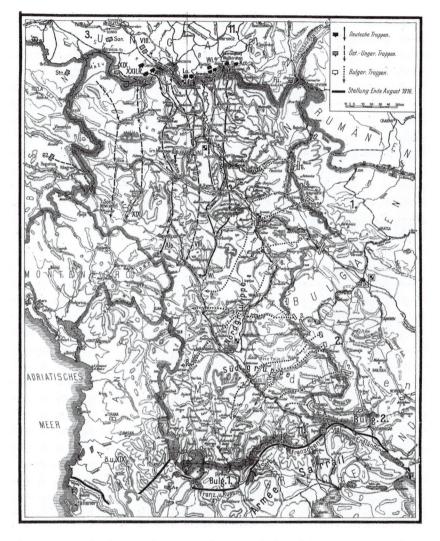

The Conquest of Serbia, October–November 1915. (Adapted from Foerster, Wolfgang, ed. *Mackensen: Briefe und Aufzeichnungen des Generalfeldmarschalls aus Krieg und Frieden*. Bonn: Wahlband der Buchgemeinde, 1938.)

government, who had requested help in the form of an entente expedition, the Army of the Orient represented the assistance that allowed Serbia defeat the latest invasion. The materialization of this aid, however, depended on the assumption that the Serbian army would be able to hold Army Group Mackensen at bay until Sarrail's forces could arrive.[85] For Mackensen and Seeckt, with the river crossing accomplished, the operation now resolved itself into a matter of bringing the Serbian forces to battle and destroying them as rapidly as possible.

Chapter 5

Fighting Storms and Serbs: October 12–22, 1915

"The *Kossava* is hindering the crossing of the Eleventh Army."

Army Group Mackensen, October 13, 1915[1]

"The Serbs, who were first effected, have adjusted to the situation as well as possible. They have come to terms with the surprise and are fighting everywhere with the greatest tenacity worthy of a warlike people."

August von Mackensen[2]

As the armies of Kövess and Gallwitz consolidated their respective bridgeheads, Mackensen and Seeckt received two major disappointments, one man-made, one natural. The military convention signed by the Central powers called for Bulgaria to begin its attack five days after the start of operations by Germany and Austria–Hungary.[3] Thus, since the preparatory bombardments for the river crossings began on October 6, the Bulgarian offensive should have begun on October 11. On the 10th, however, word arrived in Temesvár from the Bulgarian chief of the General Staff, General Nikola Zhekov, that the Bulgarians would not be able to take the offensive until October 14, 1915.[4] Mackensen took the news with his customary equanimity, simply noting that "coalition warfare always brings its share of surprises."[5]

The other disappointment was one of scale. An autumnal weather system that comes up from the southeast, the leading edge of the *Kossava* arrived over Mackensen's front on October 12, 1915; the heart of the storm hit the following day. The arrival of the *Kossava* was certainly expected.[6] The strength and intensity of the storm, however, was probably beyond what the Germans expected. By October 13 every bridge that had been built over the Save and

Danube after the crossing had either been destroyed or rendered unusable. Wind and rain lashed the Danube and the Save to the point where waves in the rivers reached heights of six feet or more. Parts of the islands in the river were flooded. The two rivers, fast flowing even in times when the weather was good, then became raging torrents. By October 14, boats or barges equipped with motors or steam engines were the only kind of water craft capable of traversing the rivers, and those kind of boats were in very short supply.[7]

The cutting of the flow of supplies across the rivers presented Mackensen and Seeckt with a serious problem. The strategic situation and the original plan called for a rapid offensive that opened up a route to Turkey. The stormy weather, which turned bridgeable rivers into major obstacles and roads into bottomless tracks of mud, then threatened to slow Mackensen's advance to a crawl. In addition, although the German Eleventh and Austro-Hungarian Third Armies each had a consolidated position on the Serbian side of the rivers, the two bridgeheads themselves were still almost 20 miles apart.

There was also a difference of opinion on how to proceed between Mackensen and his major subordinate commander. With communications across the river reduced to only a few specialized craft and concerned about the state of his artillery ammunition stocks, Gallwitz wanted to devote time to replenishing stocks of food and ammunition and then resume the offensive once the *Kossava* had abated. For Mackensen and Seeckt, however, speed mattered more. Because the Germans had calculated that it would take a British or French division only six days to move from Salonika to Niš, the offensive had to proceed, weather notwithstanding. Sensing that Gallwitz was opposed by only a few Serbian divisions, Mackensen and Seeckt thus wanted the Eleventh Army to continue pressing. Similar orders went out to the Austro-Hungarian Third Army on October 14, 1915.[8]

Having secured the Petlovo Hills, Kövess's next objective was the Avala Hills. The tallest of these, Hill 565, allowed whoever possessed it to dominate the surrounding area. The force available to Kövess for this mission was the German XXII Reserve Corps and the Austro-Hungarian VIII Corps. The principal thrust would be made by the German Forty-Third and Forty-Fourth Reserve Divisions. The Twenty-Sixth Infantry Division, having entered the bridgehead, would cover the left flank along the Save. Scheuchenstuel's VIII Corps would cover Falkenhayn's left. In addition, Mackensen subsequently wanted the Austro-Hungarian Third Army to have the Austro-Hungarian VIII Corps thrust along the south bank of the Danube to Gročka with at least a battalion, to clear the river bank and thus open up the river. The Austro-Hungarian XIX Corps would have to remain largely in place.[9]

Falkenhayn's attack on the October 13 made limited progress. Runckel's Forty-Third Reserve Division ran into a well-developed Serbian defensive position manned by the Timok II Division near the village of Rakovica that had some artillery support. The 2nd Battalion of the 202nd Reserve

Regiment took a direct hit from a Serbian piece that caused 19 casualties, including 6 killed. The regiment also took heavy machine gun fire from the Serbians, and matters were made worse when the Germans also took some short rounds from their own artillery. The 203rd Reserve Infantry Regiment had a similar experience. The Forty-Fourth Reserve Division likewise encountered tough resistance, so only local gains were made. The story was the same for Austro-Hungarian VIII Corps, whose soldiers struggled over the difficult terrain against elements of the Timok I and Morava I Divisions.[10]

Kövess's continued efforts met with success the next day. The Austro-Hungarian VIII Corps also pressed the Serbians back from their forward positions. Scheuchenstuel's troops needed help from German heavy artillery on the north bank, as the continuing *Kossava* made conditions on the river impossible for the Austro-Hungarian monitors to provide fire support. Meanwhile the German XXII Reserve Corps broke through the Serbian defenses on both sides of the railroad. Elements of the German Forty-Fourth Reserve Division and the Austro-Hungarian Fifty-Ninth Infantry Division secured the northern side of the Avala Hills by the evening of October 16. The southern side remained in Serbian hands. The German Twenty-Sixth Infantry Division also made a limited advance past Ostružnica, covering the right flank of the Forty-Fourth Reserve Division, while the Duke of Württemberg's own right flank continued to rest on the river.[11]

With the loss of the Avala line Mišić, the Serbian First Army commander, pulled his troops back over seven miles over the course of October 17, to a new line of hills centered on the Kosmaj mountain, covering the Kolubara River and the town of Valjevo. The main forces of the Austro-Hungarian Third Army could go forward only slowly, given the state of the available roads. Although the railroad ran through the sector of Falkenhayn's XXII Reserve Corps, it could not be used because several viaducts had been demolished.[12]

With the *Kossava* finally abating on October 17, the movement of men and supplies could resume. With the Serbians retreating, Kövess, prodded by Mackensen, decided to go over to the offensive, and thus ordered his forces forward, including the Austro-Hungarian XIX Corps. Although some progress was made, by the evening of the 17th, Trollmann's corps was still short of Obrenovac. Two days later, however, the German Twenty-Sixth Infantry Division right flank was able to make contact with the Austro-Hungarian Fifty-Third Infantry Division. The long trapped XIX Corps had now broken out. Groups Streith and Sorsich also then crossed the Drina and Save Rivers and began to advance on the left of Trollmann's corps opposed by Serbian rearguards. By October 22 Kövess was ready to undertake a prepared attack on the Kosmaj position. The one continuing problem was the Austro-Hungarian Sixty-Second Infantry Division, which continued to be inert on the Drina, prompting the Army Group to once again ask when some action could be expected from it.[13]

To the east, Gallwitz's Eleventh Army had the task of pressing forward to the south with the X Reserve and IV Reserve Corps. Lochow's III Corps would have to advance south as well but also send a unit westward to link up with the Austro-Hungarian VIII Corps. By the end of October 12 the three corps had linked their bridgeheads, but were still short of their immediate objectives.

The arrival of the *Kossava* served to complicate matters. With the Danube now a raging torrent, the movement of men, equipment, and supplies was then reduced to a trickle. The ability to ferry men and material across the river for the III and X Reserve Corps rested on two steamboats, the *Orsova* and the *Kornfeld*. Even though, thanks to the heroic efforts of the engineers, one pontoon bridge was rebuilt on October 14, it was nowhere near sufficient to meet the needs of the Eleventh Army.[14]

Consequently, the German Eleventh Army made only local attacks on October 13 and 14. On October 13 reconnaissance patrols from the Bavarian Eleventh Infantry Division had established that the Serbians had evacuated Požarevac, so Winckler ordered that the city be occupied the following day. The Bavarian Third Infantry Regiment moved into Požarevac on October 14. Some of the inhabitants were taken as hostages while the town's leaders were assembled in the town hall where Mackensen's proclamation was read to them. Meanwhile the Bavarian Twenty-Second Regiment, having recovered from a tough fight on the Twelfth, moved into the area west and south of the city, on both sides of the Morava River. The Bavarians counted some 200 dead Serbian soldiers, plus another 40 severely wounded.[15]

To the east of Kneussl's Bavarians, the 105th and 107th Infantry Divisions pressed to the south, into the area between the Morava and Mlava Rivers. The hilly terrain was ideally suited to defense, offering numerous flanking positions, while the cornfields provided excellent cover for trench lines. Gallwitz once again laid out his objections to the Army Group about an immediate attack. Once again, Gallwitz was overruled.[16]

Consequently, the two divisions spent several days fighting their way through successive Serbian trench lines. Esch's 105th Infantry Division had determined the main Serbian position in its sector to be located in the hills east of Lučica. Launched on October 18, the assault broke through the Serbian position, but only after overcoming stout resistance. The 129th Infantry Regiment alone lost 10 killed and 70 wounded. Serbian rearguards covered the retreat past Aleksandrovac into the more mountainous terrain a few miles to the south.[17]

Moser's 107th Infantry Division moved into the Mlava Valley. Like the 105th Infantry Division, the 107th had to fight through successive positions, first at Kalidol on October 13 and then on the line Salakovac-Smoljinac on October 16 and 17. The division's efforts were rewarded the following day, when the 232nd Reserve Regiment captured a Serbian patrol and an engineer detachment assigned to demolish the railway bridge over the Mlava.

Intelligence gleaned from the prisoners enabled the Germans to secure the railway bridge over the Mlava before it could be demolished. By the end of October 21, Winckler's IV Reserve Corps had also closed up to the Serbian positions in the mountains that marked the boundary of old Serbia.[18]

Of Gallwitz's three corps, it was Kosch's X Reserve Corps that made the most progress. To be sure there may have been some who thought that the arrival of the *Kossava* would put the war on hold, at least for a while. Kosch, however, was having none of it. On October 13, 1915, he issued a special order for his corps. Because Kosch was apparently responsible for the administration of Weisskirchen, he decided that some personnel were enjoying the civilized pleasures of the town a bit too much, while there was a war on. Thus, according to his order, all restaurants, cafés, casinos, and theaters would close nightly no later than 11 p.m. Patrols of German and Hungarian military police would make the rounds between 9 p.m. and 11 p.m., and anyone, regardless of rank, who was found on the street without an official reason would be arrested.[19]

Kosch's main concern, like those of the other German and Austro-Hungarian commanders, was getting sufficient amount of food and especially ammunition to the south bank. For transport away from the river, the local Austro-Hungarian labor detachments had to provide a number of local two-wheeled carts to the divisions. Kosch's other concern was getting himself and part of his staff across the river. The anxious corps commander noted his location in his letters to his wife with the phrase "still in Weisskirchen."[20]

Having seized the Anatema Hills, Kosch wanted to move as quickly as possible against the next hill mass on his front, the Lipovac Massif. He also wanted to capture Gradiste, located at the confluence of the Danube and Pek Rivers. The 101st Infantry Division took Gradiste, as well as the eastern part of the Lipovac Massif on October 13. Meanwhile, the 103rd Infantry Division assaulted the western part of the Lipovac Hills. Although the Serbian artillery gave the Germans some problems, including firing on advancing German infantry at ranges as close as 1,400 yards, once again the German heavy artillery provided the decisive advantage. The Seventy-First Infantry Regiment had to engage in some combat at close quarters to take a well-constructed position hidden in a cornfield. A company from the First Battalion of the Seventy-First Infantry Regiment was able to reach a position from which the Serbian guns could be taken under rifle fire, which compelled the Serbian guns to retreat. The result was that the Serbian trenches were secured and the front advanced several miles. Several villages were taken as well. Kosch's success also aided Winckler, in that the X Reserve Corps had gained control of the roads east of Winckler's major objective, Požarevac, while Kneussl's Bavarians moved in on the fortress.[21]

With the Serbian First Army having retreated to a new position in the Sapina Hills, south of Smoljinac, Kosch ordered the corps forward once again. The advance, however, was conducted at a gingerly pace. Heavy rain and a lack of suitable routes to bring forward artillery slowed the advance. These problems were exacerbated by the inaccuracy of the maps used, especially at the levels below division.[22]

Sensing that resistance, especially in Kosch's sector, was weak, the Mackensen and Seeckt ordered a major attack for October 15. Gallwitz, however, concerned about logistical issues and with the *Kossava* at its height, wanted to limit offensive activity to only local attacks. Ultimately, Gallwitz got his way, so that only the X Reserve Corps would make a limited advance.[23] Starting on October 15, Kosch's corps was able to advance on Smoljinac and Makci, and by October 17 the Germans were in possession of both places. With the *Kossava* beginning to abate, by the evening of October 16 Kosch could make preparations for establishing a command post with part of his staff on the Serbian side.[24]

The X Reserve Corps continued to press on October 18 and spent the next several days with the 103rd Infantry Division pressing toward Rasanac. The 101st Infantry Division covered the left flank. The 146th Infantry Regiment sent two battalions, plus one field artillery battery and one mountain gun battery, to advance up the Pek River Valley, a security mission that continued until December. Kosch's men brought in 500 prisoners and two guns.[25]

Over the following three days Kosch's corps continued to press the Serbs south of Boževac. An attempted Serbian counterattack against Kosch's left flank was repelled with heavy losses to the Serbs. Meanwhile Rasanac was taken by the Thirty-Second Infantry Regiment after a tough two-day fight. By October 21 the X Reserve Corps had made sufficient progress so that Kosch could look forward to linking up with the Bulgarians and thus began issuing orders needed to deal with matters concomitant with this kind of undertaking.[26]

Of all of Gallwitz's three corps, Lochow's III Corps had the toughest time. After storming Semendria castle, Lochow had to get his corps across the Jezava, a stream swollen by the heavy rains into a considerable obstacle. In addition, Lochow had the responsibility of linking up with the Austro-Hungarian Third Army. Thus, over the next several days, the Twenty-Fifth Reserve Division made a limited advance along the south bank of the Danube, trying to make contact with the left flank of Kövess's army, while the Sixth Infantry Division made short moves south toward the mountains.[27]

Like his fellow corps commanders, Lochow's troops were fighting both Serbs and storms. All along the III Corps front, the Serbians were offering stiff resistance. Villages were stoutly defended by Serbian soldiers and apparently in some cases by civilians as well. The artillery was already finding it difficult to get guns forward. One regimental historian noted that in took a full day simply to displace the guns forward a few miles.[28] The problems in getting the guns forward clearly had an impact on slowing the German advance. On October 16, for example, two companies of the Third Battalion of the

Twentieth Infantry Regiment found themselves in a difficult situation. Attempting to get across the Ralja, a swampy water course south of the Jezava, the Germans were confronted by a well-chosen Serbian position in the hills south of the stream. The excellent observation afforded to the Serbian troops by the position allowed them to keep the Germans pinned down. Fortunately for the Germans, one company had a telephone connection to the regiment. Finally, a German howitzer battery was able to get to a position from which it could lay down a suppressing fire on the Serbian defenders. Aided by the artillery and the onset of darkness, the two companies, having suffered considerably, were able to retreat from their exposed position.[29]

Ultimately, Herhudt's Sixth Division was able to cross the Ralja. On October 18 the Twentieth Infantry Regiment, which had suffered considerably two days earlier, launched a brilliant attack on a heavily defended Serbian position at Mala Krsna. Ably supported by the Third Field Artillery Regiment, the Serbian position was stormed and the defenders were driven out with heavy losses. The following two days were spent following the retreating Serbians into the hills south of the Ralja. Jarotzky's Twenty-Fifth Reserve Division, ordered to link up with Kövess's Third Army, had made some progress along the south bank of the Danube, but was still about 9 miles short of the desired objective.[30]

While the dramatic struggle played out south of the Save and Danube, the final actor entered play. Entente diplomatic and military representatives left Sofia after Bulgaria rejected the Russian ultimatum. The Bulgarians, having severed diplomatic relations with Serbia on October 13, opened their offensive the next day. Bojadiev's Bulgarian First Army, with the Sixth, Eighth, Ninth, and First Infantry Divisions deployed in a line from north to south, first had to fight its way through the mountain passes and the Sumidija II Division. Most critical for Bojadiev was the seizure of three fortified towns, Zahečar, Knjaževac, and Pirot. Once through the passes, the Bulgarian First Army would advance on the Serbian capital of Niš, located just south of the confluence of the South Morava and Nišava Rivers.[31]

Further south the Bulgarian Second Army under General Georgi Todorov, with the Third and Seventh Infantry Divisions, plus a cavalry division, would advance into Macedonia, the reason for Bulgaria's joining the Central powers. The operational object for Todorov's force was the severing of the rail line between Salonika and Niš and taking control of the Vardar Valley in Macedonia north of the border with Greece. This would serve to block any advance from Salonika by the entente forces. While Bojadiev's First Army was under Mackensen's operational control, Todorov was subject to the orders of Zhekov and the Bulgarian General Staff.[32]

Because a Bulgarian thrust on Niš was regarded as potentially lethal to Serbia, the Serbian high command reacted very sharply to the prospect. Before the onset of operations, the Serbians had posted strong forces along

Bulgarian border, including the Timok Group and the Second Army, totaling five infantry divisions and one cavalry division.[33] Consequently, Bojadiev's attack made little headway. Serbian resistance was stout, and matters were made worse by difficult terrain and bad weather, which rendered the already-inadequate road network utterly useless.[34] By October 20, 1915, the front of the Bulgarian First Army had scarcely changed. Todorov's Bulgarian Second Army had better success, having to contend mainly with just poor weather, as the Serbian forces facing them were both small and of dubious reliability. On October 19 Todorov's lead elements, consisting of cavalry and the Seventh Infantry Division, reached the Vardar at Veleš, cutting the rail line as well.[35]

While the Serbians were fighting the Germans, Austro-Hungarians, and Bulgarians, the Franco-British force, requested by the Pašić government, continued to act in a manner that reflected the uncertainty of high commands that sent it. The Serbians had requested a force of at least 120,000 men initially, and Mackensen and Seeckt had reckoned on the prospect of as many as 150,000 men appearing at Salonika.[36]

The lead element of the Army of the Orient, the French 156th Infantry Division, landed at Salonika on October 5 after the pro-entente Greek prime minister, Eleutherois Venizelos, granted permission two days earlier. The division commander, General Maurice Bailloud, received a series of contradictory orders before finally being told by the French high command to await further instructions. Meanwhile the British Twenty-Ninth Infantry Brigade also arrived the same day. The British government, however, had still not decided to commit major resources to a campaign in the Balkans.[37]

Sarrail arrived on October 12 and immediately sought to get forces moving north. His efforts were hampered by the fact that the Greek railroads were not available, as they were devoted to supporting the mobilization of the Greek army. With the railroad unavailable, Sarrail sent a regiment with some artillery north toward the Greco-Serbian border. This in turn gave the neutralist King Constantine the excuse to demand and receive Venizelos's resignation, thus creating political instability.[38]

On October 14 a second French infantry division, the Fifty-Seventh, began to disembark at Salonka, while the reinforced regiment Sarrail sent forward crossed the Serbian border. On October 21, 1915, the lead elements of the French force, plus local Serbian forces, had an indecisive skirmish with elements of the Bulgarian Second Army at the Strumica rail station, about 18 miles inside the Serbian border. The Bulgarians dug in at the nearby village of Strumica, which was just inside the Bulgarian border.[39]

For Mackensen's forces, the period after river crossings was both successful and frustrating. Some local advances had been made, at times accompanied by hard fighting, and every Serbian counterattack had been repulsed, at times with heavy losses. As before, German artillery made the difference, when it could be deployed properly.[40] Another major advantage for the Germans and Austro-Hungarians was the telephone. The ability to get telephone lines laid across the rivers allowed German and Austro-Hungarian commanders to control the operation at every level from army group down to regiment.[41] The Eleventh Army had consolidated its bridgehead, and the capture of Požarevac and Gradiste left Gallwitz's army well positioned for further offensive operations.

The Austro-Hungarian Third Army had also been able to consolidate its position with the German XXII Reserve and Austro-Hungarian VIII Corps holding a bridgehead well anchored to a river on each flank. Taking the Avala Hills forced Mišić's Serbian First Army back to the Kosmaj position covering Valjevo. The Serbian retreat also allowed the Austro-Hungarian XIX Corps to reach Obrenovac and thus escape its boggy trap on the south bank of the Save.[42]

The Bulgarian First Army's offensive, launched later than originally planned, served to tie down major Serbian forces. The potential for Bojadiev's force to drive into the Serbian rear, however, remained much more of a possibility than an actuality. Todorov's Second Army had done well against the Serbian forces in Macedonia, but how well they would do against French and British troops coming up from Salonika remained to be seen.[43]

Losses for both sides had not been light. From river crossing to October 20, the German Eleventh Army had suffered about 5,000 casualties. These were rather unevenly distributed. While Kosch's X Reserve Corps suffered relatively lightly, the III and IV Reserve Corps took a good many more casualties. The Twentieth Infantry Regiment, part of Herhudt's Sixth Infantry Division, suffered 305 casualties in its attack on Mala Krsna on October 18, which amounted to half of the losses the regiment took for the entire campaign.[44] Losses in the Austro-Hungarian Third Army was somewhat greater. The Austro-Hungarian Fifty-Ninth Infantry Division alone, for example, suffered over 1,000 casualties. By October 18, 1915, Falkenhayn's XXII Reserve Corps had taken over 3,165 casualties, over a 10th of its strength.[45] Bulgarian losses probably rivaled those of the Austro-Hungarian Third Army.

Serbian losses had been considerable. The historian of the Twentieth Infantry Regiment stated that after the hard-fought action at Mala Krsna, the village was veritably littered with the bodies of Serbian soldiers. The war diary of the Bavarian Eleventh Infantry Division likewise noted on October 12 after a Serbian counterattack had been repulsed; some 200 dead and 40 severely wounded were counted in front of one company of the Bavarian Third Infantry Regiment. A Serbian staff officer at Palanka told *New York Tribune* correspondent Gordon Gordon-Smith that three days of fighting had cost the Serbians 1,200 killed. The foreign field hospitals that constituted much of the Serbian army's medical service were now receiving wounded in large numbers.[46]

Still, the experience of the last 10 days had also been frustrating for Mackensen, Seeckt, and the troops they commanded. The *Kossava* created major supply problems for both Kövess and Gallwitz, in that the movement of material across the rivers was reduced to a trickle. Thus corps had to order their divisions to pay particular attention to matters such as ammunition consumption.[47]

The situation of the German and Austro-Hungarian troops might have been even worse when it came to food, but instead the Germans at least were pleasantly surprised. As one regimental history noted, conditions in Serbia were rather different from those found in Galicia and Poland.[48] The inhabitants of the Serbian villages and larger towns such as Požarevac, mostly women and children, proved to be welcoming enough, and only very rarely engaged in hostile actions against the German troops. This was a most pleasant surprise for German soldiers, who had been told by the Austro-Hungarians to expect the most barbarous behavior. In addition to a friendly attitude, the civilians seemed to have an endless supply of cattle, pigs, and chickens, and that most important item needed to ward off the night-time cold, slivovitz.[49]

The poor weather had other negative consequences as well. The poor condition of the roads in the area and especially in the bridgehead made it difficult to move infantry and artillery alike. The *Kossava* also grounded German aircraft. The lack of aircraft for observation and spotting impacted the accuracy of the German artillery. Occasionally, lacking good observation, German shells dropped into the positions of the German infantry.[50]

With the bridgeheads established and the Bulgarians then committed, the high commands on both sides took stock of the situation. Thus far the Serbian high command had reason to be satisfied but also cause for considerable concern. In the north, Mišić's First and Jurišić-Sturm's Third Armies had failed to stop the river crossings but had been able to preserve an intact battlefront against the Germans and Austro-Hungarians. Likewise Gojković's Timok Group and Stepanović's Second Army had stymied the Bulgarian First Army. Of more concern was the situation in the south, where Popović's force proved unable to cope with the Bulgarian Second Army, losing 2,000 prisoners. Although the forces in the north had conducted an orderly retreat to their new positions, they had taken considerable losses in doing so, losses difficult to replace.[51]

Meanwhile, the Serbian high command tried to relieve itself of some possible embarrassments. Thus the foreign medical detachments went home, although the Red Cross hospitals stayed. The foreign hospitals left early enough so that they were able to use the rail line before Todorov's forces severed it. Thus British nurse Monica Stanley left Üsküb at 8:30 p.m. on October 10, arriving at Salonika the following day. On October 12 she was invited for tea by two British officers, who were interested in her experiences in Serbia.[52]

More positively, the appearance of French forces in the Vardar Valley inside the Serbian border and the possibility of British participation had to offer the Serbs a considerable degree of hope. If Sarrail could, after negotiating the shoals presented by the tricky Greek political situation, bring up sufficient forces to break through Todorov's Bulgarian Second Army, Mackensen's offensive could be halted. Putnik's hope for this could come about only if the Serbian armies continued to maintain a front that covered Old Serbia and the critical production center of Kragujevać.[53]

For the decision makers of the Central powers, views were determined by both distance and proximity to the front. For OHL and AOK, matters in Serbia were moving far too slowly. The initial river crossing and the capture of Belgrade were greeted with jubilation and the customary drinking of pink champagne at the kaiser's table. Still, the Bulgarian delay caused concern. At AOK in Teschen, the fall of Belgrade was a cause for satisfaction, although Conrad was perhaps more occupied with his impending marriage to Gina von Reininghaus.[54] By the third week of October, however, there was considerable worry about the campaign, probably magnified by the appearance of French troops inside the Serbian border. Falkenhayn decided to make visits first to Teschen and then to Temesvár.[55]

Interestingly, what was regarded with concern at OHL was looked on as opportunity by Mackensen and Seeckt. Both men were heartened by the performance of the Bulgarian Second Army. In addition, by October 21 it was clear that every division in the Serbian army had been committed to battle. The assumption could now be made with some assurance that Putnik no longer had any operational reserves on which to draw. Before the campaign German intelligence had noted the fragility of the Serbian army.[56]

Given the situation, and with the *Kossava* abating, Mackensen and Seeckt then saw an opportunity to defeat the Serbians decisively, if not completely destroying the Serbian army. The campaign would now enter a new phase.

Chapter 6

The Fall of Kragujevać and Niš: October 22–November 5, 1915

"No good news from the Eastern Front . . . Neither the Bulgarians nor the Germans and Austrians are advancing as rapidly as we expected."

> Admiral Georg Alexander von Müller, October 18, 1915[1]

"Kragujevać has sent a deputation to the III Corps heralding submission; thus the corps will soon enter without a fight."

> Max von Gallwitz, November 1, 1915[2]

"He (Wilhelm II) was in a bad mood, which improved this evening when the news came in that the Bulgarians have taken Niš . . . "

> Admiral Georg Alexander von Müller, November 5, 1915[3]

For the Central powers, the situation by the third week of October 1915 was proof of the adage that where you stand depends on where you sit. Although Mackensen and Seeckt had contended with their share of frustrations and disappointments, the situation was then rife with opportunity. With the Serbian army fully committed to battle, a simultaneous concentric attack by the armies under Mackensen's command could bring about the destruction of the Serbian forces.[4]

For Falkenhayn, Serbia was the one dark spot in a relatively brightening picture. On the western front, Joffre's offensive in the Champagne region had fallen flat by the middle of October. The British effort at Loos, beginning in late September and extending to the middle October 1915, also foundered on the German defenses. The most notable result of the British failure was that it set the stage for the resignation of the commander of the British Expeditionary Force, Sir John French and the promotion of his replacement,

Sir Douglas Haig.[5] In the east, Ober Ost continued its offensive in the north-east, toward Riga, while also organizing the military administration of the area already occupied. Falkenhayn was not enthusiastic about the attack, as he saw no great results coming from the endeavor. Seeckt believed back in the summer that Ludendorff was the driving force behind this, suggesting that the operation was being done at the behest of pan-German interests.[6]

On other fronts the picture was positive. On the Italian front, Boroević's Austro-Hungarian Fifth Army had fought the fourth Italian Isonzo offensive to a costly standstill. In Mesopotamia, the Turkish army, commanded by Khalil Pasha and Colmar von der Goltz, had effectively stopped the British offensive toward Baghdad and soon seized the initiative. On the Gallipoli Peninsula, both sides had settled into stalemate after the failed attempt to breakout in August. Nonetheless, Turkey remained isolated.[7]

For Falkenhayn, the Serbian situation remained the fly in the ointment. As long as the Serbian army remained in the field, both Bulgaria and Turkey remained isolated. The success on other fronts, however, freed up forces for use in other theaters. The prospect of an early winter shutting down operations on the Italian front meant that Falkenhayn could then follow through on an idea he had considered before the campaign, namely committing the Bavarian Alpine Corps to Mackensen's forces. Thus, on October 20, 1915 OHL formally issued orders withdrawing the Alpine Corps from the Tyrol and sending it to Serbia. Meanwhile, Falkenhayn made visits to AOK at Teschen and Mackensen's headquarters at Temesvár.[8]

Leaving Berlin on October 22, 1915, Falkenhayn arrived in Teschen the following morning at 10:00 a.m. After a brief conference with the newlywed Conrad (who had tied the knot with Gina on the 19th), Falkenhayn departed Teschen at 1:00 p.m.[9] Traveling through Budapest, Falkenhayn arrived at Temesvár at 9:45 a.m. and a brunch conference followed. Falkenhayn informed Mackensen and Seeckt that they would indeed be reinforced with the Alpine Corps.[10]

Initially Falkenhayn wanted the Alpine Corps to be committed to Gallwitz's left flank, to help get Group Fülöpp across the Danube. Group Fülöpp, however, had crossed the Danube at Orsova on the night of October 22-23, despite attempted Romanian interference and then advanced along the river. With the Danube opened to Bulgaria, the Alpine Corps could be committed somewhere else on Mackensen's front. After casting about for several alternatives, Mackensen and Falkenhayn agreed that the Alpine Corps be directed to Kövess's Third Army, where it would relieve part of the German XXII Reserve Corps, which was not as well equipped for mountain warfare.[11]

Mackensen and Seeckt briefed OHL on the attack that had been ordered for October 24. A dinner followed, with Wilhelm II and a small coterie in attendance.[12] The next day, Falkenhayn and Tappen visited Gallwitz's headquarters at Kevevara and then went to Semendria and Temesziget Island, before returning to Temesvár. That evening Falkenhayn and Seeckt had a private meeting on Falkenhayn's train. The meeting proved more of a therapy session for Falkenhayn, who proceeded to provide Seeckt with a recitation of the difficulties he had to contend with in trying to direct Germany's war effort. With their meeting concluded, OHL's train departed at midnight for Budapest.[13]

Mackensen and Seeckt got back to running their part of the war. Even before OHL's visit, Mackensen and Seeckt had issued orders for what they thought could be the decisive effort. On the evening of October 22, 1915, the Army Group called for an attack all along the line. Gallwitz's Eleventh Army would advance south astride the Morava Valley, establishing contact with the Bulgarian First Army. Kragujevać would continue to be Gallwitz's geographic target. Kövess's Third Army would advance south as well, covering Gallwitz's right flank. The Austro-Hungarian VIII Corps and the German XXII Reserve Corps would advance against Kraljevo. The Austro-Hungarian XIX Corps would cover the right of Falkenhayn's corps. The Austro-Hungarian Sixty-Second Infantry Division would advance from Višegrad on Užice. The ultimate mission for Kövess was to prevent the Serbian forces from retreating to the west.[14]

Since operations had been going almost continuously since the *Kossava* had abated, units had to make all the normal preparations for such an undertaking while already pressing forward. Particularly problematic was getting the requisite ammunition and supplies over the still swollen rivers. Approach routes to crossing points on both sides of the river had to be improved to facilitate the passage of heavy equipment. Some divisions, such as the 101st, still did not even have all of their units across the river and would still not get them to Serbian soil for several days. Local Serbian counterattacks, such as those against the 101st Infantry Division's Forty-Fifth Infantry Regiment, had to be contended with as well.[15]

The higher commanders also had to contend with other issues. The army commanders sent reports from prisoners and other means of intelligence up the chain of command to Mackensen's headquarters. For its part, the army group headquarters wanted reports on preparation to reopen the major rail lines. Although the *Kossava* had subsided, the weather remained cloudy and rainy enough to keep aircraft grounded much of the time. Deprived of regular aerial reconnaissance, Gallwitz had to remind his units to pay more attention to the more traditional means of reconnaissance and gathering intelligence.[16]

Almost immediately Mackensen's plan had to change slightly. The biggest problem again was the Austro-Hungarian Sixty-Second Infantry Division. Although the division had finally crossed the Drina at Višegrad, the unit's advance on Užice was slowed by the combination swollen water courses and stiffening Serbian resistance, which was then being supported by troops from Montenegro. These troops were acting in accordance with a prewar agreement between Serbian and Montenegro.[17] Mackensen and Seeckt thus eliminated the division from major consideration in their planning, although they would still pester Kövess with questions about the status of the unit.[18]

With the new directive in hand, Kövess made his main effort with the Austro-Hungarian VIII Corps and the German XXII Reserve Corps. The Austro-Hungarian VIII Corps would advance via Kovačevac and across the Jasienica on Kragujevać. To Scheuchenstuel's right, the German XXII Reserve Corps would seize the dominating Rudnik massif. Trollmann's XIX Corps would cover Kövess's right flank along the Kolubara River. Group Sorsich would move against Valjevo.[19]

Kövess made slow but steady progress. He was helped by the fact that there was no enemy threat to the Austro-Hungarian XIX Corps along the Kolubara River. Trollmann's corps made sufficient progress that it drew Mackensen's approbation.[20] Meanwhile, Falkenhayn's corps moved into the mountains. While the Forty-Third Reserve Infantry Division was delayed, elements of the Forty-Fourth Reserve Infantry Division attacked successive positions on October 23 and 24. Great efforts were made to get heavy artillery into positions where the guns could support attacks. The Austro-Hungarian VIII Corps also advanced against light resistance on October 23 and 24. By the night of October 24 the Serbian forces before Kövess, consisting mainly of elements of the Danube II and Drina II Divisions from Mišić's First Army, had retreated to a position sited on the high ridges between Lazarevac and Arangelovac.[21]

Further east, Gallwitz's German Eleventh Army also made limited advances against the Serbian Second Army. The Germans had little serious fighting on October 23. Gallwitz noted that only at a couple of places Serbian dead could be counted in the hundreds. On October 23 and 24 both the III Corps and the X Reserve Corps encountered only light resistance, so in some cases regiments had only to contend with rearguards.[22] Only some elements of Esch's 105th Infantry Division, part of the IV Reserve Corps, had some serious fighting to do on October 23, driving the Serbs out of a well-prepared position covering the road in the Morava Valley south of Požarevac, after fending off a counter-attack the previous night.[23]

For the Germans the problem remained getting their guns and heavy equipment forward. By October 24 the forward lines for both Kövess and Gallwitz were a little over 30 miles south of the rivers. Although the Sun appeared on the 24th, the roads remained in an execrable state, despite the best efforts of the engineers to improve them. On average it took German artillery units about two hours to go one mile. Even using the lighter local vehicles proved of little help, and the wear on the horses was considerable. Equally problematic was the effect the weather was having on the personal equipment of the German and Austro-Hungarian soldiers.[24]

By the night of October 24, Jurišić-Sturm's Serbian Third Army had retreated to positions in a chain of hills southeast of Palanka and southwest of Rašanac. This position extended the line of Mišić's First Army to the east, blocking access to the major routes of advance for Gallwitz, the Morava and Mlava Valleys. As the German and Austro-Hungarian forces continued to move forward toward the new Serbian position, Mackensen and Seeckt issued a new directive. Mackensen discounted the prospect of Sarrail's forces bringing aid to the Serbians from Salonika. Although the outer flanks of the Austro-Hungarian Third and German Eleventh Armies continued their missions, the adjoining flanks of the two armies were directed to seize Kragujevać as rapidly as possible. Finally, perhaps thinking that the Bulgarian First Army lacked strength, Mackensen asked Zhekov to reinforce Bojadjiev with the Fifth and Eleventh Infantry Divisions.[25] A quick seizure of Kragujevać could facilitate either the envelopment of most of the Serbian forces defending in the sector or create two smaller pockets.

The renewed advance on October 25 had to contend with the difficult trio of Serbs, terrain, and weather. After a couple of days of sunny weather, heavy rain began again on October 25. Although the Austro-Hungarian XIX Corps (along with Group Sorsich) made progress sufficient to elicit congratulations from Mackensen, Falkenhayn's XXII Reserve Corps had two days of very tough fighting around Arangelovac, which was taken by the 203rd Reserve Infantry Regiment after a short firefight on October 24. Fortunately for Falkenhayn's infantry, the German artillery had gotten forward far enough to be able to bring its weight to bear. Thus by the end of October 26 Falkenhayn's troops were in possession of the positions.[26]

Once the Serbian positions in the Arangelovac area had been taken, the German XXII Reserve Corps was able to move forward without serious fighting toward the Rudnik massif. With the left flank of Mišić's Serbian First Army in retreat, Mackensen decided to press as hard as possible. As Mackensen's intelligence section judged the threat to the army group's left flank to be minor, the job of flank security could be left to Group Sorsich. Instead, the German XXII Reserve Corps, supported by the Austro-Hungarian XIX Corps, would move on Kraljevo, thus blocking one potential Serbian retreat route over the West Morava, assuming a decisive battle could still be fought around Kragujevać.[27]

While Falkenhayn's XXII Reserve Corps and Trollmann's XIX Corps struggled forward to get around the Serbian First Army's left flank, Kövess's left hand unit, the Austro-Hungarian VIII Corps, advanced on Kragujevać, moving in unison with Gallwitz's right hand, Lochow's III Corps. Scheuchenstuel's troops were helped by the fact that Austro-Hungarian supply troops and engineers had been able to create a horse-drawn railroad line from Belgrade to the south. As the Austro-Hungarian Fifty-Ninth Infantry Division approached the positions east of Arangelovac, Scheuchenstuel decided to reinforce the unit with every available heavy artillery battery. Meanwhile the Austro-Hungarian

Fifty-Seventh Infantry Division covered the Fifty-Ninth Infantry Division's left, while maintaining contact with Lochow's III Corps.[28]

Gallwitz's German Eleventh Army encountered tough resistance along much of its front on October 25. The III Corps, with the Bavarian Eleventh Infantry Division now attached to it, had to drive elements of the Sumidija II Division back over the Rača, a swampy water course. In addition, the railroad was secured between Belgrade and Palanka.[29] The IV Reserve Corps had to, because of the course shaped by the Morava River, fight its way into the mountains south and southwest of the valley. Controlling the Morava Valley and the neighboring mountains would outflank the Serbian defenses of Kragujevać from the east. Two tough days of fighting on October 24 and 25 ensued. On October 25 the III Corps reached a line with Twenty-Fifth Reserve Division on the right, holding the front from Sepci to Wisevac, the Sixth Infantry Division in the center on a front running from Bosnjani to Kosa, while the Bavarian Eleventh Infantry Division on the left reached Markovac, in the Morava Valley.[30]

Winckler's IV Reserve Corps spent October 24 and 25 fighting its way through well-constructed Serbian defenses that also enjoyed good artillery support. The Germans, however, had the benefit of artillery support as well and here the attached Austro-Hungarian mountain batteries proved particularly effective. The Germans were also discovering that once they had gotten to a position the Serbians could be engaged in close combat, meaning within pistol and bayonet range, the Serbs would generally retreat rather than fight it out. Consequently, the IV Corps elements secured the mountains between the Morava and Mlava Valleys, which placed it in position for a follow on advance against Svilajnac, near the confluence of the Morava and Rešava Rivers.[31]

Kosch's X Reserve Corps also encountered fighting in its sector, but apparently nothing near as tough as that experienced by the III and IV Reserve Corps. The 103rd Infantry Division continued to move south, along with much of the 101st Infantry Division, reaching the railroad terminus at Setonje. The detachment from the 101st Infantry Division continued its advance along the Pek River, covering Gallwitz's left flank. The detachment occupied Kučevo, seizing in accordance with corps orders quantities of copper, brass, and leather and taking 460 prisoners as well.[32]

Bojadjiev's Bulgarian First Army also made progress, finally taking Knjaževac, roughly in the center of the Serbian position. Attacks on the critical fortified locales of Pirot and Zahečar were delayed, owing to ammunition shortages. The arrival of the Austro-Hungarian Danube Flotilla at Orsova, however, raised the prospect of the Austro-Hungarians opening up the Danube to Bulgaria, which would ease the ammunition situation. Thus on October 27 Mackensen issued a renewed call for the armies to press on.[33]

Over the next two days the three armies over which Mackensen and Seeckt exercised operational control moved forward. As early as October 24, the

German Eleventh Army had identified four infantry (Danube I, Sumidija I, Morava II, and Drina I) and one cavalry division, plus several unattached regiments in its front. On October 27 and 28 these units retreated as quickly as possible to the south, leaving the rearguards to slow down the oncoming Germans. By the evening of the 28th, the forward elements of the Austro-Hungarian VIII and German III Corps were only about 15 miles north of Kragujevać Counting the divisions engaged against Kövess, including the Drina II, Danube II, and Sumidija II Divisions, almost two-thirds of the Serbian army was before the Austro-Hungarian Third and German Eleventh Armies.[34]

Other signs also boded well for Mackensen. Once the renewed offensive began on October 23, on average about 500 prisoners were being taken daily by the German Eleventh Army. On October 24, Gallwitz saw a group of 200 Serbian prisoners. They looked, in his words, "poorly clothed and malnourished." About a third of the prisoners were Macedonians. The prisoners told Gallwitz that the majority of their losses were inflicted by artillery. Owing to the heavy losses already suffered, Serbian infantry avoided close combat and when counterattacks were launched, they lacked resolve. Finally, after what amounted to almost four continuous years of war, Serbia was exhausted.[35]

Like the Germans, the Serbians were also hindered by weather and bad roads. In addition, the Serbian retreat routes were clogged with refugees. The Serbian high command confronted a difficult situation, one that presented no good alternatives. This led to wildly differing types of behavior by its leaders. King Peter was deeply depressed, severely shaken by the losses in war and the typhus epidemic. At the other end of the spectrum was Mišić. On October 27 he proposed a Kolubara type counteroffensive. Putnik, however, realized that the autumn of 1915 was quite different from the autumn of 1914, and he quickly rejected Mišić's proposal. The best that the Serbian high command could do was to hang on as best they could, while calling for a renewed entente effort to advance from Salonika.[36]

To relieve itself of other useless mouths to feed, the Serbian government requested that the entente naval missions depart from Serbia. Given that Mackensen's forces had advanced well away from the rivers and that the equipment of these units had been destroyed, these units constituted a hindrance more than anything. Thus the Serbian government's request was quite logical. The British, French, and Russian naval missions proceeded by various routes to Salonika. Only Troubridge remained, as his fluency with Serbian and French would be useful.[37]

By October 28, Mackensen had gained a better understanding of the Serbian situation. The short break in the weather allowed the Germans to get aerial reconnaissance out, and the pilots reported that the Serbians were retreating toward Kragujevać and the West Morava River. The Old Hussar's sense that there was no real threat to Kövess's right flank had proved correct. Equally positive was the fact that Group Fülöpp and the Bulgarian First

Army were then close enough to each other that the Army Group head-quarters could set a boundary line between them.[38]

With the objectives set and the thinking that the decisive battle could be at hand, the senior commanders decided that it was time to displace their respective headquarters forward. The Austro-Hungarian Third Army's battle front had moved away from the Save, Kövess quite understandably moved his headquarters from Neusatz to Belgrade. Gallwitz's headquarters also moved across the river from Kevevara to Požarevac, although Gallwitz noted that the town itself presented a depressing scene when he visited on October 23. Corps headquarters were also having to move forward a bit more quickly. Kosch, for example, by late October was relocating his headquarters about every three days, a pace slightly surpassed by division commanders such as Kneussl. Finally, Mackensen's headquarters moved from Temesvár to Semendria on October 29, although some difficulty was encountered in crossing the river. With so many arrangements to make for the liaison officers attached to the headquarters, Seeckt complained to his wife that he was becoming something of a "travel agent," as opposed to a chief of staff.[39]

With the headquarters reestablished at Semendria, Mackensen and Seeckt then refined their thinking and the final lines of the envisioned decisive battle took shape. The inner wings of the two armies, the Austro-Hungarian VIII and the German III Corps, would drive forward and capture Kragujevać. Meanwhile, the German XXII Reserve Corps would move via Gornji Milanovac against Kraljevo, while further west the Austro-Hungarian XIX Corps would take Čačak and then continue south, while also making contact with the Sixty-Second Infantry Division. The German IV Reserve Corps would move south against Jagodina and ultimately Kruševac, while the X Reserve Corps would seize Čuprija. The Bulgarian First Army would advance on a line between Paraćin and Niš and advance its left wing to Kruševac. Meanwhile, the Bulgarian Second Army would continue to cover the routes from the Morava Valley against the Serbs, while also holding the entente forces in the Vardar Valley. If everything went as planned, the majority of the Serbian First and Third Armies, plus the Timok Group, would be trapped between Austro-Hungarian, German, and Bulgarian forces on three sides. The Serbs would have their backs to the wide West Morava River, the major crossing points of which would be in Austro-Hungarian or German hands. The terrain south of the river was mountainous with few useable roads.[40]

The plan, however, never quite came to fruition. The Austro-Hungarian VIII Corps and German III Corps, who had to fix the Serbian troops north of Kragujevać, failed to do so. Scheuchenstuel's VIII Corps made very little progress against determined Serbian resistance, amply supported by artillery, on October 29. Lochow, believing he was facing three fixed fortifications, approached cautiously. Further reconnaissance revealed the Serb fortifications to be mere hastily dug trenches, but by the time the truth of the matter was discovered Lochow had lost his chance. On the morning of October 30 the Germans and Austro-Hungarians discovered only Serbian rearguards. The major Serbian forces had abandoned their works and retreated south.[41]

On the flanks matters were no better. Trollmann's XIX Corps had to contend with the elements more than the enemy. Its progress was minimal on October 28, slowed by heavy rain, swamped roads, flooded water courses, and a lack of material to build bridges capable of bearing artillery. Falkenhayn's XXII Reserve Corps had to deal with more of an enemy presence in its front. On October 28, for example, the 208th Reserve Infantry Regiment, part of the Forty-Fourth Reserve Infantry Division, had to do some tough fighting to drive Serbian forces out of Rudnik, taking four guns. Simultaneously, however, Falkenhayn's divisions also had to spend considerable effort trying to determine in the major roads in the corps' sector were capable of bearing heavy traffic. Owing to the condition of horses and roads, divisions could send only a portion of their artillery forward.[42]

Consequently, the Austro-Hungarian Third Army's right flank advanced more abreast of the corps that were moving against Kragujevać, as opposed to moving ahead. Trollmann's XIX Corps struggled forward to reach the West Morava at Čačak and to the northwest by November 1. The German XXII Reserve Corps, after some tough fighting on the 28th, found only rear-guards in front of them. Gornji Milanovac was taken on October 29, although by November 1 Falkenhayn's troops had still not reached the Čačak-Kragujevać road.[43]

Meanwhile Winckler's IV Reserve Corps, with the Bavarian Eleventh Infantry Division reassigned to it, inched its way forward toward the Morava River at Brzan. The problem was getting across the Lepenica, a small river. Beset by swamped roads, destroyed bridges, and high water, Winckler's divisions could get only limited numbers of artillery pieces across. Consequently Kneussl's attack, scheduled for October 28, had to be postponed to the next day. The attack launched on the Twenty-Ninth was a success, netting 750 prisoners and driving off a Serbian counterattack, but precious time had been lost.[44]

The adjacent 105th Infantry Division found itself delayed after taking Sviljanac by the repeated breaking of the pontoon bridge that had replaced the demolished regular bridge. Thus the division spent October 29 and 30 resting, while the engineers repaired the pontoon bridge across the Morava at Miljkov. The 107th Infantry Division was ranged behind the 105th Division. It spent two days encountering small groups of Serbian soldiers.[45]

Further east Kosch's X Reserve Corps advanced south against resistance that the Eleventh Army described as light, while Kosch called it uneven. In one case the First Battalion of the Seventy-First Infantry Regiment (103rd Infantry Division) was able to catch a retreating Serbian unit on the march, capturing 463 prisoners without a fight. The 116th Infantry Regiment had a series of small fights on October 27 and 28, netting 250 prisoners at a cost of 2 killed and

34 wounded. On Kosch's left flank, the 101st Infantry Division's advance had outstripped that of the 103rd and Kraewel had to echelon units to cover his right. The Forty-Fifth Infantry Regiment spent three days (October 26-28) fighting its way forward toward the Resava Valley at Subotica, losing 15 killed and 63 wounded. The Thirty-Second Infantry Regiment also had a tough time driving a well-entrenched Serbian force out of Rosevac on October 27, allowing the regiment to cross the river the following day.[46]

The Bulgarian First Army also made limited gains against stout Serbian defenses west of Knjaževac and west of Pirot. The taking of those two points, however, allowed for a direct advance on Niš. Also on October 29, patrols from the X Reserve Corps made contact with the Bulgarian First Army. Army Group Mackensen was then advancing on a broad, unbroken front.[47]

While the armies under Mackensen's operational control made their way forward south and west, the Bulgarian Second Army continued its advance. On October 22 the Bulgarians reached Üsküb (Skopje). This was followed by the taking of the Kačanik Gorge on October 26. The seizure of Üsküb and the Kačanik Gorge, combined with the capture of Veleš, gave Todorov a stranglehold on rail communications between Serbia and Salonika. The Bulgarian Second Army had strong positions on both sides of the Vardar.[48]

Mackensen and Seeckt, still sensing that the prize was within their grasp, issued orders for that they believed would culminate in a decisive battle at Kragujevać. The armies under Mackensen's operational control would continue their advances. Meanwhile the Bulgarian Second Army's northern group would hold Üsküb. Todorov's southern group would continue its mission of fending off any entente advance in the Vardar Valley.[49]

By the end of October 30, it was clear that the Serbian high command had reached several conclusions, each of which was as unpleasant at it was unavoidable. The first was that the Serbian position in Macedonia had collapsed. The Serbian high command had taken the calculated risk of placing its least reliable forces there, and by October 26 it was clear that the risk had become a failed gamble. The local Serbian commander, Damnjan Popović, was relieved by Putnik and replaced by Petar Bojović, but this did little to alter the situation.[50]

The second and third conclusions were related. By late October, it was abundantly clear that the entente forces from Salonika would not reach the Serbian forces fighting north of West Morava, let alone the Morava. This in turn led to the conclusion that it would be suicidal to continue to fight to hold both Niš and Kragujevać. Since the Serbian government, then located in Kraljevo, had already agreed that a separate peace was out of the question, the only hope for the Serbian army and government was retreat, either toward the entente forces to the south, or toward the Adriatic coast to the southwest.[51]

Thus, while the Austro-Hungarian VIII Corps and German III Corps continued to move forward slowly on October 30 and 31, the Serbian forces in

Kragujevać proceeded to blow up the arsenal, as well as any ammunition stocks that could be destroyed quickly. The same process was undertaken at Niš in the face of the Bulgarian First Army. After a municipal delegation visited Lochow's headquarters, Kragujevać was occupied without fighting by the 168th Infantry Regiment from Jarotzky's Twenty-Fifth Reserve Infantry Division, accompanied by the Austro-Hungarian Fifty-Seventh Infantry Division. Troops who moved through the city encountered Serbian rearguards south of town. Niš was occupied by the Bulgarians on November 5.[52]

Although the Serbian forces had largely escaped, the loss of Kragujevać and to a lesser extent Niš was a disaster for the Serbians. Because the Bulgarian Second Army controlled the railroad between Üsküb and Veleš, the Serbian army had no way to move large amounts of equipment quickly over long distances; thus the material had to be left for the Germans and Austro-Hungarians, along with 2,100 wounded soldiers. Large amounts of raw materials were also taken. Mackensen counted Serbian losses by November 1 as some 15,300 prisoners taken by the armies of Kövess and Gallwitz, plus another 6,000 brought in by the Bulgarian First Army, while the Bulgarian Second Army had taken at least several thousand prisoners. To that was added an unknown but undoubtedly considerable number of dead and wounded. About 100 guns had been taken and a number of others destroyed. Although it was difficult to quantify the extent of the losses, there was no doubt that the Putnik's forces had suffered a serious mauling. Serbian morale had also suffered severely. Captured soldiers were despondent and even the morale of officers had waned considerably.[53]

The capture of Kragujevać, however, also resulted in an old problem recurring. As with the earlier fall of Belgrade, both OHL and AOK issued announcements regarding the capture of Kragujevać, and each statement credited its own troops with seizure of the city. This time Mackensen was in no mood for any explanations from Jansa or Lustig.[54]

Although the Serbian army had escaped the clutches of Mackensen and Seeckt at Kragujevać, they still had hopes of bringing about the desired encirclement of the Serbian forces. Thus on November 1, even as the III Corps was occupying Kragujevać and reporting that it badly needed a day of rest, Mackensen and Seeckt were urging their armies on. The Austro-Hungarian Third Army was given Kraljevo as its next objective, while the German Eleventh Army would attack on both sides of the Morava toward Kruševac, at the confluence of the Morava and West Morava Rivers.[55] Rapid capture of these objectives would still allow Mackensen and Seeckt to realize the goals set forth in the original plan.

Mackensen and Seeckt, however, would have to do it without the requested additional Bulgarian forces. Zhekov was more concerned about the prospect of an entente offensive against the Bulgarian Second Army. Thus the two divisions would go to Todorov, not Bojadjiev, a decision Mackensen ultimately

endorsed, at least for the time being. Zhekov's judgment in this case was absolutely correct, as Sarrail was trying to mount such an attack against Todorov's
flank on the Crna River in early November.[56]

The advance on Kragujevać was a difficult one for the soldiers of the Central
powers. Although the Serbians did not wantonly destroy villages and towns
through which they retreated, in many cases the Serbs did take away as much
of the portable material they could carry. Thus, for example, when the 65th
Field Artillery entered Gornji Milanovac, the artillerymen found the streets clean
and well ordered, but the town was devoid of hay and straw.[57] In a few cases
some regiments, such as the Forty-Fifth (part of the 101st Infantry Division)
were in spots where the field kitchens, drawn by mules, caught up with the
infantry and were able to provide hot food. In most cases, however, infantry regiments had to supplement meager rations with locally obtained supplies. Owing
to logistical priorities, German units in the Balkans were not allowed to receive
parcels from home. The weather continued to be miserable, with days of heavy
rain followed by increasingly cold nights.[58]

Although Putnik's forces had escaped complete destruction at Kragujevać,
the fall of both Kragujevać and Niš had major strategic consequences. The tak-
ing of the two cities allowed Mackensen to claim that the strategic mission
assigned to him and Seeckt in September at Allenstein had been accomplished.
With the clearance of the Danube River, plus the taking of the railroad from
Belgrade to Niš, a landline of communications had been opened to both
Bulgaria and Turkey. German aid had already appeared in Turkey in
October, when a flight of 24 German aircraft reached Adrianople.[59]

The campaign had then reached a juncture where both sides needed to
reconsider their strategy. Since the principal objective of the Central powers
had been achieved, the issue of follow-on operations had to be considered
and what forces would be allocated to them. Matters of the administration of
the newly occupied territory had to be determined and changes in the command relationships, if any were to be made, had to be decided on.

The entente powers had much to think about as well. For the Serbians, since
the attempted stands at the rivers and then before Kragujevać and Niš had failed,
was there any place the Serbian army could make a stand? If that was not
possible, where could the army retreat? For the French and (to a lesser extent)
the British, the matter of the future of the Salonika expedition then came into
question. The campaign would now take a different direction.

Chapter 7

The Pursuit: November 6–30, 1915

"The area where our rooms are had been occupied by the King of Serbia two days earlier."

Robert Kosch, November 6, 1915[1]

"The political and military situation urgently requires that the operation against the Serbians be concluded quickly ... "

August von Mackensen, November 9, 1915[2]

"The only way out of this grave situation is a retreat to the Adriatic coast."

Serbian High Command, November 25, 1915[3]

For the Serbian government and high command, the events of late October and early November had reduced their strategic choices to a simple but elemental goal, survival. The government and at least part of the army had to survive, even in exile if necessary, to keep alive the idea of a sovereign Serbian nation, let alone a larger South Slav state. For the Serbian high command, this translated into only one operational course of action, namely retreat. Although firebrands such as Mišić would continue to press for a counteroffensive, wiser heads such as Putnik knew better. Retreat would be the order of the day. The only matter to be decided would be which direction, south, west, or southwest.

Each of these alternatives was fraught with peculiar difficulties. The southern option presented the most direct way to make contact with Sarrail's Army of the Orient. It was dependent, however, on the ability of the Serbians to break through the freshly reinforced Bulgarian Second Army. Failure to do so, or if the Serbians became hung up in trying to get through, increased the possibility that Mackensen's forces, pursuing from the north and west, could achieve the envelopment and destruction of the Serbian army that Mackensen desired. The western route led to the Albanian port of Scutari, while the southwestern route's endpoint was Durazzo, another Albanian port. Part of both of these routes ran down the Ibar Valley to Priština and the Field of Blackbirds at Kosovo, but then involved having to cross substantial mountain ranges, with some peaks as high as 6,300 feet. Thus a retreat on Priština and Kosovo was the immediate task for Putnik's forces.[4]

While the Serbians retreated, the military chiefs of the Central powers, meeting at Pless on November 6, reflected. There was indeed much to consider. The most immediate issue was to decide on the course of action regarding the campaign against the Serbian army, or what was left of it. After that, the question of future strategic choices loomed. Should an offensive be undertaken against the Army of the Orient? What about the other theaters of war and which should take precedence? Finally, how would occupied Serbia be governed and by whom?

For Falkenhayn, the defeat of the Serbian army, plus the capture of Niš and Kragujevać, fulfilled the strategic goal of opening a route to Turkey. Falkenhayn could thus proceed with his plan to shift Germany's main focus to the western front, as he had always considered the Serbian campaign to be a "subsidiary operation." The entente forces in Macedonia could be contained, as Falkenhayn regarded the idea of trying to win the war overall by a major commitment of forces to the Balkans as "wholly unsound."[5]

Conrad was the most adamant about an offensive against the Army of the Orient. He regarded the Franco-English landing at Salonika and the violation of Greek neutrality as a gross breach of international law (rather ironic given Germany's invasion of Belgium) for which the entente powers should be punished. Finally Conrad, as well as Burián, had designs on Montenegro, which both men wanted annexed by Austria-Hungary. The Bulgarians, represented by Ganchev, wanted their losses from the Second Balkan War redeemed.[6]

After a full day of wrangling and argument, replete with remarks often laced with sarcasm, some decisions were reached. The campaign against the Serbian army continued, at least for a short time. It, however, continued with fewer German forces. Falkenhayn had wanted to shift the focus of Germany's operations to the west since the late summer and that could happen then, which meant that most of the German forces allocated to Mackensen would be withdrawn relatively quickly. Occupied Serbia would be divided between Austria-Hungary and Bulgaria, with ultimately the old border between Serbia and Macedonia, along with the Morava River as the dividing line between the territory administered by Austria-Hungary and by Bulgaria. Increasing Bulgaria's role in the region was seen as the best way Germany could exert maximum influence while minimizing its own commitment of forces. The organization of rail communications to Bulgaria and Turkey was also discussed. That, like the rebuilding of the railroad and the rail bridges, would be left largely in German hands. The Greek border would not be crossed, at least for the time being. The issue of Montenegro and Albania remained undecided. Thus for the most part, Falkenhayn got his way.[7]

The major decisions had to be turned into actions by Mackensen and his cohorts. His first attempt to encircle the Serbian army had failed. Mackensen's forces were still in hot pursuit, however, and he certainly wanted to destroy the Serbian army. The difficulties of the terrain, however, brought Falkenhayn to the conclusion that a pursuit such as that demanded by Mackensen would have to be conducted only by divisions that were equipped for operations in mountainous terrain. Thus, the German forces under Mackensen's command would be reduced to four or five divisions.[8]

The decisions reached at Pless did not have an immediate impact on Mackensen, who was still seeking to trap and destroy a large part of the Serbian army between the West Morava and the mountains south of the river. On November 6, Mackensen informed Kövess that the Serbians were retreating via Kruševac to the south. Gallwitz's center (Winckler's IV Reserve Corps) would advance on Kruševac with its flanks covered by the III Corps and the X Reserve Corps, while the Bulgarian First Army continued its westward advance from Niš. Mackensen wanted the Austro-Hungarian VIII Corps to cross the West Morava and advance to Brus, in order to cut the Serbian retreat off. Scheuchenstuel's right would be covered by the German XXII Reserve Corps' advance on Kraljevo at the confluence of the West Morava and Ibar Rivers. The Army Group's right would continue to be protected by the Austro-Hungarian XIX Corps and the much maligned Austro-Hungarian Sixty-Second Infantry Division. Once the Serbians were disposed of, Mackensen hoped to launch an offensive against the Army of the Orient, the strength of which he estimated at about 80,000 men.[9]

Mackensen and Seeckt's next attempt to encircle the Serbian forces got off to a good start as the German Forty-Third Reserve Division assaulted Kraljevo, which was defended by the Drina II Division. While the 201st Reserve Infantry Regiment attacked the city, the 202nd Reserve Infantry Regiment tried to secure the bridge over the West Morava at the northern edge of Kraljevo. Although the Serbs did set off explosive charges, they failed to demolish the span completely. Using wooden planks, the 202nd was able to patch up the bridge enough to the point where it was useable. With the crossing secure, the 201st Reserve Infantry crossed the bridge and ably supported by Austro-Hungarian mountain artillery, fought its way through stiff resistance to the rail station. The seizure of the rail station broke Serbian resistance and a delegation from the municipal government surrendered the city to the Third Battalion. Meanwhile the Twenty-Sixth Infantry Division spent the day fighting its way across the West Morava at Miločaj, northwest of Kraljevo. German losses were light. The 201st Reserve Infantry Regiment, for example, lost only 6 killed and 23 wounded.[10]

The capture of Kraljevo proved a major success in two ways. First, because the Bulgarians had severed the major rail line in Serbia, once again the Serbians had no real way of moving large amounts of heavy equipment. Hence, the Germans captured a great deal of material that had been loaded on to railroad cars that had no place to go. The haul of booty included 130 guns, although a number of these were previously captured Austro-Hungarian or Turkish pieces. Large amounts of ammunition were also captured, along with numerous wagons, automobiles, searchlights, aircraft, fuel, medical equipment, and food. The rolling stock captured intact in itself would be valuable in helping getting the railroad, which by that time had reached Petrovac, back in operation.[11]

The other major advantage was that after Kraljevo was secured in the morning of November 6, the Forty-Third Reserve Infantry Division moved quickly to gain control of the area south of the city. This put the Germans in position to gain entrance to the Ibar River valley, a major Serbian retreat route and the area where Mackensen believed the Serbian government was located.[12]

While Falkenhayn's troops were taking Kraljevo, the Austro-Hungarian XIX Corps and Group Sorsich advanced on Ivanjica and the Sjenica, covering Falkenhayn's right flank. Progress was slow, as Trollmann's and Sorsich's units struggled forward against the Montenegrin forces. Scheuchenstuel's VIII Corps advanced on Trstenik, the crossing point of the West Morava about midway between Kraljevo and Kruševac. Mackensen wanted the Austro-Hungarian VIII Corps to cut off Serbian troops retreating from Kruševac.[13]

While elements of Kövess's Austro-Hungarian Third Army took Kraljevo, Gallwitz's German Eleventh Army moved against Kruševac. The advance was led by Winckler's IV Reserve Corps, advancing directly south, while Lochow's III Corps moved in support from Kragujevać. The available road network no longer allowed an advance on a broad front. As the Germans headed toward Kruševac, they encountered the signs of a defeated army. The Twentieth Infantry Regiment, part of the III Corps, marching on the road from Kragujevać to Sekuric, noted the large numbers of discarded weapons and ammunition. Destroyed and damaged vehicles as well as abandoned artillery pieces were found strewn along the road. Much of the abandoned material had fallen victim to German artillery or machine guns firing at maximum range.[14]

On the morning of November 6, Esch's 105th Infantry Division, Winckler's lead element, stormed Vavarin and later reached Jasika. From there the IV Reserve Corps' 100mm artillery batteries that had been able to go forward could take Kruševac's rail station, then crammed with material, under fire. Elements of Esch's 105th Infantry Division had to contend with relatively weak resistance. Troops of the 129th Infantry Regiment also heard demolitions being carried out in Kruševac. Meanwhile Kosch's X Reserve Corps, with the 103rd Infantry Division in the lead, reached Jovanovac, only to find yet another destroyed bridge. The 107th Infantry Division had a similar experience at Stalac. Booty taken on this day was, given the precedents of the campaign thus far, considerable. The German Eleventh Army took 2,000 prisoners, plus several thousand more men who had almost certainly deserted from the Serbian army. Material taken also included 43 locomotives and 500 rail cars. A number of ammunition wagons also fell into German hands, along with some 13,000 artillery shells and tons of small arms ammunition.[15]

The following day, troops from both the IV Reserve Corps and the X Reserve Corps converged on Kruševac. Once again there was a considerable haul of between 4,000 to 5,000 prisoners. Over 100 guns and large quantities of other types of equipment were taken, along with lots of ammunition. Of major importance were over 50 locomotives and more than 1,100 loaded rail cars.[16] With Kraljevo and Kruševac in the hands of Mackensen's forces, it looked as if the desired encirclement of most of the Serbian forces in the valley of the West Morava could be achieved, especially if Kövess could gain control of the Ibar Valley.

The second attempt at encirclement, however, also came to naught. While Bulgarian First Army's had taken Niš and had established contact with the X Reserve Corps, Bojadjiev's advance was far too slow for the taste of Mackensen and Seeckt. Thus the Serbian forces facing the Bulgarians were not being held in place. Hence, much of Timok Group and Stepanović's Second Army were able to escape the converging German and Bulgarian forces by retreating to Prokuplje and then Kuršumlija in accordance with Putnik's orders.[17]

Matters were made worse by the fact that the Bulgarian First Army was often slow in sending reports to Army Group headquarters, so Mackensen and Seeckt were not as well informed at times as they would have liked in regard to what the Bulgarians were doing. Although intelligence officers were detailed by the Army Group to Bojadjiev's headquarters to help facilitate communication, reports and messages could be sent only by aircraft or by wireless radio, with only a few sets available. Information concerning the Bulgarian Second Army was even harder to come by.[18]

The progress of the Austro-Hungarian Third Army also troubled Mackensen and Seeckt. After taking Kraljevo and Ivanjica, Kövess's forces did very little. Although the then reinforced Austro-Hungarian Sixty-Second Infantry Division had made some headway, that was of little consequence. After its exertions on November 6, the XXII Reserve Corps spent two days mostly resting. Some regiments, such as 205th Reserve Infantry (Forty-Fourth Reserve Infantry Division), engaged in costly combat on November 8 against the Serbian forces in the hills that guarded the entrance to the Ibar Valley. The 205th suffered 18 killed and 73 wounded on the 8th, but made no further advance the next day.[19]

While elements of the Forty-Forth Reserve Infantry Division were involved in combat, the Forty-Third Reserve Infantry Division rested. The soldiers of the 202nd Reserve Infantry Regiment, for example, used the welcome respite to mend clothing, and with winter coming on, gave Serbian prisoners their own worn-out footwear in exchange for the Serbians winter boots and snow-shoes, which were much better suited for the conditions. This matter was made more urgent by the fact that snow was starting to take the place of rain as the most common form of precipitation.[20]

Given that Mackensen and Seeckt maintained close communication with Gallwitz and Kövess, they quickly learned of the Austro-Hungarian Third Army's relative inaction on November 8. The next day Kövess received a blistering message from Mackensen. The message began with a brusque question: "Was not the necessity for the ruthless advance of the XIX, XXII Reserve and VIII Corps made clear?" Kövess was informed that the military and political situation demanded that the campaign be brought to a conclusion as quickly as possible. Horses that had broken down were to be replaced immediately by locally requisitioned oxen. Mackensen reinforced this with a personal telegram to Falkenhayn, demanding a rapid advance by the XXII Reserve Corps on Novi Pazar. As if to add further emphasis, Mackensen then made a personal visit to the XXII Reserve Corps on November 10.[21]

The adamant demands contained in Mackensen's message to Kövess on November 9 reflected a degree of disagreement between Mackensen and Seeckt on the one hand and the German and Bulgarian high commands on the other. For Falkenhayn and Zhekov, the capture of Niš and Kruševac signaled the end of the campaign. The goal of opening communications to Bulgaria and Turkey, after all, had been met. On November 11, Mackensen wrote to Falkenhayn, while Seeckt penned a missive to Zhekov. Both Mackensen and Seeckt argued that, while the strategic goals set before the operation had been achieved, the campaign could not be regarded as concluded, since the final victory over the Serbian army had still not been won. This would best be accomplished by a vigorous pursuit in the Ibar Valley, with the aim of fighting a decisive final battle against the Serbs in the Kosovo area near Priština. Known as the "Field of Blackbirds," it was the site of a famous battle in 1389 where the Serbians were destroyed by the Turks and later became the birthplace of Serbian nationalism.[22]

There were three unspoken concerns about the potential escape of the Serbian forces. The first was that the Serbian units could eventually reappear somewhere in the theater, either as an independent entity or as part of the entente forces in Macedonia. The second regarded Serbian nationalism. Austro-Hungarian and German intelligence regarded the Serbian army, and its officer corps in particular, as one of the bearers of Serbian nationalism. The destruction of the army, plus the removal of other nationalist elements in Serbian society, would have the effect of rendering quiet a potentially troublesome area. Finally, there were signs that Mackensen's quarry was tantalizingly close. Kosch noted in a letter written in Ćuprija to his wife on

November 6 that only two days earlier, the rooms he was staying in had been host to the king of Serbia.[23]

Mackensen and Seeckt's third attempt to encircle and destroy the Serbian army would have to be done with some reshuffled forces, owing to the decisions reached at Pless on November 6, and the topographical realities of the Serbian front. Mackensen was well aware of OHL's desire to withdraw divisions from Serbia for employment elsewhere. In addition, the roads in Serbia south of the Save and Danube converged on a few places on the West Morava River, most notably Kruševac. Also, the mountainous terrain between Kruševac and Priština had relatively few roads and was thus incapable of supporting the advance of a large force. Likewise the terrain south of Kraljevo was also mountainous, marked with peaks as high as 4,600 feet.[24]

As Gallwitz's three corps converged on Kruševac, the advance of Winckler's IV Reserve Corps, plus the advance of the Austro-Hungarian VIII Corps, effectively pinched Lochow's III Corps out of the front. In addition, the roads in Winckler's sector did not permit the employment of his full corps. Also, several of the divisions were not equipped for mountain warfare. Thus the Twenty-Fifth Reserve Infantry and Bavarian Eleventh Infantry Divisions were ordered to be withdrawn from Serbia, along with the III Corps and IV Reserve Corps headquarters. They began their marches out of Serbia on November 8, with the III Corps and the Twenty-Fifth Reserve Infantry Division going out of Serbia via Kragujevać to Kevevara, while the Kneussl's Bavarians retraced their steps first to Požarevac and then the bridge at Gradiste, respectively. The 6th and 105th Infantry Divisions remained in action under Gallwitz's direct command.[25]

Changes impacted Kövess's Third Army as well, although this involved primarily Falkenhayn's XXII Reserve Corps. The Forty-Fourth Reserve Infantry Division remained in combat in Serbia, while the Forty-Third Reserve Infantry Division occupied Kraljevo. The Twenty-Sixth Infantry Division, unequipped for mountain warfare, was ordered to withdraw from Serbia on November 8. The division, however, was replaced by the last major unit to be committed to Serbia. The German Alpine Corps had finally arrived.[26]

The Alpine Corps emerged from the discussions between Falkenhayn and Conrad in early 1915 over how to defend Austria-Hungary's Italian possessions. During the late winter of 1915 Falkenhayn had urged Austria-Hungary to buy Italy off with territorial concessions. Conrad rejected this out of hand.[27] By May 1915, the subject turned to how to deal with Italy's impending entry into the war.

With Italy then Conrad's obsession of the moment, he wanted as many as 10 German divisions for an offensive in the Tirol. Falkenhayn, seeking to minimize any German commitment, agreed after a conference at Teschen on May 18, 1915, only to send an "Alpine Corps," the first time the name was used. The next day, Falkenhayn informed Conrad that the Alpine Corps was a division size unit that would be at the Brenner Pass in the six days. What he did not tell Conrad was that the Alpine Corps did not yet exist. The day Falkenhayn gave Conrad detail about the size of the Alpine Corps, the Prussian war minister, Adolf Wild von Hohenborn sent a letter to his Bavarian counterpart, calling for the creation of an Alpine Corps.[28]

Since the Bavarian war ministry had no objection to the request from Wild, it set about creating the Alpine Corps. The unit was cobbled together by drawing together regiments from other units. The corps was officially established on May 27, 1915. The Alpine Corps was essentially an oversized division, with two brigades of two regiments each. Although the corps was relatively underequipped, especially in mountain artillery, it had a detachment of six aircraft attached to it, a rare luxury, as well as two wireless radio stations. The headquarters staff was drawn from the German Sixth Army, then commanded by Crown Prince Rupprecht of Bavaria. Lochow was supposed to be the commander of the corps, but Rupprecht wanted to keep him with the III Corps. Instead, the Bavarian war ministry named Generalmajor Konrad Krafft von Delmensingen to command the new unit.[29]

Born on 20 November 1862, Krafft's initial service in the Bavarian army was in the Bavarian Fourth Field Artillery Regiment, where he attained his initial commission in December 1883. He spent the next three decades holding a series of command and staff appointments in the Bavarian Artillery, as well as stints with the Bavarian general staff and war ministry prior to his promotion to Generalmajor on October 1, 1912. At the outbreak of war, Krafft was appointed chief of staff to Rupprecht's Sixth Army. Named commander of the Alpine Corps on May 20, 1915, it was Krafft's debut as a combat commander. Krafft was assisted by a small staff, headed by Chief of Staff Major Friedrich Wilhelm Freiherr von Willisen, a Prussian who came from the Forty-Ninth Reserve Infantry Division.[30]

Committed to the Tirol, an area Krafft was very familiar with, to act in a defensive role (as Italy had not declared war against Germany), the corps spent the summer on the Italian front. On September 21, 1915, Falkenhayn alerted Krafft to the possibility of the Alpine Corps being withdrawn for service elsewhere. One month later that possibility became a reality when, with the prospect of operations on the Italian front over for the time being, OHL ordered the Alpine Corps to Serbia. The movement began three days later.[31]

Initially assigned to the German Eleventh Army, Krafft reported to Gallwitz on October 27, as the Alpine Corps began to arrive in southern Hungary, at a pace far too slow for Gallwitz's taste. The concentration of the corps was completed by October 29. Once in Hungary, the corps received mules and handlers, plus local vehicles. The same day the corps completed its assembly in Hungary, Krafft received orders by telephone from Gallwitz. The corps was ordered to cross the Danube and march via Požarevac to Svilajnac.[32]

On November 2, the Alpine Corps crossed the Danube at Bazias and at Gradiste, using a 975 yard long pontoon bridge built by Austro-Hungarian engineers. An improved weather situation had helped improve the roads enough so that Svilajnac was reached on time and communications with the German Eleventh Army was reestablished.[33] From Svilajnac the Alpine Corps followed the line of march of the III Corps to Kragujevać. The Alpine Corps was fortunate in that engineers had been working diligently to repair and maintain bridges along the march route. The road, however, was in very poor condition and the march was hard on both men and horses. The Alpine Corps' war diary noted on November 5 that casualties among horses were becoming a problem. Maps were also inaccurate. Kragujevać was reached on November 6, where it rested.[34]

With the converging advance of Kövess's and Gallwitz's forces on Kruševac resulting in the III Corps and much of the IV Reserve Corps being pinched out of the front, Mackensen and Gallwitz agreed that the Alpine Corps be shifted to Kövess's command. Mackensen informed Kövess on November 7 that the Alpine Corps would replace Falkenhayn's XXII Reserve Corps. In a post script, Kövess was given a short description of the Alpine Corps, its organization and equipment, along with some background on Krafft. With its mission then settled, the Alpine Corps was directed to Kraljevo on November 9.[35]

There was also additional reshuffling of forces by Bulgaria, which again did not correspond to the wishes of Mackensen and Seeckt. Previously, in late October, Mackensen and Seeckt had wanted the Bulgarian high command to direct two divisions from Bulgaria to Bojadiev's Bulgarian First Army. Zhekov, however, decided to send the reinforcements to Todorov's Bulgarian Second Army.[36]

Finally, to prepare for the final push into Old Serbia, Mackensen's forces to get much lighter. The heavy artillery that had proved to be the ultimate trump card for Mackensen's troops were then something of an embarrassment, since they were so difficult to move. On November 12 and 13, the Austro-Hungarian Third Army returned seven heavy and super heavy batteries to AOK. For the Germans, the heaviest caliber to be used then was 150mm.[37]

Mackensen believed that the Serbian forces still could be surrounded and destroyed and Bulgarian First Army, advancing west from Niš, had an important role in that plan. Although perhaps as many as 80,000 men had been landed at Salonika, Mackensen and Seeckt believed that the Bulgarian Second Army was both strong enough and sufficiently well positioned to hold Sarrails's forces in check. Zhekov, however, saw the situation very differently. The chief of the Bulgarian general staff regarded the Serbian army as a broken force that was then of little consequence. The Bulgarian Second Army in Macedonia was of primary importance and required further reinforcement. Thus, Zhekov shifted the Bulgarian Sixth Division from the First Army to the Second. Zhekov also asked OHL for an additional division. Falkenhayn denied the request, but instead offered additional artillery, including heavy guns, plus some machine gun units, to the Bulgarians.[38]

Bulgarian concerns seemed justified when in early November Sarrail launched a series of attacks with the French 156th, 57th, and 122nd Infantry Divisions toward the Bulgarian border. These thrusts were aimed at out-flanking the Bulgarian defenses in the Vardar Valley. The offensive failed, owing to a stout if costly Bulgarian defense. In addition, the French were also dogged by a lack of usable roads, destroyed bridges, and inaccurate maps. The British, still plagued by a lack of certainty and indecisiveness at the highest levels of command, proved to be of little if any help. British soldiers going north toward Serbia had to contend with the same difficulties the Central powers forces had been dealing with for the past month. Fearing for the safety of Sarrail's line of communications, the French war ministry, then headed by Marne hero Joseph Gallieni, ordered Sarrail to halt his offensive and draw back to a shorter front in order to defend Salonika.[39] The Serbian army was on its own.

The final attempt to destroy the Serbian forces got off to a bad start. Aside from being slow in reporting, the Bulgarian First Army was having difficulties in getting all of its units across the West and South Morava Rivers. Bojadiev's bridging assets had not kept pace with the advance and were delayed in arriving. The Bulgarian First Division, however, was able to cross the South Morava at Leskovac, about 18 miles south of Niš. With some other units trying to cross at Niš, Mackensen ordered an all-out pursuit by the Bulgarians southwest toward Priština.[40]

The Serbian Second Army facing the Bulgarians was able to create an attacking force consisting of the Timok I, Sumidija II, and Morava II Divisions. This force was able to mount a successful counterattack on November 10 against part of Bulgarian First Division, driving it back toward Leskovac. Although some of the more fire breathing Serbian commanders wanted to expand the effort, wiser counsels prevailed. Using this respite, the Serbians continued their retreat toward Priština.[41]

The most direct pursuit of the Serbians was undertaken by an expanded X Reserve Corps with the 107th Infantry Division attached to Kosch's command. Kosch's route would take his corps across the Jastrebac Mountain, where the most direct pass was 5,200 above sea level. The highest peak reached 7,000 feet. The passes through the mountain were few and roads often nothing more than muddy tracks. Nonetheless, Kosch's lead elements were able to seize the passes against feeble Serbian resistance on November 13.[42]

With the campaign reaching its climax, Mackensen and Seeckt thought that maintaining control over the operation required closer physical proximity to the forward line. Thus on November 13 Army Group Mackensen's headquarters moved once again, this time from Semendria to Kragujevać. This was the second relocation of army group headquarters in just over two weeks. Jansa could not help but compare what he considered to be this very mobile style of command with absolute inertia that dominated Potiorek's headquarters in 1914.[43]

During the course of October, German and Austro-Hungarian air units displaced forward, crossing the river in the wake of the advancing infantry divisions. To be sure, this was no easy task. Under good circumstances, moving a German aviation detachment required 30 vehicles and 90 horses. Given the difficult conditions in Serbia, however, aviation detachments had to resort to using wagons drawn by oxen and even buffalo.[44]

For the final push against Serbia, the aviation detachments had moved up to airfields located near Vrangelovac, Kragujevać, and Svilajnac. The army aircraft park remained in Požarevac. Even then, the areas the aircraft would have to reconnoiter or attack were often over 60 miles from their airfields. Aerial reconnaissance remained dangerous, however. Although Serbian resistance was negligible, aircraft often had to operate at altitudes that were often below the height of the mountain peaks, thus making missions very dangerous. As the weather had improved slightly in early November, reconnaissance flights were able to keep Mackensen and his commanders apprised of Serbian movements. Aerial photography also gave commanders a good idea of the ruggedness of the terrain they were confronting.[45]

Mackensen and Seeckt's plan was to seize key points in the Ibar Valley, most notably Mitrovica. That would be the mission of the Austro-Hungarian Third Army. From there, Kövess's forces could approach Priština from the northwest. Gallwitz's German Eleventh Army and Bojadiev's Bulgarian First Army would advance into the Toplica Valley from the north and east, respectively. From there, Priština could be approached from the northeast and east. The ultimate goal was to destroy the Serbian army around Kosovo. Every major German, Bulgarian, or Austro-Hungarian commander understood the cultural and historical significance of Kosovo to the Serbians.[46]

If they were able to catch their quarry, the Germans had little doubt about the outcome. On November 11, Gallwitz's intelligence officer briefed the German Eleventh Army commander on the state of the Serbian forces. German intelligence had estimated the strength of Serbia's forces before the start of the campaign at about 300,000. Of this total, about 60,000 had been captured and another 90,000 killed or wounded. Of the 150,000 remaining, at most 130,000 faced Mackensen's forces. Large quantities of material had also been lost. Finally, German commanders, starting with Mackensen, recognized how war weary the population and parts of the army were.[47]

The right flank of Mackensen's forces, whose performance heretofore been disappointing, then began to advance against the Montenegrin troops. The Austro-Hungarian Sixty-Second Infantry Division finally began to make progress, giving some cover to the right flank Trollmann's XIX Corps. The Austro-Hungarian XIX Corps was able to reach Ivanjica on November 13.[48]

The Ibar River valley, which would be the focus of the Austro-Hungarian Third Army's efforts, was a narrow and winding gorge, bounded by steep hills on both sides. The principal thrust would be delivered by the German XXII

Reserve Corps to which the Alpine Corps was then attached. Although the XXII Reserve Corps was due to be withdrawn, Mackensen explained to Falkenhayn that given the importance of the thrust to Raška, about midway in the Ibar Valley between Kraljevo and Mitrovica, the corps needed to be retained for the time being.[49]

Raška was thought to be the current location of Serbian headquarters. The Forty-Fourth Reserve Infantry Division would proceed directly into the Ibar Valley. The infantry regiments would have only minimal artillery support. Because of the road conditions, only two batteries from the 44Forty-Fourth Reserve Field Artillery Regiment could go forward. Each battery could send forward only two guns, plus four ammunition wagons. Eight horses were required to draw each gun and wagon. The rest of the guns remained in Kraljevo, along with the Forty-Third Reserve Infantry Division, which remained as Kövess's reserve.[50]

Owing to the narrowness of the Ibar Valley, the Forty-Fourth Reserve Infantry Division could only send forward one regiment at a time. On its flank left in the hills, the Alpine Corps was having similar problems. On November 13 the Alpine Corps had its first action in Serbia, tangling with a rearguard from the Drina II Division. At the cost of 3 dead and 12 wounded, some 200 prisoners were taken. A captured Serbian captain stated that the Serbian high command had ordered a concentration at Mitrovica.[51]

The following two days were spent by Dorrer's infantry attacking through the Ibar Valley, with the Alpine Corps fighting their way through the Plana Hills. The advance was opposed by the Drina II and Danube II Divisions. Further east, the Austro-Hungarian VIII Corps struggled across the Kopaonik Mountains, which was the most direct route to Mitrovica. Meanwhile the X Reserve Corps continued its attack south on Kuršumlija, while the Bulgarian First Army, having recovered from its check around Leskovac, resumed the offensive, taking both prisoners and guns. The Bulgarian Second Army repulsed a weak Serbian attack southward at Gnjilane, which was aimed at opening a route toward Üsküb.[52]

The Central powers forces had a difficult time in moving forward. The Alpine Corps, for example, could only use mules to carry ammunition. Owing to the operational urgency of the situation, the troops had to go forward with only minimal rations; ammunition had absolute priority. Also the difficulty in getting artillery forward meant that Serbian rearguards often had to be dislodged with rifles and grenades. Fortunately for the Mackensen's forces, by this time the Serbian forces were in much worse shape. If the Germans especially were able to close with Serbian rearguards, they were able to bring them to battle and overcome them, inflicting casualties and taking prisoners for relatively light losses, but at the cost of precious time.[53]

The final eight days of the campaign saw the repetition of a familiar pattern. On November 16, troops of Thirty-Second Infantry Regiment from Estorff's

103rd Infantry Division approached Kuršumlija, while part of the 105th Infantry Division reached Prokuplje. It was then clear that few if any Serbian troops were on the north bank of the Toplica River and that no serious resistance would be offered. The Thirty-Second Infantry Regiment was able to get to a position where the German machine guns could engage a retreating Serbian column at long range, causing considerable havoc. After making a night approach toward Kuršumlija at 12:30 a.m. on November 17, the Thuringian infantrymen heard a shattering explosion. The next day the regiment crossed the Toplica into the town, to be met by frightened residents, who had endured looting by hungry Serbian soldiers.[54]

While the weather in October had been very rainy, it had improved enough during late October and early November to allow the German aviation detachments and Austro-Hungarian aviation companies that had recently displaced forward to send reconnaissance flights aloft. Aviation reports in early November gave Mackensen, Seeckt, and their commanders some idea as to the progress and direction of the Serbian retreat. In addition, aircraft served to facilitate communications between the German Eleventh and Bulgarian First Armies.[55]

As the advance moved toward and into the Ibar Valley, however, the weather changed again. The weather, especially at night, turned sharply colder. The first major snowstorm occurred on the night of November 16 and 17. Much of the snow melted and consequently rivers such as the Ibar and the Toplica were swamped. Conditions also made it difficult for reconnaissance aircraft to keep flying. Although the occasional reconnaissance aircraft could get airborne, it was not sufficient. Thus Krafft, like Gallwitz earlier in the campaign, had to remind his soldiers of the importance of conducting reconnaissance.[56]

With the weather and terrain worsening, Mackensen and Seeckt did their utmost to bring this final attempt at trapping the Serbian forces to a successful conclusion. The Austro-Hungarian Tenth Mountain Brigade, part of Trollmann's Austro-Hungarian XIX Corps, was shifted to the German Alpine Corps sector on November 15 and placed under Krafft's command. Command was facilitated by the bringing forward of telephone lines to Kraljevo. Because of the scarcity of roads and shortages of transport, German divisions began to create ad hoc combined arms units from elements of a division's subordinate units. On November 19, 1915, for example, Estorff created a composite regiment drawn from various companies from the 103rd Infantry Division's three regiments. The temporary unit was placed under the command of Major Radermacher, commander of the 116th Infantry Regiment. The German Alpine Corps undertook similar arrangements. The logistical needs would be handled by mules. The old hussar also called for ever greater efforts to block the retreat route of even individual Serbian divisions.[57]

In the end, however, the efforts of Mackensen, Seeckt, and the forces under their command to bring about a final decisive battle and destruction of the Serbian army came to naught. The terrain was superbly suited to the kind of delaying defense conducted by the Serbian rearguards. To be sure, the number of prisoners and especially deserters shot up considerably. Daily prisoner hauls for divisions often reached into the thousands, although that also apparently included men of military age, dressed in civilian clothing, although some showed what they claimed to be discharge papers. Large amounts of abandoned equipment were found as well.[58]

The start of the final week of the campaign also brought about yet another dustup between Mackensen and Kövess. The old hussar's hard driving of his commanders and their troops was apparently taken by Kövess that Mackensen had regarded their efforts as insufficient. Kövess communicated his indignation to army group headquarters. On November 19, Seeckt told Kövess that Mackensen had not criticized the efforts of the troops, but also noted that the potential consequences of a complete success in Serbia demanded the highest degree of effort on the part of the Austro-Hungarian Third Army.[59]

As the Germans and their allies advanced, the Serbians retreated. Although the loss of Niš, Kragujevać, Kruševac, and Kraljevo had cost the Serbians a tremendous quantity of equipment and had made a retreat inevitable, the Serbian army retained its organizational integrity. Divisions still retained distinctive identities, even though by the third week of November these units had been severely reduced. On November 23 the Austro-Hungarian Third Army informed the German Alpine Corps that according to a captured Serbian officer, the Drina II Division and the Danube II Division, both part of the Serbian First Army had been reduced to about 4,500 and 3,600 men, respectively. Both divisions still had about 20 artillery pieces each and both units had sufficient quantities of ammunition.[60]

The retreat down the Ibar and Toplica Valleys on Priština was an agonizing one for the Serbians. First, the only goal for the Serbian government and army was survival. This, plus the general war weariness that had engulfed Serbia by the late autumn of 1915, served to demoralize a good many Serbian soldiers, who were then willing to surrender or desert. There were even some suicides. This sense of demoralization increased after a second attempt to break through the Bulgarian Second Army at Kačanik Pass on 20 November proved far too weak to be effective.[61]

Still, enough of the Serbian army remained battle worthy to allow the rearguards to hold off the oncoming forces of the Central powers. In some cases Serbian rearguards were able to employ artillery. As the Forty-Fifth Infantry Regiment (part of the 101st Infantry Division)—for example, approached Priština, it encamped at Sarban, just a few miles north of Priština, on the afternoon of November 22. Almost immediately after bivouacking, the regiment spent the rest of the afternoon taking Serbian artillery fire.[62]

The Serbian retreat was guided by two practical objectives. The first was to ensure the safety of the government, since the policy was to continue the war regardless of the outcome of the campaign. The safety of King Peter was of particular concern. The king had on some occasions gotten a bit too close to the front for comfort. Prince Alexander, the government and the high command made sure that the king was kept well away from the front.[63]

Since retreat meant avoiding major combat with Mackensen's forces, as Putnik's forces retreated down the Ibar and the Toplica toward Priština, they sought to lighten themselves. Thus guns, wagons and other baggage items were either abandoned along the road or ditched in the rivers. One of the more unusual items to be discarded was the archives of the Italian legation, thrown into the Ibar by the Italian minister to Serbia, Nicola Squitti.[64]

The Serbian armies reached Priština and Kosovo ahead of their pursuers. The Serbians had also taken a large number of Austro-Hungarian prisoners with them, and there was also a great many civilian refugees. The Serbian leaders, both military and political, then reconsidered its options. They were aware that several German divisions were in the process of withdrawing from Serbia. With that in mind, the Serbians had two courses open to them, namely fight or retreat. The option to fight appealed on a couple of levels. Making a final stand on the Field of Blackbirds resonated with Serbians from a historical and national standpoint. In addition, with smaller German forces to face, the prospect of making a successful defense seemed at least possible. More aggressive commanders such as Mišić, no doubt buoyed by the recent successful counterattack against the Bulgarians at Leskovac, wanted a full counteroffensive. This might also stimulate more action from the French and British. The idea of sending a personal appeal to King Victor Emanuel of Italy and Tsar Nicholas II was also considered, but rejected as premature until the safety of the army was assured.[65]

The other alternative was to continue the retreat to Prizren and from there across the mountains to the Adriatic coast. The two principal objectives were the ports of Scutari and Durazzo, with Alessio as a secondary destination. Once on the coast, Serbia's entente partners could evacuate them to a place where the army could rest and refit. The cause of Serbian nationalism would still have its bearer. Thus Putnik gave the order to retreat on November 22. The reasoning behind the decision was set forth in the official order published by the Serbian high command on 25 November:

> The only way out of this grave situation is a retreat to the Adriatic coast. There our army will be reorganized, furnished with food, arms, munitions, clothing and all other necessities which our allies will send us, and we shall again be a fact with which our allies must reckon. The nation has not lost its being, it will continue to exist even though on foreign soil, so long as the ruler, the government and the army are there, no matter what the strength of the army may be.[66]

The publication of the communique only confirmed what was an already established fact. The Serbian armies had already retreated past Mitrovica and

Priština when the order was issued, moving toward Prizren. Although Mišić, Jurišić-Sturm, and some others initially balked at the order, Prince Alexander overruled them. Brutal reality also brought them around to acceptance of the order to retreat.[67]

In order to make the retreat work, the Serbian forces had to take three routes. The Serbian First, Second, and Third Armies went via Peć and then traced an arc running from northwest to southwest, through Montenegrin territory, skirting the northern border of Albania. The route would terminate at the Albanian port of Scutari. The rest of the Serbian forces would start from Prizren and march directly west. Once across the Vizier's Bridge, the troops who had retreated from Macedonia would continue west, through Albania, ultimately to Alessio. The Timok Group would also continue to move south and the west through Albania to Durrazzo.[68]

The final Serbian retreat began on November 24, 1915. Thus the Serbians were able to evade Mackensen's final encirclement effort. With the Ibar Valley road too congested, Kövess directed part of the Alpine Corps, plus the Austro-Hungarian Tenth Mountain Brigade, to move against Novi Pazar. From there, the German and Austro-Hungarian alpine troops could potentially interrupt the northern retreat route at Ribarić, on the Upper Ibar River. Meanwhile the Sixty-Second Infantry Division and the XIX Corps pressed into Montenegro. The rest of the German Alpine Corps and the Austro-Hungarian VIII Corps converged on Mitrovica.[69]

As the German and Bulgarian forces closed in on Priština, there was one more brief change in the command arrangements. As OHL had proposed some sort of reorganization of the X Reserve Corps, command of the forces on the verge of reaching Priština was given back to Winckler and the IV Reserve Corps headquarters. Kosch was somewhat irritated by this, but admitted to his wife frankly that "there is not much left to do."[70]

The final major acts of the campaign played out on November 23 and 24. The Austro-Hungarian Fifty-Ninth Infantry Division reached Mitrovica on November 23. The same day the IV Reserve Corps and the Bulgarian Ninth Division, having fended off a last Serbian counterattack, reached the Field of Blackbirds and Priština, securing both the next day. Large numbers of prisoners and a good deal of booty was taken in both places, as well as in Novi Pazar.[71]

The ultimate prize that Mackensen and Seeckt sought, however, eluded them. Prisoner statements indicated that the Serbian forces had retreated to Prizren and headed toward the Adriatic coast from there. Although a pursuit to Prizren was conducted that was left largely to the Bulgarians. Conditions would simply not support the use of large forces. The IV Reserve Corps in Priština had to go on half rations. The Austro-Hungarian Tenth Mountain Brigade found its route south from Ribarić blocked by a 4,921 foot high mountain with a completely iced over track as the only way through. The brigade had already lost 30 men who had frozen to death in the harsh conditions.

Confronted by these stark realities, Mackensen declared an end to the campaign on November 24, 1915.[72]

During the advance into old Serbia in November, the soldiers of the Central powers met several types of people in addition to their armed Serbian opponents. The first were the field hospitals set up by the Red Cross prior to the campaign. While the similar establishments set up by the other entente powers decided to leave Serbia once it became clear that the river lines could not be held, the people at Red Cross facilities such as the one Elsie Corbett worked in decided to stay.[73] Their belief that that they would be accorded proper treatment by Mackensen's troops proved well founded. On November 10, the Austro-Hungarians took charge of the hospital, filled with Serbian wounded. Corbett noted that, at least here, the Austrian troops were well behaved.[74]

When the Austro-Hungarian troops reached Elsie Corbett's hospital, one of the first things they did was to release the Austro-Hungarian prisoners who had been pressed into service at the hospital by the Serbians. Over the course of November, Austro-Hungarian, German, and Bulgarian soldiers increasingly ran across groups of prisoners, mainly Austro-Hungarians, who had either been released by the Serbians when they retreated or who had escaped captivity. The largest single release was at Priština, where some 2,000 prisoners, mostly Austro-Hungarians along with some Germans, were liberated.[75]

In addition to the prisoners they captured or liberated, Mackensen's soldiers also met large numbers of civilians. These were of two types. The first were Serbian civilian refugees who had fled their homes when the war came calling. Regimental histories often noted the appearance of columns of vehicles, drawn by horses or more commonly oxen, carrying women, old men, and children, showing white sheet or cloth. Although there had been only rare instances of civilian sniping at soldiers, the Germans took no chances. Such columns were regularly checked and any weapons found were confiscated. A good many deserters were also separated out and taken prisoner.[76]

The civilians who had remained in their homes were friendly. They seemed glad to see that the soldiers were Germans. The Austro-Hungarians had already established a reputation for cruelty and the Bulgarians were especially feared.[77] Soldiers from the Fifty-Second Reserve Infantry Regiment (part of Moser's 107th Infantry Division) near Kruševac recalled being invited into a home by the "white haired patriarch of the family." Once friendly intentions had been established, the soldiers were invited to table and other family members appeared with the traditional Slavic symbols of hospitality, namely bread and salt, along with fresh water. Slivovitz and plum brandy appeared soon after and requests for butter and eggs, communicated by hand gestures, resulted in the delivery of them. German offers of payment were rejected and the homeowner then escorted the soldiers to his property line and bade them farewell.[78]

Serbians who lived in isolated circumstances in the mountains presented a truly alien appearance to German soldiers. Captain Max Graf Armansperg of the Bavarian Life Regiment noted the primitive conditions in such abodes. Particularly noteworthy to Armansperg was that water was still kept in animal skins, "just like in the time of Abraham."[79]

For the Germans, the most exotic was the Muslim population within old Serbia. This group was especially numerous in Priština, an old Turkish city. The expectation that the Muslim population would welcome the Central powers troops turned out to be justified. The Muslim population of Serbia had been subject to all manner of mistreatment at the hands of the Serbian Orthodox majority during the Balkan Wars. Thus Muslims were happy to see the Germans and even the Austrians were welcomed.[80]

After Priština fell, German and Bulgarian troops were quartered, at least briefly, in the city. The 146th Regiment was situated in the Turkish quarter. Captain Behrends tried the Turkish coffee and found it very much to his dislike. Units quartered in Muslim villages noted the picturesque appearance of the older men with their turbans and the younger men who preferred the fez. Of particular curiosity were the carefully secured rooms in houses with the sign "Harem" over the doors. Austro-Hungarian troops had similar experiences, which provided a welcome break from the rigors of the Russian or Italian fronts.[81]

While the exhausted troops enjoyed a brief break after the rigors of the campaign, the commanders basked in the success of the operation. Mackensen was once again the man of the moment. The old hussar received the thanks of Francis Joseph. The elderly emperor, who had developed real affection for Mackensen during the latter's visit to Vienna in September 1915, conveyed his personal gratitude to Mackensen on November 28, 1915. Ever the diplomat, Mackensen replied the same day, expressing his thanks to Francis Joseph, while also recognizing the "brilliant" services of Kövess and Gallwitz.[82]

Likewise Wilhelm II was delighted to see one of his favorite commanders do well yet again. On November 27 the Kaiser conveyed his heartfelt thanks to Macksensen. In addition to that, Wilhelm appointed Mackensen as the proprietary colonel of the 129th (Third West Prussian) Infantry Regiment, an unusual honor normally reserved for members of a royal family. Both Mackensen and the regiment expressed delight at this. The Kaiser also sent a personal message to King Wilhelm II of Württemberg, commending the performance of the Twenty-Sixth Infantry Division. Meanwhile, in keeping with the niceties of coalition warfare, Kövess sent a gracious message to the German XXII Reserve Corps, thanking Falkenhayn's troops for their sterling service in the campaign.[83]

Within the army group's headquarters the atmosphere also lightened up. One day after the close of the campaign, prior to lunch with all the officers of the operations section, Mackensen stood before them and delivered some gracious remarks, thanking Jansa for his good work. He then awarded Jansa the Iron Cross Second Class and drank a toast to the young captain.

Jansa, both surprised and gratified, later noted rather enviously that German commanders had much more latitude in regards to giving awards than their much more bureaucratic Austro-Hungarian counterparts.[84]

The campaign was over. In less than two months, Mackensen and Seeckt had succeeded where the Austro-Hungarians under Potiorek had failed three times the year before. The price paid for putting Serbia out of the war was, by the standards of World War I, not terribly costly. The forces of the Central powers suffered about 67,000 casualties. Over half of these were from the Bulgarian First and Second Armies. Austro-Hungarian casualties totaled 18,000.[85] The Austrian official history did not give a more detailed breakdown, but presumably the lion's share of the losses were taken by Scheuchenstuel's VIII Corps. The corps had been involved in the storming of the Kalemegdan castle at Belgrade, and it later bore the onus of the Austro-Hungarian part of the advance on Kragujevać and later struggled across the Kopaonik Mountains on Mitrovica.

German casualties were the lightest, totaling about 12,000. As is usually the case, the losses were unevenly distributed across the four corps involved, but concentrated in the infantry. In the XXII Reserve Corps, for example, the 208th Reserve Infantry Regiment, part of the Forty-Fouth Reserve Infantry Division, suffered 1,295 casualties, although only a small number were killed. The 202nd Reserve Infantry Regiment of the Forty-Third Reserve Infantry Division suffered not quite as severely, losing about 800 officers and men.[86]

The same pattern held true for Gallwitz's three corps. In the IV Reserve Corps, for example, the 129th Infantry Regiment and the 122nd Fusiliers, part of Esch's 105th Infantry Division, suffered 633 and 728 casualties, respectively. Likewise the 227th Reserve Infantry Regiment of the 107th Infantry Division suffered 649 casualties. The combined casualties of the three regiments comprised over 16 percent of the total German losses. The Bavarian Eleventh Infantry Division, which suffered over 2,000 casualties, took the majority of the early in the operation, during the fight to secure the bridgehead and the subsequent advance to Požarevac.[87] By comparison most of Kosch's X Reserve Corps escaped relatively lightly. The Thirty-Second Infantry Regiment, for example, suffered a total of 473 casualties, while the Forty-Fifth Infantry Regiment took 547 casualties, concentrated in the First and Second Battalions.[88] Lochow's III Corps also took relatively light casualties. The Twentieth Infantry Regiment, part of the Sixth Infantry Division, took some 600 casualties in the campaign, although half of them were incurred on one day, October 18, when the Regiment stormed the Serbian position at Mala Krsna.[89] Given the strategic objective that was gained, the Central powers did not pay too high a price. The regimental historian of the 202nd Reserve Infantry Regiment noted that by the standards of the western front, the regiment's 800 casualties were relatively light for the gains that were made.[90]

Although the three attempts to envelop and destroy the Serbian armies had failed, the strategic objective had been obtained. The geography of the Central powers then matched its name; Germany, Austria-Hungary, Bulgaria, and Turkey controlled a solid swath of territory in the middle of the Eurasian land-mass. A military campaign, however, is not always a cleanly cut thing, particularly in a multifront war. Further strategic decisions would have to be made by both sides in the aftermath of the overrunning of Serbia.

Erich von Falkenhayn, Chief of the German General Staff in 1915. (Bain Collection, Library of Congress)

August von Mackensen, a pre-war photograph. (Bain Collection, Library of Congress)

Franz Baron Conrad von Hötzendorf, Austro-Hungarian Chief of the General. (Library of Congress)

The uneasy allies, Kaiser Wilhelm II and Conrad. (Bain Collection, Library of Congress)

Max von Gallwitz, commander of the German Eleventh Army. (Bain Collection, Library of Congress)

Robert Kosch, commander of the German X Reserve Corps and ardent photography buff. (Bain Collection, Library of Congress)

Ewald von Lochow, commander of the German III Corps. (Bain Collection, Library of Congress)

Voivode Radomir Putnik, commander of Serbia's armies. (Bain Collection, Library of Congress)

Mackensen visiting an Austro-Hungarian unit. (Bain Collection, Library of Congress)

German ground crewman attaching a bomb to an aircraft, 1915. Two things of note here are the small size of the bomb and the primitive system of attachment. (Bain Collection, Library of Congress)

Austro-Hungarian heavy howitzer. Weapons like this were Mackensen's trump card against the Serbian river defenses. (Bain Collection, Library of Congress)

Bulgarian heavy artillery. (Bain Collection, Library of Congress)

A sign of desperation: a 12-year-old Serbian artillerist, 1915. (Bain Collection, Library of Congress)

Belgrade before the war. (Bain Collection, Library of Congress)

German field artillery piece in action. (Bain Collection, Library of Congress)

A German field telephone unit in action. (Bain Collection, Library of Congress)

Serbian soldiers retreating through the mountains towards the Adriatic coast. (Bain Collection, Library of Congress)

Serbian prisoners crossing the Save into Austria-Hungary. (Bain Collection, Library of Congress)

Captured Serbian guns. (Bain Collection, Library of Congress)

Chapter 8

Aftermath: December 1915–January 1916

"The drama is over, as a Serbian army scarcely exists . . . "

Adolf Wild von Hohenborn, November 27, 1915[1]

"Everything must be done to preserve the remnants of the Serbian Army . . . "

Aristide Briand, January 1916[2]

"For us Bulgarians the war is really over. We have all we want."

Unidentified Bulgarian general officer, 1916[3]

"Divergent goals. Verdun-Italy."

Karl von Kageneck, April 27, 1916[4]

The aftermath of the campaign began with a tragedy of the war that was at the same time one of the best known and one of the least known. After Mackensen called an official halt to the campaign, the final stages of the pursuit to Prizren was handled by the Bulgarians, taking booty and prisoners as they advanced. Meanwhile the remnants of the Serbian armies, plus civilians and prisoners, struggled across the mountains through Montenegro and Albania to the Adriatic coast. Perhaps the most iconic image of the retreat was Putnik. The aged commander, still seriously ill with influenza, was carried in a sedan chair. The detail of soldiers assigned to this duty was changed every 15 minutes.[5]

While the column that took the northernmost route through Montenegrin Territory had to contend with the harsh environment, the columns going through Albania had a far worse time. First, before going their separate ways the Serbians had to cross as a single column over the Vizier's Bridge, a 600-foot-long structure that spanned the deeply gorged Drin River. The old structure, built under Turkish rule, was in considerable disrepair, and in some places the roadway was nothing more than loosely placed wooden planks that by this time had a thick coat of ice. Going into the river was lethal to any but the strongest and fastest swimmers.[6]

Once across the bridge, the column divided into two, with each taking its own route to its respective destination. The terrain was mountainous, the weather cold and snowy, and the Serbians were attacked by Albanian tribesmen. Eventually, however, the Serbian columns reached the Adriatic coast. Tired, cold, and emaciated, Serbian soldiers, civilians, politicians, and academics clustered around the ports of Scutari, Alessio, and Durazzo. They presented the appearance of walking skeletons.[7]

Far worse off were the Austro-Hungarian prisoners the Serbians had taken with them. While the retreat to the coast may have been Serbia's "Golgotha," for the Austro-Hungarian prisoners it was a death march. At the start of the campaign Serbia held about 70,000 Austro-Hungarian prisoners. Mackensen's forces had been able to free an unknown number, but one that ran well into the thousands. The rest were taken by the Serbians. Thousands died from starvation, exposure, and mistreatment at the hands of the Serbians, Montenegrins, Albanians, or any combination of the three. Only 23,000 reached the coast.[8] In retrospect, the decision to take the prisoners with them (and it is difficult to figure out who made the decision) could be considered cruel, if not criminal. Such behavior only further enflamed Austro-Hungarian feeling against the Serbians, as it confirmed the image that Austro-Hungarians held of Serbians as cruel, primitive, and even bestial.[9]

Once on the coast, the Serbians took stock. At the start of the campaign, the Serbian armies numbered anywhere from 250,000 to 270,000 men. A major mobilization of available manpower brought in hundreds of thousands more. Casualties had been severe. Some 94,000 officers and men had been killed or wounded. Mackensen's forces had captured another 124,000, and another 70,000 wounded Serbian soldiers were also taken prisoner. The common view is that perhaps 140,000 soldiers reached the coast, although some recent scholarship suggests that the number was lower, maybe 110,000. Many of them were unarmed. Amazingly, the Serbian forces had brought out 72 guns, all light pieces, but that was more a symbolic achievement than anything.[10]

The Serbians taken prisoner faced a grim fate. Generally they were moved to prisoner camps in both Austria-Hungary and Germany. Serbia did not have its own Red Cross chapter, so its prisoners did not have access to the aid the Red Cross could provide to British and French prisoners. Given the poor state many soldiers were in when they were captured, it is not surprising that the death rate for Serbian prisoners in German hands was twice that of British, French, or Belgian prisoners.[11]

Once on the coast the first matter at hand was getting food to the starving Serbians. One problem was that the northernmost unloading points for the Serbians on the Adriatic coast, San Giovanni di Medua and Alessio, were within easy reach of the Adriatic Fleet of the Austro-Hungarian Navy, which was based at Pola. Commanded by Admiral Anton Haus, the Adriatic Fleet counted 43 ships of all types, including four modern dreadnoughts.[12] Italian worries seemed confirmed when a sortie by the Adriatic Fleet into the Otranto Strait on the night of November 22-23 sank two Italian ships carrying supplies for the Serbs.[13]

Nonetheless, the entente powers organized the bringing of relief to the Serbians and soon after their evacuation Troubridge ended up being put in charge of the effort. Having shared many of the hardships of the campaign, he was trusted by the Serbians, and Troubridge was fluent in both Serbian and French.[14]

Troubridge directed Serbian civilians to San Giovanni di Medua, while the soldiers and Austro-Hungarian prisoners were directed to Durazzo. The evacuations began in January 1916. Pašić initially wanted the Serbian army to be sent to Bizerte in Tunisia for rest, refitting, and training. The army, however, was removed to Corfu, with the transfer being completed on April 5, 1916. Many of the men taken to Corfu required months to recover from their recent ordeal. A number of them died.[15]

To be sure, there were some problems with the evacuation. Italian military representatives subjected Peter I to a number of humiliations in Durazzo. Thus when he arrived in Brindisi, Peter refused to stay as a guest of Italian king Vittorio Emmanuele III preferring instead to go on to Salonika. The placing of the Serbian forces on Corfu was done without the consent of the Greek government, worsening an already tense relationship. Troubridge and his Serbian allies were fortunate in that the Adriatic Fleet made no major attempt to interfere with either the resupply operation or the evacuations. To be sure, a few raids were ordered by Haus, and a few ships were sunk, but the Austro-Hungarians employed only light surface ships, submarines, and aircraft and only in a half-hearted manner.[16]

Once the army had reached safety of the coast, and was finally situated on Corfu, the Serbian leadership immediately engaged in internal recriminations. Given the fact that Serbia had been overrun and was now under Austro-Hungarian or Bulgarian occupation, and that the army had taken staggering losses, someone had to shoulder the blame. Ultimately that role fell to the military leaders. Prince Alexander had dismissed Putnik in December 1915. Putnik's deputy Živko Pavlović was relieved a month later. Mišić was also sidelined, as much from illness as for connection with the recent disaster. The king had the good sense to steer clear of the squabbling.[17]

As to the Serbian army itself, after a period of rest and refitting in Corfu, it would be added in the form of six divisions (120,000 men) to Sarrail's forces at

Salonika. While there, the reconstituted Serbian force not only provided valuable reinforcement to Sarrail when neither France nor Britain had troops to spare but also served as a magnet for military age Serbian men fleeing occupied Serbia and for Slavic deserters from the Austro-Hungarian army.[18]

While the Serbians retreated from Serbia to the Adriatic coast, most of the German forces withdrew from Serbia. Given the paucity of roads, German divisions often found themselves having to retrace their steps back to the rivers they had crossed at the start of the campaign. Thus the German XXII Reserve Corps moved from the Ibar Valley and Kraljevo back to Belgrade.[19] Lochow's III Corps, moved back to Kevevara and Gradiste. They crossed back over the Danube on bridges built by Austro-Hungarian engineers.[20] The Bavarian Eleventh Infantry Division moved back to Gradiste via Požarevac, while the 107th Infantry Division went to Kevevara via Semendria.[21]

Some German forces would have to enjoy the civilized pleasures of the Balkans for a while more. The Alpine Corps moved back, first to Kruševac, and then to Leskovac. The 101st left a regiment in Priština and marched to Niš, where it was joined by 105th Infantry Division, which likewise had placed a regiment in Üsküb. Gallwitz's headquarters moved to Üsküb, later joined by the IV Reserve Corps headquarters. Kosch's X Reserve Corps headquarters moved back into southern Hungary. Mackensen's own headquarters completed the shifting of forces with its own move from Kragujevać to Niš on December 20.[22]

The German units, be they exiting from Serbia or merely shifting position within the theater, found the going extremely difficult, as the harsh Balkan winter was setting in. Temperatures at times fell into the teens or even single digits (in Fahrenheit), and weather systems were often punctuated with heavy snowfall. The roads were thus covered with a thick coating of snow and ice. Drifts piled the snow up to six feet or higher. The horses were not shod for ice, and often slipped in the treacherous conditions. Soldiers likewise were often not equipped with proper footwear.[23]

Having to retrace one's steps caused other problems as well. Passing back across areas that had been marched over and fought through, soldiers often came upon the detritus of war. Roads were littered with hundreds of horse corpses and broken or abandoned equipment. Columns of prisoners and returning refugees also clogged routes. Forage was also hard to come by.[24] Once the units that were moving out of Serbia had completed their marches back to the rivers, life really improved. The XXII Reserve Corps, quartered in Belgrade, enjoyed the sights. After all, when it came to Serbia in the words of one regimental history, "the land was not without its natural beauty."[25] The commanders of the Forty-Third and Forty-Fourth Reserve Divisions were invited to the opening of bridge over the Save, reestablishing communications between Belgrade and Hungary. The one rather embarrassing aspect was that the invitation sent by the Austro-Hungarian Military Governor of Belgrade, Generalmajor Josef Ritter Röhn von

Vrbas, misspelled Dorrer's name, rendering it as "Richard Dorer." Whoever read it first in Dorrer's headquarters put an exclamation point next to the name.[26]

The regiments that were redeploying out of the Balkans were generally happy to be out of the area. One soldier in the III Corps who served in a field hospital observed the exit from Serbia by penning an 18 stanza long poem about how awful the campaign was.[27] In addition, the units that crossed the rivers back into Hungary enjoyed warm welcomes afforded to them by the local population. The overrunning of Serbia had moved the war well away from them. Thus, German troops reentering Hungary were very popular. German units in both Hungary and Serbia also received about three weeks' worth of mail, as the Army Group's prohibition on the sending and receiving of mail had been lifted late in the campaign.[28]

With the campaign now over, a number of the regiments were able to receive replacements, with numbers ranging from just a few hundred to over a thousand. The regiments also refitted, received new equipment, or got back material that had been exchanged before the campaign. With replacements received, the regiments incorporated lessons from the recently concluded campaign. Time was also spent in training and focusing on marksmanship. To liven up Christmas or New Year's celebrations, regiments would hold hand grenade throwing competitions.[29] Once these activities had been completed and the units given some rest, they could be redeployed to other theaters. The details regarding these matters were worked out by Hentsch and the Austro-Hungarian officers responsible for the rear areas.[30]

Units that were posted in Niš enjoyed a pleasant experience as the Germans got on very well with the Bulgarians, who were most hospitable. Mackensen's headquarters also issued orders regarding the currency exchange rate, and promulgated caps on how many goods German soldiers could buy in Bulgaria. Regulations were also issued regarding the behavior of German soldiers on Bulgarian Territory. Efforts were also made to find Germans and Bulgarians who had facility with both languages.[31]

The regiments posted in Serbia had a rather different experience. Although there had been very few instances of guerilla activity during the campaign, troops were still directed to keep a wary eye on prisoners and refugees. Weapons and ammunition had been found among refugees, and was confiscated immediately. Troops were also told that prisoners were to be kept under a close watch before being dispatched to various collection points. Relations between German troops and Serbian civilians in places like Priština were peaceful but tense. There was also considerable concern on the part of the Germans over the prevalence of disease, most notably typhus.[32]

With combat operations concluded, a large occupied territory now had to be organized. Since the Germans had no desire to administer the area, and there was no Serbian government with which to negotiate, the task of administration would be left to the Austrians and Bulgarians. Boundary lines had been set at the meeting at Pless on November 6. In January 1916, the Austro-Hungarian army established the Military General Government of Serbia (MGG/S), under Feldmarschalleutnant Johann Ulrich Graf von Salis-Seewies, with Colonel Oskar Gallinek as his chief of staff.[33] The Bulgarians set up a military administration in their area. The one thing OHL was interested in was the railroad. Falkenhayn had gotten his way on this issue at the November 6 meeting at Pless, and that arrangement was left in place. German and Austro-Hungarian military railroad companies were still busy rebuilding demolished rail bridges. Control and operation of the railroad was left to Mackensen's headquarters, which governed traffic and set schedules. Mackensen's headquarters also issued similar regulations for river traffic.[34]

While the Serbians sorted out their own affairs, the Austro-Hungarians and Bulgarians organized their newly won possessions, and the Germans shifted their forces, both sides had a number of matters to reconsider in the aftermath of the Serbian campaign. The first matter for the Entente to consider was the future of the effort at Gallipoli. The August 1915 attack from the beachhead plus the Suvla Bay landing had not produced the desired results. With the Germans now able literally to stuff Turkey with heavy artillery and ammunition, the prospects for any kind of success coming from Gallipoli now seemed ever more remote. With the appointment of Sir William Robertson as the new Chief of the Imperial General Staff, the "westerners" in both Britain and France were now firmly in control of the direction of the war. That meant that the western front would assume the primacy of place in regards to strategic priorities. Thus the Gallipoli operation would be abandoned, starting in December 1915 and continuing through January 1916.[35]

The other major decision regarded the fate of the Army of the Orient. With the Balkans now reduced to a sideshow, some in France and Britain wanted the front shut down, so all available resources could be concentrated on the primary theater, the western front. The Superior Council of National Defense, however, ultimately decided to maintain Sarrail's forces in Greece. It would force the Central powers to maintain forces in the Balkans to guard against an offensive against Bulgaria. Finally, an entente presence in the area could still influence as yet uncommitted countries, the most important of which was Romania. Although the new military leadership in Britain also wanted to abandon the Salonika operation, a British contingent of two corps under Mahon (then promoted to lieutenant general) in Sarrail's forces were maintained in the interests of sustaining Anglo-French comity.[36]

The Central powers also had their issues to consider. The first of these was the prospect of follow-on operations. For this purpose a meeting was held at Pless on November 27, 1915. Conrad wanted to pursue operations against Montenegro and Albania. He was supported in this by Burián and the annexationists at the Ballplatz, over the concerns of Tisza. At least in regards to Montenegro, Falkenhayn regarded an invasion as understandable, even if he did not support it. Montenegro had involved its troops in combat operations against Austria-Hungary during the recent campaign. Also, the occupation of Montenegro would eliminate it as a potential base of operations for the entente. Finally, possession of Montenegro would assure the security of the Austro-Hungarian naval base at Cattaro, where German submarines were also based. Falkenhayn regarded Albania as not worth the effort or the troops required to take it, given other strategic priorities.[37]

When the entente forces retreated back into Greece, OHL requested that the Bulgarian Second Army not cross the Greek border. The Bulgarians were happy to oblige. The status of Bulgaria was one of the factors that had an impact on further action by the Central powers in the region. With the winding down of active operations in Serbia, Bulgaria had achieved all of its objectives. Obtaining Bulgarian participation for operations against Sarrail's forces at Salonika would be problematic, to say the least. With the winter coming on, however, the issue of further offensive operations into Greece could wait. One thing that could not wait, however, was Conrad's offensive into Montenegro and Albania. This was done by Kövess's Austro-Hungarian Third Army. Kövess was perfectly happy to do this. In late November, Kövess wrote a letter to Conrad demanding that his army be released from Mackensen's operational control, and subject solely to AOK. Kövess's principal complaint was that neither Mackensen nor Seeckt understood the difficulties of mountain warfare. Also he complained that German officers in general were not cognizant of the issues that faced a multiethnic army.[38]

While there is no reason to doubt that Kövess believed in what he had written, there may also have been a personal aspect to his letter. Relations between Kövess and his German superiors had become somewhat strained. Mackensen and Seeckt had no qualms about dressing down a general when they thought it necessary. In the case of Kövess, this had occurred several times. First, there was the shift of the Austro-Hungarian XIX Corps' crossing point, authorized by the Third Army but severely criticized by the Army Group. Second was the tiff between Kövess and Mackensen over the conduct of Falkenhayn's XXII Corps. Finally, there was the matter of the blistering message from Army Group Mackensen to Kövess regarding his perceived lack of urgency on November 9. Generals don't like getting chewed out, be it in person or by teletype.

Whatever the reason, Kövess got his way. Conrad removed Kövess from Mackensen's operational control on December 20, 1915, and turned the latter's forces into Montenegro and Albania. The move certainly caught Mackensen by surprise. The old hussar had been in Vienna at the invitation of Francis Joseph, who wanted to honor Mackensen on the occasion of the latter's 66th birthday. Prior to Kövess's move into Montenegro and Albania, Mackensen's forces consisted of the Austro-Hungarian Third Army, the German IV Reserve Corps plus one other German division. Conrad's removal of Kövess from Mackensen's command now reduced the army group to essentially the German Eleventh Army, which now consisted of a reinforced corps.[39]

The scope of this work does not require any detailed description of the Austro-Hungarian offensive into Montenegro and Albania. The Montenegrin forces, already in poor shape, could not do much to stop the Austro-Hungarian advance. By January 13, 1916, the Montenegrin capital of Cetinje was in Austro-Hungarian hands. Montenegro's King Nikita I and the government, like their Serbian neighbors, refused to surrender unconditionally and fled to Scutari. From there they went to Italy. A military government was established under Feldmarschalleutnant Viktor Weber. Likewise much of Albania was occupied without too much trouble.[40]

Conrad had his victory, but it came at a tremendous cost. If the Austro-Hungarian move surprised Mackensen, it outraged Falkenhayn. The Bulgarians were also angry. Any change in command arrangements required the approval of the Bulgarian high command, and Conrad had acted unilaterally. The Bulgarians were also suspicious of Austro-Hungarian aims in the Balkans. The relationship between Falkenhayn and Conrad, uneasy at the best of times, now deteriorated completely. Falkenhayn summoned Cramon to a meeting at Oderberg and "without mincing words," informed Cramon that he no longer trusted AOK and would not defend Austro-Hungarian conduct to the Bulgarians, a position supported by Sofia. Bulgarian dissatisfaction reached a point where Ferdinand returned all of his Austro-Hungarian medals to Vienna. These tensions even extended to matters as trivial as protocols observed at a dinner at Mackensen's headquarters. After AOK prohibited transit of German weapons through its territory to Bulgaria, Ferdinand actually threatened a declaration of war.[41]

The people most caught in the military and diplomatic crossfire were Mackensen and Seeckt. Jansa noted the delicate situation they were in, given that they still had to work with the Austro-Hungarians and Bulgarians on an everyday basis.[42] It was probably most fortunate for OHL that the two principal German officers on the scene were Mackensen and Seeckt. The old hussar, with his extensive experience at the Hohenzollern court and with the intricacies of coalition warfare, excelled at this kind of military diplomacy. Mackensen had developed a good relationship with the Austro-Hungarians, as noted before. In late December he went to Sofia to brief Ferdinand on the conduct and result of the recently concluded campaign. Since the military convention had specified Mackensen as the commander of the operation, he already had a good starting position. Mackensen was able to develop a good relationship with his Bulgarian counterparts. Seeckt, who was also endowed with a fair degree of diplomatic balm, likewise did his share of assuaging frayed personalities. Thus at least planning for an offensive against Salonika could continue.[43]

Over late 1915 and into early 1916 discussion and study of the prospects for an offensive against Salonika continued. Ultimately, however, they came to naught. The key items, as both Mackensen and Seeckt realized, were heavy artillery and troops; both were lacking. Although rail communications had been established, getting guns and ammunition forward from the railroad in sufficient quantities through the terrain was problematic, given the recent experiences in Serbia. In regard to troops, the German presence in the theater was now very small. With active operations in the west in the offing, Mackensen and Seeckt could not expect much in the way of reinforcements. The only logical candidate to supply troops was Bulgaria. Seeckt did not believe that Bulgaria would be willing to commit additional resources needed for such an operation, and his skepticism was justified. Gallwitz, who lacked Mackensen's flair for coalition warfare, had little taste for working with the Bulgarians, and let Mackensen know it via Seeckt.[44] Thus the only result was the erection of a defensive front along the Greek border.

Perhaps the most positive diplomatic result of the campaign concerned Romania. There had been considerable concern about the possibility of Romanian intervention in the spring of 1915, especially after the death of pro Austro-Hungarian king Carol in October 1914. Prime Minister Ion Brătianu pursued a policy much more oriented toward the entente. Victories in Russia and now the overrunning of Serbia, however, forced Brătianu and King Ferdinand to take a much more circumspect position.[45]

While the issue of Salonika festered, activity at Mackensen's headquarters continued, although there were some changes. The most notable was the departure of Bock for an assignment in the west. Mackensen kept in touch with him over the years, all the way into World War II, when Bock, himself now a Generalfeldmarschall, was one of Adolf Hitler's paladins. Bock's replacement was Lieutenant Colonel Völkers, a "very precise officer" who checked every order before it went out.[46]

With active operations over for the time being at least, some relaxation was in order. Seeckt was joined by his wife and the couple took Christmas leave in Budapest and Vienna. The ever sensitive Jansa was irritated that Seeckt was able to drive around both places at a time when gasoline was severely rationed. Meanwhile, Mackensen and his staff celebrated Christmas in Niš. Jansa was touched when Mackensen gave him a beautiful personally engraved silver cigarette case.[47]

On January 18, 1916, Wilhelm II came to visit, joined by Ferdinand of Bulgaria, along with Bulgarian Crown Prince Boris. Although the dinner at Mackensen's headquarters had its awkward moments owing to Austro-Hungarian complaints over the seating arrangements, the visit went off smoothly. The following day the Kaiser visited Belgrade, where Eugen Falkenhayn briefed him on the recent campaign, and the German XXII Reserve Corps was paraded before Wilhelm, Falkenhayn, and his division commanders.[48] In some ways, this marked the end of the Serbian campaign.

The aftermath of the campaign in Serbia abounded in ironies. The Austro-Hungarians could take some grim satisfaction in seeing the Serbian "pack of murderers" crushed. The campaign, however, could only be undertaken with a massive German presence, thus confirming Austria-Hungary's status as a junior partner, and raising fears of an expansion of German influence in the area.[49]

The final irony was the effect of victory on the Central powers in terms of the higher aspects of coalition warfare. In the spring of 1915, when an existential crisis loomed for both Austria-Hungary and Turkey, the Germans and the Austro-Hungarians entered into a period of perhaps their closest cooperation in the war. Victories on the eastern front and Serbia in 1915, along with the addition of Bulgaria to the alliance, put the Central powers in a very strong position militarily. At the same time, however, the removal of the immediate threats allowed the Central powers to enter into all manner of acrimonious discussions concerning war aims that served to damage the Central powers as an alliance. Personal antagonisms between Conrad and Falkenhayn resulted in a nearly total breakdown of communication, at a time when much closer cooperation was needed.[50] Thus, in a sense one could say that by early 1916 the Central powers had become a victim of its own success.

Chapter 9

Assessments

"The main mission of corps air detachments is to work with the staff officers of the heavy artillery in order to observe and note the effect of heavy rounds."

Army Group Temesvár, September 25, 1915[1]

"By the time the last shell is fired, the infantry must be in the enemy trenches."

Hans von Seeckt, 1915[2]

"Telephone communication is to be established ... "

German Alpine Corps, November 17, 1915[3]

By the standards of 1915, the campaign in Serbia was warfare at its most mobile. In the space of about two months, and in the most difficult terrain and weather imaginable, and against a competent opponent, Mackensen's forces had overrun Serbia. The troops under the old hussar's command had traveled a long way. The Bavarian Life Infantry Regiment, part of Krafft's Alpine Corps, from its starting point in Weisskirchen to its final objective of Obrez, covered over 320 miles. The 202nd Reserve Infantry Regiment of Falkenhayn's XXII Reserve Corps covered over 93 miles, to provide just two examples.[4]

Why had Mackensen's forces succeeded where the Austro-Hungarians had failed? The first for the success of the Central powers was the circumstances under which the campaign was mounted. Although the Serbian army had won significant victories in 1914, success came at a price of 120,000, including 22,000 dead. This combined with a virulent outbreak of typhus during the winter and spring of 1915 served to further weaken the Serbian forces.

German and Austro-Hungarian intelligence recognized correctly that the Serbian army could not sustain major casualties.[5]

In this regard, Putnik did about as well as he could have, given the situation he faced. Although severely ill himself, Putnik was able to see clearly the courses open to him as the campaign developed. He was also able to restrain the rather reckless impulses of his more aggressive subordinates, most notably Mišić. Unfortunately for Putnik, his prudence won him no favors. Blamed for the army's collapse, he was dismissed from his position after the evacuation. Sadly, Putnik never saw Serbia again. He died in Nice, France, on May 17, 1917. Ironically, command of the army eventually devolved to Mišić, after he recovered from illness and put some distance between him and the recent campaign.[6]

Another fortunate circumstance for Mackensen and Seeckt was the timing of the campaign. Everyone was aware of the impending arrival of the *Kossava*. The weather held just long enough, however, to allow the armies of Kövess and Gallwitz to execute the river crossings and establish solid bridge-heads before the *Kossava* set in. Had the storm set in earlier than expected, the feasibility of the entire project, at least in 1915, could have been called into question. When the German Third Field Artillery Regiment, for example, recrossed the Danube in its exit from Serbia in the middle of November, the Brandenburgers used a long pontoon bridge. The artillerymen noticed that after a month of heavy rains, the Danube was now over a mile wide. In addition, all of the firing positions that had been used by the regiment to support the river crossing were now completely flooded. The loss of good artillery positions, plus the lack of craft able to cross the river in stormy conditions, could have resulted in a fatal delay to the offensive, if not its outright cancellation.[7]

Aside from the fragile state of the Serbian army, there were a number of other reasons for the success of the operation. The first of these was the collection of people assigned to command it. No mere cipher for his chief of staff, August von Mackensen had clearly established himself as one of Germany's best field commanders during the campaigns in Poland and Galicia. The Serbian campaign confirmed this assessment. Mackensen's judgment of a situation was rarely wrong. He possessed the "inward eye" that Prussian theorist Carl von Clausewitz believed to be a critical necessity for a great commander. While Jansa noted that Mackensen and Seeckt reached major decisions behind closed doors, he regarded Mackensen as the ultimate decisive authority and the driving force.[8]

Certainly, Mackensen was Germany's best commander in the realm of coalition warfare. His ability to work with the Austro-Hungarians and Bulgarians was tested at times, but nonetheless was able to get them to act in accordance with his plans. At the same time, the old hussar was able to forge good personal relationships with high authorities in both Vienna and Sofia. Kövess and Jansa at times accused Mackensen (and Seeckt) of thinking solely in terms of German interests. This was somewhat unfair. Mackensen made every effort to trap and destroy the Serbian army. Since the Austro-Hungarian and German general staffs regarded the Serbian army as the bearer of Serbian nationalism, destroying it, as Mackensen wanted to do would have certainly facilitated Austro-Hungarian occupation policies, which were aimed at eradicating nationalism in Serbia.[9]

To be sure, the period after the Serbian campaign was a difficult one for Mackensen. A quintessential cavalryman who desired action, the forced inactivity once the offensive against Salonika was cancelled took its toll. Seeckt described Mackensen as an "unhappy Blücher."[10] The crisis created by Romania's entry into the war in 1916 would propel Mackensen back to prominence and his brilliant conduct of the campaign, employing troops from every member of the Central powers, would be the crowning achievement of his active service. In the words of Charles Cruttwell, Mackensen's name will always be "specially associated with enterprises demanding surprise and speed, like those against Serbia and Romania."[11]

Mackensen's alter ego Seeckt also played a critical role. As chief of staff, Seeckt oversaw the detailed planning for the operation, once the broad outlines had been formed by Hentsch. Seeckt did this by working through the most senior officers of the staff. As one of the junior officers on the staff, Major Schuch, "we were only chess pieces in his (Seeckt's) game."[12] Aside from staff planning, Seeckt was also the communications conduit to OHL, AOK, and the major subordinate commands. In this role, Seeckt was able to shield Mackensen from becoming personally involved in disagreements with his principal subordinates. Finally, there was that element of personal closeness that served to make this one of the most successful German military marriages of the war. When Seeckt moved on to another assignment in June of 1916, he admitted to his wife that the parting was "moving for both of us."[13]

Mackensen's subordinate commanders were a collection of supremely able professionals. The majority of his army, corps, and division commanders went on to higher responsibilities. After securing Montenegro and Albania, Kövess was promoted to Generaloberst in March of 1916. Kövess was later promoted to Feldmarschall and was named commander of the Austro-Hungarian army on October 22, 1918, just in time to preside over the final collapse of the dual monarchy's military situation.[14] Gallwitz moved on eventually to army and later army group command on the western front and was later considered among the possible successors to Hindenburg.[15]

Gallwitz's corps commanders also fared well. Winckler continued to be entrusted with corps commands and was promoted to General der Infanterie in 1917.[16] Krafft later commanded the Bavarian II Corps, while Kosch was later appointed deputy commander of the Ninth Army, and Lochow went on to command the Fifth Army.[17] Only Falkenhayn did not do anything of great note later in the war. Whether or not that had anything to do with his brother's dismissal as head of OHL is unclear.[18] Most of the division commanders went on to greater things. Several, such as Kraewel, attained corps command. Estorff had the distinction of being involved in the most successful amphibious landing of the war, the operation conducted by the Germans in the Baltic Islands in October 1917. The Serbian campaign was the last major action of the war for Dorrer. Gravely wounded on the western front on January 31, 1916, Dorrer died just over two months later.[19]

Mackensen and his subordinate commanders were aided in their efforts by five assets, which the Germans employed to the greatest possible advantage. The first of these was the railroad. Groener, working with the Austro-Hungarian railroad authorities, was able to amass a large force quickly and efficiently. This effort was also aided by the valuable work of the engineers and the railroad troops, who were able to prepare and expand the sidings to accommodate the number of expected troop trains.[20]

Great staff work, always a hallmark of the German army at its best, was also a factor in this campaign. The first example was the work of Hentsch and his small group that preceded Seeckt's army group staff. Seeckt's staff was able to provide general guidance and orders from Mackensen and Seeckt to Kövess, Gallwitz and (to a lesser extent) Bojadiev. Another interesting element here was the ability of Mackensen and Seeckt to exercise control over their subordinate armies under relatively mobile conditions. Jansa noted that the army group headquarters moved three times in six weeks; from Temesvár to Semendria, then Semendria to Kragujevać, and finally from Kragujevać to Niš. In no case was there a loss of control on the part of Mackensen and Seeckt. Jansa ruefully noted the difference between this campaign and Potiorek's inertia ridden style of command.[21]

The second asset that aided the Germans and Austro-Hungarians was engineer troops. The Save and Danube Rivers, and later the Morava and the Ibar, were all formidable obstacles. Once again, engineers were able to use their own material as well as local river craft to get the initial wave of infantry across. Once the troops were on the Serbian shore and the Serbian defenders driven away from the river bank, the engineers were able to build several types of bridges, some of which were capable of bearing artillery and other kinds of heavy equipment. Although the *Kossava* severely hindered the transfer of men and equipment across the Save and the Danube, once the storm had abated, the engineers were able to rebuild the bridges and restore the rail bridges. This proved critical to sustaining Mackensen's offensive.[22]

The other three assets employed by Mackensen's forces were aircraft, artillery, and the telephone. The importance of the campaign was indicated by the size of the air assets committed to the operation. As in Mackensen's earlier campaigns in Galicia, aerial reconnaissance was crucial in the run up to the start of the operation. The weather held long enough to allow the Germans and Austro-Hungarians to conduct extensive reconnaissance of the Serbian defenses along the Save and Danube. The German effort to increase the number of aircrew trained as observers in early 1915 certainly paid dividends in this regard. Faith in aerial photography was illustrated by the policy of the widest possible dissemination. In addition, once the bombardment began aircrew was charged with observing the fall of every round from heavy artillery as per previous practice in Galicia.[23] One other function performed by aircraft was communication. This was especially important in regard to facilitating communications between either Mackensen's or Gallwitz's headquarters and the Bulgarian First Army.[24]

Aside from reconnaissance and spotting, aircraft were also used in combat operations. Although bombing attacks against operational targets such as the airfield at Požarevac and strategic objectives such as the arsenal at Kragujevać were unsuccessful, one should not be too critical of the Germans here. The bomb technology available lacked reliability and destructive power to do what the Mackensen and Seeckt desired, although German and Austro-Hungarian air operations did result in the securing of air supremacy over the rivers that were to be crossed. The relative failure of the German and Austro-Hungarian pre-offensive air attacks was an example of thinking running ahead of the available technology.[25]

Once the campaign moved into central Serbia, the effectiveness of aircraft was limited by a combination of circumstances. Long stretches of bad weather kept German, Austro-Hungarian and later Bulgarian aircraft grounded. The mountainous terrain of central Serbia also made air operations hazardous. Finally, the poor state of the roads made displacing air detachments forward to new airfields a slow and difficult process.[26] It is interesting to note that the German army by this time, at least in the east, had become rather used to the idea of relying on aircraft for reconnaissance. Gallwitz had to remind his soldiers that since the availability of aircraft was limited because of weather, reconnaissance was very much their responsibility. Krafft also stressed this for the Alpine Corps after its arrival in the theater.[27]

One of the things that also deserves mention in regard to aircraft is the attitude of the senior commanders to this new technology. Mackensen and Gallwitz were not exactly youngsters. The old hussar himself turned 66 just after the campaign, and Gallwitz, born in 1852, was only three years younger than Mackensen. Nonetheless, both men saw the possibilities in the emerging technology and embraced its employment.[28]

Another critical advantage for the Germans and the Austro-Hungarians was in artillery. At the onset of the campaign, the artillery that made the difference for Mackensen's river crossing and securing of the bridgehead was heavy artillery. Gallwitz noted that his Eleventh Army was "generously reinforced" with heavy guns, defined as anything ranging from 150mm to 420mm. Between them, the Austro-Hungarian Third and German Eleventh Armies fielded 1,200 guns, including 36 batteries (normally 4 guns to a battery) of heavy artillery.[29]

Although the Serbian army did have its share of heavy artillery, the threat posed by the Bulgarians forced the Serbians to disperse it, like their few available aircraft. In the bombardment prior to the river crossings, Serbian artillery was no match for its Austro-Hungarian and German opponents. Once aerial reconnaissance had gotten a fix, Serbian artillery positions were veritably smothered by shells.[30]

With the bridgeheads established, artillery of all type was crucial in supporting infantry attacks against Serbian defenses. Two other factors were related to the artillery's ability to support the infantry, namely timing and observation. From experience gained in earlier campaigns, the timing between the lifting of the artillery barrage and the start of the infantry attack was crucial. Seeckt once explained to Jansa that this timing was the key to the success of an attack. The timing had to be so precise, Seeckt noted to the young Austro-Hungarian staff officer, that "by the time the last shell is fired, the infantry must be in the enemy trenches." If the artillery support was judged to be insufficient for the purpose of supporting the attack, the attack should not be made. Jansa called this conversation a most valuable experience. The impact of heavy artillery here again was important, both physically and psychologically, as exemplified by a 420mm hit on the Anatema Hills that literally took off the top of a hill.[31]

The ability of the artillery and infantry to work with such precise timing depended on observation. The ability to observe Serbian positions, either by air or by ground reconnaissance, was critical. This was true especially early in the campaign, as the Austro-Hungarian Third and German Eleventh Armies expanded and linked up their respective bridgeheads. On occasions where observation was lacking, German artillery would at times drop shells into German infantry positions.[32]

As the advance moved into the interior of Serbia, another kind of artillery came in to play for Mackensen's forces, namely mountain artillery. The ability to get mountain artillery forward when it became increasingly difficult to advance regular artillery proved to be another major advantage for the Central powers. This was one area where the Austro-Hungarian army excelled, and the majority of the mountain batteries employed by Mackensen's forces were provided by Austria-Hungary. These batteries were especially important when supporting the advance into or across the Morava, South Morava, and Ibar Valleys.[33] Thus, in every phase of the campaign, artillery provided a critical edge to Mackensen's forces.

The final critical technological element in Mackensen's success was the telephone. During his campaigns in Galicia and Poland, Mackensen and Seeckt had been able to use telephone successfully in coordinating the movements of as many as three armies. The weakness of the Russian artillery also facilitated the use of the telephone, as the threat of shrapnel cutting telephone wire proved to be minimal.[34]

During the Serbian campaign, the telephone once again provided the critical means by which Mackensen and Seeckt could control the operation. Jansa noted how much of the army group's headquarters activity was conducted by telephone. The extant documents at every level of command, from army group down to regiment, stressed the importance of establishing telephone communications as quickly as possible. Regimental histories often noted the importance of getting telephone wires across the rivers after the initial crossing. As in Galicia, the use of telephone here was something that would not have been possible on the western front.[35]

Finally, one must discuss the role that Bulgaria played in the success of the Central powers in the campaign. Conrad was adamant that if a fourth offensive was to be conducted against Serbia, Bulgarian participation would be absolutely essential.[36] This would be one of the few times during the war that Conrad and Falkenhayn agreed on something so readily, so the military convention was drawn up fairly quickly. In the event, although Bojadiev's Bulgarian First Army started a bit later than hoped, it did serve to tie up considerable Serbian forces in protecting the capital of Niš.[37] Todorov's Bulgarian Second Army was able to make relatively short work of the weak and poorly motivated Serbian forces in its sector, and then sever communications between Serbia and the entente forces landing at Salonika. The Bulgarians were then able to hold off Sarrail's offensive aimed at bringing relief to the Serbians. It should be noted, however, that the Bulgarian task in holding off the entente forces would have been considerably more difficult if the high commands in both France and Britain were not riven with disagreement and indecision over the prospect of a major effort in the Balkans.[38]

The situation of Serbia in the autumn of 1915 is a classic example of a minor power caught in a protracted war between military giants. While Serbia had enough staying power to make it through 1914, once Germany made a major commitment of military power to the Balkans, plus the addition of Bulgaria to the Central powers, the fragile Serbian army could not offer serious resistance against Mackensen's forces once the river line had been breached and northern Serbia lost.

Bulgaria was the new minor power in the war. Bulgaria had achieved all of its objectives in its first campaign. Given that the entente powers had decided not to pursue a major offensive campaign from Greece, and Romania effectively deterred from joining the entente, Bulgaria would be spared from having to commit major forces to further active operations, at least for the time being. Nonetheless, a defensive front would have to be maintained along the Greek border. The Bulgarian government and high command did not mind that the country's fate would be decided preferably in France, not on the Vardar.[39]

For Falkenhayn, the campaign in Serbia, combined with the previous victories in Galicia and Poland, the preconditions for his strategy had been set. The threat to Austria-Hungary from Russia had been excised, as well as any further threat to East Prussia. Mackensen's overrunning of Serbia had established the desired overland route to Turkey, bringing the Gallipoli operation to an end and helping set Turkey up for a potential victory in Mesopotamia. With these pre-conditions now met, Falkenhayn could turn to what he regarded as the main front, the western front. Matters there would be determined by undertaking an operation designed to enervate the French army.[40] The place where that would occur was at a fortified city located on the Meuse River, called Verdun.

APPENDIX

German and Austro-Hungarian General Officer Ranks

German	Austro-Hungarian	American
Generalmajor	Generalmajor	Brigadier General
Generalleutnant	Feldmarschalleutnant	Major General
General der Infanterie[a]	Feldzeugmeister[b]	Lieutenant General
Generaloberst	Generaloberst	General
Generalfeldmarschall	Feldmarschall	General of the Army

---

[a]Other equivalents include General der Kavallerie and General der Artillerie.
[b]Other equivalents include General der Artillerie, Infanterie and Kavallerie.

Notes

INTRODUCTION

1. Quoted in Holger H. Herwig, *The First World War: Germany and Austria-Hungary 1914–1918* (London: Arnold, 1997), 19.

2. Erich von Falkenhayn to Franz Baron Conrad von Hötzendorf, September 10, 1915, Armeeoberkommando (AOK) Operations Bureau, Conrad-Falkenhayn Correspondence, Russia, File 512, Österreichischer Staatsarchiv-Kriegsarchiv, Vienna, Austria. (Hereafter cited as ÖSA-KA, R512.)

3. Gunther E. Rothenberg, *The Art of War in the Age of Napoleon* (Bloomington: Indiana University Press, 1978), 34; and David G. Chandler, *The Campaigns of Napoleon: The Mind and Method of History's Greatest Soldier* (New York: Macmillan, 1966), 947.

4. Curzio Malaparte, *The Volga Rises in Europe* (London: Redman, 1957); and George F. Kennan, *The Fateful Alliance: France, Russia and the Coming of the First World War* (New York: Pantheon Books, 1984), 98.

5. For a full discussion of Bismarck's views on Germany possible involvement in various crises regarding the Balkans, see Otto Pflanze, *Bismarck and the Development of Germany*, vol. II, *The Period of Consolidation, 1871–1880*, 420 and 434, vol. III, *The Period of Fortification, 1880–1898* (Princeton: Princeton University Press, 1990), 90–91; George F. Kennan, *The Decline of Bismarck's European Order: Franco-Russian Relations, 1875–1890* (Princeton: Princeton University Press, 1975), 97–99. All ranks will be given in their German or Austro-Hungarian forms. A table of German and Austro-Hungarian ranks and their American equivalents will be included at the end of the book. In addition, all names will be given in the form standard to their country. Thus the name of the German emperor, for example, will be given as Wilhelm I, not William I.

6. Wolfgang Foerster, ed., *Mackensen: Briefe und Aufzeichnungen des Generalfeldmarschalls aus Krieg und Frieden* (Bonn: Wahlband der Buchgemeinde, 1938), 249;

Germany, Reichsarchiv, *Der Weltkrieg 1914 bis 1918* (Berlin: E.S. Mittler und Sohn, 1933), vol. 9, 275; and Jonathan E. Gumz, *The Resurrection and Collapse of Empire in Habsburg Serbia, 1914–1918* (New York: Cambridge University Press, 2009), 63.

7. Lothar Höbelt, "Österreich-Ungarns Nordfront 1914/15/," in *Die vergessene Front. Der Osten 1914/15*, ed. Gerhard P. Gross (Paderborn: Ferdinand Schöningh, 2006), 101–102; and Richard L. DiNardo, *Breakthrough: The Gorlice-Tarnow Campaign, 1915* (Santa Barbara, CA: Praeger, 2010), 29–30.

8. Herwig, *First World War*, 159; and Holger Afflerbach, *Falkenhayn: Politisches Denken und Handeln im Kaiserreich* (Munich: R. Oldenbourg Verlag, 1996), 350.

9. Gary W. Shanafelt, *The Secret Enemy: Austria-Hungary and the German Alliance, 1914–1918* (Boulder, CO: East European Monographs, 1985), 72–80; Fritz Fischer, *Germany's War Aims in the First World War* (New York: W.W. Norton & Company, Inc., 1967), 208–14; and Herwig, *First World War*, 161–62.

10. Afflerbach, *Falkenhayn*, 322.

11. General der Artillerie Richard von Berendt, "Aus grosser Zeit vor Zwanzig Jahren. Der Feldzug in Serbien," *Militär Wochenblatt* 120, no. 13 (October 4, 1935): 523. For a preliminary survey on Germany and coalition warfare, see Richard L. DiNardo and Daniel J. Hughes, "Germany and Coalition Warfare in the World Wars: A Comparative Study," *War in History* 8, no. 2 (April 2001): 166–90.

12. Colonel Charles E. Callwell, *Small Wars: Their Principles and Practice*, 3rd ed. (repr., Lincoln: University of Nebraska Press, 1996), 57.

13. General der Artillerie Max von Gallwitz, *Meine Führertätigkeit im Weltkriege 1914/1916: Belgien—Osten—Balkan* (Berlin: E. S. Mittler und Sohn, 1929), 382; Germany, Reichsarchiv, *Der Weltkrieg 1914 bis 1918*, vol. 9, 197–99; and Douglas Wilson Johnson, *Topography and Strategy in the War* (New York: Henry Holt and Company, 1917), 154–55.

14. Foerster, ed., *Mackensen*, 218–19; Hans von Seeckt, *Aus meinem Leben 1866–1917* (Leipzig: von Hase und Koehler Verlag, 1938), 220–21; and Charles R. M. F. Cruttwell, *A History of the Great War 1914–1918* (repr., Chicago: Academy Publishers, 2007), 232.

15. General Ernest von Hoeppner, *Germany's War in the Air: The Development and Operations of German Military Aviation in the World War* (repr., Nashville: The Battery Press, 1994), 46; and Lee Kennett, *The First Air War 1914–1918* (New York: The Free Press, 1991), 185.

16. Germany, Reichsarchiv, *Der Weltkrieg 1914 bis 1918*, vol. 9, 198.

17. Colonel Toepfer, "Pionierwesen," in *Die militärischen Lehren des Grossen Krieges*, ed. Generalleutnant Max Schwarte (Berlin: E.S. Mittler und Sohn, 1920), 202–3.

CHAPTER 1

1. Quoted in Mary E. Durham, *The Sarajevo Crime* (London: George Allen and Unwin, 1925), 20.

2. Quoted in Gary W. Shanafelt, *The Secret Enemy: Austria-Hungary and the German Alliance, 1914–1918* (Boulder, CO: East European Monographs, 1985), 25. Technically, Berchtold's name was actually Leopold Count von Berchtold von und

zu Ungarschitz, Fratting und Pullitz. Holger H. Herwig and Neil M. Heyman, *Biographical Dictionary of World War I* (Westport, CT: Greenwood Press, 1982), 84. For the sake of simplicity, he will be referred to as Leopold von Berchtold.

3. David G. Chandler, *The Campaigns of Napoleon: The Mind and Method of History's Greatest Soldier* (New York: Macmillan, 1966), 449; Robert A. Kann, *A History of the Habsburg Empire 1526–1918* (Berkeley: University of California Press, 1974), 221. The title of Holy Roman Emperor was bestowed originally by a grateful Pope Leo III on Charlemagne in 800, and Holy Roman Empire was comprised of most of western and central Europe east of the Pyrenees. Over the course of centuries, however, the territorial boundaries of the empire shifted to the east, while the title of Holy Roman Emperor passed into the hands of the Habsburg family, at least officially, with the coronation of Frederick III in 1440. Thereafter the empire was based on the Habsburg crown lands in Austria. By the middle of the eighteenth century, the French *Philosphe* Voltaire quipped that the Holy Roman Empire was "neither holy, nor Roman, nor an empire." Napoleon's reorganization of western Germany politically after the conclusion of the 1805 campaign put a merciful end to the defunct polity.

4. As his first wife, Josephine Beauharnais, was incapable of bearing any more children, Napoleon divorced her to marry Princess Marie Louise, the oldest daughter of Francis I, in 1810. She did give birth to an heir to Napoleon's throne in 1811. Robert A. Kann, *A History of the Habsburg Empire 1526–1918* (Berkeley: University of California Press, 1974), 225.

5. Chandler, *Campaigns of Napoleon*, 901; Kann, *History of the Habsburg Empire*, 227.

6. István Deák, "The Revolution and the War of Independence, 1848–1849," in *A History of Hungary*, ed. Peter F. Sugar, Péter Hanák, and Tibor Frank (Bloomington: Indiana University Press, 1994), 212; Kann, *History of the Habsburg Empire 1526– 1918*, 250; and Jelena Milojković-Djurić, *Panslavism and National Identity in Russia and in the Balkans 1830–1880: Images of the Self and Others* (Boulder, CO: East European Monographs, 1994), 1–2. As an amusing aside, in 1849 both Metternich and his *bete noire* Karl Marx settled in London. It would seem unlikely that they attended the same social engagements.

7. Gunther E. Rothenberg, *The Army of Francis Joseph* (West Lafayette, IN: Purdue University Press, 1976), 53–54; and Geoffrey Wawro, "An 'Army of Pigs': The Technical, Social and Political Bases of Austrian Shock Tactics, 1859–1866," *The Journal of Military History* 59, no. 3 (July 1995): 414–15.

8. Rothenberg, *Army of Francis Joseph*, 75; Kann, *History of the Habsburg Empire 1526–1918*, 320; Arthur J. May, *The Habsburg Monarchy 1867–1914* (New York: W.W. Norton, 1951), 41–43. It should be noted that in the title of May's book, the family name is rendered as "Hapsburg." For the sake of consistency, however, the version "Habsburg" will be used. Elisabeth of Bavaria was born on December 24, 1837. She was the daughter of Max Joseph, duke of Bavaria. In 1853, the 23-year-old Francis Joseph met both the 15-year-old Elisabeth and her older sister Helene. A smitten Francis Joseph courted Elisabeth, and the two married on April 24, 1854. Over the course of their long and at times difficult marriage, she bore four children, most notably Crown Prince Rudolf, born in 1858. On September 10, 1898, Elisabeth was fatally stabbed in Geneva, Switzerland, by Luigi Lucheni, a deranged Italian anarchist. Her assassination was one of a number of personal tragedies that afflicted Francis Joseph

throughout his long life. The most notable of these was the suicide of Crown Prince Rudolf at Mayerling in 1889.

9. Peter F. Sugar, "The Nature of the Non-Germanic Societies under Habsburg Rule," *Slavic Review* XXII, no. 1 (March 1963): 5.

10. Kann, *History of the Habsburg Empire 1526–1918*, 278; Luigi Albertini, *The Origins of the War of 1914*, trans. Isabella M. Massey (repr., New York: Enigma Books, 2005), vol. I, 7; Matthew S. Anderson, *The Eastern Question 1774–1923* (New York: St. Martin's Press, 1966), 180; and George F. Kennan, *The Decline of Bismarck's European Order: Franco-Russian Relations, 1875–1890* (Princeton: Princeton University Press, 1975), 29.

11. Anderson, *Eastern Question 1774–1923*, 48; Hans Kohn, *Pan-Slavism: Its History and Ideology* (Notre Dame: University of Notre Dame Press, 1953), 56. The Janissaries were children, often of Balkan ethnicity, who were taken from Christian families and raised at the court of the local Turkish ruler. They constituted a corps of, in the words of Geoffrey Parker, "elite slave soldiers." Geoffrey Parker, *The Military Revolution: Military Innovation and the Rise of the West, 1500–1800* (Cambridge: Cambridge University Press, 1988), 125. Over time, however, the Janissaries came to be emblematic of the corruption and lassitude that were regarded as the hallmarks of the Ottoman court. By the time of Karageorge's revolt, the military value of the Janissaries was a thing of the past, and the Turkish government regarded the Janissaries as a threat to the empire's internal stability. In 1826 Sultan Mahmud II disbanded the Janissaries, who then mutinied. The Sultan put down the revolt with the utmost brutality and bloodshed.

12. Anderson, *Eastern Question 1774–1923*, 50; and Albertini, *Origins of the War of 1914*, 9.

13. Milojković-Djurić, *Panslavism and National Identity in Russia and in the Balkans 1830–1880*, 47; George W. White, *Nationalism and Territory: Constructing Group Identity in Southeastern Europe* (New York: Rowman and Littlefield Publishers, 2000), 187; and Kohn, *Pan-Slavism*, 56. A German regimental history noted that in Serbian villages, the largest and most beautiful building was usually the local school, the walls of which were adorned with pictures of scenes from Serbian history. Joseph Steuer, *Das Infanterie-Regiment Generalfeldmarschall von Mackensen (3. West preussisches) Nr. 129 im Weltkriege* (Berlin: Druck und Verlag Gerhard Stalling, 1925), 141.

14. Anderson, *Eastern Question 1774–1923*, 185; Kennan, *Decline of Bismarck's European Order*, 35; and Barbara Jelavich, *A Century of Russian Foreign Policy 1814–1914* (Philadelphia: J.B. Lippincott, 1964), 178. There is still no satisfactory history of the Russo-Turkish War of 1877–1878 in English. For a preliminary look at the war from the Russian perspective, see Richard L. DiNardo, "Russian Military Operations 1877–1878," in *War and Society in East Central Europe*, vol. XVII, ed. Bela Kiraly and Gail Stokes (Boulder, CO: Social Science Monographs, 1985), 125–41; and William McElwee, *The Art of War: Waterloo to Mons* (Bloomington: Indiana University Press, 1974), 187–205. Russian planning for the war is covered in Jacob W. Kipp, "Strategic Railroads and the Dilemma of Modernization," in *Reforming the Tsar's Army: Military Innovation in Imperial Russia from Peter the Great to the Revolution*, ed. David Schimmelpenninck van der Oye and Bruce W. Menning (New York: Cambridge University Press, 2004), 95–102.

15. Kennan, *Decline of Bismarck's European Order*, 37; Volker Ullrich, *Die nervöse Grossmacht: Aufstieg und Untergang des deutschen Kaisserreichs 1871–1918*, 2nd ed. (Frankfurt-am-Main: Fischer Taschenbuch Verlag, 2010), 87; Otto Pflanze, *Bismarck and the Development of Germany*, vol. II, *The Period of Consolidation, 1871–1880*, 438; Anderson, *Eastern Question 1774–1923*, 186; and Lonnie R. Johnson, *Central Europe: Enemies, Neighbors, Friends* (New York: Oxford University Press, 1996), 173.

16. Kennan, *Decline of Bismarck's European Order*, 75.

17. Gordon A. Craig, *Germany 1866–1945* (New York: Oxford University Press, 1978), 114; May, *Habsburg Monarchy 1867–1918*, 142; and Kann, *History of the Habsburg Empire 1526–1918*, 281.

18. Bismarck had taken the precaution of garnering the support of chief of the general staff Helmuth von Moltke, Crown Prince Friedrich Wilhelm, and the rest of the Prussian cabinet before threatening resignation. Wilhelm I regarded the alliance with Austria–Hungary as a poor way to treat Russia, heretofore a valued ally. Pflanze, *Bismarck and the Development of Germany*, 507; Craig, *Germany 1866–1945*, 114; and Ullrich, *Die nervöse Grossmacht*, 89. Wilhelm's fondness for Russia may have stemmed from his formative days as a young officer in the Prussian army. He fought in the 1814 invasion of France, an effort spearheaded by Russia.

19. Kann, *History of the Habsburg Empire 1526–1918*, 406; and May, *Habsburg Monarchy 1867–1914*, 143.

20. Kennan, *Decline of Bismarck's European Order*, 75.

21. May, *Habsburg Monarchy 1867–1914*, 286; and Kennan, *Decline of Bismarck's European Order*, 142.

22. Anderson, *Eastern Question 1774–1923*, 232; Kennan, *Decline of Bismarck's European Order*, 143–44; and Kann, *History of the Habsburg Empire 1526–1918*, 409.

23. Although Alexander of Battenberg had been selected by Alexander II to be king of Bulgaria and Bulgaria was supported by Russia, Alexander of Battenberg had gotten crosswise of Tsar Alexander III soon after the tsar's ascending to the throne. Kennan, *Decline of Bismarck's European Order*, 113.

24. Craig, *Germany 1866–1945*, 131; Kennan, *Decline of Bismarck's European Order*, 313; and Ullrich, *Die nervöse Grossmacht*, 103–4.

25. Kennan, *Decline of Bismarck's European Order*, 257–58; Ullrich, *Die nervöse Grossmacht*, 104; Pflanze, *Bismarck and the Development of Germany*, 251; and Craig, *Germany 1866–1945*, 134. For a critical appraisal of the Reinsurance Treaty, see Erich Eyck, *Bismarck and the German Empire* (repr., New York: W.W. Norton, 1968), 295–96.

26. Lamar Cecil, *Wilhelm II* (Chapel Hill: University of North Carolina Press, 1989), vol. I, 130–32; and Eyck, *Bismarck and the German Empire*, 306.

27. Kennan, *Decline of Bismarck's European Order*, 410; Craig, *Germany 1866–1945*, 232; Cecil, *Wilhelm II*, 189–90; Albertini, *Origins of the War of 1914*, 63; and Ullrich, *Die nervöse Grossmacht*, 183.

28. Cecil, *Wilhelm II*, 306–308; Holger H. Herwig, *Luxury Fleet: The Imperial German Navy 1888–1918* (repr., London: The Ashfield Press, 1987), 24. For Tirpitz' early thinking on naval development, see Patrick J. Kelly, "Strategy, Tactics and Turf Wars: Tirpitz and the Oberkommando der Marine, 1892–1895," *The Journal of Military History* 66, no. 4 (October 2002): 1049–54.

29. White, *Nationalism and Territory*, 231; and Kann, *History of the Habsburg Empire 1526–1918*, 446–47.

30. Kohn, *Pan-Slavism*, 191; and Albertini, *Origins of the War of 1914*, 138–39.

31. Anderson, *Eastern Question 1774–1923*, 286; Tibor Frank, "Hungary and the Dual Monarchy, 1867–1890," in *A History of Hungary*, ed. Peter F. Sugar, Péter Hanák, and Tibor Frank (Bloomington: Indiana University Press, 1990, pb. 1994), 255; Kann, *History of the Habsburg Empire 1526–1918*, 448; and Sugar, "Nature," 24.

32. Manfred Rauchensteiner, *Der Erste Weltkrieg und das Ende der Habsburgermonarchie 1914–1918* (Vienna: Böhlau Verlag, 2013), 23; Shanafelt, *Secret Enemy*, 12; and Lawrence Sondhaus, *Franz Conrad von Hötzendorf: Architect of the Apocalypse* (Boston: Humanities Press, Inc., 2000), 104.

33. For a brief summary and analysis of the Balkan Wars, see Robert M. Citino, *Quest for Decisive Victory: From Stalemate to Blitzkrieg in Europe, 1899–1940* (Lawrence: University Press of Kansas, 2002), 101–41. The Turkish performance in the First Balkan War is covered definitively by Edward J. Erickson, *Defeat in Detail: The Ottoman Army in the Balkans, 1912–1913* (Westport, CT: Praeger Publishers, 2003). For an overview of the diplomatic aspects of the Balkan Wars, see Albertini, *Origins of the War of 1914*, 364–487. See also Jelavich, *Century of Russian Foreign Policy 1814–1914*, 269.

34. Kohn, *Pan-Slavism*, 197; Kann, *History of the Habsburg Empire 1526–1918*, 416; Rauchensteiner, *Der Erste Weltkrieg*, 28–29; Franz Baron Conrad von Hötzendorf, *Aus meiner Dienstzeit 1906–1918*, 6th ed. (Vienna: Rikola Verlag, 1921), vol. 3, 470; and Shanafelt, *Secret Enemy*, 19. Leopold von Berchtold was born on April 18, 1863, into a prosperous landowning family. Berchtold joined the Austro-Hungarian diplomatic service in 1894. Among his postings was a stint as ambassador to Russia, where he experienced the full depth of Russia's hatred toward the dual monarchy. Berchtold was appointed foreign minister on February 19, 1912, at 49 years of age, making him the youngest foreign minister in Europe. His youth and relative inexperience made him poorly suited for the position, and Berchtold's awareness of his own shortcomings made him susceptible to the more forcefully stated views of others. Although a member of the "war party" at the Ballplatz, he was never one of its leaders. Sensing the coming failure of the attempt to keep Italy out of the war, Berchtold resigned on January 13, 1915. He retired quietly to his estate in Hungary, where he died on November 21, 1942. Herwig and Heyman, *Biographical Dictionary of World War I*, 84; and Richard F. Hamilton and Holger H. Herwig, *Decisions for War, 1914–1917* (Cambridge: Cambridge University Press, 2004), 49.

35. Sondhaus, *Franz Conrad von Hötzendorf*, 133; and Johnson, *Central Europe*, 173. Nikola Pašić was born on December 18, 1845, in eastern Serbia. Desiring to become an engineer, Pašić studied in both Belgrade and Zurich. In Zurich Pašić moved in left-wing circles; among his acquaintances were Serbian socialist Svetozar Marković and anarchist leader Mikhail Bakunin. Pašić returned to Serbia and participated in the 1876 revolt against Turkey. In a new independent Serbia Pašić became a leader of the Radical Party, which put him at odds with the Obrenović dynasty, to a point where he spent a brief time in exile in Bulgaria. The return of the Karageorge family to power in the ascendance of Peter I to the throne brought Pašić to political prominence. He was prime minister when Franz Ferdinand and his wife were assassinated in Sarajevo. Although the killer, Gavrilo Princip, had received support from Serbian army officers, no direct tie between the assassins and Pašić was ever established. After personally delivering the response to the Austro-Hungarian ultimatum on July 25, 1914, Pašić

took a backseat as diplomacy yielded to military operations. He joined the government and army in the retreat to Durazzo. More a Serbian nationalist than a Pan-Slavist, Pašić was not enamored with the idea of a federal Yugoslavia that included all the South Slavs. He served two short stints as prime minister and died in Belgrade on December 10, 1926. Herwig and Heyman, *Biographical Dictionary of World War I*, 274–76.

36. Albertini, *Origins of the War of 1914*, 175; Hamilton and Herwig, *Decisions for War, 1914–1917*, 64; and Kann, *History of the Habsburg Empire 1526–1918*, 419. István Tisza de Boros-Jënö (hereafter István Tisza) was the son of the famous Hungarian statesman Kálmán Tisza. Born on April 22, 1861, in Budapest, the young Tisza studied in both Berlin and Heidelberg. Coming from a political family, Tisza entered politics via a seat in the Hungarian parliament in 1886. Over the next 15 years Tisza emerged as an ardent defender of the *Ausgleich* and the powerful position it gave to Hungary. Appointed prime minister of Hungary by Francis Joseph in 1913, his initial opposition to the idea of war with Serbia has been noted earlier. Tisza was able to expand his power by getting his friend István Count Burian appointed foreign minister after Berchtold's resignation. After Francis Joseph's death on November 21, 1916, Tisza rushed to have the new emperor Karl I crowned as king of Hungary, thus preserving the dual nature of the monarchy. Tisza, a stubborn and prickly individual, soon ran afoul of Karl and was dismissed in May 1917. After a short stint with the army, Tisza returned to Budapest. He was murdered by Hungarian communists on October 31, 1918. Herwig and Heyman, *Biographical Dictionary of World War I*, 338.

37. Hamilton and Herwig, *Decisions for War, 1914–1917*, 86; Albertini, *Origins of the War of 1914*, 165; Graydon A. Tunstall Jr., *Planning for War against Russia and Serbia: Austro-Hungarian and German Military Strategies, 1871–1914* (Boulder, CO: Social Science Monographs, 1993), 140; Rauchensteiner, *Der Erste Weltkrieg*, 76–78; Cecil, *Wilhelm II*, 200. Several generations of forest have been consumed in the production of the enormous corpus of scholarship dealing with this issue. The two original works that set forth the two contending schools of thought are Fritz Fischer, *Germany's War Aims in the First World War* (New York: W.W. Norton, 1967), 208–14; and Gerhard Ritter, *The Schlieffen Plan: Critique of a Myth* (New York: Praeger, 1958). See also Annika Mombauer, *Helmuth von Moltke and the Origins of the First World War* (Cambridge: Cambridge University Press, 2001).

38. This is another subject that has consumed several oceans worth of ink. Among a number of works worth one's attention are Tunstall, *Planning for War against Russia and Serbia*, 9–107; Norman Stone, "Moltke and Conrad: Relations between the Austro-Hungarian and German General Staffs, 1909–1914," in *The War Plans of the Great Powers, 1880–1914*, ed. Paul Kennedy (London: George Allen and Unwin, 1979), 222–51; Arden Bucholz, *Moltke, Schlieffen and Prussian War Planning* (Oxford: Berg Publishers, 1991), 256–58; Gerhard Seyfert, *Die militärischen Beziehungen und Vereinbarungen zwischen dem deutschen und österreichischen Generalstab vor und bei Beginn des Weltkrieges* (Leipzig: J. Moltzen, 1934), 53–61; General Georg Wetzell, *Der Bündniskrieg: Eine militärpolitisch operative Studie des Weltkrieges* (Berlin: E.S. Mittler und Sohn, 1937); and Richard L. DiNardo and Daniel J. Hughes, "Germany and Coalition Warfare in the World Wars: A Comparative Study," *War in History* 8, no. 2 (April 2001): 166–90.

39. Wetzell, *Der Bündniskrieg*, 4; Tunstall, *Planning for War against Russia and Serbia*, 31; Gunther E. Rothenberg, "Moltke, Schlieffen, and the Doctrine of Strategic

Envelopment," in *Makers of Modern Strategy: From Machiavelli to the Nuclear Age*, ed. Peter Paret (Princeton: Princeton University Press, 1986), 308–309; DiNardo and Hughes, "Germany and Coalition Warfare," 168; and Lothar Höbelt, "Schlieffen, Potiorek und das Ende der gemeinsam deutsch-österreich-ungarischen Aufmmarschpläne im Osten," *Militärgeschichtlichen Mitteilungen* 36 (1984): 17.

40. Helmuth von Moltke was born on May 23, 1848. He joined the German army in 1869 and fought in the Franco-Prussian War. Later in his career Moltke served as an adjutant to both his uncle and later Wilhelm II. Promoted to Generalmajor in 1899, Moltke commanded the First Guards Division and was advanced to Generalleutnant. Appointed to the general staff in 1904 under Schlieffen, two years later Moltke, then a Generaloberst, was named to succeed Schlieffen by the kaiser, even though Moltke had doubts about his suitability for the position. As chief of the general staff he introduced a greater degree of realism in the annual maneuvers. Moltke also made a number of alterations to the war plan bequeathed to him by Schlieffen that conformed to the changing international situation. Although he was one of handful of German general officers with actual combat experience in 1914, the strain of directing military operations against France proved too much for Moltke. By mid-September 1914, Moltke was a broken man, both mentally and physically. He was replaced by Erich von Falkenhayn. Later on Moltke tried to regain his old position but was thwarted by Falkenhayn. Moltke suffered a fatal heart attack on June 18, 1916. Herwig and Heyman, *Biographical Dictionary of World War I*, 257–58.

41. Generaloberst Helmuth von Moltke, *Errinerungen-Briefe-Dokumente*, ed. Eliza von Moltke (Stuttgart: Der Kommende Tag, 1922), 252; Mombauer, *Helmuth von Moltke and the Origins of the First World War*, 113; Stone, "Moltke and Conrad," 230; Conrad, *Aus meiner Dienstzeit 1906–1918*, 403–405; and Gerhard Ritter, *The Sword and the Scepter: The Problem of Militarism in Germany*, vol. 2, *The European Powers and the Wilhelminian Empire, 1890–1914* (Coral Gables, FL: University of Miami Press, 1970), 243–46.

42. John R. Schindler, "Redl—Spy of the Century?" *International Journal of Intelligence and Counter Intelligence* 18, no. 3 (Fall 2005): 498.

43. Sondhaus, *Franz Conrad von Hötzendorf*, 124–26; Conrad, *Aus meiner Dienstzeit 1906–1918*, 368; and Georg Markus, *Der Fall Redl* (Vienna: Amalthea Verlag, 1984), 221–24.

44. Tunstall, *Planning for War against Russia and Serbia*, 192.

45. Albertini, *Origins of the War of 1914*, 540–44; Tunstall, *Planning for War against Russia and Serbia*, 172–73; Hew Strachan, *The First World War*, vol. I: *To Arms* (Oxford: Oxford University Press, 2001), 294–95; Rauchensteiner, *Der Erste Weltkrieg*, 165; and Sondhaus, *Franz Conrad von Hötzendorf*, 146–47.

46. Shanafelt, *Secret Enemy*, 42; Sondhaus, *Franz Conrad von Hötzendorf*, 145; and Strachan, *First World War*, 296.

47. Herwig and Heyman, *Biographical Dictionary of World War I*, 286; Sondhaus, *Franz Conrad von Hötzendorf*, 79–80; Rothenberg, *Army of Francis Joseph*, 142; and Rauchensteiner, *Der Erste Weltkrieg und das Ende der Habsburgermonarchie 1914–1918*, 88.

48. Strachan, *First World War*, 336; Rothenberg, *Army of Francis Jospeh*, 182; and Austria, Bundesministerium für Landesverteidigung, *Österreich-Ungarns Letzter Krieg 1914–1918* (Vienna: Verlag der Militärwissenschaftlichen Mitteilungen, 1931), vol. 1, 91.

49. Strachan, *First World War*, 341; Rothenberg, *Army of Francis Joseph*, 182; Holger H. Herwig, *The First World War: Germany and Austria-Hungary 1914–1918* (London: Arnold, 1997), 88; and Austria, Bundesministerium, *Österreich-Ungarns Letzter Krieg 1914–1918*, 97–98.

50. Herwig and Heyman, *Biographical Dictionary of World War I*, 290–91.

51. Strachan, *First World War*, 340; Sondhaus, *Franz Conrad von Hötzendorf*, 150; and Herwig, *First World War*, 88.

52. Rodolphe A. Reiss, *Report upon the Atrocities Committed by the Austro-Hungarian Army during the First Invasion of Serbia* (London: Simpkin, Marshall, Hamilton, Kent and Co., Ltd., 1915), 16–17; Herwig, *First World War*, 24.

53. Rauchensteiner, *Der Erste Weltkrieg*, 190–91; Herwig, *First World War*, 88; Strachan, *First World War*, 344–45; and Austria, Bundesministerium, *Österreich-Ungarns Letzter Krieg 1914–1918*, 106.

54. Herwig, *First World War*, 88; and Hamilton and Herwig, *Decisions for War, 1914–1917*, 173.

55. Herwig, *First World War*, 88; Strachan, *First World War*, 344–45; Austria, Bundesministerium, *Österreich-Ungarns Letzter Krieg 1914–1918*, 121–22; Rothenberg, *Army of Francis Joseph*, 183; and Rauchensteiner, *Der Erste Weltkrieg*, 192.

56. Strachan, *First World War*, 346; and Austria, Bundesministerium, *Österreich-Ungarns Letzter Krieg 1914–1918*, 632.

57. Strachan, *First World War*, 346; and Austria, Bundesministerium, *Österreich-Ungarns Letzter Krieg 1914–1918*, 635.

58. Herwig, *First World War*, 111–12; Austria, Bundesministerium, *Österreich-Ungarns Letzter Krieg 1914–1918*, 712–13; and Rauchensteiner, *Der Erste Weltkrieg*, 285.

59. Gordon Gordon-Smith, *From Serbia to Jugoslavia. Serbia's Victories, Reverses and Final Triumph: 1914–1918* (New York: G.P. Putnam's Sons, 1920), 11; Army Group Temesvár, Intelligence Section, Report on the Condition of the Serbian Army, September 10, 1915, Nachlass Seeckt, File N 247/26; Bundesarchiv-Militärarchiv, Freiburg-im-Breisgau, Germany (hereafter cited as BA-MA N 247/26); Austria, Bundesministerium, *Österreich-Ungarns Letzter Krieg 1914–1918*, 759; Rauchensteiner, *Der Erste Weltkrieg*, 285; and Herwig, *First World War*, 112.

60. Austria, Bundesministerium, *Österreich-Ungarns Letzter Krieg 1914–1918*, 759; Rauchensteiner, *Der Erste Weltkrieg*, 286; Herwig, *First World War*, 112; and Karl von Kageneck Diary, September 14, 1914, BA-MA MSg 1/1914. Born on May 10, 1871, Karl von Kageneck received his lieutenant's commission in 1891. A graduate of the *Kriegsakademie* in 1904, Kaganeck was posted to Vienna as attaché in 1907. He was promoted to colonel in 1916 and reached general officer's rank before the end of the war. He died in 1967. Biographical Chronology, BA-MA MSg 109/10863.

61. Rothenberg, *Army of Francis Joseph*, 183; Strachan, *First World War*, 346; Austria, Bundesministerium, *Österreich-Ungarns Letzter Krieg 1914–1918*, 762; and Rauchensteiner, *Der Erste Weltkrieg*, 287. Potiorek officially retired on January 1, 1915. He lived in relative obscurity until his death in Klagenfurt on December 17, 1933. Herwig and Heyman, *Biographical Dictionary of World War I*, 286.

62. Austria, Bundesministerium, *Österreich-Ungarns Letzter Krieg 1914–1918*, 762; Andrej Mitronvić, *Serbia's Great War 1914–1918* (West Lafayette, IN: Purdue University Press, 2007, 102; Army Group Temesvár, Intelligence Section, Report on

the Condition of the Serbian Army, September 10, 1915, Nachlass Seeckt, BA-MA N 247/26; and Strachan, *First World War*, 346.

63. Strachan, *First World War*, 350–57; Herwig, *First World War*, 90–95; and Lothar Höbelt, "Österreich-Ungarns Nordfront 1914/15," in *Die vergessene Front. Der Osten 1914/15*, ed. Gerhard P. Gross (Paderborn: Ferdinand Schöningh, 2006), 88–91.

64. Kaganeck Diary, September 21, 1914, BA-MA MSg 1/1914; Germany, Reichsarchiv, *Der Weltkrieg 1914 bis 1918* (Berlin: E.S. Mittler und Sohn, 1933), vol. 5, 412–13; Conrad, *Aus meiner Dienstzeit 1906–1918*, 21; Rauchensteiner, *Der Erste Weltkrieg*, 277; and DiNardo, *Breakthrough*, 11–12.

65. Strachan, *First World War*, 366; Conrad, *Aus meiner Dienstzeit 1906–1918*, 791; and Herwig, *First World War*, 110.

66. Sondhaus, *Franz Conrad von Hötzendorf*, 158–59; and Herwig, *First World War*, 147.

67. Oscar Jászi, *The Dissolution of the Habsburg Monarchy* (Chicago: University of Chicago Press, 1929), 287; Kann, *History of the Habsburg Empire 1526–1918*, 419; Shanafelt, *Secret Enemy*, 12; and Sondhaus, *Franz Conrad von Hötzendorf*, 201.

68. Technically, the head of AOK was the aged Feldmarschall Archduke Friedrich (born 1856). Herwig and Heyman, *Biographical Dictionary of World War I*, 156–57; and Sondhaus, *Franz Conrad von Hötzendorf*, 167.

CHAPTER 2

1. Generalfeldmarschall Helmuth von Moltke, *Militärische Werke*, ed. German Great General Staff (Berlin: E. S. Mittler und Sohn, 1900), vol. 2, 293.

2. Holger Afflerbach, *Falkenhayn: Politisches Denken und Handeln im Kaiserreich* (Munich: R. Oldenbourg Verlag, 1996), 4; and Biographical Chronology, BA-MA MSg 109/10859.

3. Afflerbach, *Falkenhayn*, 17; Jörg Muth, *Command Culture: Officer Education in the U.S. Army and the German Armed Forces, 1901–1940, and the Consequences for World War II* (Denton: University of North Texas Press, 2011), 87; Richard L. DiNardo, *Breakthrough: The Gorlice-Tarnow Campaign, 1915* (Santa Barbara, CA: Praeger, 2010), 17; and Biographical Chronology, BA-MA MSg 109/10859.

4. Afflerbach, *Falkenhayn*, 109; Biographical Chronology, BA-MA MSg 109/10859; and Holger H. Herwig and Neil M. Heyman, *Biographical Dictionary of World War I* (Westport, CT: Greenwood Press, 1982), 145–46. Under the provisions of the constitution that established the German Empire, imperial Germany was in fact a collection of states. Three of the largest states, Prussia, Bavaria, and Württemberg, were allowed to maintain separate military establishments. Gordon A. Craig, *Germany 1866–1945* (New York: Oxford University Press, 1978), 41.

5. Afflerbach, *Falkenhayn*, 144; Volker Ullrich, *Die nervöse Grossmacht: Aufstieg und Untergang des deutschen Kaisserreichs 1871–1918*, 2nd ed. (Frankfurt-am-Main: Fischer Taschenbuch Verlag, 2010), 247–48; Lamar Cecil, *Wilhelm II* (Chapel Hill: University of North Carolina Press, 1989), vol. II, 189–94; and Erich D. Brose, *The Kaiser's Army: The Politics of Military Technology in Germany during the Machine Age, 1870–1918* (New York: Oxford University Press, 2001), 151.

6. Afflerbach, *Falkenhayn*, 188–89; and Cecil, *Wilhelm II*, 216.

7. Afflerback, *Falkenhayn*, 219; Walter Görlitz, *History of the German General Staff*, trans. Brian Battershaw (New York: Praeger, 1954), 173; Helmut Reichold, ed., *Adolf Wild von Hohenborn: Briefe und Tagebuchaufzeichnungen des preussischen Generals als Kriegsminister und Truppenführer im Ersten Weltkrieg* (Boppard-am-Rhein: Harald Boldt Verlag, 1986), 53; Robert T. Foley, *German Strategy and the Path to Verdun: Erich von Falkenhayn and the Development of Attrition; 1870–1916* (Cambridge: Cambridge University Press, 2005), 95; and Seeckt, Diary Notes, January 24, 1915, Nachlass Seeckt, BA-MA N 247/22.

8. Both Schlieffen and the younger Moltke were 58 years old when they became chiefs of the General Staff in 1891 and 1906, respectively.

9. Cecil, *Wilhelm II*, 225; and Afflerbach, *Falkenhayn*, 232.

10. DiNardo, *Breakthrough*, 13.

11. Erich Ludendorff to Helmut von Moltke, January 27, 1915; Ludendorff to Moltke, March 12, 1915, Nachlass Ludendorff, BA-MA N 77/2; Manfred Nebelin, *Ludendorff: Diktator im Ersten Weltkrieg* (Munich: Siedler Verlag, 2010), 158; and Vejas G. Liulevicius, *War Land on the Eastern Front: Culture, National Identity and German Occupation in World War I* (Cambridge: Cambridge University Press, 2000), 22–23. Seeckt also thought that a victory against Russia was achievable and would be decisive. Seeckt, Diary Notes, January 18, 1915, Nachlass Seeckt, BA-MA N 247/22.

12. Hew Strachan, *The First World War*, vol. I, *To Arms* (Oxford: Oxford University Press, 2001), 280; Foley, *German Strategy and the Path to Verdun*, 110; and Afflerbach, *Falkenhayn*, 200.

13. Graydon A. Tunstall, *Blood on the Snow: The Carpathian Winter War of 1915* (Lawrence: University Press of Kansas, 2010), 212; and DiNardo, *Breakthrough*, 25.

14. August von Cramon to Erich von Falkenhayn, March 24, 1915, 10 PM, Cramon to Falkenhayn, March 26, 1915, 10 AM BA-MA RH 61/1536; Gerhard Tappen Diary, April 6, 1915, BA-MA RH 61/986; and Germany, Reichsarchiv, *Der Weltkrieg 1914 bis 1918* (Berlin: E.S. Mittler und Sohn, 1933), vol. 7, 349.

15. Richard F. Hamilton and Holger H. Herwig, *Decisions for War, 1914–1917* (Cambridge: Cambridge University Press, 2004), 160.

16. Sean McMeekin, *The Berlin-Baghdad Express: The Ottoman Empire and Germany's Bid for World Power* (Cambridge: Harvard University Press, 2010), 111.

17. Strachan, *First World War*, 699; Hamilton and Herwig, *Decisions for War, 1914–1917*, 165–66; and McMeekin, *Berlin-Baghdad Express*, 120–21.

18. General Erich von Falkenhayn, *The German General Staff and Its Decisions, 1914–1916* (New York: Dodd, Mead, 1920), 54–56.

19. Richard Hough, *The Great War at Sea 1914–1918* (Oxford: Oxford University Press, 1983), 157; Charles R.M.F. Cruttwell, *A History of the Great War 1914–1918* (repr., Chicago: Academy Publishers, 2007), 342; Edward J. Erickson, *Gallipoli: The Ottoman Campaign* (Barnsley: Pen and Sword Books, 2010), 192; Cramon to Falkenhayn, April 8, 1915, 11:26 PM, BA-MA RH 61/1536; and Falkenhayn, *German General Staff and Its Decisions, 1914–1916*, 73.

20. The Giolitti government sought territorial compensation from Austria–Hungary in return for the dual monarchy's annexation of Bosnia–Herzegovina. Attempts to gain compensation by Italian foreign minister Tommaso Tittoni,

however, were rebuffed by both Austria–Hungary and Germany. Luigi Albertini, *The Origins of the War of 1914*, trans. Isabella M. Massey (repr., New York: Enigma Books, 2005), vol. I, 237–46.

21. Holger H. Herwig, "Strategic Uncertainties of a Nation-State: Prussia-Germany, 1871–1918," in *The Making of Strategy: Rulers, States, and War*, ed. Williamson Murray, MacGregor Knox, and Alvin Bernstein (New York: Cambridge University Press, 1994), 263; Franz Baron Conrad von Hötzendorf, *Aus meiner Dienstzeit 1906–1918*, 6th ed. (Vienna: Rikola Verlag, 1921), vol. 4, 193–94; and Generaloberst Helmuth von Moltke, *Errinerungen-Briefe-Dokumente*, ed. Eliza von Moltke (Stuttgart: Der Kommende Tag, 1922), 9.

22. Gerhard Ritter, *The Sword and the Scepter: The Problem of Militarism in Germany*, vol. 3, *The European Powers and the Wilhelminian Empire, 1890–1914* (Coral Gables, FL: University of Miami Press, 1970), 260; Lawrence Sondhaus, *Franz Conrad von Hötzendorf: Architect of the Apocalypse* (Boston: Humanities Press, 2000),176; and Afflerbach, *Falkenhayn*, 266–67.

23. August von Cramon, *Unser Österreich-Ungarischer Bundesgenosse im Weltkrieg. Erinnerungen aus meiner vierjährigen Tätigkeit als bevollmächtiger deutscher General beim k.u.k. Armeeoberkommando* (Berlin: E.S. Mittler und Sohn, 1920), 105; and Herwig and Heyman, *Biographical Dictionary of World War I*, 118–19. For details on Conrad's early life and career, see Sondhaus, *Franz Conrad von Hötzendorf*, 19–80.

24. Manfred Rauchensteiner, *Der Erste Weltkrieg und das Ende der Habsburgermonarchie 1914–1918* (Vienna: Böhlau Verlag, 2013), 23; Gary W. Shanafelt, *The Secret Enemy: Austria-Hungary and the German Alliance, 1914–1918* (Boulder, CO: East European Monographs, 1985), 12; and Sondhaus, *Franz Conrad von Hötzendorf*, 104.

25. Kaganeck Diary, April 12, 1915, BA-MA MSg 1/2514.

26. Tunstall, *Blood on the Snow*, 9.

27. Sondhaus, *Franz Conrad von Hötzendorf*, 65.

28. Cramon, *Unser Österreich-Ungarischer Bundesgenosse im Weltkrieg*, 22; Sondhaus, *Franz Conrad von Hötzendorf*, 169; Conrad to Arthur, Baron von Bolfras, April 6, 1915, ÖSA-KA MKSM 78. For an example of Conrad's writing style, see Conrad to Falkenhayn, May 18, 1915, BA-MA RH 61/962.

29. One can get a good sense of how much traveling Falkenhayn had to do in executing his duties from the diary of Gerhard Tappen, Falkenhayn's operations officer at OHL. See, for example, Tappen Diary, January 11, 1915, BA-MA RH 61/986.

30. Afflerbach, *Falkenhayn*, 256–57; and Sondhaus, *Franz Conrad von Hötzendorf*, 169. Perhaps the classic example of the terse nature of Falkenhayn's writing is Falkenhayn to Admiral Henning von Holtzendorf, March 30, 1916, BA-MA RM 28/53.

31. Josef Stürgkh, *Im deutschen Grossen Hauptquartier* (Leipzig: Paul List Verlag, 1921), 103; Afflerbach, *Falkenhayn*, 196; Conrad, *Aus meiner Dienstzeit 1906–1918*, 340; Sondhaus, *Franz Conrad von Hötzendorf*, 167; Tappen Diary, October 30, 1914, BA-MA RH 61/986; and DiNardo, *Breakthrough*, 19.

32. Germany, Reichsarchiv, *Der Weltkrieg 1914 bis 1918*, 303; and Afflerbach, *Falkenhayn*, 286.

33. Erich Ludendorff, *Meine Kriegserinnerungen 1914–1918* (Berlin: E. S. Mittler und Sohn, 1919), 106; Foley, *German Strategy and the Path to Verdun*, 132–33; Germany,

Reichsarchiv, *Der Weltkrieg 1914 bis 1918*, 303; Stürgkh, *Im deutschen Grossen Hauptquartier*, 127; Afflerbach, *Falkenhayn*, 286; and DiNardo, *Breakthrough*, 33–34.

34. Germany, Reichsarchiv, *Der Weltkrieg 1914 bis 1918*, 303–306; Gerhard Tappen, "Kriegserinneringen," unpublished, n.d., 91, BA-MA RH 61/986; Bavarian war ministry to Bavarian I, II, and III Corps, March 21, 1915, Bavarian 11th Infantry Division, Bund 52, Akt 2, Bayerisches Hauptstaatsarchiv, Abteilung IV, Kriegsarchiv, Munich, Germany (hereafter cited as BH-KA File 11/52/2); and DiNardo, *Breakthrough*, 34.

35. Cramon, *Unser Österreich-Ungarischer Bundesgenosse im Weltkrieg*, 1–3; and Biographical Chronology, BA-MA MSg 109/10858.

36. Cramon, *Unser Österreich-Ungarischer Bundesgenosse im Weltkrieg*, 104; and Cramon to Falkenhayn, April 8, 1915, 11:26 PM, BA-MA RH 61/1536. Mackensen regarded Cramon as eminently well suited to the position. Wolfgang Foerster, ed., *Mackensen: Briefe und Aufzeichnungen des Generalfeldmarschalls aus Krieg und Frieden* (Bonn: Wahlband der Buchgemeinde, 1938), 137.

37. Falkenhayn to Cramon, March 25, 1915; Cramon to Falkenhayn, March 25, 1915; Cramon to Falkenhayn, March 26, 1915, 10 AM, BA-MA RH 61/1536; Cramon, *Unser Österreich-Ungarischer Bundesgenosse im Weltkrieg*, 8; and Germany, Reichsarchiv, *Der Weltkrieg 1914 bis 1918*, 349.

38. Groener Diary Extract, Nachlass Groener, BA-MA N 46/41; Afflerbach, *Falkenhayn*, 287; and DiNardo, *Breakthrough*, 28. Wilhelm Groener was born on November 22, 1867, and obtained a commission as a second lieutenant on September 9, 1886. A graduate of the Kriegsakademie in 1896, Groener was eventually promoted to lieutenant colonel on September 13, 1912, and posted to the General Staff. At the outbreak of war in August 1914 Groener was appointed chief of the railway section and promoted to colonel a month later. Groener spent most of the next two years in administrative positions, eventually attaining the rank of Generalleutnant on November 1, 1916. On March 28, 1918, Groener was posted to Army Group Eichhorn as chief of staff. He went on to succeed Ludendorff as first quartermaster general on October 27, 1918. Groener retired from active service on September 30, 1919. He was appointed defense minister in 1928 and held that position until his resignation in May 1932. He died on May 3, 1939. Biographical Chronology, BA-MA MSg 109/10861; and Herwig and Heyman, *Biographical Dictionary of World War I*, 170–71.

39. Falkenhayn to Cramon, April 4, 1915; Cramon to Falkenhayn, April 6, 1915, BA-MA RH 61/1536; Tappen Diary, April 14, 1915, BA-MA RH 61/986; Germany, Reichsarchiv, *Der Weltkrieg 1914 bis 1918*, 361–62; and Austria, Bundesministerium für Landesverteidigung, *Österreich-Ungarns Letzter Krieg 1914–1918* (Vienna: Verlag der Militärwissenschaftlichen Mitteilungen, 1931), vol. 2, 306.

40. Conrad to Bolfras, April 6, 1915, ÖSA-KA MKSM 78/14; Falkenhayn to Cramon, April 8, 1915, BA-MA RH 61/1536; and General der Infanterie Hermann von Kuhl, *Der Weltkrieg 1914–1918* (Berlin: Verlag Tradition Wilhelm Kolk, 1929), vol. I, 119.

41. Tappen and Wild thought that the western front should continue to be the focus of Germany's military efforts. Tappen Diary, April 7, 1915, BA-MA RH 61/986; Reichold, ed., *Adolf Wild von Hohenborn*, 61; and Foley, *German Strategy and the Path to Verdun*, 132.

42. DiNardo, *Breakthrough*, 48.

43. Hans von Seeckt, *Aus meinem Leben 1866–1917* (Leipzig: von Hase und Koehler Verlag, 1938), 145; Foerster, ed., *Mackensen*, 171; Tappen Diary, May 30,

1915, BA-MA RH 61/986; Conrad to Falkenhayn, June 2, 1915, AOK Operations Bureau, Conrad–Falkenhayn Correspondence, Russia, ÖSA-KA R512; and DiNardo, *Breakthrough*, 86.

44. Falkenhayn to Conrad, June 2, 1915, AOK Operations Bureau, Conrad–Falkenhayn Correspondence, Russia, ÖSA-KA R512, Falkenhayn to German Eleventh Army, June 3, 1915, German Eleventh Army to OHL, June 3, 1915; and AOK to All Armies, June 4, 1915, BA-MA RH 61/1536; Rudolf Kundmann Diary, June 4, 1915, Conrad Archive, ÖSA-KA B/13; Hans Meier-Welcker, *Seeckt* (Frankfurt-am-Main: Bernard und Graefe Verlag für Wehrwesen, 1967), 54; and Foerster, ed., *Mackensen*, 171.

45. Cramon, *Unser Österreich-Ungarischer Bundesgenosse im Weltkrieg*, 19; Kundmann Diary, June 23, 1915, Conrad Archive, ÖSA-KA B/13, Conrad to Bolfras, June 27, 1915, ÖSA-KA MKSM 78; Rauchensteiner, *Der Erste Weltkrieg und das Ende der Habsburgermonarchie 1914–1918*, 461; and DiNardo, *Breakthrough*, 91–99.

46. German Eleventh Army, Estimate of the situation as of noon, June 15, 1915, BA-MA RH 61/1536; Seeckt, *Aus meinem Leben 1866–1917*, 153; Foerster, ed., *Mackensen*, 183–84; Tappen Diary, June 28, 1915, BA-MA RH 81/986; Kundmann Diary, June 28, 1915, Conrad Archive, ÖSA-KA B/13; and DiNardo, *Breakthrough*, 107–108.

47. Germany, Reichsarchiv, *Der Weltkrieg 1914 bis 1918*, 390; and DiNardo, *Breakthrough*, 126–30.

48. Conrad to Bolfras, June 2, 1915, ÖSA-KA MKSM 78; DiNardo, *Breakthrough*, 103; Gunther E. Rothenberg, *The Army of Francis Joseph* (West Lafayette, IN: Purdue University Press, 1976), 190.

49. Hamilton and Herwig, *Decisions for War, 1914–1917*, 176; Falkenhayn, *German General Staff and Its Decisions, 1914–1916*, 117–19; Holger H. Herwig, *The First World War: Germany and Austria–Hungary 1914–1918* (London: Arnold, 1997), 157; Falkenhayn to Conrad, June 13, 1915, BA-MA RH 61/1536; and DiNardo, *Breakthrough*, 135.

50. Richard C. Hall, *Bulgaria's Road to the First World War* (Boulder, CO: East European Monographs, 1996), 300–303; August von Mackensen, "Kriegstage in Bulgarien," November 22, 1935, Nachlass Mackensen, NA-MA N 39/310; and Hamilton and Herwig, *Decisions for War, 1914–1917*, 173–74.

51. Groener Diary Extract, Nachlass Groener, BA-MA N 46/41; and Falkenhayn to Conrad, August 5, 1915, AOK Operations Bureau, Conrad–Falkenhayn Correspondence, ÖSA-KA R512.

52. Conrad to Bolfras, April 6, 1915, ÖSA-KA MKSM 78/14; Falkenhayn to Cramon, April 8, 1915, BA-MA RH 61/1536; and Kuhl, *Der Weltkrieg 1914–1918*, 119.

53. Conrad to Falkenhayn, May 18, 1915; Conrad to Falkenhayn, May 19, 1915; Falkenhayn to Conrad, May 19, 1915; Conrad to Falkenhayn, May 23, 1915, BA-MA RH 61/962; Conrad to Bolfras, May 19, 1915; Conrad to Bolfras, May 21, 1915, ÖSA-KA MKSM 78; and Cramon, *Unser Österreich-Ungarischer Bundesgenosse im Weltkrieg*, 19.

54. Hamilton and Herwig, *Decisions for War, 1914–1917*, 199–200; Falkenhayn, *German General Staff and Its Decisions, 1914–1916*, 103; Sondhaus, *Franz Conrad von Hötzendorf*, 77; Falkenhayn to Conrad, May 16, 1915, BA-MA RH 61/962; and DiNardo, *Breakthrough*, 86.

55. Falkenhayn to Conrad, June 13, 1915, BA-MA RH 61/1536; Erickson, *Gallipoli*, 136–38; Hans von Plessen Diary, July 1, 1915, BA-MA RH 61/933; and Falkenhayn, *German General Staff and Its Decisions, 1914–1916*, 117.

56. Hall, *Bulgaria's Road to the First World War*, 303; and Lieutenant Colonel the Honorable Henry D. Napier, CMG, *The Experiences of a Military Attaché in the Balkans* (London: Drane's, 1924), 176.

57. Kundmann Diary, July 27, 1915, Conrad Archive, ÖSA-KA B/13; and Afflerbach, *Falkenhayn*, 338.

58. Kundmann Diary, July 27, 1915, Conrad Archive, ÖSA-KA B/13; Conrad to Bolfras, June 7, 1915, ÖSA-KA MKSM 78; and Shanafelt, *Secret Enemy*, 84. Bolfras was born on April 16, 1838. His service in the Austrian army extended all the way back to the Franco-Austrian War of 1859. In 1889 Bolfras was appointed head of Francis Joseph's Military Chancery, a post he held until 1916. Bolfras died in Baden on December 19, 1922. Herwig and Heyman, *Biographical Dictionary of World War I*, 90.

59. Afflerbach, *Falkenhayn*, 338; DiNardo, *Breakthrough*, 42; and Sondhaus, *Franz Conrad von Hötzendorf*, 182.

60. Tappen Diary, August 22, 1915, BA-MA RH 61/986; Hall, *Bulgaria's Road to the First World War*, 303–305; and Hamilton and Herwig, *Decisions for War, 1914–1917*, 174.

61. Herwig, *First World War*, 147–156; Erickson, *Gallipoli*, 174; Cyril Falls, *History of the Great War. Military Operations. Macedonia: From the Outbreak of War in 1914 to the Spring of 1917* (repr., Nashville: The Battery Press, 1996), 26; Cramon, *Unser Österreich-Ungarischer Bundesgenosse im Weltkrieg*, 32; and Robert A. Doughty, *Pyrrhic Victory: French Strategy and Operations in the Great War* (Cambridge: Harvard University Press, 2005), 219.

62. Falkenhayn, *German General Staff and Its Decisions, 1914–1916*, 180–81; OHL, Military Convention between Germany, Austria–Hungary and Bulgaria, September 6, 1915, BA-MA PH 5I/78; and Hall, *Bulgaria's Road to the First World War*, 305.

63. Ullrich, *Die nervöse Grossmacht*, 413; and Herwig, "Strategic Uncertainties of a Nation-State," 277.

64. Rothenberg, *The Army of Francis Joseph*, p. 190.

65. Shanafelt, *Secret Enemy*, 77; Sondhaus, *Franz Conrad von Hötzendorf*, 176; and Hall, *Bulgaria's Road to the First World War*, 305.

66. Napier, *Experiences of a Military Attaché in the Balkans*, 176.

67. Doughty, *Pyrrhic Victory*, 212–13; and Napier, *Experiences of a Military Attaché in the Balkans*, 187.

68. Alan Palmer, *The Gardeners of Salonika* (New York: Simon and Schuster, 1965), 32; Doughty, *Pyrrhic Victory*, 216–20; Napier, *Experiences of a Military Attaché in the Balkans*, 196; and Falls, *History of the Great War*, 37–39.

CHAPTER 3

1. General der Artillerie Max von Gallwitz, *Meine Führertätigkeit im Weltkriege 1914/1916: Belgien—Osten—Balkan* (Berlin: E.S. Mittler und Sohn, 1929), 379.

2. OHL, Directive for the New Army Group of Generalfeldmarschall von Mackensen, September 15, 1915, BA-MA PH 5I/78.

3. OHL, Intelligence Section, Report on the State of the Serbian Army, September 10, 1915, Nachlass Seeckt, BA-MA N 247/26.

4. OHL, Military Convention Between Germany, Austria–Hungary and Bulgaria, September 6, 1915, BA-MA PH 5I/78.

5. Conrad to Falkenhayn and Falkenhayn to Conrad, September 2, 1915, AOK Operations Bureau, Conrad Falkenhayn Correspondence, Russia, ÖSA-KA R512.

6. John R. Schindler, *Isonzo: The Forgotten Sacrifice of the Great War* (Westport, CT: Praeger, 2001), 82.

7. Austria, Bundesministerium, *Österreich-Ungarns Letzter Krieg 1914–1918* (Vienna: Verlag der Militärwissenschaftlichen Mitteilungen, 1931), vol. 3, 188; Conrad to Falkenhayn, Falkenhayn to Conrad, September 10, 1915, AOK Operations Bureau, Conrad-Falkenhayn Correspondence, Russia, ÖSA-KA R512; and Rauchensteiner, *Der Erste Weltkrieg und das Ende der Habsburgermonarchie 1914–1918*, 478.

8. Holger H. Herwig, *The First World War: Germany and Austria-Hungary 1914–1918* (London: Arnold, 1997), 147–48; Cramon to Falkenhayn, October 16, 1915, BA-MA RH 61/1536; Austria, Bundesministerium, *Österreich-Ungarns Letzter Krieg 1914–1918*, 181; and General Erich von Falkenhayn, *The German General Staff and Its Decisions, 1914–1916* (New York: Dodd, Mead, 1920), 169.

9. Ludendorff to Moltke, April 1, 1915, Nachlass Ludendorff, BA-MA N 77/2; Conrad to Bolfras, September 13, 1915, ÖSA-KA MKSM 78; Falkenhayn, *German General Staff and Its Decisions, 1914–1916*, 169; and Germany, Reichsarchiv, *Der Weltkrieg 1914 bis 1918*, (Berlin: E.S. Mittler und Sohn, 1933), vol. 9, 200.

10. Richard L. DiNardo, *Breakthrough: The Gorlice-Tarnow Campaign, 1915* (Santa Barbara, CA: Praeger, 2010), 43; and Groener Diary Extract, Nachlass Groener, BA-MA N 46/41.

11. Robert A. Doughty, *Pyrrhic Victory: French Strategy and Operations in the Great War* (Cambridge: Harvard University Press, 2005), 191–99; and Herwig, *First World War*, 171–72.

12. Herwig, *First World War*, 148; Vejas G. Liulevicius, *War Land on the Eastern Front: Culture, National Identity and German Occupation in World War I* (Cambridge: Cambridge University Press, 2000), 54; Hans Meier-Welcker, *Seeckt* (Frankfurt-am-Main: Bernard und Graefe Verlag für Wehrwesen, 1967), 62; and Seeckt to Wife, August 14, 1915, Nachlass Seeckt, BA-MA N 247/58.

13. German Army, Railroad Section, "Der Feldzug gegen Serbien im Herbst 1915," n.d., 5, BA-MA RH 61/27; Germany, Reichsarchiv, *Der Weltkrieg 1914 bis 1918*, 203; Kriegstagebuch (hereafter KTB)/Army Group Mackensen, September 16, 1915, BA-MA PH 5I/76; Wolfgang Foerster, ed., *Mackensen: Briefe und Aufzeichnungen des Generalfeldmarschalls aus Krieg und Frieden* (Bonn: Wahlband der Buchgemeinde, 1938), 213; and Gunther Hebert, *Das Alpenkorps: Aufbau, Organisation und Einsatz einer Gebirgstruppen im Ersten Weltkrieg* (Boppard-am-Rhein: Harald Boldt Verlag, 1988), 88.

14. Charles R. M. F. Cruttwell, *A History of the Great War 1914–1918* (repr., Chicago: Academy Publishers, 2007), 228–29; Conrad to Bolfras, April 6, 1915, ÖSA-KA MKSM 78; Germany, Reichsarchiv, *Der Weltkrieg 1914 bis 1918*, 201; Foerster, ed., *Mackensen*, 213; Austria, Bundesministerium, *Österreich-Ungarns Letzter Krieg 1914–1918*, 32; and British Army, General Staff, "Military Notes on the Balkan States," in *Armies of the Balkan States 1914–1918: The Military Forces of Bulgaria, Greece, Romania and Serbia*, ed. British Army, General Staff (repr., Nashville: Battery Press, 1996), 30.

15. General der Artillerie Richard von Berendt, "Aus grosser Zeit vor Zwanzig Jahren. Der Feldzug in Serbien," *Militär Wochenblatt* 120, no. 13 (October 4, 1935): 523; Oskar Regele, *Feldmarschall Conrad: Auftrag und Erfüllung, 1906–1918* (Vienna:

Verlag Herold, 1955), 309; Falkenhayn, *German General Staff and Its Decisions, 1914–1916*, 183; Austria, Bundesministerium, *Österreich-Ungarns Letzter Krieg 1914–1918*, 32; and Gallwitz, *Meine Führertätigkeit im Weltkriege 1914/1916*, 380.

16. Major Georg Paul Neumann, *Die deutschen Luftstreitkräfte im Weltkriege* (Berlin: Ernst Siegfried Mittler und Sohn, 1920), 488–89; and Lawrence Sondhaus, *The Naval Policy of Austria-Hungary, 1867–1918: Navalism, Industrial Development, and the Politics of Dualism* (West Lafayette, IN: Purdue University Press, 1994), 264.

17. Holger H. Herwig and Neil M. Heyman, *Biographical Dictionary of World War I* (Westport, CT: Greenwood Press, 1982), 235; Theo Schwarzmüller, *Zwischen Kaiser und Führer. Generalfeldmarschall August von Mackensen: Eine politische Biographie* (Paderborn: Ferdinand Schöningh, 1996), 18–91; Daniel J. Hughes, *The King's Finest: A Social and Bureaucratic Profile of Prussia's General Officers, 1871–1914* (Westport, CT: Praeger, 1987), 85; Biographical Chronology, BA-MA MSg 109/10865; and August von Mackensen, "Kriegstage in Bulgarien," November 22, 1935, Nachlass Mackensen, BA-MA N 39/310.

18. Schwarzmüller, *Zwischen Kaiser und Führer*, 82; Short Biographical Chronology, BA-MA MSg 109/10865; and Richard L. DiNardo, "Modern Soldier in a Busby: August von Mackensen, 1914–1916," in *Arms and the Man: Military History Essays in Honor of Dennis Showalter*, ed. Michael S. Neiberg (Boston: Brill, 2011), 135.

19. Dennis E. Showalter, *Tannenberg: Clash of Empires, 1914* (repr., Dulles, VA: Brassey's, 2004), 177; Schwarzmüller, *Zwischen Kaiser und Führer*, 78; Cruttwell, *History of the Great War 1914–1918*, 87; and DiNardo, "Modern Soldier in a Busby," 137–38.

20. DiNardo, *Breakthrough*, 128–29; Hans von Plessen Diary, June 22, 1915, BA-MA RH 61/933; and OHL, Military Convention Between Germany, Austria-Hungary and Bulgaria, September 6, 1915, BA-MA PH 5I/78.

21. Germany, Reichsarchiv, *Der Weltkrieg 1914 bis 1918*, 90; and DiNardo, *Breakthrough*, 38.

22. Foerster, ed., *Mackensen*, 93–94. See also Wolfgang Foerster, "Das Bild des modernen Feldherr," *Gesellschaft für Wehrpolitik und Wehrwissenschaften, Heerführer des Weltkrieges* (Berlin: E.S. Mittler und Sohn, 1939), 13–14.

23. DiNardo, *Breakthrough*, 121; and Foerster, ed., *Mackensen*, 189.

24. DiNardo, *Breakthrough*, 41; and Seeckt to Wife, April 27, 1915, Nachlass Seeckt, BA-MA N 247/57.

25. DiNardo, "Modern Soldier in a Busby," 157; Schwarzmüller, *Zwischen Kaiser und Führer*, 131; and Wolfram Wette, *Militarismus in Deutschland: Geschichte einer kriegerischen Kultur* (Frankfurt-am-Main: S. Fischer Verlag, 2008), 171.

26. Hans von Seeckt, *Aus meinem Leben 1866–1917* (Leipzig: von Hase und Koehler Verlag, 1938), 116; and Erich Ludendorff, *Meine Kriegserinnerungen 1914–1918* (Berlin: E.S. Mittler und Sohn, 1919), 109.

27. Seeckt to Wife, April 27, 1915, Nachlass Seeckt, BA-MA N 247/57, Plessen Diary, June 2, 1915, BA-MA RH 61/933; and Gallwitz, *Meine Führungtätigkeit im Weltkriege 1914/1916*, 379.

28. Kundmann Diary, June 3, 1915, Conrad Archive, ÖSA-KA B/13; and DiNardo, *Breakthrough*, 82.

29. Foerster, ed., *Mackensen*, 212; Schwarzmüller, *Zwischen Kaiser und Führer*, 121–22; and Archduke Friedrich to Mackensen, September 26, 1915, BA-MA RH 61/993.

30. Herwig and Heyman, *Biographical Dictionary of World War I*, 316; Major Bullrick, "Die Schlacht bei Vailly. Am Oktober 30, 1914, als Ausgangspunkt für der Erfolge bei Gorlice entscheidener neuer taktischer Grundsätze," Nachlass Seeckt, BA-MA N 247/22; Edgar von Schmidt-Pauli, *General von Seeckt: Lebensbild einen Deutschen Soldaten* (Berlin: Reinar Hobbing, 1937), 33; Seeckt, *Aus meinem Leben 1866-1917*, 99; and DiNardo, *Breakthrough*, 40.

31. Plessen Diary, June 22, 1915, BA-MA RH 61/933; Meier-Welcker, *Seeckt*, 55; Seeckt to Wife, June 28, 1915, Nachlass Seeckt, BA-MA N 247/57; and DiNardo, *Breakthrough*, 100.

32. John Wheeler-Bennett, *Wooden Titan: Hindenburg in Twenty Years of German History 1914-1934* (New York: William Morrow, 1936), 17; Franz Uhle-Wettler, *Erich Ludendorff in Seiner Zeit: Soldat—Stratege—Revolutionär: Eine Neubewertung* (Augsburg: Kurt Vowinckel Verlag, 1995), 177; and Basil H. Liddell Hart, *History of the First World War* (repr., London: Cassell, 1970), 197.

33. DiNardo, *Breakthrough*, 40-41; and Seeckt, *Aus meinem Leben 1866-1917*, 116.

34. DiNardo, *Breakthrough*, 41; Seeckt, *Aus meinem Leben 1866-1917*, 38; Foerster, ed., *Mackensen*, 138; and Seeckt to Wife, June 15, 1915, Nachlass Seeckt, BA-MA N 247/57.

35. Jakob Jung, *Max von Gallwitz (1852-1937): General und Politiker* (Osnabrück: Biblio Verlag, 1995), 8.

36. Herwig and Heyman, *Biographical Dictionary of World War I*, 160; and Jung, *Max von Gallwitz (1852-1937)*, 15-18.

37. Herwig and Heyman, *Biographical Dictionary of World War I*, 160; Jung, *Max von Gallwitz (1852-1937)*, 43-47; Germany, Reichsarchiv, *Der Weltkrieg 1914 bis 1918*, 351; and DiNardo, *Breakthrough*, 124.

38. Jung, *Max von Gallwitz (1852-1937)*, 16; Ludendorff, *Meine Kriegserinnerungen 1914-1918*, 102; Foerster, ed., *Mackensen*, 219; Herwig and Heyman, *Biographical Dictionary of World War I*, 160; and Gallwitz, *Meine Führungtätigkeit im Weltkriege 1914/1916*, 379.

39. Biographical Chronology, BA-MA MSg 109/10865.

40. Ibid.; and Seeckt, *Aus meinem Leben 1966-1917*, 65.

41. Biographical Chronology, BA-MA MSg 109/10861.

42. Biographical Chronology, BA-MA MSg 109/10863; and DiNardo, *Breakthrough*, 26.

43. Biographical Chronology, BA-MA MSg 109/10874; DiNardo, *Breakthrough*, 75; Robert M. Citino, *The German Way of War: From the Thirty Years' War to the Third Reich* (Lawrence: University Press of Kansas, 2005), 226-27.

44. Biological Chronology, BA-MA MSg 109/10863; DiNardo, *Breakthrough*, 44-45; and Christian Stachelbeck, *Militärische Effektivität im Ersten Weltkrieg: Die 11. Bayerische Infanteriedivision 1915 bis 1918* (Paderborn: Ferdinand Schöningh, 2010), 45.

45. Biographical Chronology, BA-MA MSg 109/10858; and DiNardo, *Breakthrough*, 122.

46. Biographical Chronology, BA-MA MSg 109/10864; Robert Kosch to Wife, February 23, 1915, Nachlass Kosch, BA-MA N 754/2; and Kosch to Wife, September 3, 1915, Nachlass Kosch, BA-MA N 745/4.

47. Biographical Chronology, BA-MA MSg 109/10864; and Larry Zuckerman, *The Rape of Belgium: The Untold Story of World War I* (New York: New York University Press, 2004), 93.

48. Michael B. Barrett, *Operation Albion: The German Conquest of the Baltic Islands* (Bloomington: Indiana University Press, 2008), 100–101; and DiNardo, *Breakthrough*, 125.

49. Biographical Chronology, BA-MA MSg 109/10866; and Gallwitz, *Meine Führertätigkeit im Weltkriege 1914/1916*, 380.

50. Mackensen's force was referred to as both Army Group Mackensen and Army Group Temesvár. See for example Army Group Temesvár, Order For Aerial Reconnaissance, September 25, 1915, BH-KA File 11/15/2; and Army Group Mackensen, Directive to Third Army, September 28, 1915, BA-MA PH 5I/78.

51. Austria, Bundesministerium, *Österreich-Ungarns Letzter Krieg 1914–1918*, 192; Rauchensteiner, *Der Erste Weltkrieg und das Ende der Habsburgermonarchie 1914–1918*, 481; and Georg Reichlin-Meldegg, *Das Kaisers Prinz Eugen? Feldmarschall Hermann Baron Kövess von Kövessháza: Der letzte Oberkommandant der K.u.K. Armee im Ersten Weltkrieg* (Graz: Ares Verlag, 2010), 126.

52. Austria, Bundesministerium, *Österreich-Ungarns Letzter Krieg 1914–1918*, 192; Rauchensteiner, *Der Erste Weltkrieg und das Ende der Habsburgermonarchie 1914–1918*, 481; and Georg Reichlin-Meldegg, *Das Kaisers Prinz Eugen? Feldmarschall Hermann Baron Kövess von Kövessháza: Der letzte Oberkommandant der K.u.K. Armee im Ersten Weltkrieg* (Graz: Ares Verlag, 2010), 126.

53. Herwig and Heyman, *Biographical Dictionary of World War I*, 211; and Reichlin-Meldegg, *Das Kaisers Prinz Eugen?* 8–29.

54. Herwig and Heyman, *Biographical Dictionary of World War I*, 211; and Reichlin-Meldegg, *Das Kaisers Prinz Eugen?* 65.

55. Herwig and Heyman, *Biographical Dictionary of World War I*, 211; Reichlin-Meldegg, *Das Kaisers Prinz Eugen?* 121–26; and Austria, Bundesministerium, *Österreich-Ungarns Letzter Krieg 1914–1918*, 29.

56. Foerster, ed., *Mackensen*, 220; and Seeckt, *Aus meinem Leben 1866–1917*, 227.

57. Austria, Bundesministerium, *Österreich-Ungarns Letzter Krieg 1914–1918*, 29–31.

58. Biographical Chronology, BA-MA MSg 109/10858.

59. Biographical Chronology, BA-MA MSg 109/10858.

60. Biographical Chronology, BA-MA MSg 109/10858; and Service Record of Eugen von Dorrer, Personal Files, File M430/2, Büschel 375, Landesarchiv Baden-Württemberg, Stuttgart, Germany. (Hereafter cited as LA-BW M430/2 Bü 375).

61. Service Record of Wilhelm von Urach, Duke of Württemberg, Personnel Files, LA-BW M430/2 Bü 2232.

62. Herwig and Heyman, *Biographical Dictionary of World War I*, 183. The most careful investigation of Hentsch's mission is Holger H. Herwig, *The Marne, 1914: The Opening of World War I and the Battle that Changed the World* (New York: Random House, 2009), 270–77.

63. Peter Broucek, ed., *Ein österreichischer General gegen Hitler. Feldmar-schalleutnant Alfred Jansa: Errinerungen* (Vienna: Böhlau Verlag, 2011), 243; and Falkenhayn, *German General Staff and Its Decisions, 1914–1916*, 186.

64. Falkenhayn to Cramon, May 26, 1915, BA-MA RH 61/1536; Colonel Scheunemann, "Pioniere im Kampf um die Donau," in *Das Ehrenbuch der Deutschen Pioniere*, ed. Paul Heinrici (Berlin: Verlag Tradition Wilhelm Kolk, 1932), 420–21; Falkenhayn, *German General Staff and Its Decisions, 1914–1916*, 186; Germany,

Reichsarchiv, *Der Weltkrieg 1914 bis 1918*, 203; and German Army, Railroad Section, "Der Feldzug gegen Serbien im Herbst 1915," 6–7, BA-MA RH 61/27.

65. Tappen Diary, September 16, 1915, BA-MA RH 61/986; OHL, Directive for the New Army Group of Generalfeldmarschall von Mackensen, September 15, 1915, BA-MA PH 5I/78; Foerster, ed., *Mackensen*, 210; and Seeckt, *Aus meinem Leben 1866–1917*, 214–15.

66. Broucek, ed., *Ein österreichischer General gegen Hitler*, 275; Austria, Bundesministerium, *Österreich-Ungarns Letzter Krieg 1914–1918*, 188; Seeckt, *Aus meinem Leben 1866–1917*, 219; Germany, Reichsarchiv, *Der Weltkrieg 1914 bis 1918*, 203; and Foerster, ed., *Mackensen*, 211–12.

67. For those unfamiliar with military terminology, a combined staff has members from two or more countries that are part of a coalition. A joint staff is homogenous in terms of nationality but has representatives from the various services of that country's armed forces.

68. Broucek, ed., *Ein österreichischer General gegen Hitler*, 276–77; and Foerster, ed., *Mackensen*, 211.

69. Broucek, ed., *Ein österreichischer General gegen Hitler*, 287.

70. Ibid.

71. Ibid., 294–96.

72. Joseph Huber, "The Forgotten City," Text of Radio Address Delivered in Munich, January 28, 1936, Nachlass Mackensen, BA-MA N 39/310; and Scheunemann, "Pioniere im Kampf um die Donau," 421.

73. Joseph Huber, "The Forgotten City," Text of Radio Address Delivered in Munich, January 28, 1936, Nachlass Mackensen, BA-MA N 39/310; and Scheunemann, "Pioniere im Kampf um die Donau," 421.

74. Liulevicius, *War Land on the Eastern Front*, 80; DiNardo, *Breakthrough*, 113–14; and First Lieutenant Herbert Ulrich, *Res.-Inf.-Regiment 52 im Weltkriege* (Cottbus: Lausitzer Druckerei und Verlagsanstalt, 1925), 227–28.

75. Wilhelm Führer, *Geschichte des Reserve Infanterie Regiments 203* (Berlin: Privately Published, 1960–1964), vol. 2, 323; Kosch to Wife, September 3, 1915, Nachlass Kosch, BA-MA N 754/4; Kosch to Wife, September 12, 1915, Nachlass Kosch, BA-MA N 754/5; and German X Reserve Corps, Special Orders, September 7, 1915, BA-MA PH 6 II/78.

76. Wilhelm Führer, *Geschichte des Reserve Infanterie Regiments 203* (Berlin: Privately Published, 1960–1964), vol. 2, 323; Kosch to Wife, September 3, 1915, Nachlass Kosch, BA-MA N 754/4; Kosch to Wife, September 12, 1915, Nachlass Kosch, BA-MA N 754/5; and German X Reserve Corps, Special Orders, September 7, 1915, BA-MA PH 6 II/78.

77. German Army, Railroad Section, "Der Feldzug gegen Serbien im Herbst 1915," 7–8, BA-MA RH 61/27; Franz Giese, *Geschichte des Reserve-Infanterie-Regiments 227 im Weltkriege 1914/18* (Privately Published, 1931), 252; and Schlawe, *Feldartillerie-Regiment General-Feldzeugmeister (1. Brandenburgisches) Nr. 3 im Weltkrieg 1914/1918*, 78.

78. German Army, Railroad Section, "Der Feldzug gegen Serbien im Herbst 1915," 7–8, BA-MA RH 61/27; Erich von Bartenwerffer and Alfred Herrmann, *Das Reserve-Infanterie-Regiment Nr. 232 im Ost und West* (Celle: Buchdruckerei W. Müller, 1927), 90; Joseph Steuer, *Das Infanterie-Regiment Generalfeldmarschall von Mackensen (3. West preussisches) Nr. 129 im Weltkriege* (Berlin: Druck und Verlag

Gerhard Stalling, 1925), 135; and Giese, *Geschichte der Reserve-Infanterie-Regiments 227 im Weltkriege 1914/18*, 252.

79. Fritz Haleck, *Das Reserve-Infanterie-Regiment Nr. 208* (Berlin: Druck und Verlag von Gerhard Stalling, 1922), 34; Franz Freiherr von Stengel, *Das K.B. 3. Infanterie-Regiment Prinz Karl von Bayern* (Munich: Verlag Bayerisches Kriegsarchiv, 1924), 40; Captain Gerok, *Das 2. Württ. Feldartillerie-Reg. Nr. 29 "Prinz Luitpold von Bayern" im Weltkrieg 1914–1918* (Stuttgart: Ehr. Belsersche Verlagsbuchhandlung, 1921), 41; Doerstling, *Kriegsgeschichte des Königlich Preussischen Infanterie-Regiments Graf Tauentzien v. Wittenberg (3. Brandenb.) Nr. 20*, 146; and German X Reserve Corps, Special Orders, October 4, 1914, BA-MA PH 6 II/79.

80. Captain Hellmut Gnamm, *Das Fusilier-Regiment Kaiser Franz Joseph von Österreich, König von Ungarn (4. württ,) Nr. 122* (Stuttgart: Ehr. Belsersche Verlagsbuchhandlung, 1921), 90; Appel, *Das Reserve-Infanterie-Regiment Nr. 205*, 101; Arthur Schöning, *Unser Regiment im Weltkriege* (Erfurt: Druck von A. Stenger, 1925), 174; Kurt Hennig, *Das Infanterie-Regiment (8. Ostpreussisches) Nr. 45 (Insterburg-Darkehmen) im Weltkriege 1914–18* (Berlin: Druck und Verlag Gerhard Stalling, 1928), 93; Ulrich, *Res.-Inf.-Regiment 52 im Weltkriege*, 232; Association of Former Officers of the Regiment, *Das 1. Masurische Infanterie-Regiment Nr. 146 1897–1919* (Berlin: Verlag Tradition Wilhelm Kolk, 1929), 131; Berendt, "Der Feldzug in Serbien," 524; and Gallwitz, *Meine Führertätigkeit im Weltkriege 1914/1916*, 389.

81. Giese, *Geschichte der Reserve-Infanterie-Regiments 227 im Weltkriege 1914/18*, 253; and Lieutenant Colonel Karl Boesser, *Geschichte des Reserve-Feldartillerie-Regiments Nr. 44* (Grossen: Rudolf Zeidler, 1932), 186. Lectures were supplemented by circulars issued by higher headquarters. See for example Bavarian Eleventh Infantry Division, Orientation on the Nature of Combat in Serbia, September 18, 1915, BH-KA 11/15/2.

82. Giese, *Geschichte der Reserve-Infanterie-Regiments 227 im Weltkriege 1914/18*, 253; Justus Scheibert, *Illustrirtes Deutsches Militär-Lexikon* (Berlin: Verlag von W. Pauli's, 1897), 169–70; Hennig, *Das Infanterie-Regiment (8. Ostpreussisches) Nr. 45 (Insterburg-Darkehmen) im Weltkriege 1914–18*, 93; Schöning, *Unser Regiment im Weltkriege*, 175; and Association of Former Officers of the Regiment, *Das 1. Masurische Infanterie-Regiment Nr. 146 1897–1919*, 131.

83. Association of Former Officers of the Regiment, *Das 1. Masurische Infanterie-Regiment Nr. 146 1897–1919*, 132.

84. Austria, Bundesministerium, *Österreich-Ungarns Letzter Krieg 1914–1918*, 199.

85. German X Reserve Corps, Corps Order, September 25, 1915 and September 29, 1915, BA-MA PH 6 II/79; and Hermann Neeff, *Das 4. Württ. Feldartillerie-Reg. Nr. 65 im Weltkrieg* (Stuttgart: Ehr. Belser AG Verlagsbuchhandlung, 1925), 52.

86. Schöning, *Unser Regiment im Weltkriege*, 173; Fritz Bergeder, *Das Reserve-Infanterie-Regiment Nr. 202 auf den Schlachtfeldern des Weltkrieges 1914–1918* (Berlin: Traditions Verlag Kolk, 1939), 94; and Hennig, *Das Infanterie-Regiment (8. Ostpreussisches) Nr. 45 (Insterburg-Darkehmen) im Weltkriege 1914–18*, 94.

87. Boesser, *Geschichte des Reserve-Feldartillerie-Regiments Nr. 44*, 184; Bergeder, *Das Reserve-Infanterie-Regiment Nr. 202 auf den Schlachtfeldern des Weltkrieges 1914–1918*, 94; Kosch to Wife, September 18, 1915, Nachlass Kosch, BA-MA N 754/5; and Giese, *Geschichte der Reserve-Infanterie-Regiments 227 im Weltkriege 1914/18*, 253. Kosch's photos are in Nachlass Kosch, BA-MA N 754/22.

88. Colonel Charles E. Callwell, *Small Wars: Their Principles and Practice*, 3rd ed. (repr., Lincoln: University of Nebraska Press, 1996), 57.

89. Mitrović, *Serbia's Great War 1914–1918*, 106–107; British Army, General Staff, "Military Notes on the Balkan States," 49; and Jonathan E. Gumz, *The Resurrection and Collapse of Empire in Habsburg Serbia, 1914–1918* (New York: Cambridge University Press, 2009), 43.

90. German Army Intelligence Section, Report on the Serbian Army, c. 1915, BH-KA 11/15/2; and German Army, Report on the State of the Serbian Army, September 10, 1915, Nachlass Seeckt, BA-MA N 247/26.

91. Mitrović, *Serbia's Great War 1914–1918*, 103; and Dimitrije Djordjević, "Radomir Putnik," in *The Serbs and their Leaders in the Twentieth Century*, ed. Peter Radan and Aleksandar Pavković (Brookfield, VT: Ashgate, 1997), 131.

92. Mitrović, *Serbia's Great War 1914–1918*, 103; and German Army Intelligence Section, Report on the Serbian Army, c. 1915, BH-KA 11/15/2.

93. British Army, General Staff, "Military Notes on the Balkan States," 50–51; German Army, Report on the State of the Serbian Army, September 10, 1915, Nachlass Seeckt, BA-MA N 247/26; and Germany, Reichsarchiv, *Der Weltkrieg 1914 bis 1918*, 197.

94. Charles E. J. Fryer, *The Destruction of Serbia in 1915* (New York: East European Monographs, 1997), 15; and British Army, General Staff, "Military Notes on the Balkan States," 41.

95. German Army, Report on the State of the Serbian Army, September 10, 1915, Nachlass Seeckt, BA-MA N 247/26; and German Army Intelligence Section, Report on the Serbian Army, c. 1915, BH-KA 11/15/2.

96. Charles E. J. Fryer, *The Royal Navy on the Danube* (Boulder, CO: East European Monographs, 1988), 39–40.

97. Herwig and Heyman, *Biographical Dictionary of World War I*, 341; Fryer, *Royal Navy on the Danube*, 34–35; and Richard Hough, *The Great War at Sea 1914–1918* (New York: Oxford University Press, 1983), 83.

98. Fryer, *Royal Navy on the Danube*, 34.

99. Mitrović, *Serbia's Great War 1914–1918*, 112; Monica M. Stanley, *My Diary in Serbia: April 1, 1915 – Nov. 1, 1915* (London: Simpkin, Marshall, Hamilton, Kent, 1916), 110; and Elsie Corbett, *Red Cross in Serbia 1915–1919: A Personal Diary of Experiences* (Banbury: Cheney and Sons, 1964), 8.

100. Herwig, *First World War*, 112; Mitrović, *Serbia's Great War 1914–1918*, 112–13; Djordjević, "Radomir Putnik," 130; German Army, Report on the State of the Serbian Army, September 10, 1915, Nachlass Seeckt, BA-MA N 247/26; Austro-Hungarian Third Army, "Serbia," September 16, 1915, LA-BW Gu117 Bü899; and Germany, Reichsarchiv, *Der Weltkrieg 1914 bis 1918*, 196–97.

101. German Army, Report on the State of the Serbian Army, September 10, 1915, Nachlass Seeckt, BA-MA N 247/26; British Army, General Staff, "Military Notes on the Balkan States," 43; and Austria, Bundesministerium, *Österreich-Ungarns Letzter Krieg 1914–1918*, 35.

102. German Army, Report on the State of the Serbian Army, September 10, 1915, Nachlass Seeckt, BA-MA N 247/26; Austria, Bundesministerium, *Österreich-Ungarns Letzter Krieg 1914–1918*, 35; and British Army, General Staff, "Military Notes on the Balkan States," 43.

103. Douglas W. Johnson, *Topography and Strategy in the War* (New York: Henry Holt, 1917), 153–54; Germany, Reichsarchiv, *Der Weltkrieg 1914 bis 1918*, 209; and Scheunemann, "Pioniere im Kampf um die Donau," 422.

104. Johnson, *Topography and Strategy in the World War*, 154–55; German Army, Railroad Section, "Der Feldzug gegen Serbien im Herbst 1915," 3, BA-MA RH 61/27; and Germany, Reichsarchiv, *Der Weltkrieg 1914 bis 1918*, 199.

105. Austria, Bundesministerium, *Österreich-Ungarns Letzter Krieg 1914–1918*, 187.

106. Germany, Reichsarchiv, *Der Weltkrieg 1914 bis 1918*, 200–202; Rauchensteiner, *Der Erste Weltkrieg und das Ende der Habsburgermonarchie 1914–1918*, 481; Johnson, *Topography and Strategy in the World War*, 148–49; and German Army, Railroad Section, "Der Feldzug gegen Serbien im Herbst 1915," 4, BA-MA RH 61/27.

107. Germany, Reichsarchiv, *Der Weltkrieg 1914 bis 1918*, 208; and Foerster, ed., *Mackensen*, 221.

CHAPTER 4

1. Hans von Seeckt, *Aus meinem Leben 1866–1917* (Leipzig: von Hase und Koehler Verlag, 1938), 229.

2. Kosch to Wife, October 10, 1915, Nachlass Kosch, BA-MA N 754/5.

3. Arthur Schöning, *Unser Regiment im Weltkriege* (Erfurt: Druck von A. Stenger, 1925), 173; Rudolf Dammert, *Der Serbische Feldzug: Erlebnisse Deutscher Truppen* (Leipzig: Verlag von Bernhard Tauchnitz, 1916), 18; and Charles E.J. Fryer, *The Royal Navy on the Danube* (Boulder, CO: East European Monographs, 1988), 125.

4. Army Group Temesvár, Order For Aerial Reconnaissance, September 25, 1915, BH-KA File 11/15/2; German X Reserve Corps, Special Order, October 1, 1915, BA-MA PH 6 II/79; Austria, Bundesministerium für Landesverteidigung, *Österreich-Ungarns Letzter Krieg 1914–1918* (Vienna: Verlag der Militärwissenschaftlichen Mitteilungen, 1931), vol. 3, 202; Germany, Reichsarchiv, *Der Weltkrieg 1914 bis 1918* (Berlin: E.S. Mittler und Sohn, 1933), vol. 9, 210; and Major Georg Paul Neumann, *Die deutschen Luftstreitkräfte im Weltkriege* (Berlin: Ernst Siegfried Mittler und Sohn, 1920), 492.

5. Colonel Hans Mayer, *Das K.B. 22. Infanterie-Regiment* (Munich: J. Lindauersche Universitäts-Buchhandlung, 1923), 48; Friedrich Appel, *Das Reserve-Infanterie-Regiment Nr. 205* (Berlin: Verlag Bernard und Graefe, 1937), 101; Wilhelm Führer, *Geschichte des Reserve Infanterie Regiments 203* (Berlin: Privately Published, 1960–1964), 331; First Lieutenant Harry Oden and First Lieutenant Friedrich Schultz, *Feldartillerie-Regiment 201: Seine Geschichte 1915–1918* (Zeulenroda: Bernhard Sporn, Buchdruckerei und Verlagsanstalt, 1931), 35; KTB/Bavarian 11th Infantry Division, September 28, 1915, BH-KA 11/15/1; and Richard L. DiNardo, *Breakthrough: The Gorlice-Tarnow Campaign, 1915* (Santa Barbara, CA: Praeger, 2010), 48.

6. Kosch to Wife, September 30, 1915, Nachlass Kosch, BA-MA N 754/5; General der Artillerie Max von Gallwitz, *Meine Führertätigkeit im Weltkriege 1914/1916: Belgien – Osten – Balkan* (Berlin: E.S. Mittler und Sohn, 1929), 382; Seeckt, *Aus meinem Leben 1866–1917*, 219; Wolfgang Foerster, ed., *Mackensen: Briefe und Aufzeichnungen des Generalfeldmarschalls aus Krieg und Frieden* (Bonn: Wahlband

der Buchgemeinde, 1938), 220; and KTB/Eleventh Army, October 4, 1915, BA-MA PH 5 II/305.

7. Jane's, *Jane's Fighting Aircraft of World War I* (repr., London: Studio, 1990), 160; Norman Franks, Frank Bailey, and Rick Duiven, *Casualties of the German Air Service 1914–1920: As Complete a List Possible Arranged Alphabetically and Chronologically* (London: Grub Street, 1999), 180; and Monica M. Stanley, *My Diary in Serbia: April 1, 1915 – Nov. 1, 1915* (London: Simpkin, Marshall, Hamilton, Kent, 1916), 102.

8. Neumann, *Die deutschen Luftstreitkräfte im Weltkriege*, 242; and Germany, Reichsarchiv, *Der Weltkrieg 1914 bis 1918*, 204.

9. Franks, Bailey, and Duiven, *Casualties of the German Air Service 1914–1920*, 180; and Stanley, *My Diary in Serbia*, 106.

10. Austro-Hungarian Third Army to 26th Infantry Division, Intelligence Summary, September 16, 1915, LA-BW Gu117 Bü899; KTB/Army Group Mackensen, September 28, 1915, BA-MA PH 5 I/76; Intelligence Section, XXII Reserve Corps, Changes During the Last Week, October 2, 1915, Nachlass Dorrer, LA-BW M660/071 Nr. 18c.

11. KTB/Army Group Mackensen, September 28, 1915, BA-MA PH 5 I/76; KTB/Bavarian Eleventh Infantry Division, September 25, 1915, BH-KA File 11/15/1; German IV Reserve Corps, Special Orders, October 2, 1915, BH-KA File 11/15/2; and Fryer, *Royal Navy on the Danube*, 16–17.

12. German X Reserve Corps, Corps Orders, October 1, 1915, BA-MA PH 6 II/79; and Bavarian 11th Infantry Division, Morning Report, October 4, 1915, BH-KA File 11/15/2.

13. Peter Broucek, ed., *Ein österreichischer General gegen Hitler. Feldmarschalleutnant Alfred Jansa: Errinerungen* (Vienna: Böhlau Verlag, 2011), 282; Georg Reichlin-Meldegg, *Das Kaisers Prinz Eugen? Feldmarschall Hermann Baron Kövess von Kövessháza: Der letzte Oberkommandant der K.u.K. Armee im Ersten Weltkrieg* (Graz: Ares Verlag, 2010), 132; General der Artillerie Richard von Berendt, "Aus grosser Zeit vor Zwanzig Jahren. Der Feldzug in Serbien," *Militär Wochenblatt* 120, no. 13 (October 4, 1935): 524; and Hans Meier-Welcker, *Seeckt* (Frankfurt-am-Main: Bernard und Graefe Verlag für Wehrwesen, 1967), 66.

14. Herbert Jäger, *German Artillery of World War One* (Wiltshire: Crowood Press, 2001), 33–34; Bavarian 11th Infantry Division, Morning Report, October 4, 1915, BH-KA File 11/15/2; Austro-Hungarian Third Army, Directive on the State of Firing Positions for the Forcing of the Danube and Save Rivers, October 4, 1915, Nachlass Dorrer, LA-BW M660/071 Nr. 18a; German IV Reserve Corps, Corps Orders for Danube Crossing, October 5, 1915, BH-KA File 11/15/2; Captain Wilhelm Schlawe, *Feldartillerie-Regiment General-Feldzeugmeister (1. Brandenburgisches) Nr. 3 im Weltkrieg 1914/1918* (Berlin: Verlag Bernard und Graefe, 1935), 80; and Fryer, *Royal Navy on the Danube*, 13.

15. KTB/Army Group Mackensen, September 28, 1915, BA-MA PH 5 I/76; Gallwitz, *Meine Führertätigkeit im Weltkriege 1914/1916*, 379; and Dammert, *Der Serbische Feldzug*, 20.

16. Holger Afflerbach, *Falkenhayn: Politisches Denken und Handeln im Kaiserreich* (Munich: R. Oldenbourg Verlag, 1996), 337; Foerster, ed., *Makensen*, 216–17; and Seeckt, *Aus meinem Leben 1866–1917*, 224.

17. Austria, Bundesministerium, *Österreich-Ungarns Letzter Krieg 1914–1918*, 187–88; and OHL, Military Convention Between Germany, Austria-Hungary and Bulgaria, September 6, 1915, BA-MA PH 5I/78.

18. Germany, Reichsarchiv, *Der Weltkrieg 1914 bis 1918*, 200–202; Douglas W. Johnson, *Topography and Strategy in the War* (New York: Henry Holt and Company, 1917), 148–49; and German Army, Railroad Section, "Der Feldzug gegen Serbien im Herbst 1915," n.d., 4, BA-MA RH 61/27.

19. Gallwitz, *Meine Führertätigkeit im Weltkriege 1914/1916*, 385.

20. Austria, Bundesministerium, *Österreich-Ungarns Letzter Krieg 1914–1918*, 201; and Germany, Reichsarchiv, *Der Weltkrieg 1914 bis 1918*, 209.

21. Gallwitz, *Meine Führertätigkeit im Weltekriege 1914/1916*, 383; KTB/Bavarian 11th Infantry Division, September 20, 1915, BH-KA File 11/15/1; Seeckt, *Aus meinem Leben 1866–1917*, 219; and German IV Reserve Corps, Corps Order, September 25, 1915, BH-KA File 11/15/2.

22. KTB/Army Group Mackensen, September 28, 1915, BA-MA PH 5I/76; KTB/ Bavarian 11th Infantry Division, BH-KA File 11/15/1; Franz Freiherr von Stengel, *Das K.B. 3. Infanterie-Regiment Prinz Karl von Bayern* (Munich: Verlag Bayerisches Kriegsarchiv, 1924), 40; and German IV Reserve Corps, Special Orders, September 29, 1915, BH-KA File 11/15/2.

23. August von Cramon, *Unser Österreich-Ungarischer Bundesgenosse im Weltkriege. Erinnerungen aus meiner vierjährigen Tätigkeit als bevollmächtiger deutsche General beim k.u.k. Armeeoberkommando* (Berlin: E.S. Mittler und Sohn, 1920), 34.

24. Reichlin-Meldegg, *Das Kaisers Prinz Eugen?* 131; Foerster, ed., *Mackensen*, 20–21; and Gallwitz, *Meine Führertätigkeit im Weltkriege 1914/1916*, 384.

25. German X Reserve Corps, Special Order, October 6, 1915, BA-MA PH 6 II/79; and DiNardo, *Breakthrough*, 88.

26. Germany, Reichsarchiv, *Der Weltkrieg 1914 bis 1918*, 206; and Austria, Bundesministerium, *Österreich-Ungarns Letzter Krieg 1914–1918*, 202.

27. Austro-Hungarian XIX Corps to German XXII Reserve Corps, October 3, 1915; Austro-Hungarian XIX Corps to Austro-Hungarian Third Army, October 4, 1915, BA-MA PH 6 II/119; Franz Giese, *Geschichte des Reserve-Infanterie Regiments 227 im Weltkriege 1914/18* (Privately Published, 1931), 254; German X Reserve Corps, Special Order, October 5, 1915, BA-MA PH 6 II/79; German 26th Infantry Division, Division Order, October 1, 1915, LA-BW Gu117 Bü900; and KTB/Eleventh Army, October 5, 1915, BA-MA PH 5 II/305.

28. Schöning, *Unser Regiment im Weltkriege*, 177–78; German XXII Reserve Corps to Austro-Hungarian Third Army, October 5, 1915, BA-MA PH 6 II/119; and German IV Reserve Corps, Corps Order for Danube Crossing, October 5, 1915, BH-KA File 11/15/1.

29. Dammert, *Der Serbische Feldzug*, 27; Gallwitz, *Meine Führertätigkeit im Weltkriege 1914/1916*, 389; and Fryer, *Royal Navy on the Danube*, 127.

30. German IV Reserve Corps, Orders for Danube Crossing, October 5, 1915, BH-KA File 11/15/2; Major Hilmer Freiherr von Bülow, *Geschichte der Luftwaffe: Eine kurz Darstellung der Entwicklung der fünften Waffe* (Frankfurt-am-Main: Verlag Moritz Diesterweg, 1934), 61; Fryer, *Royal Navy on the Danube*, 127; Neumann, *Die deutschen Luftstreitkräfte im Weltkriege*, 490; and Richard L. DiNardo, "German Air

Operations on the Eastern Front, 1914–1917," in *Essays on World War I*, ed. Peter Pastor and Graydon A. Tunstall (Boulder, CO: Social Science Monographs, 2012), 69.

31. Fryer, *Royal Navy on the Danube*, 127; and Andrej Mitrović, *Serbia's Great War, 1914–1918* (West Lafayette, IN: Purdue University Press, 2007), 145.

32. Germany, Reichsarchiv, *Der Weltkrieg 1914 bis 1918*, 212; Colonel Scheunemann, "Pioniere im Kampf um die Donau," in *Das Ehrenbuch der Deutschen Pioniere*, ed. Paul Heinrici (Berlin: Verlag Tradition Wilhelm Kolk, 1932), 428; and Fritz Haleck, *Das Reserve-Infanterie-Regiment Nr. 208* (Berlin: Druck und Verlag von Gerhard Stalling, 1922), 35–36.

33. Appel, *Das Reserve-Infanterie-Regiment Nr. 205*, 102; Scheunemann, "Pioniere im Kampf um die Donau," 428; and German XXII Reserve Corps to Austro-Hungarian Third Army, October 7, 1915, 4:45 PM, BA-MA PH 6 II/119.

34. Germany, Reichsarchiv, *Der Weltkrieg 1914 bis 1918*, 212; Führer, *Geschichte des Reserve Infanterie Regiments 203*, 339; Fritz Bergeder, *Das Reserve-Infanterie-Regiment Nr. 202 auf den Schlachtfeldern des Weltkrieges 1914–1918* (Berlin: Traditions Verlag Kolk, 1939), 95; Dammert, *Der Serbische Feldzug*, 28–28; and Scheunemann, "Pioniere im Kampf um die Donau," 428.

35. Austria, Bundesministerium, *Österreich-Ungarns Letzter Krieg 1914–1918*, 204–206; Scheunemann, "Pioniere im Kampf um die Donau," 428; and Germany, Reichsarchiv, *Der Weltkrieg 1914 bis 1918*, 212.

36. Reichlin-Meldegg, *Das Kaisers Prinz Eugen?* 131.

37. Austria, Bundesministerium, *Österreich-Ungarns Letzter Krieg 1914–1918*, 205–207; Broucek, ed., *Ein österreichischer General gegen Hitler*, 290; and Germany, Reichsarchiv, *Der Weltkrieg 1914 bis 1918*, 212.

38. Germany, Reichsarchiv, *Der Weltkrieg 1914 bis 1918*, 213; and Otto Zarn, Colonel Hayner, and Major Frantzius, *Geschichte des Reserve-Infanterie-Regiments Nr. 201* (Berlin: Verlag Bernard und Graefe, 1940), 172.

39. Austria, Bundesministerium, *Österreich-Ungarns Letzter Krieg 1914–1918*, 210; and Fryer, *Destruction of Serbia in 1915*, 59.

40. Germany, Reichsarchiv, *Der Weltkrieg 1914 bis 1918*, 217–18.

41. Ibid., 218, Zarn, Hayner, and Frantzius, *Geschichte des Reserve-Infanterie-Regiments Nr. 201*, 172; Bergeder, *Das Reserve-Infanterie-Regiment Nr. 202 auf den Schlachtfeldern des Weltkrieges 1914–1918*, 95; German Twenty-Sixth Infantry Division, Division Order, October 11, 1915, LA-BW Gu 117 Bü 900; and Austria, Bundesministerium, *Österreich-Ungarns Letzter Krieg 1914–1918*, 211.

42. Germany, Reichsarchiv, *Der Weltkrieg 1914 bis 1918*, 218; and Bergeder, *Das Reserve-Infanterie-Regiment Nr. 202 auf den Schlachtfeldern des Weltkrieges 1914–1918*, 97.

43. Austria, Bundesministerium, *Österreich-Ungarns Letzter Krieg 1914–1918*, 219–20; Lieutenant Colonel Karl Boesser, *Geschichte des Reserve-Feldartillerie-Regiments Nr. 44* (Grossen: Rudolf Zeidler, 1932), 191; Zarn, Hayner, and Frantzius, *Geschichte des Reserve-Infanterie-Regiments Nr. 201*, 173–74; Bergeder, *Das Reserve-Infanterie-Regiment Nr. 202 auf den Schlachtfeldern, des Weltkrieges 1914–1918*, 98; and Germany, Reichsarchiv, *Der Weltkrieg 1914 bis 1918*, 218.

44. German XXII Reserve Corps to Austro-Hungarian Third Army, October 11, 1915, 9:26 PM, BA-MA PH 6 II/119; Austria, Bundesministerium, *Österreich-Ungarns*

Letzter Krieg 1914–1918, 221; Germany, Reichsarchiv, *Der Weltkrieg 1914 bis 1918*, 219; and Foerster, ed., *Mackensen*, 225.

45. Seeckt, *Aus meinem Leben 1866–1917*, 234; Foerster, ed., *Mackensen*, 223; and Reichlin-Meldegg, *Das Kaisers Prinz Eugen?* 134.

46. Broucek, ed., *Ein österreichischer General gegen Hitler*, 294.

47. Dammert, *Der Serbische Feldzug*, 52; and Mitrović, *Serbia's Great War, 1914–1918*, 145.

48. Army Group Mackensen, Proclamation of the Commander of the Allied Forces, c. October 1915, LA-BW Gu 117 Bü 900.

49. Army Group Mackensen, Proclamation of the Commander of the Allied Forces, c. October 1915, LA-BW Gu 117 Bü 900.

50. Foerster, ed., *Mackensen*, 222; Gallwitz, *Meine Führertätigkeit im Weltkriege 1914/1916*, 390; and KTB/Eleventh Army, October 7, 1915, BA-MA PH 5 II/305.

51. Germany, Reichsarchiv, *Der Weltkrieg 1914 bis 1918*, 214; KTB/Eleventh Army, October 7, 1914, BA-MA PH 5 II/305; and Dammert, *Der Serbische Feldzug*, 33.

52. Schöning, *Unser Regiment im Weltkriege*, 178; and Alfred Richter, *Das 2. Thüring. Infanterie-Regiment Nr. 32* (Zeulenroda: Druck von Bernhard Spoorn, 1928), 157.

53. Schöning, *Unser Regiment im Weltkriege*, 179; Richter, *Das 2. Thüring. Infanterie-Regiment Nr. 32*, 157; and Scheunemann, "Pioniere im Kampf um die Donau," 427.

54. German 101st Infantry Division, Brief Report on Operations of the 101st Infantry Division During the Campaign in Serbia in October and November 1915, December 9, 1915, BA-MA PH 8 I/45; and Association of Former Officers of the Regiment, *Das 1. Masurische Infanterie-Regiment Nr. 146 1897–1919* (Berlin: Verlag Tradition Wilhelm Kolk, 1929), 133.

55. Schöning, *Unser Regiment im Weltkriege*, 181; and Richter, *Das 2. Thüring. Infanterie-Regiment Nr. 32*, 158.

56. Kurt Hennig, *Das Infanterie-Regiment (8. Ostpreussisches) Nr. 45 (Insterburg-Darkehmen) im Weltkriege 1914–18* (Berlin: Druck und Verlag Gerhard Stalling, 1928), 94–95; Association of Former Officers of the Regiment, *Das 1. Masurische Infanterie-Regiment Nr. 146*, 133; Schöning, *Unser Regiment im Weltkriege*, 180–81; and Richter, *Das 2. Thüring. Infanterie-Regiment Nr. 32*, 159–60.

57. Germany, Reichsarchiv, *Der Weltkrieg 1914 bis 1918*, 214; and Richter, *Das 2. Thüring. Infanterie-Regiment Nr. 32*, 159.

58. Gallwitz, *Meine Führertätigkeit im Weltkriege 1914/1916*, 393.

59. German 101st Infantry Division, Brief Report on Operations of the 101st Infantry Division During the Campaign in Serbia in October and November 1915, December 9, 1915, BA-MA PH 8 I/45; Richter, *Das 2. Thüring. Infanterie-Regiment Nr. 32*, 163; Jäger, *German Artillery of World War One*, 39; Eric D. Brose, *The Kaiser's Army: The Politics of Military Rechnology in Germany during the Machine Age, 1870–1918* (New York: Oxford University Press, 2001), 168.

60. Germany, Reichsarchiv, *Der Weltkrieg 1914 bis 1918*, 221; German 101st Infantry Division, Brief Report on Operations of the 101st Infantry Division During the Campaign in Serbia in October and November 1915, December 9, 1915, BA-MA PH 8 I/45; Hennig, *Das Infanterie-Regiment (8. Ostpreussisches) Nr. 45 (Insterburg-Darkehmen) im*

Weltkriege 1914–18, 96; Richter, *Das 2. Thüring. Infanterie-Regiment Nr. 32*, 166; and Kosch to Wife, October 10, 1915, Nachlass Kosch, BA-MA N 754/5.

61. Germany, Reichsarchiv, *Der Weltkrieg 1914 bis 1918*, 214; KTB/Bavarian Eleventh Infantry Division, October 6, 1915, BH-KA File 11/15/1; and DiNardo, *Breakthrough*, 75.

62. Germany, Reichsarchiv, *Der Weltkrieg 1914 bis 1918*, 214–15; KTB/Bavarian Eleventh Infantry Division, October 8, 1915, BH-KA File 11/15/1; Stengel, *Das K.B. 3. Infanterie-Regiment Prinz Karl von Bayern*, 41; Captain Hellmut Gnamm, *Das Fusilier-Regiment Kaiser Franz Joseph von Österreich, König von Ungarn (4. württ,) Nr. 122* (Stuttgart: Ehr. Belsersche Verlagsbuchhandlung, 1921), 92; and Joseph Steuer, *Das Infanterie-Regiment Generalfeldmarschall von Mackensen (3. West preussisches) Nr. 129 im Weltkriege* (Berlin: Druck und Verlag Gerhard Stalling, 1925), 137.

63. Stengel, *Das K.B. 3. Infanterie-Regiment Prinz Karl von Bayern*, 41; and Steuer, *Das Infanterie-Regiment Generalfeldmarschall von Mackensen (3. West preussisches) Nr. 129 im Weltkriege*, 138.

64. Steuer, *Das Infanterie-Regiment Generalfeldmarschall von Mackensen (3. West preussisches) Nr. 129 im Weltkriege*, 138; Gnamm, *Das Fusilier-Regiment Kaiser Franz Joseph von Österreich, König von Ungarn (4. württ,) Nr. 122*, 95; and First Lieutenant Herbert Ulrich, *Res.-Inf.-Regiment 52 im Weltkriege* (Cottbus: Lausitzer Druckerei und Verlagsanstalt, 1925), 233.

65. Stengel, *Das K.B. 3. Infanterie-Regiment Prinz Karl von Bayern*, 42; Germany, Reichsarchiv, *Der Weltkrieg 1914 bis 1918*, 215; and Fryer, *Destruction of Serbia in 1915*, 51.

66. Germany, Reichsarchiv, *Der Weltkrieg 1914 bis 1918*, 215; and KTB/Bavarian Eleventh Infantry Division, October 9, 1915, BH-KA File 11/15/1.

67. Germany, Reichsarchiv, *Der Weltkrieg 1914 bis 1918*, 216; Gnamm, *Das Fusilier-Regiment Kaiser Franz Joseph von Österreich, König von Ungarn (4. württ,) Nr. 122*, 95; Steuer, *Das Infanterie-Regiment Generalfeldmarschall von Mackensen (3. West preussisches) Nr. 129 im Weltkriege*, 139; and KTB/Bavarian Eleventh Infantry Division, October 9, 1915, BH-KA File 11/15/1.

68. Stengel, *Das K.B. 3. Infanterie-Regiment Prinz Karl von Bayern*, 42; Gnamm, *Das Fusilier-Regiment Kaiser Franz Joseph von Österreich, König von Ungarn (4. württ,) Nr. 122*, 95; Steuer, *Das Infanterie-Regiment Generalfeldmarschall von Mackensen (3. West preussisches) Nr. 129 im Weltkriege*, 139; and KTB/Bavarian Eleventh Infantry Division, October 9, 1915, BH-KA File 11/15/1.

69. Germany, Reichsarchiv, *Der Weltkrieg 1914 bis 1918*, 215.

70. Berendt, "Der Feldzug in Serbien," 525; Schlawe, *Feldartillerie-Regiment General-Feldzeugmeister (1. Brandenburgisches) Nr. 3 im Weltkrieg 1914/1918*, 80; and Adolf Soldan, *5. Grossherzoglich Hessischen Infanterie-Regiment Nr. 168* (Berlin: Druck und Verlag Gerhard Stalling, 1924), 66.

71. Germany, Reichsarchiv, *Der Weltkrieg 1914 bis 1918*, 215; KTB/Eleventh Army, October 9, 1915, BA-MA PH 5 II/305; Gallwitz, *Meine Führer Tätigkeit im Weltkriege 1914/1916*, 394; Soldan, *5. Grossherzoglich Hessischen Infanterie-Regiment Nr. 168*, 66; Schlawe, *Feldartillerie-Regiment General-Feldzeugmeister (1. Brandenburgisches) Nr. 3 im Weltkrieg 1914/1918*, 81; and Lieutenant Colonel Paul Doerstling, *Kriegsgeschichte des Königlich Preussischen Infanterie-Regiments Graf Tauentzien v. Wittenberg*

(3. Brandenb.) Nr. 20 (Zeulenroda: Bernhard Sporn, Buchdruckerei und Verlagsanstalt, 1933), 148.

72. Germany, Reichsarchiv, *Der Weltkrieg 1914 bis 1918*, 221; KTB/Eleventh Army, October 11, 1915, BA-MA PH 5 II/305; Gallwitz, *Meine Führer Tätigkeit im Weltkriege 1914/1916*, 397; Soldan, 5. *Grossherzoglich Hessischen Infanterie-Regiment Nr. 168*, 66; Doerstling, *Kriegsgeschichte des Königlich Preussischen Infanterie-Regiments Graf Tauentzien v. Wittenberg (3. Brandenb.) Nr. 20*, 150–51; and Scheunemann, "Pioniere im Kampf um die Donau," 430.

73. German Army, Railroad Section, "Der Feldzug gegen Serbien im Herbst 1915," 13, BA-MA RH 61/27; Kosch to Wife, October 10, 1915, Nachlass Kosch, BA-MA N 754/5; German X Reserve Corps, Special Orders, October 11, 1915, BA-MA PH 6 II/79; KTB/Army Group Mackensen, September 28, 1915, BA-MA PH 5 I/76; Scheunemann "Pioniere im Kampf um die Donau," 429; and Foerster, ed., *Mackensen*, 224.

74. Army Group Mackensen, Proclamation of the Commander of the Allied Forces, c. October 1915, LA-BW Gu 117 Bü 900; German Eleventh Army, Army Order, October 6, 1915, BH-KA File 11/15/2; German X Reserve Corps, Special Orders, October 6, 1915 and October 12, 1915, BA-MA 6 II/79.

75. Fryer, *Destruction of Serbia in 1915*, 23; Mitrović, *Serbia's Great War 1914–1918*, 111; Steuer, *Das Infanterie-Regiment Generalfeldmarschall von Mackensen (3. Westpreussisches) Nr. 129 im Weltkriege*, 141; and Bavarian Eleventh Infantry Division, Orientation on the Nature of Combat in Serbia, September 18, 1915, BH-KA File 11/15/2.

76. Tappen Diary, October 9, 1915, BA-MA RH 61/986; Plessen Diary, October 11, 1915, BA-MA RH 61/933; Lawrence Sondhaus, *Franz Conrad von Hötzendorf: Architect of the Apocalypse* (Boston: Humanities Press, 2000), 182; Gunther E. Rothenberg, *The Army of Francis Joseph* (West Lafayette, IN: Purdue University Press, 1976), 191; and Manfred Rauchensteiner, *Der Erste Weltkrieg und das Ende der Habsburgermonarchie 1914–1918* (Vienna: Böhlau Verlag, 2013), 490.

77. Broucek, ed., *Ein österreichischer General gegen Hitler*, 294; Reichlin-Meldegg, *Das Kaisers Prinz Eugen?* 135; and Seeckt, *Aus meinem Leben 1866–1917*, 235.

78. Reichlin-Meldegg, *Das Kaisers Prinz Eugen?* 135.

79. Germany, Reichsarchiv, *Der Weltkrieg 1914 bis 1918*, 211; Army Group Mackensen to Austro-Hungarian Third Army, October 10, 1915, BA-MA PH 5 I/78; Broucek, ed., *Ein österreichischer General gegen Hitler*, 290; and Gallwitz, *Meine Führer Tätigkeit im Weltkriege 1914/1916*, 394.

80. OHL, Military Convention Between Germany, Austria-Hungary and Bulgaria, September 6, 1915, BA-MA PH 5I/78; German Army, Report on the State of the Serbian Army, September 10, 1915, Nachlass Seeckt, BA-MA N 247/26; Austria, Bundesministerium, *Österreich-Ungarns Letzter Krieg 1914–1918*, 35; British Army, General Staff, "Military Notes on the Balkan States," 43; Gordon-Smith, *From Serbia to Jugoslavia*, 50; and Germany, Reichsarchiv, *Der Weltkrieg 1914 bis 1918*, 217.

81. Gallwitz, *Meine Führertätigkeit im Weltkriege 1914/1916*, 382; Neumann, *Die deutschen Luftstreitkräfte im Weltkriege*, 242; Germany, Reichsarchiv, *Der Weltkrieg 1914 bis 1918*, 204; Appel, *Das Reserve-Infanterie-Regt. Nr. 205*, 101; Oden and Schultz, *Feldartillerie-Regiment 201*, 35; German XXII Reserve Corps to Austro-Hungarian Third Army, October 7, 1915, 4:45 PM, BA-MA PH 6 II/119; and KTB/Eleventh Army, October 7, 1915, BA-MA PH 5 II/305.

82. Fryer, *Royal Navy on the Danube*, 127; Jakob Jung, *Max von Gallwitz (1852–1937) (1852–1937): General und Politiker* (Osnabrück: Biblio Verlag, 1995), 60; and Berendt, "Der Feldzug in Serbien," 525.

83. German Army, Railroad Section, "Der Feldzug gegen Serbien in Herbst 1915," 10, BA-MA RH 61/27; and Scheunemann, "Pioniere im Kampf um die Donau," 423.

84. Richter, *Das 2. Thüring. Infanterie-Regiment Nr. 32*, 157; Oden and Schultz, *Feldartillerie-Regiment 201*, 36; Reichlin-Meldegg, *Das Kaisers Prinz Eugen?* 134; and Cramon to Falkenhayn, October 12, 1915, BA-MA RH 61/1536.

85. Foerster, ed., *Mackensen*, 221; Seeckt, *Aus meinem Leben 1866–1917*, 231–32; Mitrović, *Serbia's Great War, 1914–1918*, 147; and Robert A. Doughty, *Pyrrhic Victory: French Strategy and Operations in the Great War* (Cambridge: Harvard University Press, 2005), 222.

CHAPTER 5

1. Army Group Mackensen to Austro-Hungarian Third Army, October 13, 1915, BA-MA PH 5 I/78.

2. Wolfgang Foerster, ed., *Mackensen: Briefe und Aufzeichnungen des Generalfeldmarschalls aus Krieg und Frieden* (Bonn: Wahlband der Buchgemeinde, 1938), 227.

3. OHL, Military Convention between Germany, Austria–Hungary and Bulgaria, September 6, 1915, BA-MA PH 5 I/78.

4. Born on December 25, 1864, Nikola Zhekov attended the Military Academy in Sofia and saw his first combat action against Serbia in the 1885 Serbio-Bulgarian War. After a series of staff and command assignments, Zhekov rose in the Bulgarian military. He was chief of staff for the Bulgarian Second Army in the Balkan Wars in 1912–1913. As war minister for the Radoslavov government, he prepared the Bulgarian army for war and became the commander of the army when hostilities began. Holger H. Herwig and Neil M. Heyman, *Biographical Dictionary of World War I* (Westport, CT: Greenwood Press, 1982), 363.

5. Foerster, ed., *Mackensen*, 226.

6. Hans von Seeckt, *Aus meinem Leben 1866–1917* (Leipzig: von Hase und Koehler Verlag, 1938), 231; Kosch to Wife, October 13, 1915, Nachlass Kosch, BA-MA N 754/5; and Colonel Scheunemann, "Pioniere im Kampf um die Donau," in *Das Ehrenbuch der Deutschen Pioniere*, ed. Paul Heinrici (Berlin: Verlag Tradition Wilhelm Kolk, 1932), 430.

7. Rudolf Dammert, *Der Serbische Feldzug: Erlebnisse Deutscher Truppen* (Leipzig: Verlag von Bernhard Tauchnitz, 1916), 36; KTB/Eleventh Army, October 14, 1915, BA-MA PH 5 II/305; Army Group Mackensen to Austro-Hungarian Third Army, October 13, 1915, BA-MA PH 5 I/78; Charles E.J. Fryer, *The Royal Navy on the Danube* (Boulder, CO: East European Monographs, 1988), 145; and General der Artillerie Richard von Berendt, "Aus grosser Zeit vor Zwanzig Jahren. Der Feldzug in Serbien," *Militär Wochenblatt* 120, no. 13 (October 4, 1935): 526; and Scheunemann, "Pioniere im Kampf um die Donau," 430.

8. German X Reserve Corps, Special Order, October 11, 1915, BA-MA 6 II/79; KTB/Eleventh Army, October 6, 1915, BA-MA PH 5 II/305; Jakob Jung, *Max von*

Gallwitz (1852–1937): General und Politiker (Osnabrück: Biblio Verlag, 1995), 61; and Army Group Mackensen to Austro-Hungarian Third Army, October 14, 1915, BA-MA PH 5 I/78.

9. German Twenty-Sixth Infantry Division, Division Order, October 12, 1915, 11 PM, LA-BW Gu117 Bü900; Austria, Bundesministerium für Landesverteidigung, *Österreich-Ungarns Letzter Krieg 1914–1918* (Vienna: Verlag der Militärwissenschaftlichen Mitteilungen, 1931), vol. 3, 220–21; and Army Group Mackensen to Austro-Hungarian Third Army, October 14, 1915, BA-MA PH 5 I/78.

10. Germany, Reichsarchiv, *Der Weltkrieg 1914 bis 1918* (Berlin: E.S. Mittler und Sohn, 1933), vol. 9, 219; Fritz Bergeder, *Das Reserve-Infanterie-Regiment Nr. 202 auf den Schlachtfeldern des Weltkrieges 1914–1918* (Berlin: Traditions Verlag Kolk, 1939), 99–100; Wilhelm Führer, *Geschichte des Reserve Infanterie Regiments 203* (Berlin: Privately Published, 1960–1964), vol. 2, 348–49; Lieutenant Colonel Karl Boesser, *Geschichte des Reserve-Feldartillerie-Regiments Nr. 44* (Grossen: Rudolf Zeidler, 1932), 192; and Austria, Bundesministerium, *Österreich-Ungarns Letzter Krieg 1914–1918*, 220–21.

11. Austria, Bundesministerium, *Österreich-Ungarns Letzter Krieg 1914–1918*, 223; Germany, Reichsarchiv, *Der Weltkrieg 1914 bis 1918*, 219; Friedrich Appel, *Das Reserve-Infanterie-Regiment Nr. 205* (Berlin: Verlag Bernard und Graefe, 1937), 106; Bergeder, *Das Reserve-Infanterie-Regiment Nr. 202 auf den Schlachtfeldern des Weltkrieges 1914–1918*, 103.

12. Austria, Bundesministerium, *Österreich-Ungarns Letzter Krieg 1914–1918*, 235; Charles E. J. Fryer, *The Destruction of Serbia in 1915* (New York: East European Monographs, 1997), 61.

13. Austria, Bundesministerium, *Österreich-Ungarns Letzter Krieg 1914–1918*, 233; Army Group Mackensen to Austro-Hungarian Third Army, October 19, 1915, BA-MA PH 5 I/78; German Twenty-Sixth Infantry Division, Division Order, October 19, 1915, 12:30 PM, LA-BW Gu117 Bü900; Army Group Mackensen to Austro-Hungarian Third Army, October 20, 1915, BA-MA PH 5 I/78.

14. General der Artillerie Max von Gallwitz, *Meine Führertätigkeit im Weltkriege 1914/1916: Belgien—Osten—Balkan* (Berlin: E.S. Mittler und Sohn, 1929), 399; Germany, Reichsarchiv, *Der Weltkrieg 1914 bis 1918*, 222; and Scheunemann, "Pioniere im Kampf um die Donau," 430.

15. KTB/Bavarian Eleventh Infantry Division, October 13, 1915, BH-KA 11/15/1; Franz Freiherr von Stengel, *Das K.B. 3. Infanterie-Regiment Prinz Karl von Bayern* (Munich: Verlag Bayerisches Kriegsarchiv, 1924), 43; Colonel Hans Mayer, *Das K.B. 22. Infanterie-Regiment* (Munich: J. Lindauersche Universitäts-Buchhandlung, 1923), 50; and KTB/German Eleventh Army, October 13, 1915, BA-MA PH 5 II/305.

16. Germany, Reichsarchiv, *Der Weltkrieg 1914 bis 1918*, 223; Gallwitz, *Meine Führertätigkeit im Weltkriege 1914/1916*, 403; and Foerster, ed., *Mackensen*, 225.

17. Joseph Steuer, *Das Infanterie-Regiment Generalfeldmarschall von Mackensen (3. West preussisches) Nr. 129 im Weltkriege* (Berlin: Druck und Verlag Gerhard Stalling, 1925), 142; Captain Hellmut Gnamm, *Das Fusilier-Regiment Kaiser Franz Joseph von Österreich, König von Ungarn (4. württ,) Nr. 122* (Stuttgart: Ehr. Belsersche Verlagsbuchhandlung, 1921), 98; and KTB/German Eleventh Army, October 18, 1915, BA-MA PH 5 II/305.

18. First Lieutenant Herbert Ulrich, *Res.-Inf.-Regiment 52 im Weltkriege* (Cottbus: Lausitzer Druckerei und Verlagsanstalt, 1925), 243–44; Franz Giese, *Geschichte des*

Reserve-Infanterie-Regiments 227 im Weltkriege 1914/18 (Privately Published, 1931), 262; Erich von Bartenwerffer and Alfred Herrmann, *Das Reserve-Infanterie-Regiment Nr. 232 im Ost und West* (Celle: Buchdruckerei W. Müller, 1927), 93; and KTB/ German Eleventh Army, October 21, 1915, BA-MA PH 5 II/305.

19. German X Reserve Corps, Special Orders, October 13, 1915, BA-MA PH 6 II/79.

20. Ibid.; and Kosch to Wife, October 14, 1915, Nachlass Kosch, BA-MA N 754/5.

21. German 101st Infantry Division, Brief Report on Operations of the 101st Infantry Division during the Campaign in Serbia in October and November 1915, December 9, 1915, BA-MA PH 8 I/45; Lieutenant Colonel Radermacher, *Erinnerungsblätter des Grossherzogl. Hessischen Reserve-Infanterie-Regiments Nr. 116* (Oldenburg: Druck und Verlag von Gerhard Stalling, 1929), 58; and Arthur Schöning, *Unser Regiment im Weltkriege* (Erfurt: Druck von A. Stenger, 1925), 186–87.

22. Alfred Richter, *Das 2. Thüring. Infanterie-Regiment Nr. 32* (Zeulenroda: Druck von Bernhard Spoorn, 1928), 167; Kurt Hennig, *Das Infanterie-Regiment (8. Ostpreussisches) Nr. 45 (Insterburg-Darkehmen) im Weltkriege 1914–18* (Berlin: Druck und Verlag Gerhard Stalling, 1928), 96; and Schöning, *Unser Regiment im Weltkriege*, 188.

23. Germany, Reichsarchiv, *Der Weltkrieg 1914 bis 1918*, 222; Gallwitz, *Meine Führertätigkeit im Weltkriege 1914/1916*, 402–403; and Foerster, ed., *Mackensen*, 225–26.

24. Germany, Reichsarchiv, *Der Weltkrieg 1914 bis 1918*, 222; German X Reserve Corps, Corps Staff Order, October 16, 1915, BA-MA PH 6 II/79; and Kosch to Wife, October 18, 1915, Nachlass Kosch, BA-MA N 754/5.

25. Gallwitz, *Meine Führertätigkeit im Weltkriege 1914/1916*, 405; KTB/German Eleventh Army, October 19, 1915, BA-MA PH 5 II/305; German 101st Infantry Division, Brief Report on Operations of the 101st Infantry Division during the Campaign in Serbia in October and November 1915, December 9, 1915, BA-MA PH 8 I/45; and Association of Former Officers of the Regiment, *Das 1. Masurische Infanterie-Regiment Nr. 146 1897–1919* (Berlin: Verlag Tradition Wilhelm Kolk, 1929), 135.

26. Gallwitz, *Meine Führertätigkeit im Weltkriege 1914/1916*, 410; Kosch to Wife, October 20, 1915, Nachlass Kosch, BA-MA N 754/5; Richter, *Das 2. Thuring. Infanterie-Regiment Nr. 32*, 168; German 101st Infantry Division, Brief Report on Operations of the 101st Infantry Division during the Campaign in Serbia in October and November 1915, December 9, 1915, BA-MA PH 8 I/45; and German X Reserve Corps, Firing on Aircraft, October 19, 1915, BA-MA PH 6 II/79.

27. Germany, Reichsarchiv, *Der Weltkrieg 1914 bis 1918*, 222.

28. KTB/German Eleventh Army, October 15, 1915, BA-MA PH 5 II/305; Germany, Reichsarchiv, *Der Weltkrieg 1814 bis 1918*, 223; Captain Wahrenburg, *Reserve-Infanterie-Regiment Nr. 83* (Berlin: Druck und Verlag von Gerhard Stalling, 1924), 104–105; Adolf Soldan, *5. Grossherzoglich Hessischen Infanterie-Regiment Nr. 168* (Berlin: Druck und Verlag von Gerhard Stalling, 1924), 67; and Captain Wilhelm Schlawe, *Feldartillerie-Regiment General-Feldzeugmeister (1.Brandenburgisches) Nr. 3 im Weltkrieg 1914/1918* (Berlin: Verlag Bernard und Graefe, 1935), 84.

29. Lieutenant Colonel Paul Doerstling, *Kriegsgeschichte des Königlich Preussischen Infanterie-Regiments Graf Tauentzien v. Wittenberg (3. Brandenb.) Nr. 20* (Zeulenroda: Bernhard Sporn, Buchdruckerei und Verlagsanstalt, 1933), 153–54.

30. Ibid., 155–62; Schlawe, *Feldartillerie-Regiment General-Feldzeugmeister (1. Brandenburgisches) Nr. 3 im Weltkrieg 1914/1918*, 88; KTB/German Eleventh Army, October 19, 1915, BA-MA PH 5 II/305; and Germany, Reichsarchiv, *Der Weltkrieg 1914 bis 1918*, 223.

31. Lieutenant Colonel The Honorable Henry D. Napier, CMG, *The Experiences of a Military Attaché in the Balkans* (London: Drane's, 1924), 211; Austria, Bundesministerium, *Österreich-Ungarns Letzter Krieg 1914–1918*, 227; and Douglas W. Johnson, *Topography and Strategy in the War* (New York: Henry Holt, 1917), 155–56.

32. Austria, Bundesministerium, *Österreich-Ungarns Letzter Krieg 1914–1918*, 227; Johnson, *Topography and Strategy in the War*, 150; Richard F. Hamilton and Holger H. Herwig, *Decisions for War, 1914–1917* (Cambridge: Cambridge University Press, 2004), 174; OHL, Military Convention Between Germany, Austria-Hungary and Bulgaria, September 6, 1915, BA-MA PH 5 I/78; and Robert A. Doughty, *Pyrrhic Victory: French Strategy and Operations in the Great War* (Cambridge: Harvard University Press, 2005), 223.

33. German Army, Report on the State of the Serbian Army, September 10, 1915, Nachlass Seeckt, BA-MA N 247/26; Austria, Bundesministerium, *Österreich-Ungarns Letzter Krieg 1914–1918*, 35; British Army, General Staff, "Military Notes on the Balkan States," in *Armies of the Balkan States 1914–1918: The Military Forces of Bulgaria, Greece, Romania and Serbia*, ed. British Army, General Staff (repr., Nashville: Battery Press, 1996), 43; and Johnson, *Topography and Strategy in the War*, 155.

34. Austria, Bundesministerium, *Österreich-Ungarns Letzter Krieg 1914–1918*, 227; Hans Meier-Welcker, *Seeckt* (Frankfurt-am-Main: Bernard und Graefe Verlag für Wehrwesen, 1967), 67; and Fryer, *Destruction of Serbia in 1915*, 66.

35. Austria, Bundesministerium, *Österreich-Ungarns Letzter Krieg 1914–1918*, 239; and Fryer, *Destruction of Serbia in 1915*, 67.

36. Andrej Mitrović, *Serbia's Great War 1914–1918* (West Lafayette, IN: Purdue University Press, 2007), 147; Foerster, ed., *Mackensen*, 221; and Seeckt, *Aus meinem Leben 1866–1917*, 231–32.

37. Doughty, *Pyrrhic Victory*, 222; and Cyril Falls, *History of the great war. Military Operations. Macedonia: From the Outbreak of War in 1914 to the Spring of 1917* (repr., Nashville: Battery Press, 1996), 42–43.

38. Alan Palmer, *The Gardeners of Salonika* (New York: Simon and Schuster, 1965), 38; and Hamilton and Herwig, *Decisions for War, 1914–1917*, 180.

39. Palmer, *Gardeners of Salonika*, 38; and Doughty, *Pyrrhic Victory*, 223.

40. Stengel, *Das K.B. 3. Infanterie-Regiment Prinz Karl von Bayern*, 43; Gnamm, *Das Fusilier-Regiment Kaiser Franz Joseph von Österreich, König von Ungarn (4. württ,) Nr. 122*, 97–98; Doerstling, *Kriegsgeschichte des Königlich Preussischen Infanterie-Regiments Graf Tauentzien v. Wittenberg (3. Brandenb.) Nr. 20*, 160; Schöning, *Unser Regiment im Weltkriege*, 191; and German 101st Infantry Division, Brief Report on Operations of the 101st Infantry Division during the Campaign in Serbia in October and November 1915, December 9, 1915, BA-MA PH 8 I/45.

41. Peter Broucek, ed., *Ein österreichischer General gegen Hitler. Feldmarschalleutnant Alfred Jansa: Errinerungen* (Vienna: Böhlau Verlag, 2011), 297; Gallwitz, *Meine Führertätigkeit im Weltkriege 1914/1916*, 405; Kosch to Wife, October 15, 1915,

Nachlass Kosch, BA-MA N 754/5; German Twenty-Sixth Infantry Division, Division Orders, October 19, 1915, LA-BW Gu117 Bü900; and Schöning, *Unser Regiment im Weltkriege*, 192.

42. Austria, Bundesministerium, *Österreich-Ungarns Letzter Krieg 1914–1918*, 233; and Fryer, *Destruction of Serbia in 1915*, 61.

43. Foerster, ed., *Mackensen*, 226; and Fryer, *Destruction of Serbia in 1915*, 66–67.

44. Germany, Reichsarchiv, *Der Weltkrieg 1914 bis 1918*, 223; and Doerstling, *Kriegsgeschichte des Königlich Preussischen Infanterie-Regiments Graf Tauentzien v. Wittenberg (3. Brandenb.) Nr. 20*, 162.

45. Broucek, ed., *Ein österreichischer General gegen Hitler*, 290; German XXII Reserve Corps to Austro-Hungarian Third Army, October 11, 1915, BA-MA PH 6 II/119; and German XXII Reserve Corps to Austro-Hungarian Third Army, October 19, 1915, BA-MA PH 6 II/119.

46. Doerstling, *Kriegsgeschichte des Königlich Preussischen Infanterie-Regiments Graf Tauentzien v. Wittenberg (3. Brandenb.) Nr. 20*, 162; KTB/Bavarian Eleventh Infantry Division, October 12, 1915, BH-KA 11/5/1; Gordon Gordon-Smith, *From Serbia to Jugoslavia. Serbia's Victories, Reverses and Final Triumph: 1914–1918* (New York: G.P. Putnam's Sons, 1920), 62; and Elsie Corbett, *Red Cross in Serbia 1915–1919: A Personal Diary of Experiences* (Banbury: Cheney and Sons, 1964), 39.

47. German X Reserve Corps, Special Order, October 11, 1915, BA-MA 6 II/79; Boesser, *Geschichte des Reserve-Feldartillerie-Regiments Nr. 44*, 191; German Twenty-Sixth Infantry Division, Division Order, October 14, 1915, LA-BW Gu117 Bü900.

48. Ulrich, *Res.-Inf.-Regiment 52 im Weltkriege*, 236.

49. Bavarian Eleventh Infantry Division, Orientation on the Nature of Combat in Serbia, BH-KA 11/15/2; Steuer, *Das Infanterie-Regiment Generalfeldmarschall von Mackensen (3. West preussisches) Nr. 129 im Weltkriege*, 141; Gnamm, *Das Fusilier-Regiment Kaiser Franz Joseph von Österreich, König von Ungarn (4. württ,) Nr. 122*, 96; and Schlawe, *Feldartillerie-Regiment General-Feldzeugmeister (1. Brandenburgisches) Nr. 3 im Weltkrieg 1914/1918*, 88.

50. Captain Gerok, *Das 2. Württ. Feldartillerie-Reg. Nr. 29 "Prinz Luitpold von Bayern" im Weltkrieg 1914–1918* (Stuttgart: Ehr. Belsersche Verlagsbuchhandlung, 1921), 43; Richter, *Das 2. Thüring. Infanterie-Regiment Nr. 32*, 167; Bergeder, *Das Reserve-Infanterie-Regiment Nr. 202 auf den Schlachtfeldern des Weltkrieges 1914–1918*, 99–100; and Boesser, *Geschichte des Reserve Feldartillerie-Regiments Nr. 44*, 192.

51. Fryer, *Destruction of Serbia in 1915*, 67.

52. Monica M. Stanley, *My Diary in Serbia: April 1, 1915–Nov. 1, 1915* (London: Simpkin, Marshall, Hamilton, Kent, 1916), 114–16; and Corbett, *Red Cross in Serbia 1915–1919*, 42.

53. Mitrović, *Serbia's Great War 1914–1918*, 147; Falls, *History of the great war*, 54; Fryer, *Destruction of Serbia in 1915*, 63; and Dimitrije Djordjević, "Radomir Putnik," in *The Serbs and their Leaders in the Twentieth Century*, ed. Peter Radan and Aleksandar Pavković (Brookfield, VT: Ashgate, 1997), 130.

54. Tappen Diary, October 9, 1915, BA-MA RH 61/986, Plessen Diary, October 11, 1915, BA-MA RH 61/933; and Lawrence Sondhaus, *Franz Conrad von Hötzendorf: Architect of the Apocalypse* (Boston: Humanities Press, 2000), 179–80.

55. Walter Görlitz, *The Kaiser and His Court: The Diaries, Note Books and Letters of Admiral Georg Alexander von Müller, Chief of the Naval Cabinet, 1914–1918*

(New York: Harcourt Brace and World, 1958), 115; and Tappen Diary, October 23, 1915, BA-MA RH 61/986.

56. Foerster, ed., *Mackensen*, 228; Seeckt, *Aus meinem Leben 1866–1917*, 247; Germany, Reichsarchiv, *Der Weltkrieg 1914 bis 1918*, 227; and German Army, Report on the State of the Serbian Army, September 10, 1915, Nachlass Seeckt, BA-MA N 247/26.

CHAPTER 6

1. Walter Görlitz, ed., *The Kaiser and His Court: The Diaries, Note Books and Letters of Admiral Georg Alexander von Müller, Chief of the Naval Cabinet, 1914–1918* (New York: Harcourt, Brace and World, Inc., 1958), 115.

2. General der Artillerie Max von Gallwitz, *Meine Führertätigkeit im Weltkriege 1914/1916: Belgien–Osten–Balkan* (Berlin: E.S. Mittler und Sohn, 1929), 425.

3. Görlitz, ed., *Kaiser and His Court*, 118.

4. Wolfgang Foerster, ed., *Mackensen: Briefe und Aufzeichnungen des Generalfeldmarschalls aus Krieg und Frieden* (Bonn: Wahlband der Buchgemeinde, 1938), 228; Hans von Seeckt, *Aus meinem Leben 1866–1917* (Leipzig: von Hase und Koehler Verlag, 1938), 247; Germany, Reichsarchiv, *Der Weltkrieg 1914 bis 1918* (Berlin: E.S. Mittler und Sohn, 1933), Vol. 9, 227.

5. Robert A. Doughty, *Pyrrhic Victory: French Strategy and Operations in the Great War* (Cambridge: Harvard University Press, 2005), 200–201; Holger H. Herwig, *The First World War: Germany and Austria-Hungary 1914–1918* (London: Arnold, 1997), 171–72; General Erich von Falkenhayn, *The German General Staff and Its Decisions, 1914–1916* (New York: Dodd, Mead and Company, 1920), 196.

6. [6] Manfred Nebelin, *Ludendorff: Diktator im Ersten Weltkrieg* (Munich: Siedler Verlag, 2010), 189–90; Vejas G. Liulevicius, *War Land on the Eastern Front: Culture, National Identity and German Occupation in World War I* (Cambridge: Cambridge University Press, 2000), 54–55; Falkenhayn, *German General Staff and Its Decisions, 1914–1916*, 154–56; Seeckt to Wife, August 14, 1915, Nachlass Seeckt, BA-MA N 247/58; Hans Meier-Welcker, *Seeckt* (Frankfurt-am-Main: Bernard und Graefe Verlag für Wehrwesen, 1967), 62.

7. John R. Schindler, *Isonzo: The Forgotten Sacrifice of the Great War* (Westport, CT: Praeger, 2001), 124; Sean McMeekin, *The Berlin-Baghdad Express: The Ottoman Empire and Germany's Bid for World Power* (Cambridge: Harvard University Press, 2010), 275; Edward J. Erickson, *Gallipoli: The Ottoman Campaign* (Barnsley: Pen and Sword Books, 2010), 176–77.

8. Gunther Hebert, *Das Alpenkorps: Aufbau, Organisation und Einsatz einer Gebirgstruppen im Ersten Weltkrieg* (Boppard-am-Rhein: Harald Boldt Verlag, 1988), 86–87; Falkenhayn, *German General Staff and Its Decisions, 1914–1916*, 200–201.

9. Tappen Diary, October 23, 1915, BA-MA RH 61/986; Lawrence Sondhaus, *Franz Conrad von Hötzendorf: Architect of the Apocalypse* (Boston: Humanities Press, Inc., 2000), 181.

10. In his diary Tappen called the meal breakfast, while Mackensen referred to it as lunch. Tappen Diary, October 24, 1915, BA-MA RH 61/986; Foerster, ed., *Mackensen*, 229; Meier-Welcker, *Seeckt*, 67.

11. Hebert, *Das Alpenkorps*, 87; Foerster, ed., *Mackensen*, 229; Germany, Reichsarchiv, *Der Weltkrieg 1914 bis 1918*, Vol. 9, 237.

12. Tappen Diary, October 24, 1915, BA-MA RH 61/986.

13. Gallwitz, *Meine Führertätigkeit im Weltkriege 1914/1916*, 415; KTB/German Eleventh Army, October 25, 1915, BA-MA PH 5 II/305; Tappen Diary, October 25, 1915, BA-MA RH 61/986; Seeckt, *Aus meinem Leben 1866–1917*, 250–51.

14. Army Group Mackensen to Austro-Hungarian Third Army, October 22, 1915, BA-MA PH 5 I/78; KTB/German Eleventh Army, October 22, 1915, BA-MA PH 5 II/305; Gallwitz, *Meine Führertätigkeit im Weltkriege 1914/1916*, 413; Austria, Bundesministerium für Landesverteidigung, *Österreich-Ungarns Letzter Krieg 1914–1918* (Vienna: Verlag der Militärwissenschaftlichen Mitteilungen, 1931), Vol. 3, 242–43.

15. Major Vorwerck, "Die I./Pi 18 in Serbien," *Das Ehrenbuch der Deutschen Pioniere* (Paul Heinrici, ed.) (Berlin: Verlag Tradition Wilhelm Kolk, 1932), 437; German 101st Infantry Division, Brief Report on Operations of the 101st Infantry Division During the Campaign in Serbia in October and November 1915, December 9, 1915, BA-MA PH 8 I/45; Kurt Hennig, *Das Infanterie-Regiment (8. Ostpreussisches) Nr. 45 (Insterburg-Darkehmen) im Weltkriege 1914–18* (Berlin: Druck und Verlag Gerhard Stalling, 1928), 98.

16. Austro-Hungarian Third Army to Army Group Mackensen, October 22, 1915; Army Group Mackensen to Austro-Hungarian Third Army, October 23, 1915, BA-MA PH 5 I/78; German Eleventh Army, Viewpoints on Reconnaissance in Serbia, October 23, 1915, BH-KA File 11/15/5.

17. Germany, Reichsarchiv, *Der Weltkrieg 1914 bis 1918*, Vol. 9, 236; Austria, Bundesministerium, *Österreich-Ungarns Letzter Krieg 1914–1918*, Vol. 3, 243; Srdja Pavlović, *Balkan Anschluss: The Annexation of Montenegro and the Creation of the Common South Slavic State* (West Lafayette, IN: Purdue University Press, 2008), 75.

18. Germany, Reichsarchiv, *Der Weltkrieg 1914 bis 1918*, Vol. 9, 236; Army Group Mackensen to Austro-Hungarian Third Army, October 25, 1915, BA-MA PH 5 I/78.

19. Austria, Bundesministerium, *Österreich-Ungarns Letzter Krieg 1914–1918*, Vol. 3, 244–45.

20. Ibid., 245; Army Group Mackensen to Austro-Hungarian Third Army, October 27, 1915, BA-MA PH 5 I/78.

21. Austria, Bundesministerium, *Österreich-Ungarns Letzter Krieg 1914–1918*, Vol. 3, 246–47; Friedrich Appel, *Das Reserve-Infanterie-Regiment Nr. 205* (Berlin: Verlag Bernard und Graefe, 1937), 107; German Twenty-Sixth Infantry Division, Division Order, October 23, 1915, LA-BW Gu117 Bü900; Captain Gerok, *Das 2. Württ. Feldartillerie-Reg. Nr. 29 "Prinz Luitpold von Bayern" im Weltkrieg 1914–1918* (Stuttgart: Ehr. Belsersche Verlagsbuchhandlung, 1921), 44; Germany, Reichsarchiv, *Der Weltkrieg 1914 bis 1918*, Vol. 9, 236.

22. Gallwitz, *Meine Führertätigkeit im Weltkriege 1914/1916*, 413; Lieutenant Colonel Paul Doerstling, *Kriegsgeschichte des Königlich Preussischen Infanterie-Regiments Graf Tauentzien v. Wittenberg (3. Brandenb.) Nr. 20* (Zeulenroda: Bernhard Sporn, Buchdruckerei und Verlagsanstalt, 1933), 166; Captain Wahrenburg, *Reserve-Infanterie-Regiment Nr. 83* (Berlin: Druck und Verlag von Gerhard Stalling, 1924), 106; Kosch to Wife, October 23, 1915, Nachlass Kosch, BA-MA N 754/5, KTB/German Eleventh Army, October 23, 1915, BA-MA PH 5 II/305; German 101st Infantry Division, Brief Report on Operations of the 101st Infantry Division During the

Campaign in Serbia in October and November 1915, December 9, 1915, BA-MA PH 8 I/
45; Hennig, *Das Infanterie-Regiment (8. Osrpreussisches) Nr. 45 (Insterburg-Darkehmen)
im Weltkriege 1914–18*, 98; Alfred Richter, *Das 2. Thüring. Infanterie-Regiment Nr. 32*
(Zeulenroda: Druck von Bernhard Spoorn, 1928), 171.

23. Joseph Steuer, *Das Infanterie-Regiment Generalfeldmarschall von Mackensen
(3. West preussisches) Nr. 129 im Weltkriege* (Berlin: Druck und Verlag Gerhard
Stalling, 1925), 144; Erich von Bartenwerffer and Alfred Herrmann, *Das Reserve-
Infanterie-Regiment Nr. 232 im Ost und West* (Celle: Buchdruckerei W. Müller,
1927), 94–95; Franz Freiherr von Stengel, *Das K.B. 3. Infanterie-Regiment Prinz Karl
von Bayern* (Munich: Verlag Bayerisches Kriegsarchiv, 1924), 44; Franz Giese,
Geschichte des Reserve-Infanterie-Regiments 227 im Weltkriege 1914/18 (Privately
Published, 1931), 264.

24. Germany, Reichsarchiv, *Der Weltkrieg 1914 bis 1918*, Vol. 9, 236–37; Vorwerck,
"Die I./Pi 18 in Serbien," 437; Captain Wilhelm Schlawe, *Feldartillerie-Regiment
General-Feldzeugmeister (1.Brandenburgisches) Nr. 3 im Weltkrieg 1914/1918* (Berlin:
Verlag Bernard und Graefe, 1935), 90; Otto Zarn, Colonel Hayner, and Major
Frantzius, *Geschichte des Reserve-Infanterie-Regiments Nr. 201* (Berlin: Verlag
Bernard und Graefe, 1940), 179; KTB/Bavarian Eleventh Infantry Division,
October 24, 1915, BH-KA File 11/15/1.

25. Foerster, ed. *Mackensen*, 230; Seeckt, *Aus meinem Leben 1866–1917*, 251; Army
Group Mackensen to Austro-Hungarian Third Army, October 26, 1915, BA-MA PH 5
I/78; Germany, Reichsarchiv, *Der Weltkrieg 1914 bis 1918*, Vol. 9, 238.

26. Austria, Bundesministerium, *Österreich-Ungarns Letzter Krieg 1914–1918*, Vol.
3, 248; Army Group Mackensen to Austro-Hungarian Third Army, October 27, 1915,
BA-MA PH 5 I/78; Wilhelm Führer, *Geschichte des Reserve Infanterie Regiments 203*
(Berlin: Privately Published, 1960–1964), Vol. 2, 358; Zarn, Hayner, and Frantzius,
Geschichte des Reserve-Infanterie-Regiment Nr. 201, 179; Gerok, *Das 2. Württ.
Feldartillerie-Reg. Nr. 29 "Prinz Luitpold von Bayern" im Weltkrieg 1914–1918*, 44;
Fritz Bergeder, *Das Reserve-Infanterie-Regiment Nr. 202 auf den Schlachtfeldern des
Weltkrieges 1914–1918* (Berlin: Traditions Verlag Kolk und Co., 1939), 104; Appel,
Das Reserve-Infanterie-Regt. Nr. 205, 107.

27. Army Group Mackensen to Austro-Hungarian Third Army, October 28, 1915,
BA-MA PH 5 I/78; German Twenty-Sixth Infantry Division, Division Order,
October 29, 1915, 1 AM, LA-BW Gu117 Bü900; Foerster, *Mackensen*, 231.

28. Austria, Bundesministerium, *Österreich-Ungarns Letzter Krieg 1914–1918*, Vol.
3, 247–48.

29. KTB/German Eleventh Army, October 25, 1915, BA-MA PH 5 II/305; Adolf
Soldan, *5. Grossherzoglich Hessischen Infanterie-Regiment Nr. 168* (Berlin: Druck und
Verlag Gerhard Stalling, 1924), 68; Stengel, *Das K.B. 3. Infanterie-Regiment Prinz
Karl von Bayern*, 43.

30. KTB/German Eleventh Army, October 25, 1915, BA-MA PH 5 II/305; Stengel,
Das K.B. 3. Infanterie-Regiment Prinz Karl von Bayern, 44; KTB/Bavarian Eleventh
Infantry Division, October 25, 1915, BH-KA File 11/15/1.

31. KTB/German Eleventh Army, October 25, 1915, BA-MA PH 5 II/305; First
Lieutenant Herbert Ulrich, *Res.-Inf.-Regiment 52 im Weltkriege* (Cottbus: Lausitzer
Druckerei und Verlagsanstalt, 1925), 247; Bartenwerffer and Herrmann, *Das Reserve-
Infanterie-Regiment Nr. 232 im Ost und West*, 95; Steuer, *Das Infanterie-Regiment*

Generalfeldmarschall von Mackensen (3. West preussisches) Nr. 129 im Weltkriege, 145; Gallwitz, *Meine Führertätigkeit im Weltkriege 1914/1916*, 416.

32. Kosch to Wife, October 25, 1915, Nachlass Kosch, BA-MA N 754/5; KTB/ German Eleventh Army, October 25, 1915, BA-MA PH 5 II/305; Arthur Schöning, *Unser Regiment im Weltkriege* (Erfurt: Druck von A. Stenger, 1925), 207; German 101st Infantry Division, Brief Report on Operations of the 101st Infantry Division During the Campaign in Serbia in October and November 1915, December 9, 1915, BA-MA PH 8 I/45; Richter, *Das 2. Thüring. Infanterie-Regiment Nr. 32*, 172; Lieutenant Colonel Radermacher, *Erinnerungsblätter des Grossherzogl. Hessischen Reserve-Infanterie-Regiments Nr. 116* (Oldenburg: Druck und Verlag von Gerhard Stalling, 1929), 62; Meier-Welcker, *Seeckt*, 68; German X Reserve Corps, Special Orders, October 25, 1915, BA-MA PH 6 II/79.

33. Germany, Reichsarchiv, *Der Weltkrieg 1914 bis 1918*, Vol. 9, 240; Army Group Mackensen to Austro-Hungarian Third Army, October 27, 1915, BA-MA PH 5 I/78.

34. KTB/German Eleventh Army, October 24, 1915, BA-MA PH 5 II/305; Germany, Reichsarchiv, *Der Weltkrieg 1914 bis 1918*, Vol. 9, 240; Austria, Bundesministerium, *Österreich-Ungarns Letzter Krieg 1914–1918*, Vol. 3, 248.

35. KTB/German Eleventh Army, October 26, 1915, BA-MA PH 5 II/305; Gallwitz, *Meine Führertätigkeit im Weltkriege 1914/1916*, 414; Ulrich, *Res.-Inf.-Regiment 52 im Weltkriege*, 247; Bartenwerffer and Herrmann, *Das Reserve-Infanterie-Regiment Nr. 232 im Ost und West*, 95; Steuer, *Das Infanterie-Regiment Generalfeldmarschall von Mackensen (3. West preussisches) Nr. 129 im Weltkriege*, 145.

36. Andrej Mitrović, *Serbia's Great War 1914–1918* (West Lafayette, IN: Purdue University Press, 2007, 146; Mile Bjelajac, "King Peter I Karageorge," *The Serbs and Their Leaders in the Twentieth Century*, 107; Dimitrije Djordjević, "Radomir Putnik," in *The Serbs and Their Leaders in the Twentieth Century*, ed. Peter Radan and Aleksandar Pavković (Brookfield, VT: Ashgate, 1997), 131.

37. Charles E.J. Fryer, *The Royal Navy on the Danube* (Boulder, CO: East European Monographs, 1988), 148–53.

38. Army Group Mackensen to Austro-Hungarian Third Army, October 28, 1915, BA-MA PH 5 I/78; Foerster, ed., *Mackensen*, 231; KTB/German Eleventh Army, October 28, 1915, BA-MA PH 5 II/305.

39. Georg Reichlin-Meldegg, *Das Kaisers Prinz Eugen? Feldmarschall Hermann Baron Kövess von Kövessháza: Der letzte Oberkommandant der K.u.K. Armee im Ersten Weltkrieg* (Graz: Ares Verlag, 2010), 135; Gallwitz, *Meine Führertätigkeit im Weltkriege 1914/1916*, 413; Army Group Mackensen to Austro-Hungarian Third Army, October 29, 1915, BA-MA PH 5 I/78; Paul von Kneussl Diary, 26 and October 28, 1915, Nachlass Paul von Kneussl, BH-KA NL 6; Foerster, ed., *Mackensen*, 232; Seeckt to Wife, October 28, 1915, Nachlass Seeckt, BA-MA N 247/58.

40. Army Group Mackensen to Austro-Hungarian Third Army, October 30, 1915, BA-MA PH 5 I/78; Gallwitz, *Meine Führertätigkeit im Weltkriege 1914/1916*, 423; Germany, Reichsarchiv, *Der Weltkrieg 1914 bis 1918*, Vol. 9, 243; Douglas W. Johnson, *Topography and Strategy in the War* (New York: Henry Holt and Company, 1917), 160.

41. Austria, Bundesministerium, *Österreich-Ungarns Letzter Krieg*, Vol. 3, 260–61; Germany, Reichsarchiv, *Der Weltkrieg 1914 bis 1918*, Vol. 9, 241; Wahrenburg,

Reserve-Infanterie Regiment Nr. 83, 110; Schlawe, *Feldartillerie–Regiment General Feldzeugmeister (1. Brandenburgisches) Nr. 3 im Weltkrieg 1914/1918*, 92.

42. Austria, Bundesministerium, *Österreich-Ungarns Letzter Krieg*, Vol. 3, 253; Fritz Haleck, *Das Reserve-Infanterie-Regiment Nr. 208* (Berlin: Druck und Verlag von Gerhard Stalling, 1922), 39; German Twenty-Sixth Infantry Division, Division Order, October 29, 1915, LA-BW Gu117 Bü900; Gerok, *Das 2. Württ. Feldartillerie-Reg. Nr. 29 "Prinz Luitpold von Bayern" im Weltkrieg 1914–1918*, 44.

43. Austria, Bundesministerium, *Österreich-Ungarns Letzter Krieg*, Vol. 3, 263; Germany, Reichsarchiv, *Der Weltkrieg 1914 bis 1918*, Vol. 9, 244.

44. KTB/Bavarian Eleventh Infantry Division, October 28, 1915, BH-KA File 11/15/1; Stengel, *Das K.B. Infanterie-Regiment Prinz Karl von Bayern*, 45; KTB/German Eleventh Army, October 29, 1915, BA-MA PH 5 II/305.

45. Germany, Reichsarchiv, *Der Weltkrieg 1914 bis 1918*, Vol. 9, 241; KTB/German Eleventh Army, October 29, 1915, BA-MA PH 5 II/305; Steuer, *Das Infanterie-Regiment Generalfeldmarschall von Mackensen (3. West preussisches) Nr. 129 im Weltkriege*, 146–47; Ulrich, *Res.-Inf.-Regiment 52 im Weltkriege*, 250; Giese, *Geschichte des Reserve-Infanterie Regiments 227 im Weltkriege 1914/18*, 275; Captain Hellmut Gnamm, *Das Fusilier-Regiment Kaiser Franz Joseph von Österreich, König von Ungarn (4. württ,) Nr. 122* (Stuttgart: Ehr. Belsersche Verlagsbuchhandlung, 1921), 104.

46. KTB/German Eleventh Army, October 29, 1915, BA-MA PH 5 II/305; Kosch to Wife, October 29, 1915, Nachlass Kosch, BA-MA N 754/5; Schöning, *Unser Regiment im Weltkriege*, 207; Radermacher, *Erinnerungsblätter des Grossherzogl. Hessischen Reserve-Infanterie-Regiments Nr. 116*, 63; Hennig, *Das Infanterie-Regiment (8. Osrpreussisches) Nr. 45 (Insterburg-Darkehmen) im Weltkriege 1914–18*, 98; Richter, *Das 2. Thüring. Infanterie-Regiment Nr. 32*, 173.

47. Germany, Reichsarchiv, *Der Weltkrieg 1914 bis 1918*, Vol. 9, 241–42; Kosch to Wife, October 29, 1915, Nachlass Kosch, BA-MA N 754/5.

48. Mitrović, *Serbia's Great War 1914–1918*, 146; Doughty, *Pyrrhic Victory*, 225.

49. Army Group Mackensen to Austro-Hungarian Third Army, October 30, 1915, BA-MA PH 5 I/78; Foerster, ed., *Mackensen*, 231; KTB/German Eleventh Army, October 30, 1915, BA-MA PH 5 II/305.

50. Mitrović, *Serbia's Great War 1914–1918*, 146.

51. Count Carlo Sforza, *Fifty Years of War and Diplomacy in the Balkans: Pashich and the Union of the Yugoslavs* (New York: Columbia University Press, 1940), 130; Charles E. J. Fryer, *The Destruction of Serbia in 1915* (New York: East European Monographs, 1997), 70; Mitrović, *Serbia's Great War 1914–1918*, 148.

52. Fryer, *Destruction of Serbia in 1915*, 72; Austria, Bundesministerium, *Österreich-Ungarns Letzter Krieg 1914–1918*, Vol. 3, 264; KTB/German Eleventh Army, November 1, 1915, BA-MA PH 5 II/305; Soldan, *5. Grossherzoglich Hessischen Infanterie-Regiment Nr. 168*, 69; Doerstling, *Kriegsgeschichte des Königlich Preussischen Infanterie-Regiments Graf Tauentzien v. Wittenberg (3. Brandenb.) Nr. 20*, 170; Gallwitz, *Meine Führertätigkeit im Weltkriege 1914/1916*, 425.

53. Foerster, ed., *Mackensen*, 233; Germany, Reichsarchiv, *Der Weltkrieg 1914 bis 1918*, Vol. 9, 245; Gallwitz, *Meine Führertätigkeit im Weltkriege 1914/1916*, 430.

54. Peter Broucek, ed., *Ein österreichischer General gegen Hitler. Feldmarschalleutnant Alfred Jansa: Errinerungen* (Vienna: Böhlau Verlag, 2011), 297.

55. Army Group Mackensen to Austro-Hungarian Third Army, November 1, 1915, BA-MA PH 5 I/78; KTB/German Eleventh Army, November 1, 1915, BA-MA PH 5 II/305.

56. Foerster, ed., *Mackensen*, 231; Doughty, *Pyrrhic Victory*, 225.

57. Hermann Neeff, *Das 4. Württ. Feldartillerie-Reg. Nr. 65 im Weltkrieg* (Stuttgart: Ehr. Belser AG Verlagsbuchhandlung, 1925), 55.

58. Hennig, *Das Infanterie-Regiment (8. Osrpreussisches) Nr. 45 (Insterburg-Darkehmen) im Weltkriege 1914–18*, 99; KTB/Bavarian Eleventh Infantry Division, November 3, 1915, BH-KA File 11/15/1; German X Reserve Corps, Special Orders, October 28, 1915, BA-MA PH 6 II/79; Stengel, *Das K.B. 3. Infanterie-Regiment Prinz Karl von Bayern*, 44; Bartenwerffer and Herrmann, *Das Reserve-Infanterie-Regiment Nr. 232 im Ost und West*, 96.

59. Directive for the New Army Group of Generalfeldmarschall von Mackensen, September 15, 1915, BA-MA PH 5I/78; Foerster, ed., *Mackensen*, 234; General Ernest von Hoeppner, *Germany's War in the Air: The Development and Operations of German Military Aviation in the World War* (repr., Nashville: The Battery Press, 1994), 47.

CHAPTER 7

1. Kosch to Wife, November 6, 1915, Nachlass Kosch, BA-MA N 754/5.

2. Wolfgang Foerster, ed., *Mackensen: Briefe und Aufzeichnungen des Generalfeldmarschalls aus Krieg und Frieden* (Bonn: Wahlband der Buchgemeinde, 1938), 235.

3. Quoted in John C. Adams, *Flight in Winter* (Princeton: Princeton University Press, 1942), 128.

4. Douglas W. Johnson, *Topography and Strategy in the War* (New York: Henry Holt and Company, 1917), 168–69; Germany, Reichsarchiv, *Der Weltkrieg 1914 bis 1918* (Berlin: E.S. Mittler und Sohn, 1933), vol. 9, 247; and Charles E. J. Fryer, *The Destruction of Serbia in 1915* (New York: East European Monographs, 1997), 84.

5. General Erich von Falkenhayn, *The German General Staff and Its Decisions, 1914–1916* (New York: Dodd, Mead, 1920), 207; and Tappen Diary, November 6, 1915, BA-MA RH 61/986.

6. August von Cramon, *Unser Österreich-Ungarischer Bundesgenosse im Weltkrieg. Erinnerungen aus meiner vierjährigen Tätigkeit als bevollmächtiger deutscher General beim k.u.k. Armeeoberkommando* (Berlin: E.S. Mittler und Sohn, 1920), 36; Gary W. Shanafelt, *The Secret Enemy: Austria-Hungary and the German Alliance, 1914–1918* (Boulder, CO: East European Monographs, 1985), 83–84; Manfred Rauchensteiner, *Der Erste Weltkrieg und das Ende der Habsburgermonarchie 1914–1918* (Vienna: Böhlau Verlag, 2013), 488–89; and Fryer, *Destruction of Serbia in 1915*, 79.

7. Holger Afflerbach, *Falkenhayn: Politisches Denken und Handeln im Kaiserreich* (Munich: R. Oldenbourg Verlag, 1996), 341; Rauchensteiner, *Der Erste Weltkrieg und das Ende der Habsburgermonarchie 1914–1918*, 488; Holger H. Herwig, *The First World War: Germany and Austria-Hungary 1914–1918* (London: Arnold, 1997), 179; Shanafelt, *Secret Enemy*, 84; Tappen Diary, November 6, 1915, BA-MA

RH 61/986; German Army, Railroad Section, "Der Feldzug gegen Serbien im Herbst 1915," n.d., 30–31, BA-MA RH 61/27; and Foerster, ed., *Mackensen*, 249.

8. Germany, Reichsarchiv, *Der Weltkrieg 1914 bis 1918*, 251; and Foerster, ed., *Mackensen*, 235.

9. Army Group Mackensen to Third Army, November 6, 1915, BA-MA PH 5 I/78; Austria, Bundesministerium für Landesverteidigung, *Österreich-Ungarns Letzter Krieg 1914–1918* (Vienna: Verlag der Militärwissenschaftlichen Mitteilungen, 1931), vol. 3, 278; and Foerster, ed., *Mackensen*, 234–35.

10. Germany, Reichsarchiv, *Der Weltkrieg 1914 bis 1918*, 252; Austria, Bundesministerium, *Österreich-Ungarns Letzter Krieg 1914–1918*, 276–79; Fritz Bergeder, *Das Reserve-Infanterie-Regiment Nr. 202 auf den Schlachtfeldern des Weltkrieges 1914–1918* (Berlin: Traditions Verlag Kolk, 1939), 108; Otto Zarn, Colonel Hayner, and Major Frantzius, *Geschichte des Reserve-Infanterie-Regiments Nr. 201* (Berlin: Verlag Bernard und Graefe, 1940), 184–87; and German Twenty-Sixth Infantry Division, Division Order, November 6, 1915, 10:30 PM, LA-BW Gu117 Bü900.

11. Austria, Bundesministerium, *Österreich-Ungarns Letzter Krieg 1914–1918*, 278; Germany, Reichsarchiv, *Der Weltkrieg 1914 bis 1918*, 252; Zarn, Hayner, and Frantzius, *Geschichte des Reserve-Infanterie-Regiments Nr. 201*, 185; and German Army, Railroad Section, "Der Feldzug gegen Serbien im Herbst 1915," 22, BA-MA RH 61/27.

12. Johnson, *Topography and Strategy in the War*, 160; Bergeder, *Das Reserve-Infanterie-Regiment Nr. 202 auf den Schlachtfeldern des Weltkrieges 1914–1918*, 109; Zarn, Hayner, and Frantzius, *Geschichte des Reserve-Infanterie-Regiments Nr. 201*, 187; and Army Group Mackensen to Austro-Hungarian Third Army, November 7, 1915, BA-MA PH 5 I/78.

13. Austria, Bundesministerium, *Österreich-Ungarns Letzter Krieg 1914–1918*, 282–83.

14. Germany, Reichsarchiv, *Der Weltkrieg 1914 bis 1918*, 252; Lieutenant Colonel Paul Doerstling, *Kriegsgeschichte des Königlich Preussischen Infanterie-Regiments Graf Tauentzien v. Wittenberg (3. Brandenb.) Nr. 20* (Zeulenroda: Bernhard Sporn, Buchdruckerei und Verlagsanstalt, 1933), 173; and Captain Wahrenburg, *Reserve-Infanterie-Regiment Nr. 83* (Berlin: Druck und Verlag von Gerhard Stalling, 1924), 113.

15. Germany, Reichsarchiv, *Der Weltkrieg 1914 bis 1918*, 252; Joseph Steuer, *Das Infanterie-Regiment Generalfeldmarschall von Mackensen (3. West preussisches) Nr. 129 im Weltkriege* (Berlin: Druck und Verlag Gerhard Stalling, 1925), 151; First Lieutenant Herbert Ulrich, *Res.-Inf.-Regiment 52 im Weltkriege* (Cottbus: Lausitzer Druckerei und Verlagsanstalt, 1925), 259; First Lieutenant Harry Oden and First Lieutenant Friedrich Schultz, *Feldartillerie-Regiment 201: Seine Geschichte 1915–1918* (Zeulenroda: Bernhard Sporn, Buchdruckerei und Verlagsanstalt, 1931), 47; German 101st Infantry Division, Brief Report on Operations of the 101st Infantry Division During the Campaign in Serbia in October and November 1915, December 9, 1915, BA-MA PH 8 I/45; and KTB/German Eleventh Army, November 6, 1915, BA-MA PH 5 II/305.

16. Kosch to Wife, November 7, 1915, Nachlass Kosch, BA-MA N 754/5; KTB/German Eleventh Army, November 7, 1915, BA-MA PH 5 II/305; General der

Artillerie Max von Gallwitz, *Meine Führertätigkeit im Weltkriege 1914/1916: Belgien – Osten – Balkan* (Berlin: E.S. Mittler und Sohn, 1929), 436; and Kosch to Wife, November 16, 1915, Nachlass Kosch, BA-MA N 754/5.

17. Austria, Bundesministerium, *Österreich-Ungarns Letzter Krieg 1914–1918*, 282.

18. Germany, Reichsarchiv, *Der Weltkrieg 1914 bis 1918*, 253.

19. Austria, Bundesministerium, *Österreich-Ungarns Letzter Krieg 1914–1918*, 283; and Friedrich Appel, *Das Reserve-Infanterie-Regiment Nr. 205* (Berlin: Verlag Bernard und Graefe, 1937), 116–17.

20. Bergeder, *Das Reserve-Infanterie-Regiment Nr. 202 auf den Schlachtfeldern des Weltkrieges 1914–1918*, 109; and Zarn, Hayner, and Frantzius, *Geschichte des Reserve-Infanterie-Regiments Nr. 201*, 188.

21. Army Group Mackensen to Austro-Hungarian Third Army, November 9, 1915, BA-MA PH 5 I/78; Foerster, ed., *Mackensen*, 235; and Germany, Reichsarchiv, *Der Weltkrieg 1914 bis 1918*, 264.

22. Mackensen to Falkenhayn, November 11, 1915, BA-MA PH 5 I/78; Hans von Seeckt, *Aus meinem Leben 1866–1917* (Leipzig: von Hase und Koehler Verlag, 1938), 266.

23. German Army, Intelligence Section, Report on the Serbian Army, c. 1915, BH-KA File 11/15/2; Andrej Mitrović, *Serbia's Great War 1914–1918* (West Lafayette, IN: Purdue University Press, 2007, 56–57; Jonathan E. Gumz, *The Resurrection and Collapse of Empire in Habsburg Serbia, 1914–1918* (New York: Cambridge University Press, 2009), 74; Shanafelt, *Secret Enemy*, 84; and Kosch to Wife, November 6, 1915, Nachlass Kosch, BA-MA N 754/5.

24. Foerster, ed., *Mackensen*, 235; Johnson, *Topography and Strategy in the War*, 160; and Bergeder, *Das Reserve-Infanterie-Regiment Nr. 202 auf den Schlachtfeldern des Weltkrieges 1914–1918*, 110.

25. Germany, Reichsarchiv, *Der Weltkrieg 1914 bis 1918*, 258–59; Wahrenburg, *Reserve-Infanterie-Regiment Nr. 83*, 113; Doerstling, *Kriegsgeschichte des Königlich Preussischen Infanterie-Regiments Graf Tauentzien v. Wittenberg (3. Brandenb.) Nr. 20*, 174; KTB/Bavarian Eleventh Infantry Division, November 7, 1915, BH-KA File 11/15/1; and Gallwitz, *Meine Führertätigkeit im Weltkriege 1914/1916*, 436–37.

26. Germany, Reichsarchiv, *Der Weltkrieg 1914 bis 1918*, 259; Appel, *Das Reserve-Infanterie-Regt. Nr. 205*, 114; Bergeder, *Das Reserve-Infanterie-Regiment Nr. 202 auf den Schlachtfeldern des Weltkrieges 1914–1918*, 110; and Gunther Hebert, *Das Alpenkorps: Aufbau, Organisation und Einsatz einer Gebirgstruppen im Ersten Weltkrieg* (Boppard-am-Rhein: Harald Boldt Verlag, 1988), 87.

27. Falkenhayn to Conrad, March 10, 1915 and Conrad to Falkenhayn, March 11, 1915, BA-MA RH 61/979.

28. Kundmann Diary, May 18, 1915, Conrad Archive, ÖSA-KA B/13; Conrad to Falkenhayn, May 18, 1915 and Falkenhayn to Conrad, May 19, 1915, BA-MA RH 61/979; Hebert, *Das Alpenkorps*, 14; and Afflerbach, *Falkenhayn*, 284.

29. Hebert, *Das Alpenkorps*, 15–18.

30. Biographical Chronology, BA-MA MSg 109/10864; and Hebert, *Das Alpenkorps*, 55–57.

31. Hebert, *Das Alpenkorps*, 85; KTB/Alpine Corps, October 20, 1915, BH-KA Alpenkorps 1; and Karl Paulus, *Das K.B. Jäger-Regiment Nr. 1* (Munich: Verlag Bayerisches Kriegsarchiv, 1925), 106.

32. Gallwitz, *Meine Führertätigkeit im Weltkriege 1914/1916*, 418; KTB/German Alpine Corps, October 29, 1915, BH-KA Alpenkorps 1; and German Eleventh Army to Alpine Corps, October 29, 1915, BH-KA Alpenkorps 152.

33. KTB/German Alpine Corps, November 2, 1915, BH-KA Alpenkorps 1; and Captain Max Graf Armansperg, "Feldzug in Serbien 1915," in *Das Königliche Bayerische Infanterie-Leibregiment*, ed. Officers of the Regiment (Munich: Max Schick, 1931), 103.

34. Paulus, *Das K.B. Jäger-Regiment Nr. 1*, 107; Vorwerck, "Die I/Pi 18 in Serbien," *Das Ehrenbuch der Deutschen Pioniere* (Paul Heinrici, ed.) (Berlin: Verlag Tradition Wilhelm Kolk, 1932), 438; KTB/German Alpine Corps, November 5, 1915, BH-KA Alpenkorps 1; Armansperg, "Feldzug in Serbien 1915," 106; and German Alpine Corps, Corps Order, November 6, 1915, BH-KA Alpenkorps 153.

35. Foerster, ed., *Mackensen*, 237; KTB/German Eleventh Army, November 7, 1915, BA-MA PH 5 II/305; Army Group Mackensen to Austro-Hungarian Third Army, November 7, 1915, BA-MA PH 5 I/78; and KTB/German Alpine Corps, November 9, 1915, BH-KA Alpenkorps 1.

36. Foerster, ed., *Mackensen*, 231.

37. Germany, Reichsarchiv, *Der Weltkrieg 1914 bis 1918*, 266.

38. Gallwitz, *Meine Führertätigkeit im Weltkriege 1914/1916*, 442; Germany, Reichsarchiv, *Der Weltkrieg 1914 bis 1918*, 262; and Foerster, ed., *Mackensen*, 236.

39. Robert A. Doughty, *Pyrrhic Victory: French Strategy and Operations in the Great War* (Cambridge: Harvard University Press, 2005), 226–27; Cyril Falls, *History of the Great War. Military Operations. Macedonia: From the Outbreak of War in 1914 to the Spring of 1917* (repr., Nashville: Battery Press, 1996), 55; Alan Wakefield and Simon Moody, *Under the Devil's Eye: Britain's Forgotten Army at Salonika 1915–1918* (Gloucestershire: Sutton Publishing, 2004), 14; and Alan Palmer, *The Gardeners of Salonika* (New York: Simon and Schuster, 1965), 39.

40. Germany, Reichsarchiv, *Der Weltkrieg 1914 bis 1918*, 263.

41. Austria, Bundesministerium, *Österreich-Ungarns Letzter Krieg 1914–1918*, 294; Adams, *Flight in Winter*, 110; Germany, Reichsarchiv, *Der Weltkrieg 1914 bis 1918*, 265; and Fryer, *Destruction of Serbia in 1915*, 85–86.

42. Kosch to Wife, November 13, 1915, Nachlass Kosch, BA-MA N 754/5; German 101st Infantry Division, Brief Report on Operations of the 101st Infantry Division During the Campaign in Serbia in October and November 1915, December 9, 1915, BA-MA PH 8 I/45; Alfred Richter, *Das 2. Thüring. Infanterie-Regiment Nr. 32* (Zeulenroda: Druck von Bernhard Spoorn, 1928), 179; and Kurt Hennig, *Das Infanterie-Regiment (8. Ostpreussisches) Nr. 45 (Insterburg-Darkehmen) im Weltkriege 1914–18* (Berlin: Druck und Verlag Gerhard Stalling, 1928), 103.

43. Foerster, ed. *Mackensen*, 239; Seeckt, *Aus meinem Leben 1866–1917*, 268; Rauchensteiner, *Der Erste Weltkrieg und das Ende der Habsburgermonarchie 1914–1918*, 283; and Peter Broucek, ed., *Ein österreichischer General gegen Hitler. Feldmarschalleutnant Alfred Jansa: Errinerungen* (Vienna: Böhlau Verlag, 2011), 297.

44. Major Georg Paul Neumann, *Die deutschen Luftstreitkräfte im Weltkriege* (Berlin: Ernst Siegfried Mittler und Sohn, 1920), 492–94; and General Ernest von Hoeppner, *Germany's War in the Air: The Development and Operations of German Military Aviation in the World War* (repr., Nashville: Battery Press, 1994), 46.

45. Neumann, *Die deutschen Luftstreitkräfte im Weltkriege*, 494; Hoeppner, *Germany's War in the Air*, 47; Major Hilmer Freiherr von Bülow, *Geschichte der Luftwaffe: Eine kurz Darstellung der Entwicklung der fünften Waffe* (Frankfurt-am-Main: Verlag Moritz Diesterweg, 1934), 61; and Captain Georg Paul Neumann, "Die Luftstreitkräfte," *Die militärischen Lehren des Grossen Krieges*, 275.

46. Foerster, ed., *Mackensen*, 234; Seeckt, *Aus meinem Leben 1866–1917*, 270; and Richard C. Hall, *Balkan Breakthrough: The Battle of Dobro Pole 1918* (Bloomington: Indiana University Press, 2010), 46.

47. Gallwitz, *Meine Führertätigkeit im Weltkriege 1914/1916*, 443; and Foerster, ed., *Mackensen*, 234.

48. Austria, Bundesministerium, *Österreich-Ungarns Letzter Krieg 1914–1918*, 296–97.

49. Johnson, *Topography and Strategy in the War*, 160; KTB/German Alpine Corps, November 10, 1915, BH-KA Alpenkorps 1; and Mackensen to Falkenhayn, November 11, 1915, BA-MA PH 5 I/78.

50. Lieutenant Colonel Karl Boesser, *Geschichte des Reserve-Feldartillerie-Regiments Nr. 44* (Grossen: Rudolf Zeidler, 1932), 202; Appel, *Das Reserve-Infanterie-Regiment Nr. 205*, 118; and Army Group Mackensen to Austro-Hungarian Third Army, November 11, 1915, BA-MA PH 5 I/78.

51. KTB/German Alpine Corps, November 13, 1915, BH-KA Alpenkorps 1.

52. Austria, Bundesministerium, *Österreich-Ungarns Letzter Krieg 1914–1918*, 297; KTB/German Alpine Corps, November 14, 1915, BH-KA Alpenkorps 1; and Germany, Reichsarchiv, *Der Weltkrieg 1914 bis 1918*, 267–69.

53. German Alpine Corps, "Munitionsversorgung im Ibartal," c. December 1915, BH-KA Alpenkorps 18; Paulus, *Das K.B. Jäger-Regiment Nr. 1*, 112; Appel, *Das Reserve-Infanterie-Regiment Nr. 205*, 121; and Richter, *Das 2. Thüring. Infanterie-Regiment Nr. 32*, 179.

54. KTB/German Eleventh Army, November 17, 1915, BA-MA PH 5 II/305; Richter, *Das 2. Thüring. Infanterie-Regiment Nr. 32*, 180–81; Kosch to Wife, November 18, 1915, Nachlass Kosch, BA-MA N 754/5; and Germany, Reichsarchiv, *Der Weltkrieg 1914 bis 1918*, 269.

55. Austria, Bundesministerium, *Österreich-Ungarns Letzter Krieg 1914–1918*, 299; Schöning, *Unser Regiment im Weltkriege*, 210; Germany, Reichsarchiv, *Der Weltkrieg 1914 bis 1918*, 264; and Gallwitz, *Meine Führertätigkeit im Weltkriege 1914/1916*, 441.

56. Germany, Reichsarchiv, *Der Weltkrieg 1914 bis 1918*, 270; Boesser, *Geschichte des Reserve-Feldartillerie-Regiments Nr. 44*, 201–202; Appel, *Das Reserve-Infanterie-Regiment Nr. 205*, 122; Kosch to Wife, November 17, 1915, Nachlass Kosch, BA-MA N 754/5; Neumann, *Die deutschen Luftstreitkräfte im Weltkriege*, 495; and German Alpine Corps, Corps Order, November 20, 1915, BH-KA Alpenkorps 154.

57. KTB/German Alpine Corps, November 15, 1915, BH-KA Alpenkorps 1; Austria, Bundesministerium, *Österreich-Ungarns Letzter Krieg 1914–1918*, 301; Richter, *Das 2. Thüring. Infanterie-Regiment Nr. 32*, 182; Lieutenant Colonel Radermacher, *Erinnerungsblätter des Grossherzogl. Hessischen Reserve-Infanterie-Regiments Nr. 116* (Oldenburg: Druck und Verlag von Gerhard Stalling, 1929), 67; German Alpine Corps to Group Tutschek, November 16, 1915; German Alpine Corps, Corps Order, November 17, 1915, BH-KA Alpenkorps 154; KTB/German Alpine Corps, November 16, 1915, BH-KA Alpenkorps 1; and Army Group

Mackensen to Austro-Hungarian Third Army, November 15, 1915, BA-MA PH 5 I/78.

58. Gallwitz, *Meine Führertätigkeit im Weltkriege 1914/1916*, 441; German 101st Infantry Division, Brief Report on Operations of the 101st Infantry Division During the Campaign in Serbia in October and November 1915, December 9, 1915, BA-MA PH 8 I/45; Oden and Schultz, *Feldartillerie-Regiment 201*, 47; Association of Former Officers of the Regiment, *Das 1. Masurische Infanterie-Regiment Nr. 146 1897–1919* (Berlin: Verlag Tradition Wilhelm Kolk, 1929), 140; and KTB/German Eleventh Army, November 18, 1915, BA-MA PH 5 II/305.

59. Army Group Mackensen to Austro-Hungarian Third Army, November 19, 1915, BA-MA PH 5 I/78.

60. Austro-Hungarian Third Army to German Alpine Corps, November 23, 1915, BH-KA Alpenkorps 154.

61. Fryer, *Destruction of Serbia in 1915*, 86; and Mitrović, *Serbia's Great War 1914–1918*, 148.

62. Richter, *Das 2. Thüring. Infanterie-Regiment Nr. 32*, 180; and Hennig, *Das Infanterie-Regiment (8. Ostpreussisches) Nr. 45 (Insterburg-Darkehmen) im Weltkriege 1914–18*, 107.

63. Mitrović, *Serbia's Great War 1914–1918*, 148; and Mile Bjelajac, "King Peter I Karageorge," *The Serbs and their Leaders in the Twentieth Century*, (Peter Radan and Aleksander Pavković, eds.) (Brookfield, VT: Ashgate, 1997), 107.

64. Count Carlo Sforza, *Fifty Years of War and Diplomacy in the Balkans: Pashich and the Union of the Yugoslavs* (New York: Columbia University Press, 1940), 131.

65. Fryer, *Destruction of Serbia in 1915*, 88–89; and Sforza, *Fifty Years of War and Diplomacy in the Balkans*, 133.

66. Mitrović, *Serbia's Great War 1914–1918*, 151. The order is quoted in Adams, *Flight in Winter*, 128.

67. Mitrović, *Serbia's Great War 1914–1918*, 149–50; and Branislav Gligorijević, "King Alexander I Karageorge," *The Serbs and their Leaders in the Twentieth Century*, 145.

68. Adams, *Flight in Winter*, 143–44; Mitrović, *Serbia's Great War 1914–1918*, 149; and Fryer, *Destruction of Serbia in 1915*, 99.

69. KTB/German Alpine Corps, November 20, 1915, BH-KA Alpenkorps 1; and Austria, Bundesministerium, *Österreich-Ungarns Letzter Krieg 1914–1918*, 318.

70. Germany, Reichsarchiv, *Der Weltkrieg 1914 bis 1918*, 273; and Kosch to Wife, November 22, 1915, Nachlass Kosch, BA-MA N 754/5.

71. Germany, Reichsarchiv, *Der Weltkrieg 1914 bis 1918*, 274; Austria, Bundesministerium, *Österreich-Ungarns Letzter Krieg 1914–1918*, 320; German Alpine Corps, Corps Order, November 21, 1915, BH-KA Alpenkorps 154; and KTB/German Eleventh Army, November 23, 1915, BA-MA PH 5 II/305.

72. Germany, Reichsarchiv, *Der Weltkrieg 1914 bis 1918*, 274; KTB/German Eleventh Army, November 23, 1915, BA-MA PH 5 II/305; Army Group Mackensen to Austro-Hungarian Third Army, November 24, 1915, BA-MA 5 I/78; and Gallwitz, *Meine Führertätigkeit im Weltkriege 1914/1916*, 458.

73. Elsie Corbett, *Red Cross in Serbia 1915–1919: A Personal Diary of Experiences* (Banbury: Cheney and Sons, 1964), 42; and Monica M. Stanley, *My Diary in Serbia: April 1, 1915 – Nov. 1, 1915* (London: Simpkin, Marshall, Hamilton, Kent, 1916), 115.

74. Corbett, *Red Cross in Serbia 1915–1919*, 47.

75. Ulrich, *Res.-Inf.-Regiment 52 im Weltkriege*, 266; KTB/German Eleventh Army, November 23, 1915, BA-MA PH 5 II/305; and Hennig, *Das Infanterie-Regiment (8. Ostpreussisches) Nr. 45 (Insterburg-Darkehmen) im Weltkriege 1914–18*, 108.

76. Richter, *Das 2. Thüring. Infanterie-Regiment Nr. 32*, 178; Radermacher, *Erinnerungsblätter des Grossherzogl. Hessischen Reserve-Infanterie-Regiments Nr. 116*, 68; and German Alpine Corps, Special Order, November 24, 1915, BH-KA Alpenkorps 154.

77. Tamara Scheer, *Zwischen Front und Heimat: Österreich-Ungarns Militärverwaltung im Ersten Weltkrieg* (Frankfurt-am-Main: Peter Lang, 2009), 29; and Adams, *Flight in Winter*, 80.

78. Ulrich, *Res.-Inf.-Regiment 52 im Weltkriege*, 264.

79. Armansperg, "Feldzug in Serbien 1915," 120.

80. Scheer, *Zwischen Front und Heimat*, 33; and Daniel M. Segesser, "Kriegsverbrechen auf dem Balkan und in Anatolien in der internationalisten juristischen Debatte während der Balkankriege und des Ersten Weltkriegs," in *Der Erste Weltkrieg auf dem Balkan*, ed. Jürgen Angelow (Berlin: Wissenschaft Verlag, 2011), 194.

81. Association of Former Officers of the Regiment, *Das 1. Masurische Infanterie-Regiment Nr. 146 1897–1919*, 141; Richter, *Das 2. Thüring. Infanterie-Regiment Nr. 32*, 185; and Herwig, *First World War*, 162.

82. Francis Joseph to Mackensen, November 28, 1915 and Mackensen to Francis Joseph, November 28, 1915, BA-MA RH 61/993.

83. Wilhelm II to Mackensen, November 27, 1915, BA-MA RH 61/993; Steuer, *Das Infanterie-Regiment Generalfeldmarschall von Mackensen (3. West preussisches) Nr. 129 im Weltkriege*, 156–57; and Wilhelm Führer, *Geschichte des Reserve Infanterie Regiments 203* (Berlin: Privately Published, 1960–1964), vol. 2, 378–79.

84. Broucek, ed., *Ein österreichischer General gegen Hitler*, 297–98.

85. Austria, Bundesministerium, *Österreich-Ungarns Letzter Krieg 1914–1918*, 336.

86. Fritz Haleck, *Das Reserve-Infanterie-Regiment Nr. 208* (Berlin: Druck und Verlag von Gerhard Stalling, 1922), 108; and Bergeder, *Das Reserve-Infanterie-Regiment Nr. 202 auf den Schlachtfeldern des Weltkrieges 1914–1918*, 119.

87. Steuer, *Das Infanterie-Regiment Generalfeldmarschall von Mackensen (3. West preussisches) Nr. 129 im Weltkriege*, 153; Captain Hellmut Gnamm, *Das Fusilier-Regiment Kaiser Franz Joseph von Österreich, König von Ungarn (4. württ,) Nr. 122* (Stuttgart: Ehr. Belsersche Verlagsbuchhandlung, 1921), 109; Franz Giese, *Geschichte des Reserve-Infanterie-Regiments 227 im Weltkriege 1914/18* (Privately Published, 1931), 302–303; and KTB/Bavarian Eleventh Infantry Division, October 12, 1915, BH-KA File 11/15/1.

88. Richter, *Das 2. Thüring. Infanterie-Regiment Nr. 32*, 188; and Hennig, *Das Infanterie-Regiment (8. Ostpreussisches) Nr. 45 (Insterburg-Darkehmen) im Weltkriege*, 107.

89. Doerstling, *Kriegsgeschichte des Königlich Preussischen Infanterie-Regiments Graf Tauentzien v. Wittenberg (3. Brandenb.) Nr. 20*, 162.

90. Bergeder, *Das Reserve-Infanterie-Regiment Nr. 202 auf den Schlachtfeldern des Weltkrieges 1914–1918*, 119.

CHAPTER 8

1. Helmut Reichold, ed., *Adolf Wild von Hohenborn: Briefe und Tagebuchau-fzeichnungen des preussischen Generals als Kriegsminister und Truppenführer im Ersten Weltkrieg* (Boppard-am-Rhein: Harald Boldt Verlag, 1986), 116.

2. Quoted in Andrej Mitrović, *Serbia's Great War 1914–1918* (West Lafayette, IN: Purdue University Press, 2007), 159.

3. Quoted in Alan Palmer, *The Gardeners of Salonika* (New York: Simon and Schuster, 1965), 58..

4. Kaganeck Diary, April 27, 1916, BA-MA MSg 1/2517.

5. Gordon Gordon-Smith, *From Serbia to Jugoslavia. Serbia's Victories, Reverses and Final Triumph: 1914–1918* (New York: G.P. Putnam's Sons, 1920), 153.

6. Douglas W. Johnson, *Topography and Strategy in the War* (New York: Henry Holt, 1917), 159; and John C. Adams, *Flight in Winter* (Princeton: Princeton University Press, 1942), 165–66.

7. Mitrović, *Serbia's Great War 1914–1918*, 151.

8. Ben Shepherd, *Terror in the Balkans: German Armies and Partisan Warfare* (Cambridge: Harvard University Press, 2012), 36; and Manfred Rauchensteiner, *Der Erste Weltkrieg und das Ende der Habsburgermonarchie 1914–1918* (Vienna: Böhlau Verlag, 2013), 510.

9. Shepherd, *Terror in the Balkans*, 36.

10. British Army, General Staff, "Military Notes on the Balkan States," in *Armies of the Balkan States 1914–1918: The Military Forces of Bulgaria, Greece, Romania and Serbia*, ed. British Army, General Staff (repr., Nashville: Battery Press, 1996), 49; Austria, Bundesministerium für Landesverteidigung, *Österreich-Ungarns Letzter Krieg 1914–1918* (Vienna: Verlag der Militärwissenschaftlichen Mitteilungen, 1931), 336; M. Christian Ortner, "Die Feldzüge gegen Serbien in den Jahren 1914 und 1915," *Der Erste Weltkrieg auf den Balkan*, 140; and Mitrović, *Serbia's Great War 1914–1918*, 151.

11. Robert B. Speed III, *Prisoners, Diplomats, and the Great War: A Study in the Diplomacy of Captivity* (Westport, CT: Greenwood Press, 1990), 74; and Tamara Scheer, *Zwischen Front und Heimat: Österreich-Ungarns Militärverwaltung im Ersten Weltkrieg* (Frankfurt-am-Main: Peter Lang, 2009), 34.

12. Charles W. Koburger Jr., *The Central Powers in the Adriatic, 1914–1918: War in a Narrow Sea* (Westport, CT: Prager, 2001), 15. Born June 13, 1851, Haus was the son of a Slovakian tavern owner. He joined the Austro-Hungarian Navy in 1869. Successful service in a variety of assignments brought him to the attention of Archduke Franz Ferdinand. Haus was appointed head of the Austro-Hungarian Navy in February 1913. Haus did not survive the war, dying of lung disease on February 8, 1917. Holger H. Herwig and Neil M. Heyman, *Biographical Dictionary of World War I* (Westport, CT: Greenwood Press, 1982), 181.

13. Koburger, *Central Powers in the Adriatic, 1914–1918*, 48.

14. Charles E. J. Fryer, *The Destruction of Serbia in 1915* (New York: East European Monographs, 1997), 77; and Koburger, *Central Powers in the Adriatic, 1914–1918*, 51.

15. Mitrović, *Serbia's Great War 1914–1918*, 158–59; Count Carlo Sforza, *Fifty Years of War and Diplomacy in the Balkans: Pashich and the Union of the Yugoslavs*

(New York: Columbia University Press, 1940), 140; and Fryer, *Destruction of Serbia in 1915*, 117.

16. Mile Bjelajac, "King Peter I Karageorge," *The Serbs and Their Leaders in the Twentieth Century*, 108; Richard F. Hamilton and Holger H. Herwig, *Decisions for War, 1914–1917* (Cambridge: Cambridge University Press, 2004), 180–81; and Koburger, *Central Powers in the Adriatic, 1914–1918*, 55.

17. Mitrović, *Serbia's Great War 1914–1918*, 162–63; Herwig and Hamilton, *Biographical Dictionary of World War I*, 256; and Bjelajac, "King Peter I Karageorge," 108.

18. Palmer, *Gardeners of Salonika*, 61; Mitrović, *Serbia's Great War 1914–1918*, 164; and Shepherd, *Terror in the Balkans*, 36.

19. German Twenty-Sixth Infantry Division, Division Order, November 21, 1915, LA-BW Gu117 Bü900; Friedrich Appel, *Das Reserve-Infanterie-Regiment Nr. 205* (Berlin: Verlag Bernard und Graefe, 1937), 125; Fritz Bergeder, *Das Reserve-Infanterie-Regiment Nr. 202 auf den Schlachtfeldern des Weltkrieges 1914–1918* (Berlin: Traditions Verlag Kolk, 1939), 117; and Captain Gerok, *Das 2. Württ. Feldartillerie-Reg. Nr. 29 "Prinz Luitpold von Bayern" im Weltkrieg 1914–1918* (Stuttgart: Ehr. Belsersche Verlagsbuchhandlung, 1921), 46.

20. Captain Wahrenburg, *Reserve-Infanterie-Regiment Nr. 83* (Berlin: Druck und Verlag von Gerhard Stalling, 1924), 114; and Captain Wilhelm Schlawe, *Feldartillerie-Regiment General-Feldzeugmeister (1.Brandenburgisches) Nr. 3 im Weltkrieg 1914/1918* (Berlin: Verlag Bernard und Graefe, 1935), 94–95.

21. KTB/Bavarian Eleventh Infantry Division, November 7, 1915, BH-KA File 11/15/1; Kneussl Diary, November 14, 1915, Nachlass Kneussl, BH-KA NL 6; and First Lieutenant Herbert Ulrich, *Res.-Inf.-Regiment 52 im Weltkriege* (Cottbus: Lausitzer Druckerei und Verlagsanstalt, 1925), 276.

22. KTB/German Alpine Corps, November 30, 1915, BH-KA Alpenkorps 1; Gunther Hebert, *Das Alpenkorps: Aufbau, Organisation und Einsatz einer Gebirgstruppen im Ersten Weltkrieg* (Boppard-am-Rhein: Harald Boldt Verlag, 1988), 88; German 101st Infantry Division, Brief Report on Operations of the 101st Infantry Division During the Campaign in Serbia in October and November 1915, December 9, 1915, BA-MA PH 8 I/45; Association of Former Officers of the Regiment, *Das 1. Masurische Infanterie-Regiment Nr. 146 1897–1919* (Berlin: Verlag Tradition Wilhelm Kolk, 1929), 144; Captain Hellmut Gnamm, *Das Fusilier-Regiment Kaiser Franz Joseph von Österreich, König von Ungarn (4. württ,) Nr. 122* (Stuttgart: Ehr. Belsersche Verlagsbuchhandlung, 1921), 114; Joseph Steuer, *Das Infanterie-Regiment Generalfeldmarschall von Mackensen (3. West preussisches) Nr. 129 im Weltkriege* (Berlin: Druck und Verlag Gerhard Stalling, 1925), 155; KTB/German Eleventh Army, November 18, 1915, BA-MA PH 5 II/305; and Wolfgang Foerster, ed., *Mackensen: Briefe und Aufzeichnungen des Generalfeldmarschalls aus Krieg und Frieden* (Bonn: Wahlband der Buchgemeinde, 1938), 249.

23. Franz Giese, *Geschichte des Reserve-Infanterie-Regiments 227 im Weltkriege 1914/18* (Privately Published, 1931), 301; KTB/German Alpine Corps, November 30, 1915, BH-KA Alpenkorps 1; Kurt Hennig, *Das Infanterie-Regiment (8. Ostpreussisches) Nr. 45 (Insterburg-Darkehmen) im Weltkriege 1914–18* (Berlin: Druck und Verlag Gerhard Stalling, 1928), 110; and Kosch to Wife, November 28, 1915, Nachlass Kosch, BA-MA N 754/5.

24. Captain Max Graf Armansperg, "Feldzug in Serbien 1915," in *Das Königliche Bayerische Infanterie-Leibregiment*, ed. Officers of the Regiment (Munich: Max Schick, 1931), 127; Hennig, *Das Infanterie-Regiment (8. Osrpreussisches) Nr. 45 (Insterburg-Darkehmen) im Weltkriege 1914–18*, 109; Giese, *Geschichte der Reserve-Infanterie-Regiments 227 im Weltkriege 1914/18*, 301; and Ulrich, *Res.-Inf.-Regiment 52 im Weltkriege*, 274.

25. Gerok, *Das 2. Württ. Feldartillerie-Reg. Nr. 29 "Prinz Luitpold von Bayern" im Weltkrieg 1914–1918*, 46; and Bergeder, *Das Reserve-Infanterie-Regiment Nr. 202 auf den Schlachtfeldern des Weltkrieges 1914–1918*, 120.

26. Generalmajor Josef Ritter Röhn von Vrbas to Generalleutnant Richard Dorer, December 29, 1915, Personal Files, Nachlass Dorrer. LA-BW M 660/071 Nr. 18e.

27. Hermann Neeff, *Das 4. Württ. Feldartillerie-Reg. Nr. 65 im Weltkrieg* (Stuttgart: Ehr. Belser AG Verlagsbuchhandlung, 1925), 57; and K. Drautz, "Bursstag 1915 in Serbien," BA-MA PH 6 I/204.

28. Adolf Soldan, *5. Grossherzoglich Hessischen Infanterie-Regiment Nr. 168* (Berlin: Druck und Verlag Gerhard Stalling, 1924), 70; Giese, *Geschichte der Reserve-Infanterie-Regiments 227 im Weltkriege 1914/18*, 301; Franz Freiherr von Stengel, *Das K.B. 3. Infanterie-Regiment Prinz Karl von Bayern* (Munich: Verlag Bayerisches Kriegsarchiv, 1924), 47; and Schlawe, *Feldartillerie-Regiment General-Feldzeugmeister (1. Brandenburgisches) Nr. 3 im Weltkrieg 1914/1918*, 94.

29. Armansperg, "Feldzug in Serbien 1915," 129; Fritz Haleck, *Das Reserve-Infanterie-Regiment Nr. 208* (Berlin: Druck und Verlag von Gerhard Stalling, 1922), 40; Bergeder, *Das Reserve-Infanterie-Regiment Nr. 202 auf den Schlachtfeldern des Weltkrieges 1914–1918*, 120; Christian Stachelbeck, *Militärische Effektivität im Ersten Weltkrieg: Die 11. Bayerische Infanteriedivision 1915 bis 1918* (Paderborn: Ferdinand Schöningh, 2010), 93–94; Stengel, *Das K.B. 3. Infanterie-Regiment Prinz Karl von Bayern*, 47; Lieutenant Colonel Radermacher, *Erinnerungsblätter des Grossherzogl. Hessischen Reserve-Infanterie-Regiments Nr. 116* (Oldenburg: Druck und Verlag von Gerhard Stalling, 1929), 69; and Ulrich, *Res.-Inf.-Regiment 52 im Weltkriege*, 277.

30. Peter Broucek, ed., *Ein österreichischer General gegen Hitler. Feldmarschalleutnant Alfred Jansa: Errinerungen* (Vienna: Böhlau Verlag, 2011), 299.

31. Hennig, *Das Infanterie-Regiment (8. Ostpreussisches) Nr. 45 (Insterburg-Darkehmen) im Weltkriege 1914–18*, 111; Army Group Mackensen, Order of the Day Nr. 21, December 3, 1915, BA-MA PH 5 I/77; and Army Group Mackensen, Order of the Day Nr. 26, December 24, 1915, BA-MA PH 5 I/77.

32. German Alpine Corps, Special Orders, November 24, 1915, BH-KA Alpenkorps 154; and Association of Former Officers of the Regiment, *Das 1. Masurische Infanterie-Regiment Nr. 146*, 146.

33. Gerhard Ritter, *The Sword and the Scepter: The Problem of Militarism in Germany* (Coral Gables, FL: University of Miami Press, 1970), 86; Scheer, *Zwischen Front und Heimat*, 331–32; and Jonathan E. Gumz, *The Resurrection and Collapse of Empire in Habsburg Serbia, 1914–1918* (New York: Cambridge University Press, 2009), 63.

34. Army Group Mackensen, Order of the Day Nr. 21, December 3, 1915, BA-MA PH 5 I/77; German Army, Railroad Section, "Der Feldzug gegen Serbien im Herbst 1915," 33, BA-MA RH 61/27; and Army Group Mackensen, Order of the Day Nr. 22, December 6, 1915, BA-MA PH 5 I/77.

35. Lothar Höbelt, "Der Balkan und die Strategie der Entente," *Der Erste Weltkrieg auf dem Balkan* (Jürgen Angelow, ed.) (Berlin: Wissenschaft Verlag, 2011) 66; Edward J. Erickson, *Gallipoli: The Ottoman Campaign* (Barnsley: Pen and Sword Books, 2010), 178–79; Elizabeth Greenhalgh, *Victory through Coalition: Britain and France during the First World War* (Cambridge: Cambridge University Press, 2005), 36; and Robert A. Doughty, *Pyrrhic Victory: French Strategy and Operations in the Great War* (Cambridge: Harvard University Press, 2005), 240.

36. Greenhalgh, *Victory through Coalition*, 36; Palmer, *Gardeners of Salonika*, 59; Doughty, *Pyrrhic Victory*, 238–39; Höbelt, "Der Balkan und die Strategie der Entente," 65–66; and Alan Wakefield and Simon Moody, *Under the Devil's Eye: Britain's Forgotten Army at Salonika 1915–1918* (Gloucestershire: Sutton Publishing, 2004), 32. Over the course of October and November, three other British divisions had arrived in Salonika. Cyril Falls, *History of the Great War. Military Operations. Macedonia: From the Outbreak of War in 1914 to the Spring of 1917* (repr., Nashville: Battery Press, 1996), 103.

37. General Erich von Falkenhayn, *The German General Staff and Its Decisions, 1914–1916* (New York: Dodd, Mead, 1920), 229; Ritter, *Sword and the Scepter*, vol. 3, 86; and Lawrence Sondhaus, *Franz Conrad von Hötzendorf: Architect of the Apocalypse* (Boston: Humanities Press, 2000), 183.

38. Georg Reichlin-Meldegg, *Das Kaisers Prinz Eugen? Feldmarschall Hermann Baron Kövess von Kövessháza: Der letzte Oberkommandant der K.u.K. Armee im Ersten Weltkrieg* (Graz: Ares Verlag, 2010), 138.

39. Foerster, ed., *Mackensen*, 248; Hans von Seeckt, *Aus meinem Leben 1866–1917* (Leipzig: von Hase und Koehler Verlag, 1938), 290; Hans Meier-Welcker, *Seeckt* (Frankfurt-am-Main: Bernard und Graefe Verlag für Wehrwesen, 1967), 72; Theo Schwarzmüller, *Zwischen Kaiser und Führer. Generalfeldmarschall August von Mackensen: Eine politische Biographie* (Paderborn: Ferdinand Schöningh, 1996), 125; and Broucek, ed., *Ein österreichischer General gegen Hitler*, 299.

40. Austria, Bundesministerium, *Österreich-Ungarns Letzter Krieg 1914–1918*, vol. 3, 575–76; Cramon to Falkenhayn, January 13, 1916, BA-MA RH 61/1536; Srdja Pavlović, *Balkan Anschluss: The Annexation of Montenegro and the Creation of the Common South Slavic State* (West Lafayette, IN: Purdue University Press, 2008), 76–78; and Heiko Brendel, "Der geostrategische Rahmen der österreichisch-ungarischen Besatzung Montenegros im Ersten Weltkrieg," *Der Erste Weltkrieg auf dem Balkan*, 168.

41. August von Cramon, *Unser Österreich-Ungarischer Bundesgenosse im Weltkriege. Erinnerungen aus meiner vierjährigen Tätigkeit als bevollmächtiger deutsche General beim K.u.K. Armeeoberkommando* (Berlin: E.S. Mittler und Sohn, 1920), 45; Broucek, ed., *Ein österreichischer General gegen Hitler*, 300; and Holger H. Herwig, *The First World War: Germany and Austria-Hungary 1914–1918* (London: Arnold, 1997), 159.

42. Broucek, ed., *Ein österreichischer General gegen Hitler*, 299.

43. OHL, Military Convention Between Germany, Austria-Hungary and Bulgaria, September 6, 1915, BA-MA PH 5 I/78; Mackensen, "Kriegstage in Bulgarien," November 22, 1935, Nachlass Mackensen, BA-MA N 39/310; Broucek, ed., *Ein österreichischer General gegen Hitler*, 301; and Meier-Welcker, *Seeckt*, 73.

44. Johnson, *Topography and Strategy in the War*, 173–74; Seeckt, *Aus meinem Leben 1866–1917*, 307; Meier-Welcker, *Seeckt*, 73; Jung, *Max von Gallwitz (1852–1937)*, 64; and DiNardo, "Modern Soldier in a Busby," 153.

45. Hamilton and Herwig, *Decisions for War. 1914–1917*, 176; Lamar Cecil, *Wilhelm II* (Chapel Hill: University of North Carolina Press, 1989), 228; and Ritter, *Sword and the Scepter*, vol. 3, 79.

46. Broucek, ed., *Ein österreichischer General gegen Hitler*, 299; and Schwarzmüller, *Zwischen Kaiser und Führer*, 386.

47. Broucek, ed., *Ein österreichischer General gegen Hitler*, 300.

48. Görlitz, ed., *The Kaiser and His Court*, 127–28; Seeckt, *Aus meinem Leben 1866–1917*, 312–13; Foerster, ed., *Mackensen*, 254; Broucek, ed., *Ein österreichischer General gegen Hitler*, 300; Lieutenant Colonel Karl Boesser, *Geschichte des Reserve-Feldartillerie-Regiments Nr. 44* (Grossen: Rudolf Zeidler, 1932), 214–16; and Bergeder, *Das Reserve-Infanterie-Regiment Nr. 202 auf den Schlachtfeldern des Weltkrieges 1914–1918*, 120.

49. Sondhaus, *Franz Conrad von Hötzendorf*, 182; Gary W. Shanafelt, *The Secret Enemy: Austria-Hungary and the German Alliance, 1914–1918* (Boulder, CO: East European Monographs, 1985), 84; and Rauchensteiner, *Der Erste Weltkrieg und das Ende der Habsburgermonarchie 1914–1918*, 488.

50. Herwig, *First World War*, 205.

CHAPTER 9

1. Army Group Temesvár, Order For Aerial Reconnaissance, September 25, 1915, BH-KA File 11/15/2.

2. Quoted in Peter Broucek, ed., *Ein österreichischer General gegen Hitler. Feldmarschalleutnant Alfred Jansa: Errinerungen* (Vienna: Böhlau Verlag, 2011), 302.

3. German Alpine Corps, Corps Order, November 17, 1915, BH-KA Alpenkorps 154.

4. Captain Max Graf Armansperg, "Feldzug in Serbien 1915," in *Das Königliche Bayerische Infanterie-Leibregiment*, ed. Officers of the Regiment (Munich: Max Schick, 1931), 128; and Fritz Bergeder, *Das Reserve-Infanterie-Regiment Nr. 202 auf den Schlachtfeldern des Weltkrieges 1914–1918* (Berlin: Traditions Verlag Kolk, 1939), 116.

5. Manfred Rauchensteiner, *Der Erste Weltkrieg und das Ende der Habsburgermonarchie 1914–1918* (Vienna: Böhlau Verlag, 2013), 286; M. Christian Ortner, "Die Feldzüge gegen Serbien in den Jahren 1914 und 1915," *Der Erste Weltkrieg auf dem Balkan* (Jürgen Angelow, ed.) (Berlin: Wissenschaft Verlag, 2011), 136; German Army, Report on the State of the Serbian Army, September 10, 1915, Nachlass Seeckt, BA-MA N 247/26; and Austro-Hungarian Third Army, "Serbia," September 16, 1915, LA-BW Gu117 Bü899.

6. Holger H. Herwig and Neil M. Heyman, *Biographical Dictionary of World War I* (Westport, CT: Greenwood Press, 1982), 291; and Andrej Mitrović, *Serbia's Great War 1914–1918* (West Lafayette, IN: Purdue University Press, 2007), 313.

7. Hans von Seeckt, *Aus meinem Leben 1866–1917* (Leipzig: von Hase und Koehler Verlag, 1938), 231; General der Artillerie Max von Gallwitz, *Meine Führertätigkeit im*

Weltkriege 1914/1916: Belgien–Osten–Balkan (Berlin: E.S. Mittler und Sohn, 1929), 388; Kosch to Family, October 7, 1915, Nachlass Kosch, BA-MA N 754/5; Captain Wilhelm Schlawe, *Feldartillerie-Regiment General-Feldzeugmeister (1.Brandenburgisches) Nr. 3 im Weltkrieg 1914/1918* (Berlin: Verlag Bernard und Graefe, 1935), 95; Gallwitz, *Meine Führertätigkeit im Weltkriege 1914/1916*, 399; Germany, Reichsarchiv, *Der Weltkrieg 1914 bis 1918* (Berlin: E.S. Mittler und Sohn, 1933), 222; and Colonel Scheunemann, "Pioniere im Kampf um die Donau," in *Das Ehrenbuch der Deutschen Pioniere*, ed. Paul Heinrici (Berlin: Verlag Tradition Wilhelm Kolk, 1932), 430.

8. Richard L. DiNardo, *Breakthrough: The Gorlice-Tarnow Campaign, 1915* (Santa Barbara, CA: Praeger, 2010), 138; Carl von Clausewitz, *On War*, eds. and trans. Michael Howard and Peter Paret (Princeton: Princeton University Press, 1976), 102; and Broucek, ed., *Ein österreichischer General gegen Hitler*, 297.

9. Georg Reichlin-Meldegg, *Das Kaisers Prinz Eugen? Feldmarschall Hermann Baron Kövess von Kövessháza: Der letzte Oberkommandant der K.u.K. Armee im Ersten Weltkrieg* (Graz: Ares Verlag, 2010), 137; Broucek, ed., *Ein österreichischer General gegen Hitler*, 291; German Army, Report on the State of the Serbian Army, September 10, 1915, Nachlass Seeckt, BA-MA N 247/26; Austro-Hungarian Third Army, "Serbia," September 16, 1915, LA-BW Gu117 Bü899; and Jonathan E. Gumz, *The Resurrection and Collapse of Empire in Habsburg Serbia, 1914–1918* (New York: Cambridge University Press, 2009), 68.

10. Hans Meier-Welcker, *Seeckt* (Frankfurt-am-Main: Bernard und Graefe Verlag für Wehrwesen, 1967), 84.

11. Richard L. DiNardo, "Modern Soldier in a Busby: August von Mackensen, 1914–1916," in *Arms and the Man: Military History Essays in Honor of Dennis Showalter*, ed. Michael S. Neiberg (Boston: Brill, 2011), 155; and Charles R. M. F. Cruttwell, *A History of the Great War 1914–1918* (repr., Chicago: Academy Publishers, 2007), 173.

12. Meier-Welcker, *Seeckt*, 81.

13. Seeckt, *Aus meinem Leben 1866–1917*, 250–51; Jakob Jung, *Max von Gallwitz (1852–1937): General und Politiker* (Osnabrück: Biblio Verlag, 1995), 65; and Seeckt to Wife, June 27, 1915, Nachlass Seeckt, BA-MA N 247/58.

14. Herwig and Hamilton, *Biographical Dictionary of World War I*, 211–12; and Reichlin-Meldegg, *Das Kaisers Prinz Eugen?* 233–34.

15. Herwig and Hamilton, *Biographical Dictionary of World War I*, 160–61.

16. Biographical Chronology, BA-MA MSg 109/10874.

17. Biographical Chronology, BA-MA MSg 109/10864; and Biographical BA-MA MSg 109/10865.

18. Biographical Chronology, BA-MA MSg 109/10858.

19. Biographical Chronology, BA-MA MSg 109/10864; Richard L. DiNardo, "Huns with Web-Feet: Operation Albion, 1917," *War in History* 12, no. 4 (November 2005): 414; and Chaplain J. Boesch, Forty-Fourth Reserve Infantry Division, Eulogy for Generalleutnant von Dorrer, April 2, 1916, Nachlass Dorrer, LA-BW M430/2 Bü375.

20. Scheunemann, "Pioniere im Kampf um die Donau," 420–21; General Erich von Falkenhayn, *The German General Staff and Its Decisions, 1914–1916* (New York: Dodd, Mead, 1920), 186; Germany, Reichsarchiv, *Der Weltkrieg 1914 bis 1918*, vol. 9, 203; and German Army, Railroad Section, "Der Feldzug gegen Serbien im Herbst 1915," 6–7, BA-MA RH 61/27.

21. Broucek, ed., *Ein österreichischer General gegen Hitler*, 297.

22. Justus Scheibert, *Illustrirtes Deutsches Militär-Lexikon* (Berlin: Verlag von W. Pauli's, 1897), 114–16; Joseph Huber, "The Forgotten City," Text of a Radio Address Delivered in Munich, January 28, 1936, Nachlass Mackensen, BA-MA N 39/310; and KTB/Bavarian Eleventh Infantry Division, October 14, 1915, BH-KA File 11/15/1.

23. Army Group Temesvár, Order for Aerial Reconnaissance, September 25, 1915, BH-KA File 11/15/2; Austria, Bundesministerium für Landesverteidigung, *Österreich-Ungarns Letzter Krieg 1914–1918* (Vienna: Verlag der Militärwissenschaftlichen Mitteilungen, 1931), 202; Germany, Reichsarchiv, *Der Weltkrieg 1914 bis 1918*, vol. 9, 210; Major Hilmer Freiherr von Bülow, *Geschichte der Luftwaffe: Eine kurz Darstellung der Entwicklung der fünften Waffe* (Frankfurt-am-Main: Verlag Moritz Diesterweg, 1934), 60; and DiNardo, *Breakthrough*, 49.

24. Germany, Reichsarchiv, *Der Weltkrieg 1914 bis 1918*, vol. 9, 253; and Major Georg Paul Neumann, *Die deutschen Luftstreitkräfte im Weltkriege* (Berlin: Ernst Siegfried Mittler und Sohn, 1920), 496.

25. Jane's, *Jane's Fighting Aircraft of World War I* (repr., London: Studio, 1990), 160; Neumann, *Die deutschen Luftstreitkräfte im Weltkriege*, 242; and Germany, Reichsarchiv, *Der Weltkrieg 1914 bis 1918*, vol. 9, 204.

26. Bülow, *Geschichte der Luftwaffe*, 61; Neumann, *Die deutschen Luftstreitkräfte im Weltkriege*, 492; and General Ernest von Hoeppner, *Germany's War in the Air: The Development and Operations of German Military Aviation in the World War* (repr., Nashville: Battery Press, 1994), 46–47.

27. Bavarian Eighth Reserve Infantry Division, Excerpt From Campaign Experiences of the German Eastern Army, June 1915, BH-KA File 8R/11/1; German Eleventh Army, Viewpoints on Reconnaissance in Serbia, October 23, 1915, BH-KA File 11/15/5; and German Alpine Corps, Corps Order, November 20, 1915, BH-KA Alpenkorps 154.

28. Wolfgang Foerster, ed., *Mackensen: Briefe und Aufzeichnungen des Generalfeldmarschalls aus Krieg und Frieden* (Bonn: Wahlband der Buchgemeinde, 1938), 240; Jung, *Max von Gallwitz (1852–1937)*, 33; and DiNardo, "Modern Soldier in a Busby," 162.

29. General der Artillerie Richard von Berendt, "Aus grosser Zeit vor Zwanzig Jahren. Der Feldzug in Serbien," *Militär Wochenblatt* 120, no. 13 (October 4, 1935): 523; Gallwitz, *Meine Führertätigkeit im Weltkriege 1914/1916*, 379–80; and Herbert Jäger, *German Artillery of World War One* (Wiltshire: Crowood Press, 2001), 34.

30. Charles E. J. Fryer, *The Royal Navy on the Danube* (Boulder, CO: East European Monographs, 1988), 127; and Andrej Mitrović, *Serbia's Great War 1914–1918* (West Lafayette, IN: Purdue University Press, 2007), 145.

31. Alfred Richter, *Das 2. Thüring. Infanterie-Regiment Nr. 32* (Zeulenroda: Druck von Bernhard Spoorn, 1928), 163; and Broucek, ed., *Ein österreichischer General gegen Hitler*, 302.

32. Lieutenant Colonel Paul Doerstling, *Kriegsgeschichte des Königlich Preussischen Infanterie-Regiments Graf Tauentzien v. Wittenberg (3. Brandenb.) Nr. 20* (Zeulenroda: Bernhard Sporn, Buchdruckerei und Verlagsanstalt, 1933), 155–62; Schlawe, *Feldartillerie-Regiment General-Feldzeugmeister (1. Brandenburgisches) Nr. 3 im Weltkrieg 1914/1918*, 88; Captain Gerok, *Das 2. Württ. Feldartillerie-Reg. Nr. 29 "Prinz Luitpold von Bayern" im Weltkrieg 1914–1918* (Stuttgart: Ehr. Belsersche

Verlagsbuchhandlung, 1921), 43; Richter, *Das 2. Thüring. Infanterie-Regiment Nr. 32,* 167; Bergeder, *Das Reserve-Infanterie-Regiment Nr. 202 auf den Schlachtfeldern des Weltkrieges 1914–1918,* 99–100; and Lieutenant Colonel Karl Boesser, *Geschichte des Reserve-Feldartillerie-Regiments Nr. 44* (Grossen: Rudolf Zeidler, 1932), 192.

33. Bergeder, *Das Reserve-Infanterie-Regiment Nr. 202 auf den Schlachtfeldern des Weltkrieges 1914–1918,* 108; and Otto Zarn, Colonel Hayner, and Major Frantzius, *Geschichte des Reserve-Infanterie-Regiments Nr. 201* (Berlin: Verlag Bernard und Graefe, 1940), 184–87.

34. DiNardo, *Breakthrough,* 140.

35. Broucek, ed., *Ein österreichischer General gegen Hitler,* 297; Arthur Schöning, *Unser Regiment im Weltkriege* (Erfurt: Druck von A. Stenger, 1925), 177–78; German XXII Reserve Corps to Austro-Hungarian Third Army, October 5, 1915, BA-MA PH 6 II/119; German IV Reserve Corps, Corps Order for Danube Crossing, October 5, 1915, BH-KA File 11/15/1; German Twenty-Sixth Infantry Division, Division Order, October 11, 1915, LA-BW Gu117 Bü900; Richter, *Das 2. Thüring. Infanterie-Regiment Nr. 32,* 159; and DiNardo, *Breakthrough,* 140.

36. Conrad to Bolfras, April 6, 1915, ÖSA-KA MKSM 78/14; Falkenhayn to Cramon, April 8, 1915, BA-MA RH 61/1536; and General der Infanterie Hermann von Kuhl, *Der Weltkrieg 1914–1918* (Berlin: Verlag Tradition Wilhelm Kolk,1929), 119.

37. German Army, Report on the State of the Serbian Army, September 10, 1915, Nachlass Seeckt, BA-MA N 247/26; Austria, Bundesministerium, *Österreich-Ungarns Letzter Krieg 1914–1918,* vol. 3, 35; and British Army, General Staff, "Military Notes on the Balkan States," in *Armies of the Balkan States 1914–1918: The Military Forces of Bulgaria, Greece, Romania and Serbia,* ed. British Army, General Staff (repr., Nashville: Battery Press, 1996), 43.

38. Mitrović, *Serbia's Great War 1914–1918,* 146; Robert A. Doughty, *Pyrrhic Victory: French Strategy and Operations in the Great War* (Cambridge: Harvard University Press, 2005), 212–13; and Cyril Falls, *History of the Great War. Military Operations. Macedonia: From the Outbreak of War in 1914 to the Spring of 1917* (repr., Nashville: Battery Press, 1996), 42–43.

39. Richard C. Hall, *Balkan Breakthrough: The Battle of Dobro Pole 1918* (Bloomington: Indiana University Press, 2010), 60–61.

40. Holger Afflerbach, *Falkenhayn: Politisches Denken und Handeln im Kaiserreich* (Munich: R. Oldenbourg Verlag, 1996), 357; and Falkenhayn, *German General Staff and Its Decisions, 1914–1916,* 296.

Bibliography

ARCHIVAL MATERIAL

Austria

Österreichisches Staatsarchiv—Kriegsarchiv, Vienna

78—Military Chancery of His Majesty
512—AOK Operations Bureau, Conrad-Falkenhayn Correspondence, Russia
B/13—Rudolf Kundmann Diary, Conrad Archive

Germany

Bayerisches Hauptstaatsarchiv—Kreigsarchiv, Munich

Nachlass Paul von Kneussl
NL 5
NL 6
Bavarian 8th Reserve Division
File 8R Bund 11 Akt1
Bavarian 11th Infantry Division
File 11 Bund 15 Akt 1
File 11 Bund 15 Akt 2
File 11 Bund 15 Akt 5
German Alpine Corps
Alpenkorps 1
Alpenkorps 18
Alpenkorps 152
Alpenkorps 153

Alpenkorps 154
Bundesarchiv-Militärarchiv, Freiburg-im-Breisgau
MSg 1/1914—Karl von Kaganeck Diary
MSg 1/2514—Karl von Kaganeck Diary
MSg 109—Biographical Chronologies
N 39—Nachlass Mackensen
N 46—Nachlass Groener
N 77—Nachlass Ludendorff
N 247—Nachlass Seeckt
N 754—Nachlass Kosch
PH 5—Army Group Mackensen
PH 6—German IV and X Reserve Corps
PH 8—German 101st Infantry Division
PH 305—German Eleventh Army
RH 61/27 German Army Railroad Section
RH 61/933 Hans von Plessen Diary and Various Correspondence
RH 61/979 Falkenhayn Correspondence
RH 61/986 Gerhard Tappen Diary
RH 61/1536 OHL Ost Operationen 1915
Landesarchiv-Baden-Württemberg, Stuttgart
M 430—Service Record of Wilhelm von Urach, Duke of Württemberg
M 660—Service Record of Eugen von Dorrer
Gu 117—German 26th Infantry Division

PUBLISHED WORKS

Adams, John C. *Flight in Winter.* Princeton: Princeton University Press, 1942.
Afflerbach, Holger. *Falkenhayn: Politisches Denken und Handeln im Kaiserreich.*
    Munich: R. Oldenbourg Verlag, 1996.
Albertini, Luigi. *The Origins of the War of 1914.* 3 Vols. Translated by Isabella M.
    Massey. Reprint, New York: Enigma Books, 2005.
Anderson, Matthew S. *The Eastern Question 1774–1923.* New York: St. Martin's
    Press, 1966.
Angelow, Jürgen, ed. *Der Erste Weltkrieg auf dem Balkan.* Berlin: Wissenschaft
    Verlag, 2011.
Appel, Friedrich. *Das Reserve-Infanterie-Regiment Nr. 205.* Berlin: Verlag Bernard und
    Graefe, 1937.
Association of Former Officers of the Regiment. *Das 1. Masurische Infanterie-
    Regiment Nr. 146 1897–1919.* Berlin: Verlag Tradition Wilhelm Kolk, 1929.
Austria, Bundesministerium für Landesverteidigung. *Österreich-Ungarns Letzter Krieg
    1914–1918.* 7 Vols. Vienna: Verlag der Militärwissenschaftlichen Mitteilungen,
    1931–1938.
Barret, Michael B. *Operation Albion: The German Conquest of the Baltic Islands.*
    Bloomington: Indiana University Press, 2008.
Bartenwerffer, Erich, and Alfred Herrmann. *Das Reserve-Infanterie-Regiment Nr. 232
    im Ost und West.* Celle: Buchdruckerei W. Müller, 1927.

Berendt, General der Artillerie Richard von. "Aus grosser Zeit vor zwanzig Jahren: Der Feldzug in Serbien." *Militär Wochenblatt* 120, no. 13 (October 4, 1915): 523–27.

Bergeder, Fritz. *Das Reserve-Infanterie-Regiment Nr. 202 auf den Schlachtfeldern des Weltkrieges 1914–1918.* Berlin: Traditions Verlag Kolk, 1939.

Bernhardi, General der Kavallerie Friedrich von. *Deutschlands Heldenkampf 1914–1918.* Munich: J.F. Lehmanns Verlag, 1922.

Boesser, Lieutenant Colonel Karl. *Geschichte des Reserve-Feldartillerie-Regiments Nr, 44.* Grossen: Rudolf Zeidler, 1932.

British Army, General Staff. *Armies of the Balkan States 1914–1918: The Military Forces of Bulgaria, Greece, Romania and Serbia.* Reprint, Nashville: Battery Press, 1996.

Brose, Eric D. *The Kaiser's Army: The Politics of Military Technology in Germany during the Machine Age.* New York: Oxford University Press, 2001.

Broucek, Peter, ed. *Ein österreichischer General gegen Hitler. Feldmarschalleutnant Alfred Jansa: Erinnerungen.* Vienna: Böhlau Verlag, 2011.

Bucholz, Arden. *Moltke, Schlieffen and Prussian War Planning.* Oxford: Berg Publishers, 1991.

Bülow, Major Hilmar Freiherr von. *Geschichte der Luftstreitkräfte: Eine Kurze Darstellung der Entwicklung der fünften Waffe.* Frankfurt-am-Main: Verlag Moritz Diesterweg, 1934.

Callwell, Colonel Charles E. *Small Wars: Their Principles and Practice.* 3rd ed. Reprint, Lincoln: University of Nebraska Press, 1996.

Cecil, Lamar. *Wilhelm II.* 2 Vols. Chapel Hill: University of North Carolina Press, 1989–1996.

Chandler, David G. *The Campaigns of Napoleon: The Mind and Method of History's Greatest Soldier.* New York: Macmillan, 1966.

Citino, Robert M. *The German Way of War: From the Thirty Years' War to the Third Reich.* Lawrence: University Press of Kansas, 2005.

Citino, Robert M. *Quest for Decisive Victory: From Stalemate to Blitzkrieg in Europe, 1899–1940.* Lawrence: University Press of Kansas, 2002.

Clausewitz, Carl von. *On War.* Translated and edited by Michael Howard and Peter Paret. Princeton: Princeton University Press, 1976.

Conrad von Hötzendorf, Franz Baron. *Aus meiner Dienstzeit 1906–1918.* 5 Vols. 6th ed. Vienna: Rikola Verlag, 1921–1925.

Corbett, Elsie. *Red Cross in Serbia 1915–1919: A Personal Diary of Experiences.* Banbury: Cheney and Sons, 1964.

Craig, Gordon A. *Germany 1866–1945.* New York: Oxford University Press, 1978.

Cramon, August von. *Unser Österreich-Ungarischer Bundesgenosse im Weltkrieg. Erinnerungen aus meiner vierjährigen Tätigkeit als bevollmächtiger deutsche General beim K.u.K. Armeeoberkommando.* Berlin: E.S. Mittler und Sohn, 1920.

Cruttwell, Charles R.M.F. *A History of the Great War 1914–1918.* Reprint, Chicago: Academy Publishers, 2007.

Dammert, Rudolf. *Der Serbische Feldzug: Erlebnisse Deutscher Truppen.* Leipzig: Verlag von Bernhard Tauchnitz, 1916.

DiNardo, Richard L. *Breakthrough: The Gorlice-Tarnow Campaign, 1915.* Santa Barbara, CA: Praeger, 2010.

DiNardo, Richard L., and Daniel J. Hughes. "Germany and Coalition Warfare in the World Wars: A Comparative Study." *War in History* 8, no. 2 (April 2001): 166–90.

DiNardo, Richard L. "Huns with Web-Feet: Operation Albion, 1917." *War in History* 12, no. 4 (November 2005): 396–417.

Doerstling, Lieutenant Colonel Paul. *Kriegsgeschichte des Königlich Preussischen Infanterie-Regiments Graf v. Tauentzien (3. Brandenb.) Nr. 20.* Zeulenroda: Bernhard Sporn Buchdruckerei und Verlagsanstalt, 1933.

Doughty, Robert A. *Pyrrhic Victory: French Strategy and Operations in the Great War.* Cambridge, MA: Harvard University Press, 2005.

Dunham, Mary E. *The Sarajevo Crime.* London: George Allen and Unwin, 1925.

Erickson, Edward J. *Defeat in Detail: The Ottoman Army in the Balkans, 1912–1913.* Westport, CT: Praeger Publishers, 2003.

Erickson, Edward J. *Gallipoli: The Ottoman Campaign.* Barnsley: Pen and Sword, 2010.

Eyck, Erich. *Bismarck and the German Empire.* Reprint, New York: W.W. Norton, 1968.

Falkenhayn, General Erich von. *The German General Staff and Its Decisions, 1914–1916.* New York: Dodd, Mead, 1920.

Falls, Cyril. *Military Operations: Macedonia. From the Outbreak of War to the Spring of 1917.* Reprint, Nashville: Battery Press, 1996.

Fischer, Fritz. *Germany's War Aims in the First World War.* New York: W.W. Norton, 1967.

Foerster, Wolfgang, ed. *Mackensen:Briefe und Aufzeichnungen des Generalfeld-marschalls aus Krieg und Frieden.* Bonn: Wahlband der Buchgemeinde, 1938.

Foley, Robert T. *German Strategy and the Path to Verdun: Erich von Falkenhayn and the Development of Attrition; 1870–1916.* Cambridge: Cambridge University Press, 2005.

Franks, Norman, Frank Bailey, and Rick Duiven. *Casualties of the German Air Service 1914–1920: As Complete a List Possible Arranged Alphabetically and Chronologically.* London: Grub Street, 1999.

Fryer, Charles E. J. *The Destruction of Serbia in 1915.* New York: East European Monographs, 1997.

Fryer, Charles E. J. *The Royal Navy on the Danube.* Boulder, CO: East European Monographs, 1988.

Führer, Wilhelm. *Geschichte des Reserve Infanterie Regiments 203.* 4 Vols. Berlin: Privately Published, 1960–1964.

Gallwitz, General der Artillerie Max von. *Meine Führertätigkeit im Weltkriege 1914–1916: Belgien-Osten-Balkan.* Berlin: E.S. Mittler und Sohn, 1929.

Germany, Reichsarchiv. *Der Weltkrieg 1914 bis 1918.* 14 Vols. Berlin: E.S. Mittler und Sohn, 1925–1944.

Gerok, Captain. *Das 2. württ. Feldartillerie-Reg. Nr. 29 "Prinz Luitpold von Bayern" im Weltkrieg 1914–1918.* Stuttgart: Ehr. Belsersche Verlagsbuchhandlung, 1921.

Gesellschaft für Wehrpolitik und Wehrwissenschaft. *Heerführer des Weltkrieges.* Berlin: E.S. Mittler und Sohn, 1939.

Giese, Franz. *Geschichte des Reserve-Infanterie-Regiments 227 im Weltkriege 1914/18.* Privately Published, 1931.

Gnamm, Captain Hellmut. *Der Fusilier-Regiment Kaiser Franz Joseph von Österreich, König von Ungarn (4. württ.) Nr. 132.* Stuttgart: Ehr. Belsersche Verlagsbuch-handlung, 1921.

Gordon-Smith, Gordon. *From Serbia to Jugoslavia: Serbia's Victories, Reverses and Final Triumph: 1914-1918.* New York: G.P. Putnam's Sons, 1920.

Görlitz, Walter. *History of the German General Staff.* Translated by Brian Battershaw. New York: Praeger, 1954.

Görlitz, Walter. *The Kaiser and His Court: The Diaries, Note Books and Letters of Admiral Georg Alexander von Müller, Chief of the Naval Cabinet, 1914-1918.* New York: Harcourt, Brace and World, 1958.

Greenhalgh, Elizabeth. *Victory through Coalition: Britain and France during the First World War.* Cambridge: Cambridge University Press, 2005.

Gross, Gerhard P., ed. *Die vergessene Front: Der Osten 1914/15.* Paderborn: Ferdinand Schöningh, 2006.

Gumz, Jonathan E. *The Resurrection and Collapse of Empire in Habsburg Serbia, 1914-1918.* New York: Cambridge University Press, 2009.

Haleck, Fritz. *Das Reserve-Infanterie-Regiment Nr. 208.* Berlin: Druck und Verlag von Gerhard Stalling, 1922.

Hall, Richard C. *Balkan Breakthrough: The Battle of Dobro Pole 1918.* Bloomington: Indiana University Press, 2010.

Hamilton, Richard F., and Holger Herwig. *Decisions for War, 1914-1917.* Cambridge: Cambridge University Press, 2004.

Heinrici, Paul, ed. *Das Ehrenbuch der Deutschen Pioniere.* Berlin: Verlag Tradition Wilhelm Kolk, 1932.

Hennig, Kurt. *Das Infanterie-Regiment (8. Ostpreussisches) Nr. 45 (Insterburg-Darkehmen) im Weltkriege 1914-18.* Berlin: Druck und Verlag Gerhard Stalling, 1928.

Herbert, Gunther. *Das Alpenkorps: Aufbau, Organization und Einsatz einer Gebirgstruppen im Ersten Weltkrieg.* Boppard-am-Rhein: Harald Boldt Verlag, 1988.

Herwig, Holger H. *The First World War: Germany and Austria-Hungary 1914-1918.* London: Arnold, 1997.

Herwig, Holger H. *Luxury Fleet: The Imperial German Navy 1888-1918.* Reprint, London: Ashfield Press, 1997.

Herwig, Holger H. *The Marne: The Opening of World War I and the Battle that Changed the World.* New York: Random House, 2009.

Herwig, Holger H., and Neil M. Heyman. *Biographical Dictionary of World War I.* Westport, CT: Greenwood Press, 1982.

Höbelt, Lothar. "Schlieffen, Potiorek und das Ende der gemeinsam deutsch-österreichungarischen Aufmarschpläne im Osten." *Militärgeschichtlichen Mitteilungen* 36 (1984): 7-30.

Hoeppner, General Ernst von. *Germany's War in the Air: The Development and Operations of German Military Aviation in the World War.* Reprint, Nashville: Battery Press, 1994.

Hough, Richard. *The Great War at Sea 1914-1918.* New York: Oxford University Press, 1983.

Hughes, Daniel J. *The Kings Finest: A Social and Bureaucratic Profile of Prussia's General Officers, 1871-1914.* Westport, CT: Praeger, 1987.

Hupchick, Dennis P. *The Balkans: From Constantinople to Communism.* New York: Palgrave, 2002.

Jäger, Herbert. *German Artillery of World War One*. Wiltshire: Crowood Press, 2001.

Janes's. *Jane's Fighting Aircraft of World War I*. Reprint, London: Studio, 1990.

Jászi, Oscar. *The Dissolution of the Habsburg Monarchy*. Chicago: University of Chicago Press, 1929.

Jelavich, Barbara. *A Century of Russian Foreign Policy 1814–1814*. Philadelphia: J.B. Lippincott, 1964.

Jobst, 1st Lieutenant. "Ulanen-Regiment König Wilhelm I (2. Württembergisches) Nr. 20." In *Die Tradition des deutschen Heeres: Traditionsheft*. Nr. 370 (1938), 870–73.

Johnson, Douglas W. *Topography and Strategy in the War*. New York: Henry Holt, 1917.

Johnson, Lonnie R. *Central Europe: Enemies, Neighbors, Friends*. New York: Oxford University Press, 1996.

Jung, Jakob. *Max von Gallwitz (1852–1937): General und Politiker*. Osnabrück: Biblio Verlag, 1995.

Kann, Robert A. *A History of the Habsburg Empire 1526–1918*. Berkeley: University of California Press, 1974.

Kelly, Patrick J. "Strategy, Tactics and Turf Wars: Tirpitz and the Oberkommando der Marine, 1892–1895." *The Journal of Military History* 66, no. 4 (October 2002): 1033–60.

Kennan, Geroge F. *The Decline of Bismarck's European Order: Franco-Russian Relations, 1875–1890*. Princeton: Princeton University Press, 1975.

Kennan, Geroge F. *The Fateful Alliance: France, Russia and the Coming of the First World War*. New York: Pantheon Books, 1984.

Kennedy, Paul, ed. *The War Plans of the Great Powers, 1880–1914*. London: George Allen and Unwin, 1979.

Kennett, Lee. *The First Air War 1914–1918*. New York: Free Press, 1991.

Kiraly, Bela, and Gail Stokes, eds. *War and Society in East Central Europe*. Vol. XVII. Boulder, CO: Social Science Monographs, 1995.

Koburger, Charles W., Jr. *The Central Powers in the Adriatic, 1914–1918: War in a Narrow Sea*. Westport, CT: Praeger, 2001.

Kohn, Hans. *Pan-Slavism: Its History and Ideology*. Notre Dame: University of Notre Dame Press, 1953.

Kuhl, General der Infanterie Hermann von. *Der Weltkrieg 1914–1918*. 2 Vols. Berlin: Verlag Tradition Wilhelm Kolk, 1929.

Liddell Hart, Basil H. *History of the First World War*. Reprint, London: Cassell, 1970.

Liulevicius, Vejas G. *War Land on the Eastern Front: Culture, National Identity and German Occupation in World War I*. Cambridge: Cambridge University Press, 2000.

Ludendorff, Erich. *Meine Kriegserinnerungen 1914–1918*. Berlin: E.S. Mittler und Sohn, 1919.

Malaparte, Curzio. *The Volga Rises in Europe*. London: Redman, 1957.

Markus, Georg. *Der Fall Redl*. Vienna: Amalthea Verlag, 1984.

May, Arthur, Jr. *The Habsburg Monarchy 1867–1914*. New York: W.W. Norton, 1951.

Mayer, Colonel Hans. *Das K.B. 22. Infanterie-Regiment*. Munich: J. Lindauersche Universitäts-Buchhandlung, 1923.

McElwee, William. *The Art of War: Waterloo to Mons*. Bloomington: Indiana University Press, 1974.

Meier-Welcker, Hans. *Seeckt*. Frankfurt-am-Main: Bernard und Graefe Verlag für Wehrwesen, 1967.

Milojković-Djurić, Jelena. *Panslavism and National Identity in Russia and the Balkans 1830–1880: Images of the Self and Others*. Boulder, CO: East European Monographs, 1994.

Mitrović, Andrej. *Serbia's Great War 1914–1918*. West Lafayette, IN: Purdue University Press, 2007

Mohr, Eike. *Heeres- und Truppengeschichte des Deutschen Reiches und Seiner Länder 1806 bis 1918: eine Bibliographie*. Osnabrück: Biblio Verlag, 1989.

Moltke, Generalfeldmarschall Helmuth von. *Militärische Werke*. Edited by German Great General Staff. 14 Vols. Berlin: E.S. Mittler und Sohn, 1892–1912.

Moltke, Generaloberst Helmuth von. *Erinnerungen-Briefe-Dokumente*. Edited by Eliza von Moltke. Stuttgart: Der Kommende Tag, 1922.

Mombauer, Annika. *Helmuth von Moltke and the Origins of the First World War*. Cambridge: Cambridge University Press, 2001.

Morser, Generalleutnant Otto von. *Kurzer Strategischer Überblick über den Weltkrieg 1914–1918*. Berlin: E.S. Mittler und Sohn, 1921.

Muth, Jörg. *Command Culture: Officer Education in the U.S. Army and the German Armed Forces, 1901–1940, and the Consequences for World War II*. Denton: University of North Texas Press, 2011.

Napier, Lieutenant Colonel the Honorable Henry D., CMG. *The Experiences of a Military Attaché in the Balkans*. London: Drane's, 1924.

Nebelin, Manfred. *Ludendorff: Diktator im Ersten Weltkrieg*. Munich: Siedler Verlag, 2010.

Neeff, Hermann. *Das 4. Württ. Feldartillerie Reg. Nr. 65 im Weltkrieg*. Stuttgart: Ehr. Belser A.G., Verlagsbuchhandlung, 1925.

Neiburg, Michael S., ed. *Arms and the Man: Military History Essays in Honor of Dennis Showalter*. Boston: Brill, 2011.

Neumann, Major Georg P. *Die deutschen Luftstreitkräfte im Weltkriege*. Berlin: Ernst Siegfried Mittler und Sohn, 1920.

Oden, 1st Lieutenant Harry and 1st Lieutenant Friedrich Schultz. *Feldartillerie-Regiment 201: Seine Geschichte 1915–1918*. Zeulenroda: Bernhard Sporn, Buchdruckerei und Verlagsanstalt, 1931.

Officers of the Regiment, ed. *Das Königliche Bayerische Infanterie-Leibregiment*. Munich: Max Schick, 1931.

Palmer, Alan. *The Gardeners of Salonika*. New York, Simon and Schuster, 1965.

Paret, Peter, ed. *Makers of Modern Strategy: From Machiavelli to the Nuclear Age*. Princeton: Princeton University Press, 1986.

Parker, Geoffrey. *The Military Revolution: Military Innovation and the Rise of the West, 1500–1800*. Cambridge: Cambridge University Press, 1988.

Pastor, Peter, and Garydon Tunstall, eds. *Essays on World War I*. Boulder, CO: Social Science Monographs, 2012.

Paulus, Karl. *Das K.B. Jäger-Regiment Nr. 1*. Munich: Bayerisches Kriegsarchiv, 1925.

Pavlović, Srdja. *Balkan Anschluss: The Annexation of Montenegro and the Creation of the Common South Slavic State*. West Lafayette, IN: Purdue University Press, 2008.

Pflanze, Otto. *Bismarck and the Development of Germany.* 3 Vols. Princeton: Princeton University Press, 1990.

Radan, Peter, and Aleksander Pavković. *The Serbs and Their Leaders in the Twentieth Century.* Brookfield, VT: Ashgate, 1997.

Radermacher, Lieutenant Colonel. *Erinnerungsblätter des Grossherzogl. Hessischen Reserve-Infanterie-Regiment Nr. 116.* Oldenbourg: Druck und Verlag von Gerhard Stalling, 1929.

Rauchensteiner, Manfred. *Der Erste Weltkrieg und das Ende der Habsburgmonarchie.* Vienna: Böhlau Verlag, 2013.

Regele, Oskar. *Feldmarschall Conrad: Auftrag und Erfüllung, 1906–1918.* Vienna: Verlag Herold, 1955.

Reichlin-Meldegg, Georg. *Das Kaisers Prinz Eugen? Feldmarschall Hermann Baron Kövess von Kövessháza: Der letzte Oberkommandant der K.u.K. Armee im Ersten Weltkrieg.* Graz: Ares Verlag, 2010.

Reichold, Helmut, ed. *Adolf Wild von Hohenborn: Briefe und Tagebuchaufzeichnungen des preussischen Generals als Kriegsminister und Truppenführer im Ersten Weltkrieg.* Boppard-am-Rhein: Harald Boldt Verlag, 1986.

Reiss, Rodolphe A. *Report upon the Atrocities Committed by the Austro-Hungarian Army during the First Invasion of Serbia.* London: Simpkin, Marshall, Hamilton, Kent, 1915.

Richter, Alfred. *Das 2. Thüring. Infanterie-Regiment Nr. 32.* Zeulenroda: Druck von Bernhard Spoorn, 1928.

Ritter, Gerhard. *The Schlieffen Plan: Critique of a Myth.* New York: Praeger, 1958.

Ritter, Gerhard. *The Sword and the Scepter: The Problem of Militarism in Germany.* 4 Vols. Coral Gables, FL: University of Miami Press, 1970.

Rothenberg, Gunther E. *The Army of Francis Joseph.* West Lafayette, IN: Purdue University Press, 1976.

Rothenberg, Gunther E. *The Art of War in the Age of Napoleon.* Bloomington: Indiana University Press, 1978.

Scheer, Tamara. *Zwischen Front und Heimat: Österreich-Ungarns Militärverwaltung im Ersten Weltkrieg.* Frankfurt-am-Main: Peter Lang, 2009.

Schimmelpennick van der Oye, David, and Bruce W. Menning, eds. *Reforming the Tsar's Army: Military Innovation in Imperial Russia from Peter the Great to the Revolution.* New York: Cambridge University Press, 2004.

Schindler, John R. *Isonzo: The Forgotten Sacrifice of the Great War.* Westport, CT: Praeger, 2001.

Schindler, John R. "Redl—Spy of the Century?" *International Journal of Intelligence and Counter Intelligence* 18, no. 3 (Fall 2005): 483–507.

Schlawe, Captain Wilhelm. *Feldartillerie-Regiment General-Feldzeugmeister (1. Brandenburgisches) Nr. 3 in Weltkrieg 1914/1918.* Berlin: Verlag Bernard und Graefe, 1935.

Schmidt-Pauli, Edgar von. *General von Seeckt: Lebensbild einen Deutschen Soldaten.* Berlin: Reinar Hobbing, 1937.

Schöning, Arthur. *Unser Regiment im Weltkrieg.* Erfurt: Druck von A. Stenger, 1925.

Schwarte, Generalleutnant Max, ed. *Die militärischen Lehren des Grossen Krieges.* Berlin: E.S. Mittler und Sohn, 1920.

Schwarzmüller, Theo. *Zwischen Kaiser und Führer. Generalfeldmarschall August von Mackensen: Eine Politische Biographie.* Paderborn: Ferdinand Schöningh, 1996.

Seeckt, Hans von. *Aus meinem Leben 1866–1917.* Leipzig: von Hase und Kohler Verlag, 1938.

Seyfert, Gerhard. *Die militärischen Beziehungen und Vereinbarungen zwischen dem deutschen und österreichischen Generalstab vor und bei Beginn des Weltkrieges.* Leipzig: J. Moltzen, 1934.

Sforza, Count Carlo. *Fifty Years of War and Diplomacy in the Balkans: Pashich and the Union of the Yugoslavs.* New York: Columbia University Press, 1940.

Shanafelt, Gary W. *The Secret Enemy: Austria-Hungary and the German Alliance, 1914–1918.* Boulder, CO: East European Monographs, 1985.

Shepherd, Ben. *Terror in the Balkans: German Armies and Partisan Warfare.* Cambridge, MA: Harvard University Press, 2012.

Showalter, Dennis E. *Tannenberg: Clash of Empires, 1914.* Reprint, Dulles, VA: Brassey's, 2004.

Soldan, Adolf. *5. Grossherzoglich Hessischen Infanterie-Regiment Nr. 168.* Berlin: Druck und Verlag Gerhard Stalling, 1924.

Sondhaus, Lawrence. *Franz Conrad von Hötzendorf: Architect of the Apocalypse.* Boston: Humanities Press, 2000.

Sondhaus, Lawrence. *The Naval Policy of Austria-Hungary 1867–1918: Navalism, Industrial Development, and the Politics of Dualism.* West Lafayette, IN: Purdue University Press, 1994.

Speed, Robert B., III. *Prisoners, Diplomats, and the Great War: A Study in the Diplomacy of Captivity.* Westport, CT: Greenwood Press, 1990.

Stachelbeck, Christian. *Militärische Effektivität im Ersten Weltkrieg: Die 11. Bayerische Infanteriedivision 1915 bis 1918.* Paderborn: Ferdinand Schöningh, 2010.

Stanley, Monica M. *My Diary in Serbia: April 1, 1915—Nov. 1, 1915.* London: Simpkin, Marshall, Hamilton, Kent, 1916.

Stengel, Franz Freiherr von. *Das K.B. 3. Infanterie-Regiment Prinz Karl von Bayern.* Munich: Verlag Bayerisches Kriegsarchiv, 1924.

Steuer, Joseph. *Das Infanterie-Regiment Generalfeldmarschall von Mackensen (3. West preussisches) Nr. 129 im Weltkriege.* Berlin: Druck und Verlag Gerhard Stalling, 1925.

Strachan, Hew. *The First World War*, Vol. I. *To Arms.* Oxford: Oxford University Press, 2001.

Sugar, Peter F. "The Nature of the Non-Germanic Societies under Habsburg Rule." *Slavic Review* XXII, no. 1 (March 1963): 1–30.

Sugar, Peter F., Peter Hánák, and Frank Tibor, eds. *A History of Hungary.* Bloomington: Indiana University Press, 1994.

Tunstall, Graydon A., Jr. *Blood on the Snow: The Carpathian Winter War of 1915.* Lawrence: University Press of Kansas, 2010.

Tunstall, Graydon A. *Planning for War against Russia and Serbia: Austro-Hungarian and German Military Strategies, 1871–1914.* Boulder, CO: Social Science Monographs, 1993.

Uhle-Wettler, Franz. *Erich Ludendorff in Seiner Zeit: Soldat—Stratege—Revolutionär: Eine Neubewertung.* Augsburg: Kurt Vowinckel Verlag, 1995.

Ullrich, Volker. *Die nervöse Grossmacht: Aufstieg und Untergang des deutschen Kaiserreichs 1871–1918.* 2nd ed. Frankfurt-am-Main: Fischer Taschenbuch Verlag, 2010.

Ulrich, 1st Lieutenant Herbert. *Res.-Inf.-Regiment 52 im Weltkriege.* Cottbus: Lausitzer Druckerei und Varlagsanstalt, 1925.

Wahrenburg, Captain. *Reserve-Infanterie-Regiment Nr. 83.* Berlin: Druck und Verlag von Gerhard Stalling, 1924.

Wakefield, Alan, and Simon Moody. *Under the Devil's Eye: Britain's Forgotten Army at Salonika 1915–1918.* Gloucestershire: Sutton Publishing, 2004.

Wawro, Geoffrey. "An 'Army of Pigs': The Technical, Social, and Political Bases of Austrian Shock Tactics, 1859–1866." *The Journal of Military History* 59, no. 3 (July 1995): 407–33.

Wette, Wolfram. *Militarismus in Deutschland: Geschichte einer Kriegerischen Kultur.* Frankfurt-am-Main: S. Fischer Verlag, 2008.

Wetzell, General Georg. *Der Bündniskrieg:Eine militärpolitisch operative Studie des Weltkrieges.* Berlin: E.S. Mittler und Sohn, 1937.

Wheeler-Bennett, John. *Wooden Titan: Hindenburg in Twenty Years of German History 1914–1934.* New York: William Morrow, 1936.

White, George W. *Nationalism and Territory: Constructing Group Identity in Southeastern Europe.* New York: Rowman and Littlefield Publishers, 2000.

Zarn, Otto, Colonel Hayner, and Major Frantzius, *Geschichte des Reserve-Infanterie-Regiments Nr. 201.* Berlin: Verlag Bernard und Graefe, 1940.

Zuckerman, Larry. *The Rape of Belgium: The Untold Story of World War I.* New York: New York University Press, 2004.

Index

Abraham, 118

Adrianople, 100

Adriatic Sea, 9, 98, 101, 115, 116, 121, 123, 124

Aegean Sea, 9, 13

aircraft, 3, 39, 42, 56, 59, 61, 87, 100, 105, 111, 113, 134; effectiveness of, 60, 61, 75; German reliance on, 60, 91, 113, 135

Albania, 8, 13, 103, 116, 121, 126, 127, 128, 133

Aleksandrovac, 81

Alessio, 115, 116, 122, 123

Alexander of Battenberg, King of Bulgaria, 10, 11

Alexander, Prince of Serbia, 115, 116, 123

Alexander I, Tsar of Russia, 6

Alexander II, Tsar of Russia, 9, 10,

Alexander III, Tsar of Russia, 1, 10

Allenstein, 27, 50, 100

Alsace-Lorraine, 26

Anatema Hills, 69, 70, 82

Andrássy, Julius, 10

Arangelovac, 92, 93

Armansperg, Captain Max Graf, 117, 118

Army, Austro-Hungarian, 25, 26, 34, 37, 51, 124, 126, 133; High Command (AOK), 16, 17, 18, 19, 20, 25, 27, 29, 33, 34, 37, 41, 46, 47, 49, 62, 64, 68, 88, 90, 99, 109, 127, 128, 133; Units, Armies: First, 19; Second, 15, 16, 17, 19, 20, 30, 47; Third, 29, 38, 39, 46, 47, 48, 54, 57, 62, 63, 64, 66, 67, 75, 79, 80, 83, 84, 86, 90, 91, 93, 95, 96, 97, 99, 104, 105, 106, 107, 109, 111, 114, 127, 135, 136; Fourth, 29, 37; Fifth, 15, 17, 18, 19, 31, 90; Sixth, 15, 17, 18; Aviation Companies: 3rd, 39; 6th, 39; 9th, 39; 15th, 39; Corps: VI, 31; VIII, 47, 48, 61, 66, 67, 75, 79, 80, 81, 86, 91, 92, 93, 95, 96, 98, 103, 104, 106, 107, 112, 116, 119; XII, 47; XIX, 47, 48, 66, 67, 68, 75, 79, 80, 86, 91, 92, 93, 96, 97, 103, 104, 106, 111, 113, 116, 127; Divisions, Cavalry: 2nd, 37; 9th, 37; Divisions, Infantry: 53rd, 48, 66, 80; 57th, 47, 67, 94, 99; 59th, 37, 47, 66, 67, 74, 80, 86, 93, 94, 116; 61st, 37; 62nd, 48, 64, 67, 68, 74, 75, 80, 91, 96, 103, 105, 111, 116; Groups (Division Equivalents): Fülöpp, 46, 69, 90, 95; Sorsich, 48, 80, 92, 93, 104;

About the Author

RICHARD L. DINARDO, PhD, professor of National Security Affairs at the Marine Corps Command and Staff College, Quantico, Virginia, has written extensively on a wide variety of topics in military history. He completed his bachelor's degree in history at Bernard Baruch College, City University of New York (CUNY), and his doctorate in history at the CUNY Graduate School and University Center. Prior to his arrival at Quantico in 1998, he taught at St. Peter's College and also spent two years as visiting professor at the Air War College in Maxwell AFB. DiNardo is the author or editor of six books including ABC-CLIO's *Breakthrough: The Gorlice–Tarnow Campaign, 1915*, which won honorable mention in the Western Front Association's Tomlinson Book Prize for 2010. DiNardo's other published works include *Germany and the Axis Powers: From Coalition to Collapse* and *Mechanized Juggernaut or Military Anachronism?: Horses and the German Army of World War II*. He is also the author or editor of a number of articles on the American Civil War and coeditor of *James Longstreet: The Man, the Soldier, the Controversy*.